Cruise Ships

William Mayes

Published by Overview Press Ltd
MAYES HOUSE, VANSITTART ESTATE, ARTHUR ROAD,
WINDSOR, BERKS, ENGLAND, SL4 1SE
TEL: +44 (0) 1753 620237   FAX: +44 (0) 1753 832430

the **leading** *guide to the cruise industry*

contents

ISBN 978 0 9547206 4 3

First edition published September 2005.

Second edition published August 2007.

This third edition fully revised and updated, published September 2009.

Front cover: The **Saga Ruby** at Sharm El Sheikh *(William Mayes)*

Frontispiece: The **Queen Elizabeth 2** in Southampton Water *(William Mayes)*

Back cover: The **Maxim Gorkiy** at Flam *(William Mayes)*

Design by Miles Cowsill and Lily Publications Limited, PO Box 33, Ramsey, Isle of Man IM99 4LP

Advertising sales Stephen Macey +44 (0) 1202 701053 email smacey4@btinternet.com

Printed by Gomer Press, Wales

the **leading** *guide to the cruise industry*

introduction

O nce again I would like to express my thanks to all of those who have made encouraging and helpful remarks, supplied new information and photographs, and assisted in other ways to create what I sincerely believe to be the most comprehensive and accurate single written source of information on the world's passenger ships today. In this edition I have included a few more interesting coastal and inland ships; while maintaining the entry level at 30 berths, the number of vessels covered has increased to almost 700 passenger-carrying ships.

It is now just four years since I was putting the finishing touches to the first edition of this book, and in that time the changes that have taken place have been astonishing. The pace of change continues unchecked, and since the second edition there have been some surprising developments, including the change of control of NCL from Star Cruises to Apollo Management, the bankruptcy of Club Cruise, the closure of Island Cruises and the impending closure of Ocean Village. Other operators appeared for the first time in the second edition, but had gone by the time this edition was being prepared.

The effects of the worldwide problems in the financial markets have filtered through to the cruise industry, and it can be seen from the section detailing changes since the last edition, that many companies are no longer trading. Indeed several never even got as far as starting. A number of companies currently have vessels under arrest, and it is likely that some will not trade again.

A few ships have gone for scrap, and again one was lost through sinking. The scrapping of older ships is expected to accelerate as the SOLAS changes that come into effect in 2010 take their toll. Clearly for those of us that prefer the more traditional cruise experience on a 'real' ship the choice is becoming rather limited.

Among the information sources on which I rely, I mention again Sea-Web, the on-line ship register from Lloyds Register-Fairplay, without which the updating of this book would have been almost impossible.

I would once more like to express particular thanks to Andy Kilk and Ted Scull, both good friends for many years, for their encouragement and for searching out pictures from their collections; to Mark Amielanczyk, who has once again provided much additional information from his many years of research into passenger ships; John-ward Phillips who has again helped with some obscure name derivations; to Jonathan Boonzaier who has supplied pictures and expertise in connection with operators and ships in South East Asia; and to Matthew Davies, Alf Sims, Richard Seville, Ben Lyons and Martin Grant all of whom sent in numerous pictures. Finally I'd like to thank Rick Frendt once again for his generous supply of images.

Many thanks to other friends who have been kind enough to supply information and pictures, allowing a good geographical coverage to be maintained.

The text is as correct as possible as at 31 July 2009.

William Mayes
Mayes House
Windsor
England
SL4 1SE

william.mayes@overviewpress.co.uk

the **leading** *guide to the cruise industry*

a brief review of the cruise industry

The combined effects of the changes to the SOLAS requirements, which come into force in 2010, the general economic downturn and the recent Swine Flu pandemic have all taken their toll on an industry that has seen spectacular growth over many years. While it is only the Spanish market that has contracted between 2007 and 2008, others are expected to follow between now and when the major economies start to grow again. On top of these problems, there is the Alaska tourist tax and a worldwide press ready to leap on, and blow out of proportion, other difficulties such as Norovirus. The final nail in the coffin for some ships and operators, however, may be the introduction of Emission Control Areas, where so called 'dirty' ships may not be able to trade unless they use a lighter fuel, at a significantly higher cost. Cruises in and around Canada and New England could be seriously affected as ships withdraw due to increased expense, estimated by the cruise companies to add US$15 per person per day to an average fare. This, all at a time when the local government in the areas affected is spending vast sums to attract more cruise business. Joined up thinking, this is not.

The recession coming so soon after the opening of new casinos in Macau has led to a serious decline in the Hong Kong gambling cruise business, and with large casinos due to open in Singapore in the coming years, this could be the end of a business that has absorbed surplus ships from other parts of the world.

A number of classic ships have gone, or are about to come out of service. These include the SAGA ROSE, BLACK PRINCE, REGAL EMPRESS, QUEEN ELIZABETH 2, MAXIM GORKIY and THE TOPAZ. Even the iconic QE2 is not safe in her new role, as it seems that there is no money, in one of the richest parts of the world, to carry out the works that will transform her into the tourist attraction that she was due to become.

Orders for all types of new ship, but particularly cruise ships, have all but dried up and many shipyards are facing an uncertain future. There may be bargains to be had by the first cruise operators to break ranks and place new orders, but there may also be fewer yards with which to contract.

While the larger companies are able to weather the storm and reduce prices to keep ships full, this is not possible for smaller operators, several of which have gone out of business, and it is widely expected that others will follow, thus removing a possible depository for older tonnage from the large companies. Having said that, as we went to press Gerry Herrod's new venture had just been announced, bringing back into service a ship that had been laid up for several years. This is a further addition to the soft expedition or cultural cruise fleet and one wonders if this market has any further room for expansion.

So, all in all, it is gloomy picture for the operators and lovers of smaller and older ships. We hope that by the time the next edition of this book appears, in 2011, the situation will be much brighter.

Bringing in the tenders on the **Eurodam** *(Richard Mayes)*

the **leading** *guide to the cruise industry*
a guide to using this book

Criteria for Inclusion In compiling this book I have attempted to include in the main section all sea-going passenger cruise ships listed as having overnight accommodation for more than 30 passengers. All roll-on roll-off vessels, regardless of their passenger capacity, have been excluded unless, at the time of compilation, the ship was in use exclusively as a cruise ship. Overnight passenger vessels that previously provided cabin accommodation, but which in their current roles (day cruise or gambling ships, generally) no longer do so are included within the other sections. In addition, a few significant passenger-carrying vessels that have never had overnight accommodation and some interesting vessels with fewer than 30 berths have been included. A small number of the more important river and canal operations are also included.

Order The companies and groups of companies are listed in alphabetical order in all sections. Note that the definite article and words meaning company do not count. Companies are listed under their popularly known names where these differ from their official names, although the official name is shown in the text. Where companies are part of a larger grouping they are listed under the parent company, so Holland America Line appears under Carnival Corporation. There is a company index in addition to current and former ship name indices.

Company Information Some general company information and a little historical background are given here. Some of the smaller companies may only have some basic information in this section, but as this work progresses through new editions the detail will be expanded.

Address This is generally the location of the company's administrative headquarters.

Contact Details The telephone and fax numbers given are the contact numbers for the administration offices. These numbers are expressed in the form + (access code for international calls) followed by the country code and then the telephone number within the country, normally with the first digit omitted. Most companies can be e-mailed through their websites so separate e-mail addresses are not given.

Areas Operated The areas of operation have been listed here. It is not always possible to tie particular ships to any one area, but where practical the area has been shown at the end of each ship history.

Place Names All countries, cities and towns have been given the English version of their name most commonly used, unless the local version is now generally used by English speakers.

List of Vessels The layout is as follows:

Name	Gross Tonnage	Year Built	Service Speed (knots)	Prop. method Screws	Passenger Capacity Normal Max.		Crew Number	Length	Beam All in Metres	Draft	Flag
VESSEL NAME	5619gt	1965	16.0k	D2	280p	302p	91c	116.8m	16.5m	5.3m	HR

Gross Tonnage is now mainly listed under the 1969 convention, and is a measure of the volume of the ship. The tonnages used are generally those given by Lloyds Register, unless the author has reason to doubt those figures, in which case other sources have been used. In theory, all vessels laid down or significantly altered since 1982 and employed on international voyages, should be measured under the 1969 convention, but this is not always the case. Where a tonnage figure is given which is not is accordance with the 1969 convention the entry is marked with a ‡. Gross tonnage is now a unit-less measure of the volume of all of a ship's enclosed spaces from the keel to the funnel, measured to the inside of the hull framing. This volume is then multiplied by a factor, which is dependent upon the type of ship, to give a figure for gross tonnage. It is technically incorrect to refer to gross tons or tons, but for ease of reference the gross tonnage column figures have a gt after them.

Service Speed is generally that quoted by the company, and may be significantly less than the ship's top speed.

Machinery and Screws Machinery types are shown as follows with the number of screws after the type code.

Steam Turbine	ST	Steam Turbine with Electric Drive	SE
Steam Reciprocating	SR	Diesel	D
Diesel with Electric Drive	DE	Sail with Diesel Assistance	SD

A recent phenomenon has been the use of pod propulsion systems. These feature rotateable pods incorporating the propellers, and cut down on the need for separate directional thrusters. Pod technology is relatively new and ships incorporating this drive system have not been without technical difficulties. Ships with pods are indicated with a P and those with gas turbines have a G. The letter N indicates a nuclear reactor.

Normal Passenger Capacity, **Maximum Passenger Capacity** and **Crew Numbers** are again those quoted by the company, where possible, or from other authoritative sources if these are considered more reliable. In some cases the numbers quoted are berthed (b) and deck or unberthed (d). For school ships or training ships (s) is used to denote students or trainees. Passenger and crew numbers change from time to time, so the figures quoted here are a snapshot at the time of publication.

Dimensions are given in metres to one decimal place. Length is overall length. Beam is moulded breadth, which may be less than the width of the ship above the hull. Draught is full load draught.

Flag (and country codes) used throughout this book are the ISO 3166 standard code as follows.

AE	United Arab Emirates	FI	Finland	KN	St Kitts & Nevis	PL	Poland
AN	Netherlands Antilles	FJ	Fiji	KP	North Korea	PT	Portugal
AR	Argentina	FO	Faroes	KR	South Korea	RU	Russia
AU	Australia	FR	France	KY	Cayman Islands	SE	Sweden
AX	Aland Islands	GB	United Kingdom	KZ	Kazakhstan	SG	Singapore
BB	Barbados	GD	Grenada	LR	Liberia	SL	Sierra Leone
BE	Belgium	GE	Georgia	LU	Luxembourg	SN	Senegal
BM	Bermuda	GI	Gibraltar	MH	Marshall Islands	TH	Thailand
BR	Brazil	GL	Greenland	MM	Myanmar	TR	Turkey
BS	Bahamas	GR	Greece	MT	Malta	TT	Trinidad & Tobago
BZ	Belize	HK	Hong Kong	MX	Mexico	TV	Tuvalu
CA	Canada	HN	Honduras	MY	Malaysia	TZ	Tanzania
CK	Cook Islands	HR	Croatia	NI	Norwegian	UA	Ukraine
CL	Chile	ID	Indonesia		International	US	United States
CN	China	IL	Israel	NL	Netherlands	VC	St Vincent &
CY	Cyprus	IN	India	NO	Norway		Grenadines
DE	Germany	IS	Iceland	NZ	New Zealand	VE	Venezuela
DK	Denmark	IT	Italy	OM	Oman	VN	Vietnam
EC	Ecuador	JP	Japan	PA	Panama	VU	Vanuatu
EG	Egypt	KI	Kiribati	PF	French Polynesia	WF	Wallis & Futuna
ES	Spain	KM	Comoros	PH	Philippines	ZA	South Africa

Ownership of many vessels is complicated. Some ships are owned by their operator or one of its associated companies, while others are chartered in and some are owned by banks and finance companies. Within this book ships are only listed as chartered if they are chartered from a company that is not part of the same group, as many ships are owned by one-ship companies within a group but operated by other group companies.

Many ships are chartered from owners unconnected with the operator. I have tried to list these ships under the operator with whom they spend most time. One area where it has been particularly difficult to decide how to best present the information is the Arctic and Antarctic expedition ships, especially those owned by Russian companies but marketed throughout the world by a number of tour operators. In all cases I have tried to present the information in the most logical and accessible way, but suggestions for future improvement will be welcomed. There are some occasions when a ship appears more than once, under different operators. Examples of reasons why this happens are where a ship is to be transferred or sold part way through the currency of this book and, where the sale is already known about before the book closed for press or in a situation where a ship is chartered to different operators at different times of the year.

Some companies are not currently operating or have no ships. Where there is a good likelihood that operations will resume the company has been included in the relevant section. Similarly, some vessels were laid up. Those with a good chance of going back into service have also been included in the main sections.

Residential Cruise Ships are currently being advertised in both the United States of America and the United Kingdom. Only one such ship, THE WORLD, is currently in service and although others are projected, at the time of publication none had ordered or acquired a ship. Therefore Condo Cruise Line, Four Seasons Hotels and Resorts, Orphalese Global Strategies and Residential Cruise Line have not been included in this edition.

Names of ships are shown in capitals throughout this book. Ship name derivations are given where known and relevant either to the sphere of operation or to the owner. Some of these derivations are continuations of earlier themes and are perhaps less relevant today than formerly, but serve to link the current operation with earlier history of the owner.

Acknowledgements

I would like to thank the following individuals, without whose help this would have been a less good book.

Mark Amielanczyk, Jonathan Boonzaier, Miles Cowsill, Douglas Cromby, Matthew Davies, Egidio Ferrighi, Rick Frendt, Martin Grant, Clive Harvey, John Hendy, Andy Kilk, Bill Lawes, Doreen Lawes, Mick Lindsay, David Littlejohn, Ben Lyons, Stephen Macey, Chris Mason, John May, Lizette May, Brenda Mayes, Richard Mayes, Phil Neumann, Douglas Newman, Bruce Peter, Allan Ryszka-Onions, John-ward Phillips, Gillian Ridgway, Ted Scull, Oliver Sesemann, Richard Seville, Alf Sims, Frank Stainer, Matthew Sudders, Willem van der Leek, Nick Widdows, John Wiseman and Martin Wright.

The **Astor** at Oban *(Bruce Peter)*

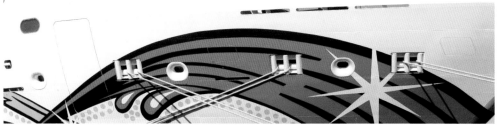

The **Norwegian Jewel** *(William Mayes)*

The **Saga Ruby**, northbound in the Suez Canal *(William Mayes)*

The **Rotterdam** comes home *(William Mayes)*

the **leading** *guide to the cruise industry*

section I Cruise Ships

7107 ISLANDS CRUISE

The Company 7107 Islands Cruise is a Filipino cruise line that was formed in 2008 by Filipino businessman Esteban C Tajanlangit. The company operates domestic cruises around the Philippine archipelago. In June 2009 the ship was seized by the Philippine tax department because of a dispute over unpaid import duties. The future of the company remains uncertain at the time of publishing.

Address Palawan Centre, 2nd Floor, 832 Arnaiz Ave, San Lorenzo, Makati City, Philippines 1223

Telephone +63 2 887 7107 **Fax** +63 2 887 4590

Website www.7107islandscruise.net

Area operated Philippines

ISLANDS CRUISE	5113gt	1968	17.0k	D2	274p	342p	137c	106.9m	16.2m	5.0m	PH

ISLANDS CRUISE was built as the Spanish car and passenger ferry VICENTE PUCHOL by Union Naval de Levante (yard number 101) at Valencia, Spain. She was delivered to Compania Trasmediterranea in December 1968. In 1987 she was sold to Attica Shipping of Greece and renamed ARCADIA. She appears to have been renamed ANGELINA LAURO for a single season in 1990, but reverted to ARCADIA during the following year. In 1997 she passed to Golden Sun Cruises of Greece without a change of name, but was re-acquired by Attica Shipping in 2000. In 2001 she was chartered to Great Lakes Cruises, and following a voyage to the Great Lakes from Europe, her charterers encountered difficulties and were forced to abandon their programme of cruises in the lakes. She was laid up in Montreal for 15 months before being sold at auction to Anaconda Maritime. She was renamed CARIBIC STAR and was to have been chartered to Megawest Cruises of Australia in 2004 for Pacific cruising as the TROPICAL ISLANDER, but that transaction failed to materialise. It then appeared that she may be destined for World Yacht Club as a condominium ship, but that never happened. In 2005 she was acquired by Danish company C&C Marine (Coco Explorer Cruises) and put into service in the Philippines. However, she was not successful and within a short time was laid up for sale. Taiwanese company Inluck International Cruise Group announced its purchase of the vessel in 2006, and its intention to rename her ASIA AND PACIFIC STAR. However this transaction was never completed. She was renamed ISLANDS CRUISE in April 2009, but was seized by the Philippines Customs Bureau in June 2009 for alleged failure to pay approximately $400,000 in import duty. IMO 6816970

ABERCROMBIE & KENT

The Company Abercrombie & Kent is a British-American tour operator specialising in luxury tours to exotic destinations, which was founded in 1962 by Geoffrey Kent and his parents Valerie and Colonel John Kent. The company, initially based in Nairobi, Kenya, specialised in long distance tours through East and Central Africa, but when American Jorie Butler joined the partnership in 1971, four years after John and Valerie Kent retired from active participation, horizons were expanded beyond Africa. The company also owns and operates the Nile cruise ships SUN BOAT III and SUN BOAT IV, and offers other cruises worldwide on the CLIPPER ODYSSEY and Antarctic cruises on the MINERVA. Abercrombie & Kent sells cruises on other 'adventure' type vessels.

Chairman and CEO Geoffrey Kent **Vice-Chairman** Jorie Butler Kent **Managing Director** Redmond Walsh

Address St George's House, Ambrose Street, Cheltenham, Gloucestershire GL50 3LG England
1520 Kensington Road, Suite 212, Oakbrook, Illinois 60523 –2156, United States of America

Telephone +44 845 6182200 **Fax** +44 845 0700607
+1 630 954 2944 **Fax** +1 630 954 3324

Website www.abercrombiekent.co.uk and www.abercrombiekent.com

Area operated Antarctica (MINERVA) Worldwide (CLIPPER ODYSSEY)

CLIPPER ODYSSEY	5218gt	1989	18.0k	D2	120p	120p	70c	103.0m	15.4m	4.3m	BS

Adriatic Cruises' **Dalmacija** *(Ivo Batricevik)*

Aegean Experience's **Aegean I** in Piraeus *(Matthew Davies)*

MINERVA	12449gt	1996	16.0k	D2	200p	200p	146c	133.0m	20.0m	5.1m	BS

CLIPPER ODYSSEY For details see under Zegrahm Expeditions (TUI).

MINERVA For details see under Swan Hellenic (All Leisure Group). Passenger numbers limited to 200 on Antarctic itineraries.

ADRIATIC CRUISES

The Company Adriatic Cruises was set up in 2006 by Croatian bus operator Autotrans to acquire the DALMACIJA from her former operator. A programme of Adriatic cruises was advertised for 2007, but in March it was announced that the ship had been chartered to Hansa Kreuzfahrten for the summer of 2007. During 2008 the company operated an itinerary with boarding points in Izmir and Split, but dropped the calls at ports north of Split. The new service included Corinth Canal transits in both directions and a call at Durres in Albania. However as this edition was closing for press there were reports that the company was seeking bankruptcy protection and that the ship was laid up.

Managing Director Theodor Candrlic

Address PO Box 288, HR 51000, Rijeka, Croatia

Telephone +385 51 660300

Website www.adriaticcruises.hr

Area operated The Dalmatian Coast of Croatia from Split and Izmir (not thought to be operating currently)

DALMACIJA	5619gt	1965	16.0k	D2	260p	302p	91c	116.8m	16.5m	5.3m	HR

DALMACIJA was built at the Brodogradiliste Uljanik Shipyard (yard number 243) at Pula, in what was then Yugoslavia, for the coastal cruising services of Yugoslavian state operator Jadrolinija. She also made a number of summer cruises in Northern Europe and Scandinavia. She passed to Intercruise in about 1991, underwent a major renovation in 1999, and was acquired by Uljanik Plovidba in 2001. She underwent another major rebuild in 2002, but retained much of her elegant profile. In 2006 Uljanik Plovidba pulled out of cruising in order to concentrate on its tanker business, and sold the DALMACIJA to Autotrans. She was refurbished in Pula and is now chartered to Adriatic Cruises. For the summer of 2007 she was chartered to Hansa Kreuzfahrten. Dalmacija (English Dalmatia) is a coastal region of Croatia, stretching from Rab in the north to the Gulf of Kotor in the south. IMO 6411964

ADVENTURE CRUISE LINES

The Company Adventure Cruise Lines is a US company.

Address 3419 Via Lido 632, Newport Beach, California 92663, United States of America

Telephone +1 310 987 9893 **Fax** +1 866 543 6054

Website www.adventurecruiselines.net

Area operated California, Hawaii, Washington and Alaska

PACIFIC MONARCH	336gt	1981	11.0k	D1	54p	80p	17c	41.1m	8.5m	2.3m	US

PACIFIC MONARCH was built by Blount Marine Corporation, Warren, Rhode Island as the NEW SHOREHAM I. She was acquired by Cruise West in 2000 and renamed SPIRIT OF GLACIER BAY. In 2006 she became Adventure Cruise Lines' PACIFIC MONARCH. IMO 8963739

AEGEAN EXPERIENCE

The Company The Aegean Experience is a Greek registered company established in 2008. It is believed that the ship is owned by Gerry Herrod, the founder of Orient Lines and Discovery World Cruises.

Address 1 Sirangiou Street, 18534 Piraeus, Greece

Telephone +30 210 413 5938 **Fax** +30 210 452 8950

Area operated Not currently operating; the ship is undergoing conversion in Greece

AEGEAN I	11563gt	1973	17.0k	D2	576p	682p	190c	140.5m	20.8m	6.6m	GR

AEGEAN I began life as the ro-ro cargo ship NARCIS of Zim Israel Navigation of Haifa. She was built by Santierul Naval Galatz (yard number 617) at Galatz, Romania. In 1985 she was acquired by Dolphin Hellas Shipping and renamed ALKYON. She was substantially refitted at Perama, Greece and re-delivered in 1988 as the AEGEAN DOLPHIN. During the following year she was renamed as the DOLPHIN, but she reverted to her previous name in 1990. In 1996 she was renamed AEGEAN I and operated at least one cruise for Discovery Cruises. She also undertook a charter to Renaissance Cruises in that year. In 1998 she commenced cruising for Golden Star Cruises. Following an ownership dispute involving Louis Cruise Lines the ship was laid up in 2006. IMO 7225910

ALL LEISURE GROUP

The Company All Leisure Group is the holding company of All Leisure Holidays, in turn the owner of Voyages of Discovery, Swan Hellenic and Discover Egypt. In April 2009 the business of Hebridean Island Cruises was bought out of administration.

Chairman Roger Allard **Chief Executive Officer** Ross Jobber

Address Lynnem House, 1 Victoria Way, Burgess Hill, West Sussex, RH15 9NF, England

Telephone +44 1444 462103 **Fax** +44 1444 462161

Website www.allleisuregroup.com

HEBRIDEAN ISLAND CRUISES

The Company Hebridean Island Cruises was established in 1988 to purchase and convert the car ferry COLUMBA for operation as the small luxury cruise ship HEBRIDEAN PRINCESS in the waters of Western Scotland. The company was a subsidiary of Hebridean Cruises plc, which purchased Hebridean Island Cruises from its previous owner in 1998. An expansion of operations occurred in 2001 with the acquisition of the former Renaissance Cruises' ship RENAISSANCE SIX, which was refitted and renamed HEBRIDEAN SPIRIT. The new ship operated on worldwide itineraries. In 2006 the company was renamed as Hebridean International Cruises Limited. In August 2007 58% of the share capital was acquired by Stonefield Castle Group. With the economic downturn in the United Kingdom biting hard, the company sold the HEBRIDEAN SPIRIT at short notice in the spring of 2009, and returned to its roots. The sale of the HEBRIDEAN SPIRIT was completed on 7 April 2009 and on the following day the company went into administration. Within three weeks, the business and the ship was sold to All Leisure Group and renamed as Hebridean Island Cruises. The Hebrides, after which the company is named, is an archipelago off the Western coast of Scotland, comprising the Inner and Outer Hebrides. They include Skye, Lewis, Harris and Islay.

Chairman The Lord Sterling of Plaistow

Address Kintail House, Carleton New Road, Skipton, North Yorkshire, BD23 2DE

Telephone +44 1756 704700 **Fax** +44 1756 704794

Website www.hebridean.co.uk

Area operated Scotland, the Scottish Isles and occasionally Norway

| HEBRIDEAN PRINCESS | 2112gt | 1964 | 14.5k | D2 | 49p | 49p | 38c | 71.6m | 13.3m | 2.7m | GB |

HEBRIDEAN PRINCESS, the former MacBrayne car ferry COLUMBA underwent a massive transformation in 1989 to become one of the most exclusive cruise ships in the world. Hall Russell (yard number 912) at Aberdeen, Scotland built her as one of a trio of side-loading car ferries for service to the Western Isles from Oban. In 1973 David MacBrayne and the Caledonian Steam Packet Company (both British Government owned) were merged into Caledonian MacBrayne, and the ship eventually re-registered under that organisation. In 1988 she was sold to Leisure and Marine Holdings (trading as Hebridean Island Cruises) and converted into the luxury country house style cruise ship HEBRIDEAN PRINCESS. In 1998 the company and the ship were sold to Hebridean Cruises plc, but the style of operation remained unchanged. During the summer of 2006 HM Queen Elizabeth II chartered the ship for a week of Scottish cruising. IMO 6409351

SWAN HELLENIC

The Company The origins of what is now Swan Hellenic go back to the 1930's when the Hellenic Travellers Club ran cruises and tours to Greece and Asia Minor. Following the end of the Second World

All Leisure Group's **Hebridean Princess** *(Bruce Peter)*

All Leisure Group's **Minerva** *(Bill Lawes)*

War, W F & R K Swan, who then owned the club, re-introduced Hellenic cruises. The first of these cruises was undertaken in 1954 aboard the 1,700 ton 1952-built MIAOULIS, chartered from Nomikos Lines. It was in the following year that Sir Mortimer Wheeler, the celebrated archaeologist, began his connection with the firm, of which he was later to become Chairman. In that year the company operated its second cruise aboard the AEGAEON, owned by the Greek Typaldos Lines, and by then more than 40 years old. W F & R K Swan (Hellenic) Ltd, trading as Swans Hellenic Cruises used another of that company's ships, the MEDITERRANEAN, between 1956 and 1958. Typaldos also provided the ADRIATIKI for ten cruises between 1957 and 1961. By the early 1960's a pattern of three early and three late season cruises aboard the ANKARA, chartered from Turkish Maritime Lines, had emerged. At the start of the next decade the number of cruises undertaken each year had steadily increased and a replacement was sought for the ANKARA, which was by now more than 45 years old, and only partly air-conditioned. The vessel selected was the ORPHEUS of Epirotiki, and she served Swans well for 22 years. In the meantime, P&O had bought Swans Hellenic Cruises in 1983 from Trust House Forte (who had acquired the company in 1968), and continued to develop the business by gradually extending the cruising season. Later the company was restyled as Swan Hellenic. In 1995, the ORPHEUS was replaced by the newly built MINERVA, based on the hull of an unwanted Russian research vessel, but completed and fitted out as a very suitable ship to take the business forward. Initially taken on a four-year charter, this was extended to the spring of 2003, when the laid-up R EIGHT, renamed as the MINERVA II, replaced her. Ken Swan died in August 2005, and subsequently Carnival Corporation (the then owner of Swan Hellenic) decided to transfer the MINERVA II to Princess Cruises as the ROYAL PRINCESS. In February 2007 Carnival announced that the Swan Hellenic brand was not going to be revived. Just three weeks later Lord Sterling acquired Swan Hellenic from Carnival, but within a short time had sold the brand to Voyages of Discovery. The company started trading again in spring 2008, using the company's earlier ship, the MINERVA, on which a six-year charter had been secured. Swan Hellenic has subsequently re-entered the river cruise market.

Chairman The Lord Sterling of Plaistow

Address Lynnem House, 1 Victoria Way, Burgess Heath, West Sussex, RH15 9NF, England

Telephone +44 845 246 9700 **Fax** +44 1444 462181

Website www.swanhellenic.com

Areas operated Mediterranean Sea, Northern Europe, Scandinavia, Africa and Antarctica

MINERVA	12449gt	1996	16.0k	D2	362p	394p	157c	133.0m	20.0m	5.1m	BS

MINERVA was partially constructed by the Sudostroitelnyy Zavod Okean Shipyard (yard number 1) at Nikolaev in the Ukraine as the research vessel OKEAN. Her keel was laid in 1987 and she was launched in 1989 but not completed. She was purchased by V-Ships and towed to the Mariotti shipyard in Genoa for completion as a passenger ship. On completion in 1996 she was chartered to the Peninsular and Oriental Steam Navigation Company for use by Swan Hellenic Cruises, as a replacement for the smaller ORPHEUS, and given the name MINERVA. At the end of her charter in 2003, she was returned to V-Ships, who succeeded in setting two new charters for her. For the summer of 2003 she became the SAGA PEARL for the 'over 50' tour operator, Saga Holidays, and in the winter she took the name EXPLORER II for Abercrombie & Kent's expedition cruises. For summer 2004 she was operated by Saga again, reverting to her Saga name. In November 2004 she took up winter employment with Abercrombie & Kent, but for the summer she operated for Phoenix Reisen as the ALEXANDER VON HUMBOLDT. In January 2007 it was announced that Voyages of Discovery had taken the ship on long-term charter. Some six months later the group acquired Swan Hellenic and so the perfect match was to return the renamed MINERVA to that organisation. The ship will continue to serve her winters in the Antarctic where she is marketed in conjunction with Abercrombie and Kent, and where passenger numbers are limited to 200. Minerva is the Roman name for Athena, the Greek goddess of (amongst other things) wisdom. MINERVA is chartered to Phoenix Reisen for the return leg of her Antarctic season in spring 2010. IMO 9144196

VOYAGES OF DISCOVERY

The Company Voyages of Discovery is a brand of the United Kingdom registered All Leisure Group. Its origins are in the Schools Abroad business that started offering educational cruises in 1984. The cruises, mostly run during school holidays and using a variety of chartered Greek ships were popular with both adults and children and so the company expanded into the mainstream cruise market. For a while, in the early 1990s, the company was Greek-owned and operated the EMERALD SEAS, although in that era the company was known as Discovery Cruises. The Greek company failed in the mid 1990s and came back under UK control. Voyages of Discovery has chartered a number of ships over the years including the AEGEAN I and the AEGEAN SPIRIT (formerly Costa's ENRICO C). Until 2004 the company operated the DISCOVERY from May to November on charter from Discovery World Cruises (founded by Gerry Herrod), but now also markets itself under that name in the USA following its recent acquisition of that business, together with the DISCOVERY. For 2008 the company also operated the OCEAN MAJESTY under exclusive charter between March and May on a series of Mediterranean, Black Sea and Red Sea Cruises. Voyages of Discovery still operates at least one schools cruise each year, with those in 2009 and 2010 being to the Eastern Mediterranean in the October half-term.

Managing Director David Yellow

Address Lynnem House, 1 Victoria Way, Burgess Hill, West Sussex, RH15 9NF, England

Telephone +44 1444 462150 **Fax** +44 1444 462160

Website www.voyagesofdiscovery.com

Area operated Europe, Red Sea, Scandinavia, The Americas, Antarctica, South Pacific and the Galapagos Islands

DISCOVERY	20216gt	1971	18.0k	D2	698p	758p	350c	168.7m	24.6m	7.5m	BM

DISCOVERY was built by Rheinstahl Nordseewerke (yard number 414) at Emden in Germany as the ISLAND VENTURE for Norwegian Cruiseships (a joint venture between Fearney & Eger and Lorentzen), to be chartered to Flagship Cruises for service between New York and Bermuda, along with her sister, the SEA VENTURE. The service could not support two ships, so the ISLAND VENTURE was put up for charter. Princess Cruises was in search of a replacement for the CARLA C, so chartered the ISLAND VENTURE and renamed her as the ISLAND PRINCESS in 1972. She passed to The Peninsular & Oriental Steam Navigation Company, with Princess Cruises in 1974. In 1999 she was sold to Ringcroft Investment and chartered to Hyundai Merchant Marine as the HYUNDAI PUNGAK for cruising from South Korea. Having acquired three ships, the market could not sustain this number of berths and the ship was laid up before being sold to Gerry Herrod, the founder of Orient Lines. She was taken to Tuzla in Turkey and refitted as the PLATINUM in 2001. From 2002 she operated for Herrod's own Discovery World Cruises on South American itineraries in winter and on Voyages of Discovery educational cruises in summer, as the DISCOVERY in both roles. Herrod retired in 2004 and Voyages of Discovery now operate the ship under its own name and as Discovery World Cruises. The most famous ship to bear the name DISCOVERY was undoubtedly that of Captain Robert Falcon Scott, used as the ship for the National Antarctic Expedition of 1901-1904. That ship is currently preserved in Dundee, Scotland. IMO 7108514

AMBASSADORS INTERNATIONAL

The Company Ambassadors International is a US travel, events and marine services group. In early 2007, Ambassadors International acquired Windstar Cruises from Carnival Corporation. What little is left of Majestic America Line is currently for sale, along with other assets, as the company seeks to focus on Windstar Cruises.

MAJESTIC AMERICA LINE

The Company Majestic America Line is part of Ambassadors International. In 2006 the company acquired both the American West Steamboat Company and the Delta Queen Steamboat Company and these began to trade as Majestic America Line during 2007.

The American West Steamboat Company, owned by Oregon Rail Holdings of Portland, Oregon, was established in 1995, with the new QUEEN OF THE WEST reintroducing sternwheeler cruising to the Columbia, Willamette and Snake Rivers after an absence of almost 80 years. The 2,000-mile long Columbia River is the second longest river in the USA and saw its first sternwheeler, the JENNIE CLARK, in 1855. In 2006 the company was acquired by Ambassadors International and incorporated into Majestic America Line.

The origins of the Delta Queen Steamboat Company can be traced back to 1890, when Captain Greene established the Greene Line of Steamers with the purchase at auction of the riverboat H K BEDFORD. Freight services began on the upper Ohio and Kanahwa Rivers, but before long the company started to offer passenger services. In 1948, the DELTA QUEEN entered service for the company, having been bought at auction from the US Navy's reserve fleet. In the early 1950's the company was facing a very

All Leisure Group's **Discovery** *(Harwich International Port)*

Majestic America Line's **American Queen** at Point Pleasant *(Andrew Kilk)*

Majestic America Line's **Columbia Queen** at Portland *(Andrew Kilk)*

Majestic America Line's **Empress of the North** at Portland *(Andrew Kilk)*

uncertain future, but California businessman Richard Simonton stepped in and with the help of publicist Betty Blake, soon had the company thriving again. Following an emotional campaign, the DELTA QUEEN, with her vast quantities of wood, was granted Congressional exception to SOLAS. The company was acquired by Overseas National Airways in 1969, and adopted its current name five years later. In the early 1990's, after another change of ownership, the company acquired the troubled American Hawaii Cruise Line and both companies then became part of the newly formed holding company, American Classic Voyages. Following severe financial difficulties after the September 11th attacks on the World Trade Centre the company collapsed, but the steamboat side of the business was rescued by Delaware North Companies Inc. In 2006 this company was acquired by Ambassadors International and incorporated into Majestic America Line. During 2008 it was clear that the American river cruising business of the company was in dire straits. The MISSISSIPPI QUEEN renovation was abandoned and what remains of the vessel is little more that a hulk that is unlikely to re-enter passenger service. The DELTA QUEEN, unable for the time being to gain further exemption from safety regulations, has temporarily become a hotel on the Tennessee River at Chattanooga. The EMPRESS OF THE NORTH and the CONTESSA were surrendered to the creditor United States Maritime Administration and the AMERICAN QUEEN was thought to be heading the same way. The remainder of the Majestic America fleet is likely to be sold off piecemeal. The fleet is listed here for convenience, pending final disposal.

Address 2101 Fourth Avenue, Suite 1150, Seattle, Washington, WA98121 United States of America

Telephone +1 206 292 9606 **Fax** +1 206 340 0975

Website www.majesticamericaline.com

Area operated Columbia, Willamette and Snake Rivers and Alaska's Inside Passage and the Mississippi, Arkansas and Ohio Rivers in the Deep South and Heartland of the USA (not currently operating)

AMERICAN QUEEN	10159gt	1995	10.0k	SR1	444p	481p	180c	127.5m	25.9m	2.6m	US
COLUMBIA QUEEN	1599gt	2000	11.0k	D2	150p	150p	57c	66.4m	19.5m	2.1m	US
CONTESSA	490gt	1986	22.0k	D2	48p	48p	15c	32.0m	9.4m	2.0m	US
EMPRESS OF THE NORTH	3388gt	2003	14.0k	DE2	231p	235p	84c	109.7m	16.4m	3.8m	US
MISSISSIPPI QUEEN	‡3364gt	1976	12.0k	SR1	414p	414p	157c	114.6m	20.4m	3.4m	US
QUEEN OF THE WEST	2115gt	1994	11.0k	DE1	150p	163p	47c	70.15m	15.2m	2.1m	US

AMERICAN QUEEN was built by the McDermott Shipyard (yard number 296) in Amelia, Louisiana, USA for the Delta Queen Steamboat Company. She is currently laid up near New Orleans. IMO 9084542

COLUMBIA QUEEN was built for the Delta Queen Steamboat Company at the time that it was part of American Classic Voyages. The ship was built by the Leevac Shipyard (yard number 311) at Jennings, Louisiana, USA. When the American Classic Voyages group collapsed in 2001, the ship was laid up and not reactivated until 2005, when put into service by Great American River Journeys. That operation ceased after a single season and the ship was laid up again. She was acquired by Majestic America Line in October 2006 and soon afterwards commenced a series of cruises in the Northwest Rivers. She is laid up at Portland, Oregon. IMO 8643303

CONTESSA was built by Nichols Brothers Boatbuilders (yard number S 81) at Freeland, Washington for Glacier Bay Cruises and Tours as the EXECUTIVE EXPLORER. She was acquired by Ambassadors International at the end of 2005, but did not enter service until the autumn of 2006. The CONTESSA was surrendered to MARAD on the bankruptcy of Majestic America Line in 2008. IMO 8978679

EMPRESS OF THE NORTH was built at the Nichols Boatbuilders Yard (yard number S142) at Freeland in Washington State, USA. She is currently laid up in Portland. IMO 9263538

MISSISSIPPI QUEEN was built by Jeffboat Inc (yard number 2999) at Jeffersonville, Indiana, USA for the Mississippi Queen Steamboat Company. The ship was to undergo a major refurbishment, but although the strip-out has occurred, no rebuilding work has been done. The shell of this vessel remains laid up in New Orleans and is unlikely to return to passenger service. IMO 8643066

QUEEN OF THE WEST was built at the Nichols Brothers Boatbuilders Yard (yard number S110) at Freeland, Washington State, USA. She is laid up at Portland. IMO 8642957

Majestic America Line's **Mississippi Queen** at St Louis *(Andrew Kilk)*

Majestic America Line's **Queen of the West** *(Majestic America Line)*

WINDSTAR CRUISES

The Company Windstar Cruises Inc. has its origins in the formation in 1984 of Windstar Sail Cruises Limited, a Bahamas registered company set up by Karl Gosta Andren to build and operate the first large commercial sailing vessels since the 1920's. The first two ships were ordered in October 1985 and a third shortly afterwards with an option for a fourth ship, never exercised. The WIND STAR was delivered in October 1986, followed six months later by the WIND SONG. Unfortunately, the company's marketing failed to generate the passenger volume required to fill their ships, so in June 1987 Holland America took on this role, at the same time acquiring a 50% stake in the company. The remaining 50% was purchased in September 1988 and although the company retained an outward appearance of independence, there was a certain amount of integration behind the scenes. In 1994 the head office was moved to Holland America's address in Seattle and the company name was changed to Windstar Cruises Inc. In early 2003 the WIND SONG, suffered an engine room fire and was declared a constructive total loss. She was subsequently scuttled. Windstar Cruises became part of Ambassadors International in early 2007, when it was acquired from Carnival Corporation. In mid 2009, the company took over the management of its vessels from V-Ships.

Address 300 Elliott Avenue West, Seattle, WA 98119, United States of America

Telephone +1 206 281 3535 **Fax** +1 206 286 3229

Website www.windstarcruises.com

Areas operated Mediterranean and Caribbean

WIND SPIRIT	5736gt	1988	14.0k	SD1	148p	168p	91c	134.2m	15.8m	4.1m	BS
WIND STAR	5703gt	1986	12.0k	SD1	148p	168p	91c	134.2m	15.5m	4.1m	BS
WIND SURF	14745gt	1989	12.0k	SDE2	308p	397p	178c	187.2m	20.0m	5.0m	BS

WIND SPIRIT was built, along with her sisters the WIND STAR and the recently lost WIND SONG, by Societe Nouvelle des Ateliers et Chantiers du Havre (yard number 272) at Le Havre, France, as a motorised sailing yacht capable of being schooner rigged. She is the fastest of the trio of ships built for the company. Wind assisted she can make 17 knots and has sailed predominantly in the Mediterranean and Caribbean, but did spend part of the 1988 season in Alaska. Clara van der Vorm, wife of the then chairman of Holland America Line, christened her. IMO 8603509

WIND STAR was delivered in March 1987 by Societe Nouvelle des Ateliers et Chantiers du Havre (yard number 269) and following a positioning cruise spent a season in French Polynesia. Her godmother was Louise Andren, the wife of the line's founder. She generally operates in the Caribbean and Mediterranean. IMO 8420878

WIND SURF was built by Societe Nouvelle des Ateliers et Chantiers du Havre (yard number 274) for Club Mediterranee SA (Club Med) of France and on delivery at the beginning of 1990 was registered in Fort de France, Martinique, thus qualifying her for French state subsidies. Wind assisted she is capable of making 14 knots. She operated in the Caribbean and Mediterranean as the CLUB MED 1 until June 1997 when she was bought by Windstar Cruises and renamed WIND SURF. Her operational areas remain unchanged. IMO 8700785

AMERICAN CANADIAN CARIBBEAN LINE

The Company American Canadian Caribbean Line was founded in 1966 by Captain Luther Blount to serve the demand for small ship cruising in American coastal waters. The ships are all shallow draft, have retractable wheelhouses to allow access to rivers that would otherwise be inaccessible, and are fitted with a bow ramp to allow direct disembarkation onto secluded beaches. Luther Blount died in 2006, at the age of 90. In November 2006, the company's third ship, the NIAGARA PRINCE, passed into the ownership of three colleges, a $6.5 million legacy from inventor and philanthropist Blount. However, she remained unused so the company bought her back in 2008.

President Nancy Blount

Address 461 Water Street, PO Box 368, Warren, Rhode Island 02885, United States of America

Telephone +1 401 247 0955 **Fax** +1 401 247 2350

Website www.accl-smallships.com

Area operated Caribbean and Central America (winter), East Coast USA and Canada (summer)

GRANDE CARIBE	761gt	1997	10.0k	D2	100p	100p	17c	55.6m	11.9m	2.0m	US
GRANDE MARINER	829gt	1998	10.0k	D2	100p	100p	17c	56.0m	11.9m	1.9m	US
NIAGARA PRINCE	667gt	1994	10.0k	D2	84p	94p	17c	53.0m	12.2m	2.0m	US

All three ships were built for the company by Blount Industries (yard numbers 294, 298 and 287) at Warren, Rhode Island, USA. IMO 8978631 8978643 and 8978629

AMERICAN CRUISE LINES

The Company American Cruise Lines was established in 2000.

President P Booth **Vice-Chairman** R Alim

Address 741 Boston Post Road, Suite 200, Guildford, Connecticut 06437-2743, United States of America

Telephone +1 203 453 6800 **Fax** +1 203 453 0417

Website www.americancruiselines.com

Area operated East Coast USA from New England to Florida

AMERICAN EAGLE	1148gt	2000	12.5k	D2	49p	49p	22c	51.2m	13.1m	2.0m	US
AMERICAN GLORY	1148gt	2002	12.5k	D2	49p	49p	22c	51.2m	13.1m	2.0m	US
AMERICAN SPIRIT	1973gt	2005	14.0k	D1	100p	100p	27c	65.2m	13.9m	2.0m	US
AMERICAN STAR	1973gt	2007	14.0k	D1	100p	100p	27c	65.2m	13.9m	2.0m	US

AMERICAN EAGLE was built by Chesapeake Shipbuilding (yard number 78) at Salisbury, Maryland, USA for the company. At the time of writing the AMERICAN EAGLE was sale-listed on Chesapeake Shipbuilding's website. IMO 8972340

AMERICAN GLORY was built for the company by Chesapeake Shipbuilding (yard number 80). IMO 8972338

AMERICAN SPIRIT was built by Chesapeake Shipbuilding (yard number 82). IMO 9283124

AMERICAN STAR was delivered by Chesapeake Shipbuilding (yard number 86) in the summer of 2007. IMO 9427615

Cruise ship on order

INDEPENDENCE	3000gt	2010	14.0k	D2	104p	104p	c	73.0m	15.4m	m	US

INDEPENDENCE is under construction at Chesapeake Shipbuilding and is due for delivery in the spring of 2010.

PEARL SEAS CRUISES

The Company Pearl Seas Cruises is a subsidiary of American Cruise Lines. The order placed with the Irving Shipyard was for two vessels, but with the long delays in completing the first ship, the order for the second was cancelled.

Chaiman and Chief Executive Officer Charles Robertson

Address 741 Boston Post Road, Suite 200, Guildford, Connecticut 06437, United States of America

Telephone +1 203 453 4211 **Fax** +1 203 453 5072

Website www.pearlseascruises.com

Area operated East Coast America from Canada (including the Great Lakes) to the Caribbean

PEARL MIST	4985gt	2009	17.0k	D2	210p	210p	c	99.0m	16.8m	3.5m	MH

PEARL MIST was built by the Irving Shipyard (yard number 6092) in Halifax, Nova Scotia. The order was originally for two ships, but serious delays in the delivery of the PEARL MIST led to the cancellation of the second ship, and at the time of writing the PEARL MIST had still not been delivered. All cabins on the ship have private balconies. IMO 9412701

Windstar Cruises' **Wind Star** at Tortuga *(Rick Frendt)*

Windstar Cruises' **Wind Surf** in the Adriatic Sea *(John May)*

American Canadian Caribbean Line's **Grande Caribe** *(ACCL)*

American Cruise Lines' **American Spirit** at Clarkston *(Ben Lyons)*

AMERICAN SAFARI CRUISES

The Company American Safari Cruises is a US company, established in 1997. The company also operates two smaller vessels that do not qualify for inclusion.

Address 3826 18th Avenue West, Seattle, WA98119, United States of America

Telephone +1 206 284 0300 **Fax** +1 206 283 9322

Website www.amsafari.com

Area operated California, Mexico, Washington and Alaska

SAFARI EXPLORER	695gt	1998	10.0k	D2	36p	40p	16c	45.7m	11.6m	m	US

SAFARI EXPLORER was built by Freeport Shipbuilding and Marine Repair (yard number 151) at Freeport, Florida as the research and survey vessel RAPTURE. She was converted for cruising in 2001, and was acquired by her current owner in 2008 and renamed SAFARI EXPLORER. IMO 8964654

ANEDIN LINE

The Company Rederi AB Allandia (Anedin Linjen), is a Swedish company operating a single overnight cruise ship between Stockholm and Mariehamn on the Finnish Aland Islands. The company, whose trading name is thought to be a Swedish version of Onedin Line – the title of a popular British television drama series of the 1970's about a 19th century ship owner – had begun running this service in that decade using the chartered ACHILLEUS. Ownership of the company passed through a number of hands over the years, including Sally Line and Effjohn International.

Address Vasagatan 6, 11181 Stockholm, Sweden

Telephone +46 8 456 2200 **Fax** +46 8 100 741

Website www.anedinlinjen.com

Area operated 24 hour cruises from Stockholm, Sweden

BIRGER JARL	3564gt	1953	15.0k	D1	340p	369p	c	92.7m	14.2m	4.9m	SE

BIRGER JARL was built under that name by Finnboda Varf (yard number 351) in Stockholm, Sweden as a steam powered ferry for Stockholms Rederi AB Svea for service on the routes from Stockholm to Helsinki and Turku. By 1973, when she was sold to Bore Line subsidiary Jakob Lines, she had been wearing the corporate livery of the Silja Line consortium for a number of years. Her new owner set her to work in the north of the Gulf of Bothnia and renamed her as the BORE NORD. In the following summer she operated cruises for Bore Line between Turku and Visby, Gotland. She later served as an accommodation ship at Stavanger, Norway. Her next move was to Mini Carriers in 1977, for use on a new Baltic Sea service as the MINISEA; this service never materialised. In 1978 she was sold to the perhaps inappropriately named Caribbean Shipping Company of Panama as a replacement for the ACHILLEUS, referred to above. She began her new career under the name BALTIC STAR and a little later was re-engined with diesels. She has proved to be a very popular ship, despite the impressive tonnage against which she competes. In 2002, she reverted to her original name. Birger Jarl is said to have been the founder of what we now know as the city of Stockholm, in about 1250. IMO 5044893

ANTARCTIC SHIPPING CORPORATION

The Company Antarctic Shipping Corporation is a Chilean company founded in 2002 by a group of former naval officers.

Address Ebro 2740, Office 602, Las Condes, Santiago, Chile

Telephone +56 2 481 6910 **Fax** +56 2 481 6917

Website www.antarctic.cl

Area operated Antarctica and Patagonia

ANTARCTIC DREAM	2180gt	1959	10.0k	D3	78p	78p	40c	82.0m	11.9m	4.6m	BZ

ANTARCTIC DREAM was built by Haarlemsche Scheepsbouw (yard number 552) at Haarlem in the Netherlands as the PILOTO PARDO for the Chilean Navy. In 1998 she was sold to Paoa Naviera and renamed as the HOTU MATUA. She joined her current owner, Dreamright Investment, in 2003 and adopted the name ANTARCTIC DREAM for her new cruise services. During 2009 she is expected to cruise around Spitzbergen in the summer. IMO 5278432

ANTARCTICA XXI

The Company Antarctica Travels is a Chilean Tour operator specializing in fly cruises to Antarctica from Punta Arenas, with flights to King George Island in the South Shetland Islands.

Address Lautaro Navarro 987, 2do Piso, Punta Arenas, Chile

Telephone +56 61 614100 **Fax** +56 61 614105

Website www.antarcticaxxi.com

Area operated Antarctica

PROFESSOR MULTANOVSKIY	1753gt	1982	9.0k	D2	52p	52p	23c	71.6m	12.8m	4.5m	RU

PROFESSOR MULTANOVSKIY was built for the Government of Russia's Hydrometeorological Institute by Oy Laivateollisuus (yard number 346) at Turku, Finland. The ship is now operated by the Arctic and Antarctic Research Institute to whom she passed in 1994. She is named after Professor Boris Multanovskiy (1876-1946), an eminent meteorologist and polar researcher. Antarctica XXI operates the ship from November 2009 to January 2010. IMO 8010362

ANTARPPLY EXPEDITIONS

The Company Antarpply Expeditions is an Argentinean Tour operator specializing in cruises to Antarctica.

Address Gob Paz 633, 1st Floor, 9410 Ushuaia, Argentina

Telephone +54 2901 433636 **Fax** +54 2901 437728

Website www.antarpply.com

Area operated Antarctica

USHUAIA	‡2802gt	1970	14.0k	D2	82p	84p	38c	84.8m	15.6m	5.5m	PA

USHUAIA was built as the US Government research vessel RESEARCHER by the American Shipbuilding Co (yard number 198) at Lorain, Ohio, USA. Launched in 1968, she was not completed until 1970. She was renamed as the MALCOLM BALDRIGE in 1988 and was sold to Argentinean company Ushuaia Adventure in 2001, when she took her current name. Cruise North seasonally chartered her from 2005, but she now appears to be operating on charter to Antarpply Expeditions. Ushuaia is the capital city of the Argentine province of Tierra del Fuego and is the world's southernmost city. IMO 6901907

APOLLO MANAGEMENT

The Company Apollo Management is a New York-based investment group. Oceania Cruises was acquired in February 2007 and during 2008 Regent Seven Seas Cruises was purchased from Carlson. Both of these companies are now part of Apollo's Prestige Cruise Holdings division. Also during 2008 Apollo entered into an agreement to acquire 50% of NCL, including NCL America for which a separate agreement was in force, allowing Star Cruises to pull out if certain profit levels were not achieved. Star Cruises exercised its option in the autumn of 2008, leaving NCL America entirely under the control of Apollo. Although NCL is still 50% owned by Star Cruises, Apollo Management has control.

Chief Executive Officer Leon Black

NCL AMERICA

The Company NCL America is a US based former subsidiary of Star Cruises specifically set up to operate US registered and crewed ships in the Hawaiian Islands. Passenger numbers did not meet expectations, leading to the PRIDE OF HAWAI'I being withdrawn from service and repositioned to Europe for 2008. In late 2008 NCL America became wholly owned by Apollo Group, following the withdrawal by Star Cruises, and the PRIDE OF ALOHA was returned to Star.

Address Suite 900, 900 Bishop Street, Honolulu, United States of America

Telephone +1 808 527 3800 **Fax** +1 808 527 3801

Anedin Line's **Birger Jarl** in Stockholm *(Rick Frendt)*

Antarctic Shipping Corporation's **Antarctic Dream** at Ushuaia *(Bill Lawes)*

Antarctica XXI's **Professor Multanovskiy** in Antarctica *(Bill Lawes)*

NCL America's **Pride of America** at Kauai *(Rick Frendt)*

Website www.ncl.com

Areas Operated Hawaii

PRIDE OF AMERICA	80439gt	2005	21.0k	DEP2	2146p	2300p	900c	281.3m	32.2m	8.0m	US
UNITED STATES	53329gt	1952	35.0k	ST4	1382P	1928P	1093c	301.8m	30.9m	9.8m	US

PRIDE OF AMERICA was ordered by the new United States Lines (part of the American Classic Voyages grouping) from the Ingalls Shipbuilding Yard (yard number 7671) at Pascagoula, Mississippi, USA as one of a pair of what were to be the first ocean passenger ships to be constructed in a US shipyard for more than 40 years. As in other histories in this book, the events of September 11, 2001 had a devastating effect on American Classic Voyages and the company filed for bankruptcy. Norwegian Cruise Line later purchased what there was of these two ships and had the parts towed to Bremerhaven where both ships were to have been completed for the Hawaiian cruise market. The ship was lengthened by 25 metres at this time. While being completed, the PRIDE OF AMERICA as she was now named, was partially sunk during a storm on 14 January 2004. The shipyard subsequently filed for bankruptcy and it is thought that what little there was of the second ship has now been scrapped or incorporated into another ship. As an 'American built' and US flagged ship she is able to operate in the Hawaii Islands without the need to call at a foreign port. Her godmother was Elaine Chao, then US Secretary of Labour. IMO 9209221

UNITED STATES, the fastest passenger liner ever built, has been languishing in various ports for more than 35 years, since she was withdrawn from service in 1969. She was built by the Newport News Shipbuilding and Drydock Company (yard number 488) in Newport News, Virginia, USA for the transatlantic service of United States Lines to partner the older and smaller AMERICA. She gained the Blue Riband for the fastest westbound and eastbound crossings of the North Atlantic in 1952 with an eastbound average speed of 35.53 knots, a speed not subsequently beaten by a conventional passenger ship. Withdrawn from transatlantic service in November 1969, she was laid up first in Newport News and later in Hampton Roads and then Norfolk. In June 1992 she was towed to Istanbul and in November 1993 moved to Sevastopol for the removal of asbestos. In May 1994 she returned to Istanbul (Tuzla) and in July 1996 was towed to Philadelphia. Norwegian Cruise Line acquired the UNITED STATES in April 2003, although it is extremely unlikely that she will ever re-enter commercial service, and she remains laid up. IMO 5373476

NORWEGIAN CRUISE LINE

The Company The origins of Norwegian Cruise Line date from 1966 when the Norwegian Klosters Rederi ordered a car ferry from a Bergen shipyard to fill what was perceived as a gap in the ferry market, a route from Southern England to Spain. Due to external difficulties the route was quickly abandoned and alternative work was sought for the 11,000 ton SUNWARD. Under the Norwegian Caribbean Line banner she was placed in a new cruise service to the Caribbean, based in Miami, Florida. Such was the success that a second, slightly larger vessel was ordered, the STARWARD, and then another, the SKYWARD. Two further ships were ordered in 1970 from an Italian yard, but after the first (the SOUTHWARD) was delivered the building cost of the second ship escalated dramatically and the company abandoned her. She was subsequently completed as P&O's SPIRIT OF LONDON and is Singapore Star Shipping's FLAMENCO 1. In 1979 the Klosters company acquired the long laid-up transatlantic liner FRANCE and after a major refit she became the world's largest cruise ship – the NORWAY. Further expansion occurred in 1984 with the acquisition by Klosters of another Norwegian owned company, Royal Viking Line, together with its three luxury ships. That company ran for a while as a separate entity, but by 1991 its earlier ships had been absorbed into Norwegian Caribbean Line and Royal Viking Line was left with just two new ships, both of which were eventually sold to units of the now Carnival Group. Royal Cruise Line together with its one remaining ship, the CROWN ODYSSEY, joined the group in 1990. Transfers to that fleet over the next four years included two of the original Royal Viking trio, together with the last ever RV ship, the ROYAL VIKING QUEEN. More new ships came on stream during the 1990's and in a restyling the company adopted the title Norwegian Cruise Line. Following a battle for the company between Carnival Holdings and Star Cruises, the protagonists agreed to take split ownership of Norwegian Cruise Line and its then subsidiary, Orient Lines, in the ratio of 40 to 60. Subsequently Carnival withdrew and control passed to Star Cruises in 2000. Recently, several of Star's new-buildings have been allocated to the company, and two of NCL's smaller ships have gone in the opposite direction. In 2007 Star Cruises sold 50% of Norwegian Cruise Line (together with control) to Apollo Management.

President Kevin Sheehan

Address 7665 Corporate Centre Drive, Miami, Florida 33126, United States of America

Telephone +1 305 436 4000 **Fax** +1 305 436 4120

Website www.ncl.com

Areas Operated North America, Caribbean Sea, South America and Europe

NORWEGIAN DAWN	92250gt	2002	24.0k	DEP2	2224p	2683p	1126c	294.1m	32.2m	8.2m	BS
NORWEGIAN DREAM	50764gt	1992	21.0k	D2	1726p	2156p	614c	229.8m	28.5m	6.8m	BS
NORWEGIAN GEM	93530gt	2007	24.0k	DEP2	2384p	2750p	1154c	294.1m	32.2m	8.2m	BS
NORWEGIAN JADE	93558gt	2006	24.0k	DEP2	2224p	2750p	1100c	294.1m	32.2m	8.6m	BS
NORWEGIAN JEWEL	93502gt	2005	24.0k	DEP2	2376p	2750p	1130c	294.1m	32.2m	8.2m	BS
NORWEGIAN MAJESTY	40876gt	1992	21.0k	D2	1460p	1790p	550c	207.3m	27.6m	5.8m	BS
NORWEGIAN PEARL	93530gt	2007	24.0k	DE2	2384p	2750p	1154c	294.1m	32.2m	8.2m	BS
NORWEGIAN SKY	77104gt	1999	23.0k	DEP2	2002p	2450p	800c	258.7m	32.3m	8.0m	BS
NORWEGIAN SPIRIT	75338gt	1998	24.0k	DE2	1960p	2975p	1100c	268.6m	32.2m	7.9m	BS
NORWEGIAN STAR	91740gt	2001	24.0k	DEP2	2240p	2683p	1126c	294.1m	32.2m	8.0m	BS
NORWEGIAN SUN	78309gt	2001	22.6k	DE2	2002p	2400p	968c	258.6m	32.3m	7.6m	BS

NORWEGIAN DAWN was ordered for Star Cruises from Jos. L. Meyer (yard number 649) at Papenburg, Germany as the SUPERSTAR SCORPIO but allocated to Norwegian Cruise Line while under construction. Her area of operation is principally the Caribbean and the US East Coast, although in 2009 and 2010 she will undertake a number of cruises from New York to Bermuda during the summer. The NORWEGIAN DAWN is owned by Star Cruises. IMO 9195169

NORWEGIAN DREAM was built as the DREAMWARD for Kloster Cruise Line of Nassau (Norwegian Caribbean Line) by Chantiers de l'Atlantique (yard number C30) at St Nazaire, France. When built the ship was 39,217 gross tons and had a length of 190 metres. In 1998 she followed her sister, the NORWEGIAN WIND, into the Lloydwerft shipyard in Bremerhaven, Germany to have a new 40 metre mid section fitted, and was renamed NORWEGIAN DREAM for the now re-styled Norwegian Cruise Line. During the following year while on passage to Dover, England at the end of a cruise she was involved in a serious collision with the Evergreen container ship EVER DECENT. After disembarking her passengers at Dover she proceeded to Lloydwerft at Bremerhaven for repairs. The NORWEGIAN DREAM spent a number of summer seasons cruising from Dover to Baltic and Scandinavian destinations, but then moved to the Caribbean and Alaska. She returned to Europe in the summer, cruising from Dover. In 2008 she was expected to be replaced by the NORWEGIAN JADE, and a sale (which later fell through) was agreed with Louis Cruise Lines. She is currently not in service, and is probably the youngest cruise ship to be laid up at the time of writing. Owned by Star Cruises, she may eventually head east for service as a gambling ship, along with her sister, the SUPERSTAR AQUARIUS. IMO 9008419

NORWEGIAN GEM was built by Meyer Werft (yard number 670) and following her naming in New York by Cindy Cardella in December 2007 was positioned to the US East Coast. For 2009 and 2010 she operates in the Mediterranean and Caribbean Seas. IMO 9355733

NORWEGIAN JADE was built by Meyer Werft (yard number 668) at Papenburg, Germany as the PRIDE OF HAWAI'I for NCL America. With passenger numbers on her Hawaii services not meeting expectations; following a refit in Cadiz she was moved to Europe in 2008 under the name NORWEGIAN JADE, and for 2009 cruises from Southampton in the summer. For the 2010 season she will be based in Venice. IMO 9304057

NORWEGIAN JEWEL commenced her career with three cruises from Dover, England following delivery from Jos. L. Meyer (yard number 667) at Papenburg, Germany. She then operated a series of cruises on the East Coast of North America before positioning to the Caribbean where she was christened by Melania Trump in Miami. She now cruises in Europe and the Caribbean. IMO 9304045

NORWEGIAN MAJESTY was laid down for Birka Line of Mariehamn, Aland Islands by Wartsila (yard number 1312) at Turku, Finland. She was to have been named BIRKA QUEEN. Following the failure of Wartsila, the ship was completed by Kvaerner Masa Yards for Majesty Cruise Line as the ROYAL MAJESTY and made her maiden voyage from Southampton to New York in July 1992. She was 32,396 tons and 173.5 metres long as built and subsequently operated for Dolphin Cruise Line. She passed to Norwegian Cruise Line in 1997 and was renamed NORWEGIAN MAJESTY. In 1999 she was lengthened by 33.8 metres by Lloydwerft at Bremerhaven, Germany by means of a new mid-section constructed

NCL America's **United States** at Philadelphia *(Rick Frendt)*

Norwegian Cruise Line's **Norwegian Dawn** at New York *(Theodore W Scull)*

Norwegian Cruise Line's **Norwegian Jewel** in Copenhagen *(William Mayes)*

Norwegian Cruise Line's **Norwegian Majesty** off Grand Cayman *(Rick Frendt)*

Norwegian Cruise Line's **Norwegian Sky** at Miami *(Rick Frendt)*

Norwegian Cruise Line's **Norwegian Star** at San Francisco *(Andrew Kilk)*

Norwegian Cruise Line's **Norwegian Sun** at San Francisco *(Andrew Kilk)*

by Aker MTW at Wismar, Germany. She was sold to Louis Cruise Lines in 2008, but continued to operate on East coast USA itineraries for NCL until delivered to Louis in 2009. IMO 8814744

NORWEGIAN PEARL was built by Meyer Werft (yard number 669) at Papenburg, Germany. She was named by American talk show host Rosie O'Donnell and now operates in the Caribbean and Alaska. IMO 9342281

NORWEGIAN SKY was laid down for Costa Crociere in 1996 as the COSTA OLYMPIA by Bremer Vulkan (yard number 108) at Vegesack, Germany but not completed due to the bankruptcy of the shipyard. The partially built hull was acquired by Norwegian Cruise Line and moved to Lloydwerft at Bremerhaven, Germany to be completed as the NORWEGIAN SKY. She was renamed as the PRIDE OF ALOHA following the partial sinking of the still incomplete PRIDE OF AMERICA in the shipyard at Bremerhaven, and entered service for NCL America in the Hawaiian islands. Following a disappointing market performance the PRIDE OF HAWAI'I was withdrawn, followed soon after by the PRIDE OF ALOHA, which went back to Norwegian Cruise Line as the NORWEGIAN SKY. She now operates 3- and 4- day Bahamas trips from Florida. The NORWEGIAN SKY is owned by Star Cruises. IMO 9128532

NORWEGIAN SPIRIT was built by Meyer Werft (yard number 646) at Papenburg, Germany as the SUPERSTAR LEO, the first new ship for Star Cruises. She was transferred to Norwegian Cruise Line in 2004 and renamed NORWEGIAN SPIRIT. She is a sister to the SUPERSTAR VIRGO. Her itineraries include East Coast USA and the Caribbean. The NORWEGIAN SPIRIT is owned by Star Cruises. IMO 9141065

NORWEGIAN STAR was laid down as the SUPERSTAR LIBRA by Meyer Werft (yard number 648) at Papenburg, Germany for Star Cruises, but switched to subsidiary, Norwegian Cruise Line before completion. She currently cruises in Alaska, West Coast USA and the Mexican Riviera, and is owned by Star Cruises. IMO 9195157

NORWEGIAN SUN's hull was built by Aker MTW (yard number 005) at Wismar, Germany and she was completed by Lloydwerft (yard number 109) at Bremerhaven, Germany. She currently operates in Alaska, the Pacific Ocean and South America, but in 2010 will be based in Dover. IMO 9218131

Cruise ship on order

NORWEGIAN EPIC	c153000gt	2009	22.0k	DE2	4200p	p	2200c	329.5m	40.0m	8.7m	BS

NORWEGIAN EPIC is on order from Aker Yards (Yard number C33) at St Nazaire, France. She is one of a pair of ships ordered, with an option of a third. However, in the autumn of 2008 the order for the second ship was cancelled and the option for a third will not be exercised. IMO 9410569

PRESTIGE CRUISE HOLDINGS

The Company Prestige Cruise Holdings was set up by Apollo Management to hold the group's interests in its premier and luxury cruise businesses, currently Oceania Cruises and Regent Seven Seas Cruises.

Chairman Frank Del Rio

OCEANIA CRUISES

The Company Oceania Cruises was founded in 2002 by cruise industry veterans Joe Watters and Frank Del Rio. Renaissance Cruises collapsed in September 2001 and all of its ships were laid up, many of them at Gibraltar. Subsequently they were all acquired by Cruiseinvest, an investment company connected with the ship builder, as that organisation still had financial commitments. Oceania Cruises subsequently entered into charters for the three ships listed below, introducing them one at a time. In 2006 the company purchased the three ships. In February 2007 private equity firm Apollo Management acquired a majority stake in the company. Shortly afterwards two new ship orders were announced.

President Bob Binder **Founding Chairman** Joe Watters **Chairman and CEO** Frank Del Rio

Address 8300 North West 53rd Street, Suite 308, Miami, Florida 33122 United States of America

Telephone +1 305 514 2300

Website www.oceaniacruises.com and www.oceaniacruises.co.uk

Area operated Europe, South America and the Caribbean Sea, the Far East and China

INSIGNIA	30277gt	1998	20.0k	DE2	680p	812p	373p	181.0m	25.5m	5.9m	MH

Oceania Cruises' **Regatta** in the Kiel Canal *(Oliver Sesemann)*

Regent Seven Seas Cruises' **Paul Gauguin** at Bora Bora *(Rick Frendt)*

Regent Seven Seas Cruises' **Seven Seas Mariner** *(Rick Frendt)*

Regent Seven Seas Cruises' **Seven Seas Navigator** at Cabo San Lucas *(Rick Frendt)*

Regent Seven Seas Cruises' **Seven Seas Voyager** at Kusadasi *(Rick Frendt)*

NAUTICA	30277gt	2000	20.0k	DE2	680p	812p	373p	181.0m	25.5m	5.9m	MH
REGATTA	30277gt	1998	20.0k	DE2	680p	812p	373p	181.0m	25.5m	5.9m	MH

INSIGNIA was the first of the second generation cruise ships built for Renaissance Cruises by Chantiers de l'Atlantique (yard number H31) at St Nazaire, France as the rather unimaginatively named R ONE. This series of eight ships was decorated in the elegant style of the Edwardian ocean liners. INSIGNIA, christened in Monte Carlo by Virginia Watters, entered service for Oceania Cruises in 2004. IMO 9156462

NAUTICA was built as the R FIVE, the first member of the second quartet of ships for Renaissance Cruises by Chantiers de l'Atlantique (yard number P31) at St Nazaire, France. She operated for Pullmantur as the BLUE DREAM in 2004, although not officially renamed. NAUTICA began sailing for Oceania Cruises in 2005 and was christened in Istanbul by Miami philanthropist and civic leader Fana Holtz. IMO 9200938

REGATTA was built by Chantiers de l'Atlantique (yard number I31) at St Nazaire, France as the R TWO for Renaissance Cruises. REGATTA entered service for Oceania Cruises in 2003, and was christened in Barcelona by Marcia Del Rio. IMO 9156474

Cruise ships on order

MARINA	c65000gt	2010	20.0k	DE2	1252p	1252p	780c	251.5m	32.2m	7.0m	MH
RIVIERA	c65000gt	2011	20.0k	DE2	1252p	1252p	780c	251.5m	32.2m	7.0m	MH

MARINA & RIVIERA were ordered from Fincantieri in March 2007 and will be built at the Sestri yard in Genoa. IMO 9438066 and 9438078

REGENT SEVEN SEAS CRUISES

The Company Regent Seven Seas Cruises, formerly Radisson Seven Seas Cruises, was a complicated structure of organisations, partly a joint venture between the US leisure group Carlson (owners of Radisson) and Vlassov (owners of V Ships of Monaco). The company's origins go back to 1992, when Carlson set up a new subsidiary, Diamond Cruise Line, later Radisson Diamond Cruises, to operate the RADISSON DIAMOND. The company later took over Seven Seas Cruises, with its single ship the SONG OF FLOWER, changing its name at that time to Radisson Seven Seas Cruises, and later took on the lease of the PAUL GAUGUIN. The V Ships joint venture began in 1999 with the delivery of the SEVEN SEAS NAVIGATOR. The company was renamed as Regent Seven Seas Cruises in 2006. In 2008 the company was acquired by Apollo Management and placed in its Prestige Cruises division. Until the recent economic downturn took effect it was planned that the company would order another 700-passenger ship.

Address 1000 Corporate Drive, Suite 500, Fort Lauderdale, FL 33334, United States of America

Telephone +1 800 477 7500 **Fax** +1 954 351 2119

Website www.rssc.com

Areas operated Worldwide

PAUL GAUGUIN	19170gt	1997	19.0k	DE2	320p	320p	211c	156.0m	22.0m	5.2m	BS
SEVEN SEAS MARINER	48075gt	2001	20.0k	DEP2	700p	780p	447c	216.0m	28.8m	7.0m	BS
SEVEN SEAS NAVIGATOR	28550gt	1999	19.5k	D2	490p	542p	324c	170.6m	24.0m	7.3m	BS
SEVEN SEAS VOYAGER	42363gt	2003	20.0k	DEP2	700p	769p	445c	206.5m	28.8m	7.1m	BS

PAUL GAUGUIN was built by Chantiers de l'Atlantique (yard number G31) at St Nazaire, France for Services et Transports – Tahiti. She was to have been named TAHITI NUI, but was built with her current name. She was christened by Carole Poylo, in the presence of Maria Gauguin, granddaughter of the famous painter. Initially hotel services were to be provided by Radisson Seven Seas Cruises, but the company then operated the ship under lease. The ship was sold to a consortium incorporating the respective owners of Grand Circle Travel and Vantage Travel (both based in Boston, Massachusetts) in 2005, but until at least 2010 the ship will be operated by RSSC in conjunction with that organization on her French Polynesian itineraries. Paul Gauguin (1848-1903) was one of the leading French painters of the post impressionist period. From 1891 until his death he lived in French Polynesia. IMO 9111319

SEVEN SEAS MARINER was built by Chantiers de l'Atlantique (yard number K31) at St Nazaire, France for Radisson Seven Seas Cruises, with a hull based on that of Festival Cruises' MISTRAL. IMO 9210139

SEVEN SEAS NAVIGATOR's hull was built in St Petersburg, Russia by Admiralteyskiy Sudostroitelnyy Zavod (yard number 02510) as the Ukrainian research vessel AKADEMIK NICOLAY PILYUGIN. Unfinished, the hull was purchased by V-Ships (renamed BLUE SEA) and transferred to the Mariotti shipyard at Genoa for completion as the SEVEN SEAS NAVIGATOR. IMO 9064126

SEVEN SEAS VOYAGER's hull was built by Cantieri Nav. Visentini at Donada, Italy under sub-contract to T. Mariotti of Genoa (yard number MAR001), who completed the construction of the ship. The ship was christened in Monaco in the presence of His Serene Highness Prince Albert II by Barbara Carlson Gage. IMO 924714

ARCTIC UMIAQ LINE

The Company Arctic Umiaq Line is a Greenland owned company, which was founded in 1774 as Den Kongelige Gronlandske Handel (Royal Greenland Trading Company) and first started operating ships on its own account in 1797. In 1985 the company was taken over by the Greenland Home Rule Administration and then became Gronlands Handel (Greenland Trading) The company was later restyled as KNI Service and subsequently KNI Pilersvisoq. In January 1993 the company was split into two, with the container shipping going to the newly formed Royal Arctic Line and the passenger ships being placed with another new company, Arctic Umiaq Line. Both companies remained Greenland Government owned. Arctic Umiaq Line ceased trading on 31 March 2006 as it was then decided to maintain links along the Greenland coast by air rather than by sea. The company was then sold to Arctic Travel Group, a new company established by three Danish travel agencies. The service lasted only until September 2006, when the company collapsed due to financial difficulties. Two ships quickly found buyers, but the third did not. As a result the Greenland Government required Royal Arctic Line and Air Greenland to jointly form a new Arctic Umiaq Line to operate the ship on the west coast of Greenland.

Administration Director Soren Andersen

Address Aqqusinersuaq 52, PO Box 1580, DK 3900 Nuuk, Greenland

Telephone +299 349190 **Fax** +299 322450

Website www.aul.gl

Area operated Cruises and passenger services on the west coast of Greenland

SARFAQ ITTUK	2118gt	1992	13.0k	D1	104p	246p	22c	72.8m	11.3m	3.3m	GL

SARFAQ ITTUK was built by the Orskov Shipyard (yard number 156) in Frederikshavn, Denmark for the Greenland Government owned KNI Pilersvisoq, as a coastal passenger ship with a capacity for 150 passengers. In 1999/2000 the ship was lengthened by 23 metres by Stocznia Remontowa at Gdansk, Poland. IMO 8913899

ATOLL EXPLORER CRUISES

The Company Atoll Explorer Cruises is a trading name of Universal Enterprises, a Maldives based company that also operates a supply ship in the islands. The company previously owned the ISLAND EXPLORER (ex NORDNORGE), which was used initially as a cruise ship, and later as a static hotel and diving ship. That ship has now been sold for scrap.

Address 39 Orchid Magu, PO Box 2015, Male 20-02, Maldive Islands

Telephone +960 332 2246 **Fax** +960 333 3618

Website www.atollexplorer.com

Area operated Maldive Islands

ATOLL EXPLORER	297gt	1964	13k	D2	40p	40p	c	50.3m	11.6m	3.0m	MV

ATOLL EXPLORER was built by the Burton Shipyard (yard number 357) at Port Arthur, Texas, USA as CAMPECHE SEAL. In 1986 she became the AQUANAUT EXPLORER for Cayman Islands based Dive and Sail Holidays. She was renamed as THE EXPLORER in 1993 and took her current name in 1995, when acquired by Universal Enterprises. IMO 7101231

Arctic Umiak Line's **Sarfaq Ittuk** at Qaqortoq *(Rick Frendt)*

Aurora Expeditions' **Polar Pioneer** at Ushuaia *(Bill Lawes)*

AURORA EXPEDITIONS

The Company Aurora Expeditions is an Australian adventure company specialising in small group expeditions.

Co-Founders and Directors Greg Mortimer and Margaret Werner **Chief Executive Officer** Lisa Bolton

Address Level 2, 88 George Street, The Rocks, NSW 2000, Australia

Telephone +61 2 9252 1033 **Fax** +61 2 9252 1373

Website www.auroraexpeditions.com.au

Area operated Antarctica, generally from Argentina between November and March and the Arctic in summer

MARINA SVETAEVA	4575gt	1989	14.3k	D1	90p	100p	41c	90.0m	17.2m	5.3m	RU
POLAR PIONEER	1753gt	1982	12.0k	D1	54p	56p	c	71.6m	12.8m	4.5m	RU

MARINA SVETAEVA was built by Stocznia im Komuny Paryskiej (yard number B961/03) at Gdynia, Poland for Glavmorneft. Her current owner is Morskaya Kompaniya Sakhalin-Kurily. Her registered name is MARINA TSVETAYEVA, and she is named after the poet, born in Moscow in 1892, later considered to be one of the finest Russian poets. (The MARINA TSVETAYEVA also operates cruises for Poseidon Arctic Voyages). IMO 8509181

POLAR PIONEER was built by Oy Laivateollisuus Ab (yard number 342) at Turku, Finland as the AKADEMIK SHULEYKIN for the Russian Hydrometeorological Institute. She was transferred to the Arctic and Antarctic Research Institute in 1994 and to the Russian Government controlled Marine Service in 1997. In 2001 she was refitted as a polar expedition ship and renamed POLYARNYY PIONER. Although she carries the name POLAR PIONEER, she appears to still be registered as the POLYARNYY PIONER. IMO 8010324

AYRAVATA CRUISES

The Company Ayravata is an operator of river cruise ships in Myanmar (Burma)..

Address Number 25, Ground Floor, 38th Street, Kyauktada Township, Yangon, Myanmar.

Website www.ayravatacruises.com

Area operated The rivers of Myanmar

PANDAW	gt	1947	11.0k	D1	32p	32p	c	47.7m	11.5m	0.8m	MM
PAUKAN	gt	2007	12.0k	D1	55p	55p	30c	55.8m	11.6m	1.1m	MM

PANDAW was one of six similar vessels commissioned by the Burmese Government-owned Inland Water Transport Board. She was built by Yarrows on the River Clyde in Scotland as a river passenger and cargo vessel. In 1998 she underwent conversion to a luxury river cruise ship and was operated for five years by a new Irrawaddy Flotilla Company. That charter ended and she was subjected to another major refit for her current operator.

PAUKAN was built by the Myanmar Shipyard at Yangon (Rangoon), Myanmar for the company. Paukan is the old name for Bagan, a city on the banks of the Irrawaddy River, the capital city of the First Myanmar Empire.

BIRKA CRUISES

The Company Birka Line is a Finnish (Aland Island) owner of ro-ro freighters that also operates a cruise ship on 22 hour duty free and party cruises from Stockholm. For a while the company owned the BIRKA QUEEN, built as the ROYAL VIKING SKY, but her operation was not totally successful and she was chartered to Princess Cruises as the GOLDEN PRINCESS before being sold to Star Cruises. The Baltic cruise business began in 1971, but stepped up a gear with the arrival of the purpose built BIRKA PRINCESS in 1986. That ship was sold to Louis Cruise Lines in 2006, becoming the SEA DIAMOND and sinking in April 2007 following contact with rocks off the Greek island of Santorini. Birka Line was taken over by Aland Island ferry operator, Eckero Line in 2007.

Address Stadsgardsterminalen, Box 15131, SE10465 Stockholm, Sweden

Telephone +46 8 702 7200 **Fax** +46 8 643 9246

Website www.birka.se

Area operated 24 hour cruises from Stockholm, Sweden plus some longer Baltic Sea cruises

BIRKA PARADISE	34728gt	2004	21.0k	D2	1468p	1800p	219c	176.9m	28.0m	6.6m	AX

BIRKA PARADISE was built by Aker Finnyards (yard number 442) at Rauma, Finland for Birka Line. She has been designed to attract a younger clientele than that usually associated with her former fleet mate, the BIRKA PRINCESS. IMO 9273727

BLU CRUISES

The Company Blu Cruises, part of the Alilauro Group of high-speed ferry operating companies, operates 3- and 4-day cruises in the Bay of Naples.

Telephone +39 081 497 2222

Website www.blucruises.it

Area operated The Bay of Naples

CAPRI	900gt	1962	13.5k	D2	56p	56p	c	62.0m	9.8m	2.8m	PT

CAPRI was built by Cantieri Navale Cassaro (yard number 115) at Messina, Sicily as the general cargo ship BASILUZZO for Societa di Navigazione NAVISARMA Spa. She later became part of the Si.Re.Mar. fleet. She was acquired by Cycladic Cruises in 1985 and renamed CITY OF ANDROS, with the intention of having her rebuilt as a cruise ship. That was eventually completed in 1992 in Piraeus. In 2003 she was acquired by Blu Cruises and renamed as the CITALIA after an extensive refit. She was renamed as the CAPRI in 2007. IMO 5037644

BLUE DREAM SHIPPING

The Company Blue Dream Shipping is a trading name of Loral Ltd, a Turkish-owned Greek registered company founded in 2005 to acquire the TDI KARADENIZ from Turkish Maritime Lines as part of the Turkish Government privatisation scheme.

Area operated The Mediterranean coast of Turkey, the Black Sea and the Eastern Mediterranean

DREAM	4326gt	1997	16.8k	D2	180p	180p	62c	93.0m	15.8m	3.9m	MT

DREAM was built by the Halic Shipyard (yard number 303) in Istanbul, Turkey as the overnight passenger vessel and cruise ship TDI KARADENIZ for Turkish Maritime Lines. Latterly she has operated summer cruising seasons in the Eastern Mediterranean. As part of the Turkish Government's privatisation policy, the ship was sold to her current owner in early 2005. IMO 9005871

BLUE LAGOON CRUISES

The Company Blue Lagoon Cruises was founded in 1950 by New Zealander, Captain Trevor Withers, initially as a tuna boat charter business. In 1966 he sold the business to Captain Claude Miller, a well-known New Zealand ship owner.

Chief Executive Officer Gerrard Harvey

Address PO Box 130, 183 Vitogo Parade, Lautoka, Fiji Islands

Telephone +679 666 1622 **Fax** +679 666 4098

Website www.bluelagooncruises.com

Area operated Fiji

FIJI PRINCESS	1258gt	1998	15.0k	D2	68p	76p	20c	55.5m	15.0m	2.1m	FJ
LYCIANDA	‡385gt	1984	12.0k	D2	42p	60p	16c	39.5m	7.8m	1.8m	FJ
MYSTIQUE PRINCESS	1533gt	1996	11.5k	D2	72p	108p	24c	55.3m	12.5m	2.8m	FJ
NANUYA PRINCESS	394gt	1988	11.0k	D2	50p	75p	18c	42.6m	8.5m	2.0m	FJ

FIJI PRINCESS was built by Chantiers Navale (yard number B234) at Marseilles, France as the RIVAGE MARTINIQUE for Rivages Croisieres. She was renamed PEARL OF SEYCHELLES in 2001 and joined the fleet of her present owner in 2004 as the FIJI PRINCESS. IMO 9199907

Birka Cruises' **Birka Paradise** in the Stockholm Archipelago *(Bruce Peter)*

Aida Cruises' **Aidabella** at Civitavecchia *(William Mayes)*

Aida Cruises' **Aidacara** in the Kiel Canal *(Oliver Sesemann)*

LYCIANDA was built for Blue Lagoon Cruises by Industrial & Marine Engineering (yard number 31) at Suva, Fiji. IMO 8401987

MYSTIQUE PRINCESS was built by Astilleros Servicios Navales (yard number 111) at Valdivia, Chile for Blue Lagoon Cruises. IMO 9131395

NANUYA PRINCESS was built by the Fiji Marine Shipyard & Slipways (yard number 84) at Suva, Fiji for the company. Nanuya is a Fijian island in the western Yasawa group of islands. IMO 8908014

CANADIAN SAILING EXPEDITIONS

The Company Canadian Sailing Expeditions is a Canadian company.

Address PO Box 2613, Halifax, Nova Scotia, B3J 3N5, Canada

Telephone +1 902 429 1474 **Fax** +1 902 429 1475

Website www.canadiansailingexpeditions.com

Area operated Atlantic Canada and the Caribbean Sea

CALEDONIA		955gt	1947	10.0k	SD1	62p	77p	20c	59.4m	9.2m	4.6m	CA

CALEDONIA was built by Cook, Welton and Gemmell (yard number 779) of Beverley, England as the trawler AKUREY for Canadian owners. She subsequently bore the names PETREL and PETREL V. She was converted to a square-rigged barquentine in 1977. In 2000 she passed to Canadian Sailing Expeditions and was renamed CAPE HARRISON. She was renamed again, this time as the CALEDONIA, in 2002. IMO 5007508

CANODROS

The Company Canodros SA is an Ecuador registered company operating a single ship within the Galapagos Islands. The company was established in 1987 by Carlos Perez Perasso.

General Manager Marco Pino Palacios

Address Urnabizacion Santa Leonor, Manzana 5, Solar No 10, Guayaquil, Ecuador

Telephone +593 4 228 5711 **Fax** +593 4 228 7561

Website www.canodros.com

Area operated Galapagos Islands

GALAPAGOS EXPLORER II	4077gt	1990	14.5k	D2	100p	100p	67c	88.3m	15.3m	4.0m	EC

GALAPAGOS EXPLORER II was built by Cantieri Navali Ferrari (yard number 45) at La Spezia, Italy as the RENAISSANCE THREE for Renaissance Cruises. She was purchased by her current owner in 1997, as a replacement for the GALAPAGOS EXPLORER. IMO 8708660

CAPTAIN COOK CRUISES

The Company Captain Cook Cruises is an Australian family-owned business, established in the 1970's to operate sightseeing cruises in Sydney Harbour. The company now operates 16 ships, but those not listed here are day cruise vessels.

Chief Executive Officer Trevor Haworth

Address Level 6, 37 Pitt Street, Sydney, New South Wales 2000, Australia

Telephone +61 2 9206 1122 **Fax** +61 2 9251 4725

Website www.captaincook.com.au

Area operated Great Barrier Reef, Murray River, Sydney Harbour and Fiji

CAPTAIN COOK'S EXPLORER	1160gt	1979	8.0k	D1	116p	120p	23c	52.5m	11.0m	1.2m	AU
MURRAY PRINCESS	c1500gt	1986	6.0k	D1	120p	120p	30c	67.0m	15.0m	1.2m	AU
REEF ENDEAVOUR	3125gt	1996	13.5k	D2	150p	168p	35c	73.6m	14.0m	3.7m	AU
REEF ESCAPE	1815gt	1987	9.0k	D2	120p	138p	28c	69.7m	13.5m	1.5m	FJ

CAPTAIN COOK'S EXPLORER was built as the MURRAY EXPLORER. She operates occasional overnight and weekend cruises from Sydney.

MURRAY PRINCESS was built at Goolwa, Australia as a stern-wheel river cruise ship, and is currently operating in the Murray River.

REEF ENDEAVOUR was built at the Fiji Marine Shipyard & Slipways (yard number 920) at Suva, Fiji. She operates cruises to the Great Barrier Reef. IMO 9012666

REEF ESCAPE was built by Carrington Slipways (yard number 182) at Newcastle, New South Wales, Australia as the LADY HAWKESBURY. She was renamed REEF ESCAPE in 1990 when purchased by Captain Cook Cruises. In 1997 she was registered under the Fijian flag as DRO KI CAKAU, but reverted to the name REEF ESCAPE in 2004. She cruises in the Fiji Islands. IMO 8512475

The company also operates the day sailing vessels RA MARAMA and SPIRIT OF THE PACIFIC in the Fiji Islands, and a fleet of day boats around Sydney Harbour.

CARNIVAL CORPORATION and PLC

The Company In 1972, entrepreneur Ted Arison purchased the 1960 built Canadian Pacific Steamships' transatlantic liner EMPRESS OF CANADA, renamed her MARDI GRAS, and began operating her on cruises from Miami. Arison had been involved in Norwegian Caribbean Lines, so was no stranger to the Caribbean cruise trade. Who, in 1972, could have foreseen that from these modest beginnings Carnival would, by the end of the century, have become the largest cruise-ship owning group in the world. This transformation has come about not only by building new ships, but also by means of an ambitious acquisition programme. Commencing with the purchase of Holland America Line in 1989, Seabourn in 1992, a 50% stake in Costa Crociere (Airtours had the other 50% and Carnival acquired just under 30% of Airtours) in 1997, Cunard in 1998 and finishing (to date) with the acquisition of the remaining 50% share in Costa Crociere in 2001. There was also the hard fought merger with P&O Princess Cruises in 2003 to form a dual listed company (on the London and New York stock exchanges). P&O Princess itself was a relatively new company, albeit with a long and impressive pedigree, having been formed as recently as the autumn of 2000 when P&O (The Peninsular and Oriental Steam Navigation Company) de-merged its cruising businesses. One potential acquisition that did not happen was the purchase of Premier Cruise line in 1991, following uncertainty over earnings in the wake of the first Gulf War. The operational name Carnival Corporation came into use in 1993. Where not operating for an international clientele the marketing area of each subsidiary is shown after the company name. The operating companies within the group are shown in alphabetical order, but the section headed 'structure' may be useful for viewing how this conglomerate developed. In late 2006 Carnival Corporation announced its intention to enter into a joint venture with Germany's TUI AG, under which the latter company would have owned 5% of the new business. However, the proposal fell foul of the regulatory process and did not proceed. In 2007 Carnival Corporation entered into a joint venture with Spain's Iberojet, under which Carnival now owns 75% of that business. This would seem to serve two purposes in that it gives Carnival a toehold in the Spanish market, hot on the heels of Royal Caribbean's acquisition of Pullmantur, and also provides another outlet within the group for ships that are no longer considered to be 'front line' vessels. Shortly after this acquisition Carnival sold Wind Star Cruises to Ambassadors International's Majestic America Line. Carnival Corporation's ships carried more than 8.1 million passengers in 2008.

Chairman and Chief Executive Officer Micky Arison **Vice-Chairman and Chief Operating Officer** Howard Frank

Address   Carnival Place, 3655 N.W. 87th Avenue, MIAMI, FL 33178 United States of America

Mountbatten House, Grosvenor Square, Southampton, SO15 2BF, England

Website www.carnivalplc.com or www.carnivalcorp.com

Structure Holding Company Carnival Corporation and plc

Carnival Cruise Lines, Costa Crociere, Holland America Line, Princess Cruises and Seabourn report directly to Carnival Corporation.

Cunard Line, Ocean Village, P&O Cruises and P&O Cruises Australia report through Princess Cruises.

Aida Cruises and Iberocruceros report through Costa Crociere.

AIDA CRUISES

The Company The origins of Aida Cruises can be traced back to 1991, when one of the results of German reunification was the acquisition of former East German Deutsche Seereederei and its single ship, the ARKONA, by West German investors. In 1994 the order was placed for the first new ship, a radically different vessel from the ARKONA, and one that was intended to offer the German equivalent of Club Med at sea. At this time the ARKONA was on charter to another German company, Seetours, then part of TUI, but later acquired by Deutsche Seereederei. At the end of September 1999 it was announced that P&O and Seetours, as the German cruising business was now styled, had agreed to form a new venture, Aida Cruises, to develop the German cruise market. The company had been operating the AIDA since 1996, but lacked the finance to invest in further ships; indeed the AIDA had been sold to NCL in 1997 and chartered back. The AIDA was reacquired and almost immediately P&O placed the order for two similar, but slightly larger ships. All three Aida vessels were then registered in London. With the merger of P&O Princess and Carnival Corporation, Aida Cruises was moved from the control of P&O Princess to Costa Cruises, and the ships were re-registered from London to Genoa. With the demise of A'Rosa's ocean cruise business that organisation's single ocean cruise ship (AIDABLU – formerly CROWN PRINCESS) was transferred to Aida. It had been intended that the A'Rosa brand would also operate her sister, the REGAL PRINCESS, but that ship remained with Princess Cruises, latterly being transferred to P&O Cruises (Australia). Germany is the world's third largest market for cruise passengers, justifying the order for a further quartet of ships, the first of which replaced the AIDABLU, transferred within the Carnival Group to Ocean Village. That order for four ships was later extended to six vessels. Aida Cruises caters only for German speaking passengers.

President Michael Thamm **Senior Vice President Operations** Michael Ungerer

Address Am Strande 3d, 18055 Rostock, Germany

Telephone +49 381 4440 **Fax** +49 381 444 8888

Website www.aida.de

Areas operated Mediterranean, Atlantic Isles, Scandinavia, Middle East and the Caribbean

AIDAAURA	42289gt	2003	19.4k	DE2	1266p	1582p	418c	203.2m	28.1m	6.2m	IT
AIDABELLA	69203gt	2008	21.0k	DE2	2050p	2500p	646c	252.0m	32.2m	7.2m	IT
AIDACARA	38557gt	1996	21.0k	D2	1180p	1230p	370c	193.3m	27.6m	6.2m	IT
AIDADIVA	69203gt	2007	21.8k	DE2	2050p	2500p	646c	252.0m	32.2m	7.2m	IT
AIDALUNA	69203gt	2009	21.0k	DE2	2050p	2500p	646c	252.0m	32.2m	7.2m	IT
AIDAVITA	42289gt	2002	19.4k	DE2	1266p	1582p	418c	203.2m	28.1m	6.2m	IT

AIDAAURA was built by the Aker MTW Yard (yard number 4) in Wismar, Germany for Aida Cruises and named by Heidi Klum. For summer 2009 she cruises in Northern Europe, then moves to the Mediterranean, and spends the winter in the Caribbean. IMO 9221566

AIDABELLA was delivered by the Meyer shipyard (yard number 660) in the spring of 2008, and named by Eva Padberg. The AIDABELLA spends the winter months in the Canary Islands and the summer in the Mediterranean Sea. IMO 9334868

AIDACARA was built by Kvaerner Masa Yards (yard number 1337) at Turku, Finland for Arkona Touristik of Germany as the AIDA. Her godmother was Christiane Herzog. As a result of the financial difficulties of her owners, the ship was sold to Norwegian Cruise Line in 1997, but chartered back. She was re-purchased by Arkona Touristik in 1999, and the operating company was restyled as Aida Cruises. The AIDA was renamed AIDACARA in 2001 in anticipation of the delivery of the first of the pair of ships under construction in Germany. In 2009 she starts the season in Southern Europe, then moves north and for the winter heads to the Far East. IMO 9112789

AIDADIVA is the first of a series of four ships ordered from the Meyer shipyard (yard number 659) at Papenburg, Germany. The order was later amended with the addition of two more ships with a slightly higher passenger capacity, and at that time the fourth ship in this series had her specification changed to match the new pair. The ship was named in Hamburg on 20 April 2007 by Maria Galleski, winner of a competition held in conjunction with the local newspaper Hamburger Abendblatt. The AIDADIVA spent her first season in the Mediterranean based at Palma de Majorca and later in the Canary Islands, based in Tenerife. She now winters in the Arabian Gulf and spends the summer in the Mediterranean Sea. IMO 9334856

AIDALUNA is the last of the first series of three ships built by Meyer (yard number 666) and was named in Palma, Majorca on 4 April 2009 by model Franziska Knuppe. She then repositioned to Northern Europe before spending the winter in the Canary Islands. IMO 9362542

Aida Cruises' **Aidavita** at St John's Antigua *(Rick Frendt)*

Carnival Cruise Lines' **Carnival Destiny** at Bridgetown *(Andrew Kilk)*

Carnival Cruise Lines' **Carnival Imagination** at Miami *(Rick Frendt)*

AIDAVITA was built at Wismar in Germany by Aker MTW (yard number 3) for Aida Cruises. She was christened by Doris Shroder-Kopf. The AIDAVITA spends summer in the Mediterranean Sea, and moves to the Caribbean in winter. IMO 9221554

Cruise ships on order

AIDABLU	c71000gt	2010	21.0k	DE2	2174p	2500p	646c	252.0m	32.2m	7.2m	IT
NEWBUILDING 2	c71000gt	2011	21.0k	DE2	2174p	2500p	646c	252.0m	32.2m	7.2m	IT
NEWBUILDING 3	c71000gt	2012	21.0k	DE2	2174p	2500p	646c	252.0m	32.2m	7.2m	IT

AIDABLU is the first ship in a series of three vessels that are slightly larger than the AIDADIVA class. She is under construction by Meyer Werft (yard number 680) at Papenburg, Germany. She will be based in Northern Europe for the first part of 2010, following her naming on 9 February by international designer Jette Joop. IMO 9398888

NEWBUILDING 2 as above with yard number 689. IMO 9490040

NEWBUILDING 3 as above with yard number 690. IMO 9490052

CARNIVAL CRUISE LINES

The Company Carnival Cruise Lines began operations in 1972 with the MARDI GRAS (formerly the EMPRESS OF CANADA), an inauspicious start as she ran aground on her maiden voyage. In 1979 she undertook a series of Pacific cruises from Los Angeles, and earlier had undertaken an epic 41-day Mediterranean cruise. Her former running mate on Canadian Pacific's transatlantic service, the EMPRESS OF BRITAIN, suitably renamed CARNIVALE, joined her at the end of 1975. A third ship, the S A VAAL of the South African Marine Corporation (earlier the TRANSVAAL CASTLE of the Union Castle Mail Steamship Company), renamed FESTIVALE, joined the fleet in 1977 following her closing the joint Union Castle/Safmarine service between Southampton and South Africa. The first new ship was ordered shortly afterwards, and entered service in January 1982 as the TROPICALE. All of these ships have now left the Carnival Cruise Lines fleet. The delivery of the TROPICALE, however, signalled the start of what has proved to be the most expansive passenger shipbuilding programme of the past 50 years, and by 1987 Carnival Cruise Lines was carrying more passengers than any other cruise line. Carnival Cruise Lines has developed a strong affiliation with Italian shipbuilder Fincantieri, who have built eight of the most recent twelve ships. The company employs around 36,000 staff and in 2008 carried almost 3.7 million passengers.

President and Chief Executive Officer Gerald Cahill

Address Carnival Place, 3655 N.W. 87th Avenue, Miami, FL 33178-2428, United States of America

Telephone +1 305 599 2600 **Fax** +1 305 406 4779

Website www.carnival.com

Areas operated Caribbean, Mexico, Alaska, East Coast USA, Mediterranean

CARNIVAL CONQUEST	110239gt	2002	22.5k	DE2	2974p	3783p	1170c	290.2m	35.5m	8.2m	PA
CARNIVAL DESTINY	101353gt	1996	19.0k	DE2	2642p	3360p	1040c	272.2m	35.5m	8.2m	BS
CARNIVAL DREAM	c130000gt	2009	22.5k	DEP2	3646p	4200p	1367c	304.2m	37.0m	8.2m	PA
CARNIVAL ECSTASY	70367gt	1991	19.5k	DE2	2040p	2634p	920c	260.8m	31.5m	7.8m	PA
CARNIVAL ELATION	70390gt	1998	19.5k	DEP2	2040p	2634p	920c	260.8m	31.5m	7.8m	PA
CARNIVAL FANTASY	70367gt	1990	19.5k	DE2	2040p	2634p	920c	260.8m	31.5m	8.0m	PA
CARNIVAL FASCINATION	70367gt	1994	19.5k	DE2	2040p	2594p	920c	260.8m	31.5m	7.8m	BS
CARNIVAL FREEDOM	110320gt	2007	22.5k	DE2	2974p	3783p	1170c	290.2m	35.5m	8.2m	PA
CARNIVAL GLORY	110239gt	2003	22.5k	DE2	2974p	3783p	1170c	290.2m	35.5m	8.2m	PA
CARNIVAL IMAGINATION	70367gt	1995	19.5k	DE2	2040p	2634p	920c	260.8m	31.5m	7.8m	BS
CARNIVAL INSPIRATION	70367gt	1996	19.5k	DE2	2040p	2634p	920c	260.8m	31.5m	7.8m	BS
CARNIVAL LEGEND	85942gt	2002	22.0k	DEP2	2124p	2667p	930c	292.5m	32.2m	7.8m	PA
CARNIVAL LIBERTY	110320gt	2005	22.5k	DE2	2974p	3783p	1170c	290.2m	35.5m	8.2m	PA
CARNIVAL MIRACLE	85942gt	2004	22.0k	DEP2	2124p	2680p	930c	292.5m	32.2m	8.0m	PA
CARNIVAL PARADISE	70390gt	1998	19.5k	DEP2	2040p	2594p	920c	260.8m	31.5m	7.8m	PA
CARNIVAL PRIDE	85920gt	2001	22.0k	DEP2	2124p	2680p	930c	292.5m	32.2m	7.8m	PA
CARNIVAL SENSATION	70367gt	1993	19.5k	DE2	2040p	2634p	920c	260.8m	31.5m	7.8m	BS
CARNIVAL SPIRIT	85920gt	2001	22.0k	DEP2	2124p	2680p	930c	292.5m	32.2m	7.8m	PA
CARNIVAL SPLENDOR	113323gt	2008	22.5k	DE2	2974p	3540p	1118c	290.0m	25.5m	8.2m	PA

Carnival Cruise Lines' **Carnival Liberty** at Philipsburg, St Maarten *(Andrew Kilk)*

Carnival Cruise Lines' **Holiday** at Cozumel *(Rick Frendt)*

Carnival Cruise Lines' **Carnival Pride** at Cabo San Lucas *(Rick Frendt)*

CARNIVAL TRIUMPH	101509gt	1999	19.0k	DE2	2758p	3360p	1040c	272.2m	35.5m	8.2m	BS
CARNIVAL VALOR	110239gt	2004	22.5k	DE2	2974p	3783p	1170c	290.2m	35.5m	8.2m	PA
CARNIVAL VICTORY	101509gt	2000	19.0k	DE2	2758p	3360p	1040c	272.2m	35.5m	8.2m	PA
HOLIDAY	46052gt	1985	21.5k	D2	1452p	1800p	660c	221.6m	28.0m	7.5m	BS

CARNIVAL CONQUEST was built by Fincantieri (yard number 6057) at Monfalcone, Italy. Interestingly, the forward section of the hull was built at the Sestri yard in Genoa and towed to Monfalcone for completion. The CARNIVAL CONQUEST cruises the Eastern and Western Caribbean from Galveston, Texas. IMO 9198355

CARNIVAL DESTINY was Carnival Cruise Lines' first 100,000+ gross ton cruise ship. At the time of her delivery by Fincantieri's Monfalcone, Italy yard (yard number 5941) in 1996 she was the largest passenger ship ever built. She now works on 4-, and 5-day Eastern Caribbean itineraries from Miami. IMO 9070058

CARNIVAL DREAM is on order from Fincantieri (yard number 6151) and is due for delivery in September 2009. She then operates cruises in the Mediterranean Sea before moving to New York for a series of cruises and then takes up station at Port Canaveral for alternate 7-day Eastern and Western Caribbean itineraries. IMO 9378474

CARNIVAL ECSTASY was built by the Helsinki, Finland shipyard of Masa Yards (yard number 480) and delivered in 1991 as the ECSTASY, the second of the 'Fantasy' class. Following her naming ceremony in New York, she began cruising from Miami in June 1991. The Carnival prefix was added to her name in November 2007. She now operates to the Western Caribbean from Galveston, Texas. IMO 8711344

CARNIVAL ELATION is the seventh ship in the 'Fantasy' class and was delivered in 1998 by Kvaerner Masa Yards (yard number 491), Helsinki, Finland as the ELATION. She was the first large passenger ship to use pod propulsion. She was renamed as the CARNIVAL ELATION in November 2007. Her itineraries include short cruises to the Mexican Riviera from San Diego. In spring 2010 she has been chartered by the Royal Canadian Mounted Police for use as an accommodation ship at Vancouver in connection with the Winter Olympic Games. IMO 9118721

CARNIVAL FANTASY is the first ship in an eight ship series ordered from Wartsila and its successors in Finland. She was delivered as the FANTASY by Masa Yard's Helsinki shipyard (yard number 479) in 1990, following the failure of Wartsila Marine Industries, and was immediately employed on cruises from Miami. She was renamed with the Carnival prefix in 2007. She now cruises to the Western Caribbean from New Orleans until November when she transfers to Mobile as a replacement for the HOLIDAY. IMO 8700773

CARNIVAL FASCINATION is the fourth of the 'Fantasy' class (yard number 487), delivered by Masa Yards, Helsinki, Finland and entered service as the FASCINATION in 1994. Renamed in October 2007, the CARNIVAL FASCINATION is now employed on short cruises from Jacksonville. IMO 9041253

CARNIVAL FREEDOM was built by Fincantieri (yard number 6129) at the Breda Shipyard in Venice. After being named by businesswoman Kathy Ireland, her first season featured Mediterranean cruises followed by a repositioning trip to the Caribbean. She now operates Eastern and Western Caribbean cruises from Fort Lauderdale. IMO 9333149

CARNIVAL GLORY is another product of the Monfalcone, Italy shipyard of Fincantieri (yard number 6059). The CARNIVAL GLORY now serves the 7-night Eastern and Western Caribbean cruise market from her base in Port Canaveral or Miami, Florida. IMO 9198367

CARNIVAL IMAGINATION is the fifth member of the 'Fantasy' class (yard number 488) and was delivered to Carnival Cruise Lines as the IMAGINATION by Masa Yards, Helsinki, Finland in 1995. Her cruises from Miami to the Western Caribbean and the Bahamas are of 4 and 3 nights duration respectively. IMO 9053878

CARNIVAL INSPIRATION entered service with Carnival as the INSPIRATION in 1996. She was renamed as the CARNIVAL INSPIRATION in late 2007 and now operates 4- and 5-day cruises to the Western Caribbean from Tampa, Florida, and is the sixth ship to be constructed by Masa Yards, Helsinki, Finland in the 'Fantasy' class (yard number 489). IMO 9087489

CARNIVAL LEGEND was delivered in 2002 by Kvaerner Masa Yards (yard number 501) at Helsinki, Finland, as the third of the 'Spirit' class for Caribbean cruising. Following her naming by Dame Judi Dench, she was the first Carnival ship to cruise in Europe as she undertook a number of voyages from

Harwich, England prior to heading for New York. She now covers Western Caribbean itineraries from Tampa. IMO 9224726

CARNIVAL LIBERTY was built by Fincantieri (yard number 6111) at Monfalcone, Italy. After being christened by actress Mira Sorvino in Civitavecchia, Italy on 19 July 2005, the ship commenced a series of summer cruises in the Mediterranean, based at that port. Her current employment is Western and Eastern Caribbean cruises from Miami. IMO 9278181

CARNIVAL MIRACLE was built by Kvaerner Masa Yards (yard number 503) in Helsinki, Finland. She now cruises to the Eastern Caribbean from New York, and the Southern and Western Caribbean from Fort Lauderdale. IMO 9237357

CARNIVAL PARADISE is the final member of the eight ship 'Fantasy' class (yard number 494), and when delivered to Carnival Cruise Lines as the PARADISE in 1998 became the world's first totally smoking-free ship (funnel excepted, we assume). She later quietly dropped her non-smoking status. She had the Carnival prefix added to her name in 2007 and now sails to Mexico on short cruises from Los Angeles. IMO 9120877

CARNIVAL PRIDE is the second of the 'Spirit' class ships and was delivered by the Helsinki, Finland shipyard of Kvaerner Masa Yards (yard number 500) at the end of 2001 for alternate 7-day Eastern and Western Caribbean cruising based at Port Canaveral, Florida. She now operates a variety of itineraries on the US east coast. IMO 9223954

CARNIVAL SENSATION is the third member of the 'Fantasy' class. Following the failure of Wartsila Marine Industries in November 1989, the order was cancelled. The contract was renewed with Masa Yards, Helsinki, Finland (yard number 484) in 1991 and the ship joined Carnival's growing Caribbean fleet as the SENSATION in 1993. She was renamed as the CARNIVAL SENSATION in 2007 and now sails to the Bahamas from Port Canaveral. In early 2009 she had 98 balconies added. IMO 8711356

CARNIVAL SPIRIT is the name-ship of the 'Spirit' class. When delivered by Kvaerner Masa Yards (yard number 499) of Helsinki, Finland in 2001, she became Carnival Cruise Lines' first ship to serve the Alaska and Hawaii markets. In addition, she now cruises to Mexico from San Diego. IMO 9188647

CARNIVAL SPLENDOR is the first ship in a new class, built by Fincantieri (yard number 6135), at the Sestri yard at Genoa, Italy. Following her delivery she was named by broadcaster and musician Myleene Klass in Dover on 10 July 2008 and was based in the UK for a summer season of cruises in Northern Europe. The ship now serves the Mexican market from Los Angeles. IMO 9333163

CARNIVAL TRIUMPH was built by Fincantieri (yard number 5979) at Monfalcone, Italy and delivered in 1999, as the second ship in the 'Destiny' class. She currently cruises to the Western Caribbean from New Orleans and Miami, but during the summer of 2009 will operate a series of Canada and New England cruises from New York. IMO 9138850

CARNIVAL VALOR was built by Fincantieri (yard number 6082) at Monfalcone, Italy. The CARNIVAL VALOR is employed on Western Caribbean cruises from Miami. IMO 9236389

CARNIVAL VICTORY is the third member of the 'Destiny' class, built by Fincantieri (yard number 6045) at Monfalcone, Italy and was delivered in 2000. She now operates from San Juan and Barbados to the Southern Caribbean. IMO 9172648

HOLIDAY is the second new ship ordered by Carnival Cruise Lines, being delivered from the Aalborg Vaerft shipyard (yard number 246) at Aalborg, Denmark in June 1985. She now does short cruises to the Western Caribbean from Mobile, Alabama until October 2009, after which she will be refitted to join the Iberocruceros fleet as the GRAND HOLIDAY. IMO 8217881

Cruise ships on order

CARNIVAL MAGIC	c130000gt	2011	22.5k	DEP2	3648p	4200p	1367c	304.2m	37.0m	8.2m	PA

CARNIVAL MAGIC is on order from Fincantieri's Monfalcone shipyard (yard number 6167). IMO 9378486

COSTA CRUISES

The Company The origins of the Costa Line date from 1924 when the brothers Federico, Eugenio and Enrico Costa bought their first cargo ship. It was not until after the Second World War that the business entered passenger shipping. In 1947 the small MARIA C, and in 1948 the ANNA C and ANDREA C were the first passenger ships for what had now become known as Linea C. The company

Carnival Cruise Lines' **Carnival Splendor** in Istanbul *(William Mayes)*

Costa Cruises' **Costa Concordia** at Barcelona *(William Mayes)*

Costa Cruises' **Costa Europa** at Barcelona *(William Mayes)*

was initially involved in the post-war migrant trades, but subsequently built up a route network linking South America with Mediterranean ports. In 1959 the FRANCA C (built in 1914 and still sailing as the mission ship DOULOS) became the first Costa Line ship to be exclusively allocated to American cruising. This major Italian passenger line was re-styled Costa Armatori S.p.A. in 1967 and in the following year the company introduced Caribbean fly-cruises based in San Juan. In 1986, in response to changed markets, the company was renamed Costa Crociere S.p.A. and thereafter was involved solely in cruise operations. In 1993 the French Croisieres Paquet became part of Costa, and two years later the company began cruises to Havana. In December 1996 the shareholders accepted a joint bid by Airtours of the United Kingdom and Carnival Corporation, and so the last major Italian passenger ship operator ceased to be independent. In spring 2001 Carnival Corporation acquired Airtours' holding in Costa, and the latter company then became a full subsidiary. Subsequently Costa has taken control of both Aida Cruises and Iberocruceros for management purposes. In 2010 a new Paquet Croisieres will begin operation using the COSTA ALLEGRA. It is thought that Costa has licenced the Paquet name to a new French operator.

Chairman and Chief Executive Officer Pier Luigi Foschi **President** Gianni Onorato

Address Via de Marini 60, 16149 Genoa, Italy

Telephone +34 010 54831 **Fax** +34 010 5483290

Website www.costacruises.co.uk and www.costacruise.com

Areas operated Mediterranean, Scandinavia, Middle East, Far East, South America and the Caribbean

COSTA ALLEGRA	28597gt	1969	20.0k	D2	800p	1030p	418c	187.7m	25.8m	8.2m	IT
COSTA ATLANTICA	85619gt	2000	22.0k	DEP2	2112p	2680p	902c	292.5m	32.2m	8.0m	IT
COSTA CLASSICA	52926gt	1991	19.8k	D2	1308p	1783p	650c	220.6m	30.8m	7.3m	IT
COSTA CONCORDIA	114147gt	2006	19.6k	DE2	3000p	3780p	1100c	290.2m	35.5m	8.2m	IT
COSTA EUROPA	54763gt	1986	22.5k	D2	1494p	1773p	642c	243.2m	29.7m	6.5m	IT
COSTA FORTUNA	102587gt	2003	20.0k	DE2	2718p	3470p	1068c	272.2m	35.5m	8.2m	IT
COSTA LUMINOSA	92720gt	2009	21.6k	DEP2	2260p	2828p	921c	294.0m	32.3m	8.1m	IT
COSTA MAGICA	102587gt	2004	20.0k	DE2	2718p	3470p	1068c	272.2m	35.5m	8.2m	IT
COSTA MARINA	25558gt	1969	20.0k	D2	763p	1025p	391c	174.2m	25.8m	8.2m	IT
COSTA MEDITERRANEA	85619gt	2003	22.0k	DEP2	2114p	2680p	920c	292.5m	32.2m	8.0m	IT
COSTA PACIFICA	114500gt	2009	19.6k	DE2	3000p	3780p	1100c	290.2m	35.5m	8.3m	IT
COSTA ROMANTICA	53049gt	1993	19.8k	D2	1356p	1787p	650c	220.5m	30.8m	7.3m	IT
COSTA SERENA	114500gt	2007	19.6k	DE2	3000p	3780p	1100c	290.2m	35.5m	8.2m	IT
COSTA VICTORIA	75166gt	1996	23.0k	DE2	1928p	2394p	792c	252.9m	32.3m	7.8m	IT

COSTA ALLEGRA was built by Wartsila (yard number 1170) at Turku in Finland as one of a class of five container ships for the Johnson Line of Sweden in 1969. As the ANNIE JOHNSON she served Johnson Line's North American service to Northern Europe until 1985, when she was sold to Peleus Marine Company of Cyprus (a company owned by Greek ship-owner Antonis Lelakis) who planned to convert her and two sisters into cruise-ships. She was renamed the REGENT MOON, but these plans eventually fell through, and in 1988 she was sold to the Swiss-based Mediterranean Shipping Company and renamed the ALEXANDRA. In 1990, following the successful conversion of the COSTA MARINA, Costa approached MSC and bought the ship, which was sent to the Mariotti shipyard in Genoa for conversion. In addition to the conversion the ship was lengthened by 13.5 metres and equipped with new engines, being re-delivered to Costa Crociere in September 1992 as the COSTA ALLEGRA. The COSTA ALLEGRA is based in South East Asia, but returns to the Mediterranean Sea for summer 2010, when she will be chartered to a new Paquet Croisieres. IMO 6916885

COSTA ATLANTICA is the first example within Carnival Corporation of similar designs being used for ships built for more than one operator. The COSTA ATLANTICA is a sister to the CARNIVAL SPIRIT class of ships and was delivered to the company by Kvaerner Masa Yards (yard number 498), Helsinki, Finland in June 2000. Her sister ship, the COSTA MEDITERRANEA, was delivered during 2003. The COSTA ATLANTICA operates cruises in Northern Europe in summer and the Caribbean Sea in winter. IMO 9187796

COSTA CLASSICA, ordered in July 1987, was the first new passenger ship to be built for Costa Line since the elegant EUGENIO C of 1966. Built by Fincantieri (yard number 5877) at Venice, Italy, she was floated out of her building dock in February 1991 and delivered at the end of that year. She has operated in both the Mediterranean and Caribbean markets. In 2000 she was due to have been

Costa Cruises' **Costa Fortuna** at Naples *(Matthew Davies)*

Costa Cruises' **Costa Marina** in Istanbul *(William Mayes)*

lengthened by Cammell Laird at Birkenhead, England, but while the ship was on her way to the shipyard a dispute arose and the lengthening didn't take place, despite the shipyard having constructed the new centre section. The COSTA CLASSICA is now based in the Far East. IMO 8716502

COSTA CONCORDIA was ordered from Fincantieri in 2004, and was built in the Sestri yard (yard number 6122) at Genoa, Italy. For 2009 she spends most of the year in the Mediterranean Sea, from her homeport at Savona. IMO 9320544

COSTA EUROPA was built for Home Lines by Jos. L. Meyer (yard number 610) at Papenburg, Germany and delivered in 1986 as the HOMERIC. She operated for Home Lines on their summer service between New York and Hamilton, Bermuda, but spent her winters cruising in the Caribbean. Home Lines was acquired by Holland America Line in 1988 and on 2 November the HOMERIC was renamed WESTERDAM. Her duties were now split between the Caribbean (winter) and Alaska cruises from Vancouver (summer). In October 1989 the ship was returned to her builders to have a 39.6 metre mid section inserted, resuming service in March 1990 and subsequently being re-registered to the Dutch flag in 1996. She was transferred to Costa Crociere during 2002 and renamed COSTA EUROPA. During a refit in 2007 the area over the bridge that was previously a cinema was converted into six grand suites with oval balconies. She currently spends most of the year operating in the Mediterranean and Red Seas. From April 2010 she is chartered to Thomson Cruises as the THOMSON DREAM. IMO 8407735

COSTA FORTUNA was built by Fincantieri at the Sestri yard (yard number 6086) in Genoa, Italy. She spends the summers based in Venice and operates Caribbean itineraries in the winter. IMO 9239783

COSTA LUMINOSA was built by Fincantieri (yard number 6155) at the Breda yard in Venice. She sails in Northern and Southern Europe and the Red Sea. IMO 9398905

COSTA MAGICA was built by Fincantieri at the Sestri yard (yard number 6087) in Genoa, Italy. She currently operates in the Baltic, Caribbean and Mediterranean Seas. IMO 9239795

COSTA MARINA was the first in a series of five container ships built by Wartsila (yard number 1169) at Turku, Finland for Johnson Line of Sweden; a sister to the ANNIE JOHNSON, she was named the AXEL JOHNSON. In 1985 she was sold to Lelakis-owned company Universal Glow Inc. and renamed the REGENT SUN. The plan to convert the ship for cruising was abandoned in 1986 and she was sold and renamed ITALIA. Two years later she was sold to Costa company Mediterranean Cruise Lines and renamed the COSTA MARINA. A further two years elapsed before the new cruise ship emerged from the Mariotti shipyard at Genoa. She has subsequently operated in the Caribbean, Europe, Scandinavia and South America. From spring 2002 the COSTA MARINA became the first Carnival group ship to be dedicated to the growing German cruise market, offering cruises in the Mediterranean and Baltic Seas. Pioneering again, the COSTA MARINA became the first of the company's ships to be based in the Far East in 2006, returning to the Mediterranean Sea for the bulk of 2007, and where she is now scheduled to operate until at least late 2010. IMO 6910544

COSTA MEDITERRANEA was built by Kvaerner Masa Yards (yard number 502) at Helsinki, Finland. The COSTA MEDITERRANEA currently operates in the Caribbean Sea in winter and the Mediterranean and Baltic Seas in summer. IMO 9237345

COSTA PACIFICA was built by Fincantieri (yard number 6148) at the Sestri yard, Genoa. She will spend her first 18 months in the Mediterranean Sea on a variety of itineraries. IMO 9378498

COSTA ROMANTICA is a near sister to the COSTA CLASSICA and was delivered to the company by the Venice shipyard of Fincantieri (yard number 5899) in September 1993. In winter 2006/7 she cruised from South American and Caribbean ports, returning to Europe for the summer. In 2009 she spends the summer in the Mediterranean Sea before moving on to the east coast of Africa en route to the Far East where she will be based in 2010. IMO 8821046

COSTA SERENA was built by Fincantieri (yard number 6130) at Sestri, Genoa. The COSTA SERENA spends all of her time in the Mediterranean Sea. IMO 9343132

COSTA VICTORIA is one of a pair of ships ordered from Bremer Vulkan at Bremen, Germany (yard number 107) at the end of 1993. Her keel was laid in November 1994 and she was floated out of her building dock less than ten months later. She was delivered in July 1996. The second ship of this pair (to have been named COSTA OLYMPIA) was not delivered due to the bankruptcy of the shipyard, but was later bought and completed for Norwegian Cruise Line as the NORWEGIAN SKY. The COSTA VICTORIA spends most of her time cruising in the Mediterranean Sea, but in 2007 and 2008 wintered in the Red Sea. In 2009 she will spend the winter in South America. IMO 9109031

Costa Cruises' **Costa Mediterranea** at Venice *(William Mayes)*

Costa Cruises' **Costa Romantica** at Toulon *(Andrew Kilk)*

Costa Cruises' **Costa Serena** in Istanbul *(William Mayes)*

Cruise ships on order

COSTA DELIZIOSA	c92700gt	2010	21.6k	DEP2	2260p	2828p	921c	294.0m	32.3m	8.1m	IT
NEWBUILDING 2	c114500gt	2011	19.6k	DE2	3012p	3780p	1100c	290.2m	35.5m	8.3m	IT
NEWBUILDING 3	c114500gt	2012	19.6k	DE2	3012p	3780p	1100c	290.2m	35.5m	8.3m	IT

COSTA DELIZIOSA is on order from Fincantieri (yard number 6164) and the forward section will be built in Ancona, while the after section will come from the Breda yard in Venice. IMO 9398917

NEWBUILDING 2 and **3** are on order from Fincantieri (yard numbers 6188 and 6189) and will be built in the Marghera yard. IMO 9479852 and 9479864

CUNARD LINE

The Company In 1840 Samuel Cunard's British and North American Royal Mail Steam Packet Company inaugurated the first North Atlantic steamship mail service under a contract with the Admiralty for which the latter would pay the sum of £55,000 per annum. This company soon became known as the Cunard Line. The 1,135-ton wooden paddle steamer BRITANNIA took the first sailing on 4th July 1840 between Liverpool, Halifax and Boston. By 1848 Cunard Line was operating a weekly transatlantic service using nine steamers. During the 1850's Mediterranean services were established and by the time of Samuel Cunard's death in 1865 the company had built up an impressive route network served by modern ships. To raise capital for new ships, the company, along with its associated companies, was merged into the new Cunard Steam Ship Company Limited in 1878, and two years later the public were invited to subscribe for £800,000 of the issued capital of £2,000,000. The next 50 years was a period of growth, spurred on to a great extent by the rivalry between the many emerging European and American shipping companies. In 1881, Cunard's SERVIA was the first ship to be lit by electric light, and twelve years later the CAMPANIA was the company's first twin-screw vessel. Steam turbines began to power the fleet in 1905 with the arrival of the CARMANIA. In 1907, the company's largest and most prestigious ships to date, the 31,000 gross ton sisters LUSITANIA and MAURETANIA entered service, each taking the 'Blue Riband' for Cunard. In fact, with the exception of the UNITED STATES, the MAURETANIA was the ship that held the record for the longest – from 1907 to 1929. With the arrival in 1914 of the 45,000-ton AQUITANIA the company could maintain the weekly New York service with just these three ships. After the end of the First World War, Cunard acquired the former German owned 52,000 ton IMPERATOR and renamed her BERENGARIA. During the depression of the early 1930's it became necessary for Cunard Line to merge with the White Star Line to form Cunard-White Star Limited in order to secure British Government finance to pay for the building of the 81,000 ton QUEEN MARY. In order to maintain the New York service with just two ships a second 'Queen' was ordered in 1936, but due to the outbreak of war the QUEEN ELIZABETH did not enter Cunard service until 1946. The company's first ship designed with cruising in mind was the 1949 built CARONIA; painted in three shades of green, she served the lucrative American market. The QUEEN MARY made her last transatlantic voyage in 1967 and was sold eventually for use as a hotel and museum at Long Beach, California. The last voyage of the QUEEN ELIZABETH took place the following year, and in early 1969 the QUEEN ELIZABETH 2 made her debut on the North Atlantic. Trafalgar House Investments Limited acquired Cunard in 1971, and in the same year the first of Cunard's new generation of cruise ships, the 14,000-ton sisters CUNARD ADVENTURER and CUNARD AMBASSADOR began sailing in the Caribbean. The former was sold to Klosters (the forerunner of Norwegian Cruise Line) in 1976 and the latter was converted for use as a livestock carrier following a fire in 1974. The CUNARD PRINCESS (launched as the CUNARD CONQUEST) and the CUNARD COUNTESS, both 18,000 tons, were the next cruise ships to join the fleet and were again used in the Caribbean. These were sold to other operators in 1995/96. Norwegian America Cruises, together with the elegant near-sisters SAGAFJORD and VISTAFJORD, was acquired in 1983 and retained as a separate brand for a number of years. Trafalgar House Investments was taken over towards the end of 1996 by the Norwegian construction and engineering group Kvaerner, and thus Cunard became Norwegian owned. Cunard didn't fit well into the Kvaerner group, so was sold to a consortium led by Carnival in May 1998. That company subsequently acquired the remaining shares from the other members of the consortium. Cunard's first new vessel subsequent to the acquisition, the QUEEN MARY 2, entered service in January 2004, thus ending almost a quarter of a century of no investment in new ships. The CARONIA (formerly VISTAFJORD) left the Cunard fleet in the autumn of 2004 when she began a new career with Saga Holidays, leaving this most famous of all the Atlantic lines with just the two 'Queens'.

The previously announced QUEEN VICTORIA, due for delivery in 2005 never materialised in the Cunard fleet, instead being diverted to P&O Cruises as the ARCADIA. Subsequently the new QUEEN VICTORIA was ordered from Fincantieri. Before the entry into service of the new ship, the disposal of the QUEEN ELIZABETH 2 was announced. She had been sold to a company owned by the Government of Dubai for $100 million, to become a hotel, conference centre, museum and tourist attraction, and undertook her final, one way, cruise to Dubai in November 2008. A new QUEEN ELIZABETH joins the fleet in October 2010.

Management of Cunard has been transferred to Carnival UK and the head office is now in Southampton.

President and Managing Director Peter Shanks

Address Mountbatten House, Grosvenor Square, Southampton SO15 2BF United Kingdom

Telephone +44 845 071 0300 **Fax** +44 2380 657353

Website www.cunard.com or www.cunard.co.uk

Areas operated Europe, the Caribbean, the Americas and World Cruises (QUEEN MARY 2 also Atlantic crossings)

QUEEN MARY 2	148528gt	2003	29.3k	GDEP4	2620p	3090p	1292c	345.0m	41.0m	10.3m	GB
QUEEN VICTORIA	90049gt	2007	22.0k	DEP2	1980p	2144p	818c	294.0m	32.3m	7.9m	GB

QUEEN MARY 2 was built by Chantiers de l'Atlantique (yard number G32) at St Nazaire in France in 2003 as the first traditionally hulled liner for more than a quarter of a century. She was delivered at the end of the year and made a triumphant entrance to the Port of Southampton for the first time on 26 December 2003. Following her maiden voyage to Fort Lauderdale on 12 January 2004 she spent the spring in the Caribbean before undertaking a varied programme of cruises from both Southampton and New York, between which she undertook Atlantic crossings. In 2006 she undertook a trip around South America, which attracted rather more adverse publicity than might have been thought necessary after she put one pod out of action on leaving Fort Lauderdale. In 2007 she undertook her first World Cruise. IMO 9241061

QUEEN VICTORIA was ordered as a replacement for the previous ship intended to carry this name (now P&O Cruises' ARCADIA), from Fincantieri (yard number 6127) at Monfalcone, Italy. Her keel was laid in May 2006 and the ship floated out in January 2007. Her Royal Highness The Duchess of Cornwall named the QUEEN VICTORIA in Southampton on 10 December 2007. During her first season she operated a series of fly cruises based in the Mediterranean, but has subsequently been firmly based in Southampton. IMO 9320556

Cruise ship on order

QUEEN ELIZABETH	c92000gt	2010	22.0k	DEP2	2014p	2200p	820c	294.0m	32.3m	7.9m	GB

QUEEN ELIZABETH is currently under construction by Fincantieri (yard number 6187) at Monfalcone, near Venice, Italy. Her keel-laying ceremony was held on 2 July 2009. IMO 9477438

HOLLAND AMERICA LINE

The Company The Nederlandsch Amerikaansche Stoomvaart Maatschappij (Netherlands American Steamship Company) came into being on 18 April 1873 to operate transatlantic liner services in competition with the other already well-established European steamship lines. The company gradually built up its services, fleet and reputation, and in 1898 adopted the yellow, green and white funnel colours which were to identify its ships for more than 70 years. The company was officially established as De Holland Amerika Lijn N.V. (The Holland America Line Ltd.) in 1896, a name by which it had been known unofficially for many years. The company was able to operate during most of the First World War as The Netherlands was a neutral country, but that didn't stop the loss of a number of ships to mines and later to submarine and surface attack. After the war, the Depression began to set in and the operations of the company started to be scaled back at the end of the 1920's. However, Holland America's passenger shipping was less severely affected than that of some other liner companies and by 1934 the STATENDAM was in need of a running mate on the New York service. That running mate was to be the NIEUW AMSTERDAM of 1938, Holland America's most elegant ship and certainly one of the best looking passenger liners ever built.

At the beginning of the Second World War the company moved its headquarters from Rotterdam to Willemstad, Curacao even though The Netherlands attempted to remain neutral. In 1940 Germany overran its small neighbour and in the accompanying air raids the Holland America office was

Costa Cruises' **Costa Victoria** at Aqaba *(William Mayes)*

Cunard Line's **Queen Mary 2** at Southampton *(William Mayes)*

Cunard Line's **Queen Victoria** in Istanbul *(William Mayes)*

Holland America Line's **Eurodam** off St Peter Port *(Richard Mayes)*

destroyed. After the end of the war the first new passenger ships were the predominantly tourist class ships RYNDAM (1951) and MAASDAM (1952), for the North Atlantic service. The company then began to think more positively about using ships for cruising in the off-season. Although the NIEUW AMSTERDAM had already proved successful in this role, the newer ships were not really suitable. The next delivery, however, had been built with an eye to cruising and entered service in 1956 as the STATENDAM. A running mate was now required for the NIEUW AMSTERDAM, and thus the ROTTERDAM with her revolutionary profile and thin uptakes in place of a funnel arrived in 1959. During the 1960's and 1970's cruising increased its importance to the company's revenues and a pair of former Moore McCormack liners were acquired for this purpose. As if to add emphasis to the change in direction, a new house flag, hull colour and an orange and blue funnel marking were introduced. The grand old NIEUW AMSTERDAM made the last scheduled transatlantic crossing for the Holland America Line in 1971, bringing to an end almost 100 years of the Rotterdam to New York passenger service. She remained in a cruising role for a further two years before being sold to Taiwanese breakers at the end of 1973. That year also saw the entry into service of the first new passenger ship for almost a quarter of a century, the 9,000-ton PRINSENDAM. Sadly she was to have a very short life as she was lost in the Gulf of Alaska on 11th October 1980 following an engine room fire. However, she had established the popularity of Alaskan cruising and in the following year both the ROTTERDAM and the STATENDAM served this market. In 1983, just before the delivery of the new NOORDAM and NIEUW AMSTERDAM, the company merged fully with its recently acquired subsidiary, Westours Inc., to form Holland America Westours Inc. In 1985 this name was further changed to Holland America Line – Westours Inc. July 1987 saw the new holding company Holland America Line N.V. take a 50% stake in Windstar Cruises Inc. and in the following year the company acquired Home Lines Inc. with its two ships, the ATLANTIC (not operated by Holland America and later sold to Premier Cruise Lines) and the HOMERIC, renamed the WESTERDAM. Later in 1988 Holland America purchased the remaining 50% of Windstar.

In November 1988 agreement was reached for Carnival Holdings Ltd to acquire the cruise and tour businesses of the Holland America group for $625 million. The first major effect of the takeover was the ordering of three (later increased to four) new ships from Fincantieri, beginning with the STATENDAM, delivered in 1993. The 1959-built ROTTERDAM was retired in September 1997; her replacement, delivered shortly afterwards was the sixth ship to bear that name. The WESTERDAM left the fleet in 2002 and joined fellow Carnival subsidiary Costa in Europe. Thereafter a steady stream of new-buildings joined the premier brand fleet of Holland America. In recent years the company has diversified its itineraries and now commits more ships to Europe each summer.

President and Chief Executive Officer Stein Kruse

Address 300 Elliott Avenue West, Seattle, WA 98119-4198, United States of America

Telephone +1 206 281 3535 **Fax** +1 206 281 7110

Website www.hollandamerica.com

Areas operated Worldwide

AMSTERDAM	62735gt	2000	22.5k	DEP2	1380p	1872p	615c	237.8m	32.2m	8.1m	NL
EURODAM	86273gt	2008	21.9k	DEP2	2104p	2671p	929c	285.2m	32.2m	8.0m	NL
MAASDAM	55575gt	1993	20.3k	DE2	1258p	1625p	580c	219.2m	30.8m	7.7m	NL
NOORDAM	82318gt	2006	22.0k	GDEP2	1918p	2388p	820c	285.2m	32.2m	8.0m	NL
OOSTERDAM	81769gt	2003	22.0k	GDEP2	1848p	2388p	815c	285.2m	32.2m	8.0m	NL
PRINSENDAM	37983gt	1988	21.8k	D2	793p	870p	443c	204.0m	28.9m	7.2m	NL
ROTTERDAM	59652gt	1997	22.5k	DE2	1316p	1708p	600c	237.9m	32.2m	7.5m	NL
RYNDAM	55819gt	1994	20.3k	DE2	1270p	1633p	580c	219.2m	30.8m	7.7m	NL
STATENDAM	55819gt	1993	20.3k	DE2	1258p	1621p	580c	219.2m	30.8m	7.7m	NL
VEENDAM	57092gt	1996	20.3k	DE2	1258p	1621p	580c	219.2m	30.8m	7.7m	NL
VOLENDAM	61214gt	1999	20.2k	DE2	1432p	1837p	615c	237.0m	32.3m	8.1m	NL
WESTERDAM	81811gt	2004	22.0k	GDEP2	1916p	2388p	817c	285.2m	32.2m	8.0m	NL
ZAANDAM	61396gt	2000	20.2k	DE2	1432p	1837p	615c	237.0m	32.3m	8.1m	NL
ZUIDERDAM	82305gt	2002	22.0k	GDEP2	1916p	2388p	817c	285.4m	32.2m	7.8m	NL

AMSTERDAM is the third ship to be named in honour of the capital city of The Netherlands, and was delivered to Holland America by Fincantieri (yard number 6052), Venice, Italy during 2000. Initially she was named AMSTERDAM I as there was already a ship on the Bahamas register named AMSTERDAM. Following her 2002 world cruise she was deployed on cruises to Alaska and the

Caribbean Sea. The AMSTERDAM undertakes a world cruise each year and in 2009 and 2010 cruises in Alaska and the Pacific, including some departures from Sydney. IMO 9188037

EURODAM was built by the Breda (Venice) yard of Fincantieri (yard number 6149). She is the first ship of the so-called Signature Class, a development of the Vista class of ship, and was named by Her Majesty Queen Beatrix of the Netherlands in Rotterdam on 1 July 2008. The EURODAM is in Northern Europe for the summer of 2009 and then repositions via New England to the Caribbean Sea. IMO 9378448

MAASDAM is the second of three ships ordered from Fincantieri (yard number 5882) at Monfalcone, Italy on 25 November 1989, and the fifth MAASDAM to have been in the Holland America line fleet. The ship entered service under the Bahamas flag in December 1993 and was transferred to the Dutch flag in 1996. Maasdam is a village situated to the south of Rotterdam. MAASDAM cruises in the Caribbean, east coast USA and Canada and Europe in 2009/10. IMO 8919257

NOORDAM has a name incorporating the northerly compass point together with the traditional Holland America 'Dam' ending. She is the second ship of this name and the last in a series of four vessels built for the company by Fincantieri (yard number 6079) in Italy. Her godmother was actress Marlee Matlin at a dedication ceremony in New York on 22 February 2006. The NOORDAM cruises in the Mediterranean and Caribbean Seas in 2009/10. IMO 9230115

OOSTERDAM was built by Fincantieri (yard number 6076) in Italy as the second ship in what has emerged as a four ship series (with a fifth similar ship eventually becoming P&O Cruises' ARCADIA). Her name is derived from the easterly point of the compass. HRH Princess Margriet of The Netherlands named her in Rotterdam. The OOSTERDAM cruises to Mexico and in the Mediterranean Sea in 2009/10. IMO 9221281

PRINSENDAM was built by Wartsila Marine Industries (yard number 1296) at their Turku, Finland yard, for Kloster's Royal Viking Line of Oslo as the ROYAL VIKING SUN. She was to be the penultimate ship built for this company, which had been owned since 1984 by Norwegian Caribbean Line. In 1994 she was sold to Cunard Line but retained her name. Following the partial amalgamation of Cunard and Seabourn, she was transferred to the Seabourn fleet and renamed the SEABOURN SUN. Considered to be unsuitable as a fleet-mate for the trio of yacht-like ships in the Seabourn fleet, she was transferred to fellow Carnival subsidiary Holland America Line as the second PRINSENDAM. For her current season she cruises in Europe, the Caribbean Sea, South America and Africa. During late 2009 and early 2010 the ship will have a major refit that includes the addition of 22 cabins and a new bar. IMO 8700280

ROTTERDAM was ordered in January 1995 from the Marghera, Venice yard of Fincantieri in Italy (yard number 5980) as a larger and faster version of the STATENDAM class, but particularly as a replacement for the much-loved 1959-built ROTTERDAM. She was named by HRH Princess Margriet and is the sixth Holland America ship to bear the name of the second largest city and busiest seaport in The Netherlands. She cruises in South America, through the Panama Canal and undertakes a world voyage in 2009/10. IMO 9122552

RYNDAM is the final member of the trio of cruise ships (and the third ship to bear this name) ordered from the Monfalcone, Italy yard of Fincantieri (yard number 5883) on 25 November 1989. She began her commercial career under the Bahamas flag with a ten day Caribbean cruise on 20 October 1994, after being named by Madeleine Arison, wife of Micky Arison. She was re-flagged to the Netherlands in 1996, and cruises Alaska, the Sea of Cortez and the Caribbean Sea in 2009/10. IMO 8919269

STATENDAM is the lead ship in a series of three sisters ordered from Fincantieri (yard number 5881) at Monfalcone, Italy on 25 November 1989. She was the first ship to be ordered for Holland America Line following the takeover by Carnival, and entered service on 25 January 1993, the fifth ship to bear this name, the origins of which are unclear. The name may refer to a settlement near the Dutch town of Geertruideaberg, but is more likely a reference to the Staten, the Government in the early days. She was originally registered under the ownership of Windsurf Ltd of Nassau, Bahamas but was transferred to the Dutch flag under Holland America Line ownership in 1996. In her current season the STATENDAM cruises to Alaska, Mexico and the Caribbean Sea. In spring 2010 she has been chartered by the Royal Canadian Mounted Police for use as an accommodation ship at Vancouver in connection with the Winter Olympic Games. IMO 8919245

VEENDAM became the fourth member of the STATENDAM class when ordered from Fincantieri's Marghera shipyard (yard number 5954) in Venice, Italy on 3 December 1993. She was delivered in May 1996 and, after being named by the actress Debbie Reynolds, entered commercial service at the end

Holland America Line's **Amsterdam** *(Theodore W Scull)*

Holland America Line's **Maasdam** at Halifax NS *(William Mayes)*

Holland America Line's **Oosterdam** at Civitaveccia *(William Mayes)*

of that month. She had a large complement of British deck and engineering officers due to a shortage of suitable Dutch personnel. She retained her Bahamas registry for a number of years before switching to the Dutch flag. She was partially rebuilt in 2009, resulting in a gross tonnage increase of 1,300. The VEENDAM is named in honour of a town in the eastern part of The Netherlands, close to Groningen. The VEENDAM cruises in the Caribbean Sea, to Alaska and to Bermuda in 2009/10. IMO 9102992

VOLENDAM, named after a small town on the coast of the inland sea, Ijssel-Meer, was delivered by the Venice, Italy yard of Fincantieri (yard number 6035) in 1999. The VOLENDAM cruises in south east Asia, Australasia and Alaska, and in 2010 will undertake a 34-day round Australia cruise. Tennis player Chris Evert christened the ship on 12 November 1999 in Fort Lauderdale. IMO 9156515

WESTERDAM was built by Fincantieri (yard number 6077) in Italy as the third ship in a series of four. Her name is derived from the western point of the compass and her godmother was actress Renee Soutendijk in a ceremony held in Venice on 25 April 2004. The WESTERDAM cruises in Alaska and the Caribbean Sea in 2009/10. IMO 9226891

ZAANDAM takes her name from a town that now forms part of the northern suburbs of Amsterdam. Delivered by the Venice yard of Fincantieri, (yard number 6036), she operates to Hawaii and Alaska in 2009/10. IMO 9156527

ZUIDERDAM has a name incorporating the southern compass point together with the traditional Holland America 'Dam' suffix. This ship is the first of a series of five vessels (then six – one of which was cancelled and one of which is P&O Cruises' ARCADIA) ordered from Fincantieri (yard number 6075) in Italy. American journalist Joan Lunden named the ship in Fort Lauderdale on 14 December 2002. The ZUIDERDAM cruises in the Caribbean Sea and to Alaska and Europe in 2009/10. IMO 9221279

Cruise ships on order

NIEUW AMSTERDAM	c86000gt	2010	21.9k	DEP2	2104p	2671p	929c	285.2m	32.2m	8.0m	NL
NEWBUILDING 2	c86000gt	2011	21.9k	DEP2	2104p	2671p	929c	285.2m	32.2m	8.0m	NL

NIEUW AMSTERDAM is on order from the Sestri yard of Fincantieri (yard number 6181). She will be moved to the Marghera yard for outfitting. After a rather unfortunate choice of name for the preceding ship, the company has revived a traditional name. She will be the fourth of the company's ships to bear this former name for New York City. IMO 9378450

NEWBUILDING 2 is the third ship in the so-called Signature class, although the construction and yard number is currently unconfirmed. IMO 9454929

Holland America Line also owns the THOMSON CELEBRATION, chartered to Thomson Cruises and recently sold the THOMSON SPIRIT to Louis Cruise Lines.

IBEROCRUCEROS

The Company Iberojet was, until February 2007, part of Orizonia Corporation, Spain's largest travel company. Iberojet was a relative newcomer to the growing market for cruising amongst Spaniards. During the early part of 2005 the company was also operating the GRAND LATINO, now Fred. Olsen's BOUDICCA. In February 2007, Carnival Corporation signed a letter of intent with Iberojet's owners to form a joint venture targeting the Spanish Market. The fleet is to be grown by cascading older units from the various Carnival Corporation fleets. Under the terms of the agreement, Carnival Corporation owned 75% of the joint venture, with the remainder in the hands of Orizonia. Costa Crociere manages the company, and in 2009 acquired the remaining 25% of Iberocruceros. Carnival Cruise Lines' HOLIDAY will join the fleet in 2010 as the GRAND HOLIDAY. Iberocruceros caters for Spanish speaking passengers.

Managing Director Alfredo Serrano

Address 23 Grand Via Asima Poligon Son Castillo, 07009 Palma de Mallorca, Spain

Telephone +34 971 788220 **Fax** +34 971 282585

Website www.iberocruceros.es

Area operated Mediterranean

GRAND CELEBRATION	47262gt	1987	21.5k	D2	1498p	1896p	620c	223.3m	28.0m	7.6m	PT
GRAND MISTRAL	48200gt	1999	19.0k	DE2	1248p	1667p	470c	216.0m	28.8m	6.9m	IT

Holland America Line's **Prinsendam** at Bridgetown *(Andrew Kilk)*

Holland America Line's **Rotterdam** at Dover *(William Mayes)*

Holland America Line's **Statendam** in Hong Kong *(Bruce Peter)*

Holland America Line's **Zaandam** in Vancouver *(Andrew Kilk)*

Iberocruceros' **Grand Celebration** in Livorno *(William Mayes)*

Iberocruceros' **Grand Mistral** in Civitavecchia *(William Mayes)*

GRAND VOYAGER	24391gt	2000	28.0k	D2	836p	920p	360c	180.4m	25.5m	7.3m	IT

GRAND CELEBRATION was built by Kockums (yard number 597), at their Malmo, Sweden shipyard. She was delivered in 1987 as the CELEBRATION to Carnival Cruise Lines for that company's Caribbean cruising operation. In 1989 the CELEBRATION collided with, and sank, the Cuban vessel CAPITAN SAN LOUIS but sustained only minor damage herself. She was transferred within the group to Iberocruceros in July 2008 and renamed GRAND CELEBRATION. IMO 8314134

GRAND MISTRAL, the first new ship for Festival Cruises, was delivered by Chantiers de l'Atlantique (yard number J31), St Nazaire, France as the MISTRAL. Following the collapse of Festival Cruises she was purchased by her builder, now part of the Alstom Group and eventually chartered to Iberojet. She was marketed initially as the IBEROSTAR MISTRAL. Subsequently she was renamed as the GRAND MISTRAL in 2004. The Mistral is a strong wind from the northwest affecting the southern coast of France, predominantly from Marseilles to St Tropez. IMO 9172777

GRAND VOYAGER, another first new ship, was built as one of a pair of high-speed cruise ships for Royal Olympic Cruises of Greece by Blohm & Voss (yard number 961) in Hamburg as the OLYMPIC VOYAGER. Political unrest in the Eastern Mediterranean meant that her intended service was curtailed and she was put on to work more mundane than the 'Three Continents in a Week' circuit for which she was built. Difficulties with the International Olympic Organisation led to the company restyling itself as Royal Olympia Cruises and the ship was renamed OLYMPIA VOYAGER. The company within ROC that owned the ship filed for bankruptcy, starting the process that led to the complete failure of the group. The ship was auctioned and acquired by the V-Ships group. Renamed VOYAGER, she was chartered to Iberojet, initially being marketed as GRAND VOYAGER. She was formally renamed in late 2005. IMO 9183506

OCEAN VILLAGE

The Company Ocean Village is a division within P&O Cruises, having commenced operation in the spring of 2003 as a company providing, bizarrely, 'cruises for people who don't do cruises'. In a fairly radical departure from the accepted cruise concept, Ocean Village was seeking to adopt a resort style in order to attract a younger and more active type of passenger, and includes self-service meals and a vast range of sporting and other active pursuits. The concept appeared to have been successful, as the AIDABLU joined the Ocean Village fleet in spring 2007. However, in the summer of 2008 it was announced that the company would be closed down by the end of the summer of 2010 European season and the ships transferred to P&O Cruises in Australia.

Address Richmond House, Terminus Terrace, Southampton SO14 3PN, England

Telephone +44 845 358 5000 **Fax** +44 2380 523720

Website www.oceanvillageholidays.co.uk

Areas operated Mediterranean and Caribbean

OCEAN VILLAGE	63524gt	1989	19.5k	DE2	1578p	1856p	514c	245.6m	32.2m	7.7m	GB
OCEAN VILLAGE TWO	70310gt	1990	19.5k	DE2	1664p	2014p	677c	245.1m	32.3m	7.9m	GB

OCEAN VILLAGE was laid down in May 1988 as the SITMAR FAIRMAJESTY by Chantiers de l'Atlantique (yard number B29) at St Nazaire, France for the Sitmar Line. That company passed into the ownership of the P&O Group in September 1988, and the ship was subsequently delivered as the STAR PRINCESS in the spring of 1989 for service within P&O's Princess Cruises division. In late 1997 the ship was transferred to P&O Cruises for operation within the UK passenger fleet and renamed ARCADIA, thus reviving a traditional P&O name. She cruised from the UK in the summer and in the Caribbean during the winter until the spring of 2003, when she was transferred to Ocean Village and renamed OCEAN VILLAGE in a ceremony performed by Ulrika Jonsson. She is now based in the Mediterranean in summer and the Caribbean in winter. She will transfer to P&O Cruises Australia in 2010 as the PACIFIC PEARL. IMO 8611398

OCEAN VILLAGE TWO is one of the last pair of ships ordered by Sitmar Line in 1988 prior to that company being acquired by P&O. Built by Fincantieri (yard number 5839) at Monfalcone, Italy, she was delivered to Princess Cruises in 1990 as the CROWN PRINCESS. Princess employed her on a variety of itineraries including European cruises until the summer of 2002, when she was transferred within the Group to the newly formed A'Rosa Cruises of Germany, taking the name A'ROSA BLU. On the sale of A'Rosa's river cruise business in 2004, she was transferred to Aida Cruises and renamed

Iberocruceros' **Grand Voyager** in Villefranche *(William Mayes)*

Ocean Village at Bridgetown *(Rick Frendt)*

Ocean Village Two *(Richard Seville)*

as the AIDABLU. In spring 2007 she passed to Ocean Village and following a three week refit emerged as the OCEAN VILLAGE TWO. She will transfer to P&O Cruises Australia in 2009 as the PACIFIC JEWEL. IMO 8521220

P&O CRUISES

The Company As the ownership of this company changes over the years since its de-merger from the Peninsular and Oriental Steam Navigation Company, it is easy to forget that this is the descendant of the company that invented cruising. Its history of passenger services goes back to 1837 and the formation of the Peninsular Steam Navigation Company (the peninsula being Iberia), which later became The Peninsular and Oriental Steam Navigation Company, or P&O as it was both universally and affectionately known. The company was founded as the Peninsular Steam Navigation Company to fulfil the new British Admiralty-controlled mail contract serving Vigo, Oporto, Lisbon, Cadiz and Gibraltar from Falmouth. The first mail steamer, the DON JUAN, was lost on the homeward leg of her maiden mail voyage, but the reputation of the company was little damaged as all of the passengers, crew, mail and cargo were saved. In 1839 the company won the tender for the mail contract from Falmouth to Alexandria, via Gibraltar and Malta, but had insufficient capital for new ships. The answer came in the form of a merger with the Trans-Atlantic Steamship Company of Liverpool, bringing two large ships to the fleet. In 1840, a new company was set up with liability limited by Royal Charter; the Peninsular and Oriental Steam Navigation Company had been born. P&O invented cruising in 1844 when it advertised a 'Grand Tour' by sea from Southampton to Gibraltar, Malta, Athens, Smyrna, Jaffa and Alexandria utilising three ships, the LADY MARY WOOD, the TAGUS and the IBERIA. This voyage was recorded in William Makepeace Thackeray's 'Notes of a Journey from Cornhill to Grand Cairo'. Subsequently round trips from Southampton to destinations such as Constantinople and Alexandria were offered.

Throughout the second half of the nineteenth century the ships of the P&O became larger and more luxurious as the company increased its routes to cover the far-flung corners of the British Empire. Australia, the Indian Sub-Continent and the Far East became the most important routes for the company, and it was on these that the newest and largest ships served. The company was also an important supplier of vessels for use as troopships, both for overseas campaigns and on long-term contract.

Innovation continued apace with the RAVENNA of 1880 being the first passenger ship to be built with a full steel superstructure, and four years later the VALETTA was the first of the company's ships to use electric light.

In 1904 the company advertised its first proper cruise on a ship refitted specifically for that purpose. The 6,000-ton VECTIS had been adapted to carry just 150 first-class passengers. Ten years later, after the company had merged with the British India Steam Navigation Company, its fleet totalled 197 ships. That year also saw the company relieved of almost two-thirds of its fleet for war service as hospital ships, troop transports and armed merchant cruisers. P&O lost 17 ships during the First World War, and subsidiary companies lost a further 68.

In December 1918 one of the most significant acquisitions took place when P&O purchased 51% of the share capital of the Orient Steam Navigation Company. The Orient Line had been a joint operator with P&O on the Australian Mail Contract for some time. By 1921 the company had reintroduced its long haul services to India (weekly), China (fortnightly) and Australia (four-weekly). In the 1920's P&O and Orient Line between them took delivery of more than twenty new passenger liners, most of which were used on the Australian service. Cruising began again in 1925 when the RANCHI undertook a cruise to Norway as her maiden voyage. For the 1929 season, P&O offered a total of 15 cruises, including some aboard the new VICEROY OF INDIA, the first turbo-electric ship for the company.

The combined fleets of the companies within the P&O Group peaked in the mid 1920's, when more than 500 ships ranging from the excursion vessels and coasters of the General Steam Navigation Company, to the modern refrigerated cargo ships of New Zealand Shipping Company and Federal Steam Navigation, and the state of the art passenger liners of P&O and Orient Line were owned.

The Second World War took its toll on the P&O Group with the loss of 156 ships including such passenger liners as the VICEROY OF INDIA, RAWALPINDI, CATHAY, STRATHALLAN, ORONSAY and ORCADES. By the late 1940's commercial aviation was beginning to take a hold, so the passenger fleet renewal programme concentrated on fewer but larger and faster ships. When these ships came on stream between 1947 and 1954 they cut the sailing time to Australia from five to four weeks.

P&O Cruises' **Arcadia** at Bridgetown *(William Mayes)*

P&O Cruises' **Aurora** off Elba *(William Mayes)*

In 1955 both P&O and Orient Line ordered what were to be their last passenger liners, the CANBERRA and the ORIANA. These were fast ships and shaved another week off the Australian run; ORIANA recorded a speed of 30.64 knots on trials. These two ships came under full common ownership in 1961 when P&O acquired the remaining minority interests in Orient Line and restyled its passenger operations as P&O-Orient Lines. The 1960's saw a general downturn in line voyages and a reduction in the number of ships operated, a trend that was to continue into the 1970's when cruising became a vital employment for ships between line voyages.

In 1971 the company underwent a massive re-organisation when the activities of more than 100 subsidiaries operating 239 ships were structured into a number of operating divisions. The Passenger Division, the forerunner of P&O Cruises, commenced with 13, including the last two large ships of British India, NEVASA and UGANDA. During the early 1970's times were really bad for the passenger liner with relatively young ships being sent for scrap becoming a regular occurrence. Princess Cruises was acquired in 1974 and the almost new SPIRIT OF LONDON was transferred to that company. By the late 1970's the CANBERRA and ORIANA served the UK cruise market and the ARCADIA was employed in Australia. In 1981 the ORIANA replaced the ARCADIA in Australia, and the UK was left with just the CANBERRA and the SEA PRINCESS, newly transferred from Australia. CANBERRA was out of P&O service for much of 1982 when she was requisitioned for use in the Falklands War. In 1986 SEA PRINCESS was switched to the Princess Cruises fleet, leaving just the CANBERRA to service the UK.

With the withdrawal of the CANBERRA imminent, P&O Cruises ordered its first new ship for the British market, the ORIANA, which set the standard for all that followed when she was delivered in 1995. CANBERRA was scrapped in 1997 and her replacement was the ARCADIA (formerly STAR PRINCESS and now OCEAN VILLAGE). The P&O Cruises fleet had grown at an impressive rate and the 2005 brochure offered cruises on six ships (including the ADONIA, now transferred back to Princess Cruises as the SEA PRINCESS), a choice not seen since the early 1970's.

P&O Princess Cruises became an independent company on its demerger from the Peninsular & Oriental Steam Navigation Company in 2000. In early 2003 P&O Princess began talks with Royal Caribbean on a possible merger, but shareholders eventually voted for a merger with Carnival Corporation, which occurred in the autumn of that year. As a result of that merger it is now unlikely that there will be any more ships designed specifically for P&O Cruises. The most recent fleet additions have either come from Princess Cruises or are based on Princess Cruises design.

Chief Executive Officer David Dingle **Managing Director** Carol Marlow

Address Richmond House, Terminus Terrace, Southampton, SO14 3PN, England

Telephone +44 2380 534200 **Fax** +44 2380 227920

Website www.pocruises.co.uk

Areas operated Mediterranean, Scandinavia, positioning voyages to the Caribbean and world cruises, all from Southampton. Fly cruises in the Caribbean and South America

ARCADIA	83781gt	2005	22.0k	DEP2	1848p	2388p	866c	285.1m	32.2m	7.8m	BM
ARTEMIS	44588gt	1984	21.5k	D2	1200p	1318p	520c	230.6m	29.2m	7.8m	BM
AURORA	76152gt	2000	25.0k	DE2	1874p	2290p	850c	270.0m	32.2m	7.9m	BM
OCEANA	77499gt	2000	21.0k	DE2	2004p	2272p	875c	261.0m	32.3m	8.0m	BM
ORIANA	69153gt	1995	24.0k	D2	1814p	1928p	800c	260.0m	32.2m	7.9m	BM
VENTURA	116017gt	2008	22.5k	DE2	2592p	3574p	1239c	289.6m	36.0m	8.5m	BM

ARCADIA was laid down for Holland America Line (yard number 6078) by Fincantieri at Marghera, Venice in Italy. Prior to delivery she was transferred to the Cunard line as the QUEEN VICTORIA. In the spring of 2004, she was again transferred – this time to P&O Cruises as part of a major fleet reorganisation within the British parts of Carnival – to become the ARCADIA when delivered in April 2005. ARCADIA is based in Southampton during the spring, summer and autumn, and usually spends winter in the Caribbean. She continues the tradition established by the previous ship of this name as an adults-only vessel. Named by Dame Kelly Holmes, she is the fourth P&O ship to bear the poetic name for an area of what is now the Greek Peloponnese, the peninsula south of the Isthmus of Corinth that makes up the southern part of Greece. In late 2008 the ship received a new block of cabins at the stern, thereby increasing their number by 34, during a refit at the Lloydwerft shipyard at Bremerhaven. IMO 9226906

ARTEMIS was the first purpose built cruise ship to be ordered by the P&O Group. She was built by Wartsila (yard number 464) at Helsinki, Finland as the ROYAL PRINCESS and delivered in late 1984. Initially used on US based itineraries for Princess Cruises, she has more recently undertaken trips around South America, but spent the summer in European waters. For 2003/2004 she undertook an interesting set of worldwide itineraries, including much of Africa, South America, Antarctica, the Amazon and Europe. In a major redeployment within the British division of Carnival she was transferred to P&O Cruises in spring 2005 as the ARTEMIS, a rather clever, if not entirely appropriate renaming, reflecting her connection with Diana, Princess of Wales, who named the ship in 1984. Artemis, daughter of Zeus and Lato, and twin sister of Apollo was a Greek goddess of the chase and protectoress of children and young animals; the Roman equivalent was Diana. The ARTEMIS now cruises from Southampton for much of the year, but in winter incorporates a long voyage to exotic destinations into her itinerary. IMO 8201480

AURORA was built by Jos. L. Meyer (yard number 640) at Papenburg, Germany as the second purpose built cruise ship for the British market. Ordered in 1998, she was delivered in the spring of 2000 and after an abortive maiden voyage has settled down as a successful member of the P&O Cruises fleet, undertaking an annual World Cruise in addition to her European itineraries from Southampton. Engine problems at the start of her World Cruise in 2005 gained much press coverage, but despite the best journalistic efforts it proved extremely difficult to find anyone with a bad word to say about either the company or the ship. During her 2008 world cruise she again suffered mechanical problems, leading to the loss of several port calls. Aurora, goddess of the dawn, was the name chosen for the ship as a link to the dawning of a new millennium. IMO 9169524

OCEANA was built by Fincantieri (yard number 6044) at Monfalcone, Italy as the OCEAN PRINCESS for Princess Cruises' operations in the Caribbean and to Alaska. In the autumn of 2002 she was renamed OCEANA and transferred to P&O Cruises to serve the British market, operating predominantly from the United Kingdom. Her first season commenced with Caribbean fly-cruises before she took up her Southampton based itinerary. The second ship to bear the name, Oceana is the feminine form of Oceanus, the Roman god of the ocean. The OCEANA usually spends winter in the Caribbean. IMO 9169550

ORIANA was the first purpose built cruise ship for the British market, and when she entered service in 1995 she very quickly became a favourite and set the standard that many others have yet to achieve. This sturdily built, classically elegant ship was ordered from the Jos. L. Meyer yard (yard number 636) at Papenburg in 1993, becoming, at the time of her delivery, the largest passenger ship to be built in Germany. HM Queen Elizabeth II named her in Southampton. In addition to cruises from Southampton, the ORIANA has undertaken a number of world cruises, but for the 2004 UK winter season pioneered a new programme in the Caribbean and around South America. This is the second ORIANA to have served the company, a name given to the poetic huntress and heroine; a character associated with Queen Elizabeth I of England by contemporary writers. Her regular cruising pattern now centres on Southampton, with a winter World Cruise. In 2006, following a major refit, the ORIANA was moved from the UK registry to that of Bermuda in order to allow weddings to be performed on board. IMO 9050137

VENTURA was built by Fincantieri (yard number 6132) at the Monfalcone shipyard in Italy, and based on a design that can be traced back to the first 100,000+ ton ship for Princess Cruises, the GRAND PRINCESS. She spends summer based at Southampton, England and winters in the Caribbean Sea. IMO 9333175

Cruise ship on order

AZURA	c116000gt	2010	22.5k	DE2	3076p	3600p	1200c	289.6m	36.0m	8.5m	BM

AZURA was ordered late in 2006 from Fincantieri (yard number 6166) and will be built at Monfalcone. IMO 9424883

P&O CRUISES AUSTRALIA

The Company Although P&O had always had a cruising presence in Australia, until the mid-1970's with regular line voyages and 'between voyage cruising' and in later years with the 1954-built ARCADIA and subsequently the 1960-built ORIANA, the permanent presence ended with the sale of the latter ship to Japan at the end of 1986. That all changed in 1988, however, when P&O acquired Sitmar Line and its Australian based cruise ship, the FAIRSTAR (built in 1957 as the Bibby Line troopship OXFORDSHIRE). A one-ship operation continued with the FAIRSTAR until 1997, then the FAIR

P&O Cruises' **Artemis** in Southampton *(Bruce Peter)*

P&O Cruises' **Oceana** leaving Southampton *(William Mayes)*

P&O Cruises' **Oriana** at St John's Antigua *(William Mayes)*

PRINCESS until 2000, followed by the PACIFIC SKY until 2003 when the PACIFIC PRINCESS (see Princess Cruises) joined the fleet on a part time basis. Subsequently, the company has benefited from the replacement programmes elsewhere within the group with Carnival's JUBILEE and Costa's COSTA TROPICALE joining the growing fleet. For management purposes the company has recently been re-styled as Carnival (Australia), but it is too soon to know whether the P&O Cruises Australia marketing name is likely to disappear in the immediate future. In 2006 the PACIFIC SKY was sold to Spanish operator Pullmantur and renamed SKY WONDER. In 2009 the OCEAN VILLAGE TWO joins the fleet as the PACIFIC JEWEL, and one year later the OCEAN VILLAGE follows her as the PACIFIC PEARL, thus reuniting the last three Sitmar ordered ships in the same fleet for the first time since 1997.

Chief Executive Officer Ann Sherry

Address Level 9, 203 Pacific Highway, St Leonard's, NSW 2605, Australia

Telephone +61 2 132469 **Fax** +61 2 8424 9161

Website www.pocruises.com.au

Areas operated Australasia, South East Asia and the Pacific Islands

PACIFIC DAWN	70285gt	1991	19.5k	DE2	1590p	2050p	696c	245.1m	32.3m	8.1m	GB
PACIFIC JEWEL	70310gt	1990	19.5k	DE2	1664p	2014p	677c	245.1m	32.3m	7.9m	GB
PACIFIC PEARL	63524gt	1989	19.5k	DE2	1578p	1856p	514c	245.6m	32.2m	7.7m	GB
PACIFIC SUN	47546gt	1986	21.5k	D2	1486p	1896p	670c	223.2m	28.0m	7.5m	GB

PACIFIC DAWN was the last ship ordered by Sitmar Line, but was delivered to the P&O Group for service with Princess Cruises as the REGAL PRINCESS by the Monfalcone yard of Fincantieri (yard number 5840). In recent years she has undertaken interesting South East Asian itineraries, and was due to be transferred to fellow group company A'Rosa Cruises in 2004. This transfer did not occur and she remained in the Princess fleet. However, she was then due to transfer to Ocean Village in November 2006. This transfer did not take place either as her sister the AIDA BLU (formerly CROWN PRINCESS) was transferred instead. She joined the P&O Cruises Australia fleet in the autumn of 2007, as the PACIFIC DAWN. IMO 8521232

PACIFIC JEWEL is one of the last pair of ships ordered by Sitmar Line in 1988 prior to that company being acquired by P&O. Built by Fincantieri (yard number 5839) at Monfalcone, Italy, she was delivered to Princess Cruises in 1990 as the CROWN PRINCESS. Princess employed her on a variety of itineraries including European cruises until the summer of 2002, when she was transferred within the Group to the newly formed A'Rosa Cruises of Germany, taking the name A'ROSA BLU. On the sale of A'Rosa's river cruise business in 2004, she was transferred to Aida Cruises and renamed as the AIDABLU. In spring 2007 she passed to Ocean Village and following a three-week refit emerged as the OCEAN VILLAGE TWO. She will transfer to P&O Cruises Australia in 2009 as the PACIFIC JEWEL. IMO 8521220

PACIFIC PEARL was laid down in May 1988 as the SITMAR FAIRMAJESTY by Chantiers de l'Atlantique (yard number B29) at St Nazaire, France for the Sitmar Line. That company passed into the ownership of the P&O Group in September 1988, and the ship was subsequently delivered as the STAR PRINCESS in the spring of 1989 for service within P&O's Princess Cruises division. In late 1997 the ship was transferred to P&O Cruises for operation within the UK passenger fleet and was renamed ARCADIA, thus reviving a traditional P&O name. She cruised from the UK in the summer and in the Caribbean during the winter until the spring of 2003, when she was transferred to Ocean Village and renamed OCEAN VILLAGE in a ceremony performed by Ulrika Jonsson. She is now based in the Mediterranean in summer and the Caribbean in winter. She will transfer to P&O Cruises Australia in 2010 as the PACIFIC PEARL. IMO 8611398

PACIFIC SUN floated out of her building dock at the Kockums shipyard (yard number 596), Malmo, Sweden in October 1985, and was delivered eight months later to Carnival Cruise Lines as the JUBILEE. In 2004 she was transferred within the group to P&O Cruises Australia and renamed PACIFIC SUN by Olympian Lisa Curry-Kenny. On the arrival of the PACIFIC DAWN, the PACIFIC SUN moved from Sydney to Brisbane. IMO 8314122

PRINCESS CRUISES

The Company Princess Cruises began operation in December 1965 when Stanley McDonald, a Seattle industrialist, chartered the 1949-built, Canadian Pacific Railway ship PRINCESS PATRICIA, from where the new company took its name. The first cruises were to the west coast of Mexico, and they

P&O Cruises' **Ventura** sailing from Southampton *(Chris Mason)*

P&O Cruises' **Pacific Dawn** in Sydney *(Alf Sims)*

P&O Cruises' **Pacific Sun** in Sydney *(Alf Sims)*

were so successful that the ship was chartered again the following year. By the 1967/68 season a larger ship was needed, and the company was fortunate to obtain the charter of the recently completed 12,000-ton ITALIA, marketed as PRINCESS ITALIA but not renamed. During the next season a second ship, Costa Line's CARLA C, marketed as PRINCESS CARLA, joined the ITALIA, allowing that ship to inaugurate cruises to Alaska. In the autumn of 1970 her owners needed the CARLA C, so Princess Cruises was again a one-ship company. The recently built ISLAND VENTURE became unexpectedly available for charter in late 1972, and renamed ISLAND PRINCESS she quickly established her position in the Princess fleet, where she remained for 27 years. In 1973 the ITALIA was returned to her owners, and in the following year the Peninsular & Oriental Steam Navigation Company, in a move designed to strengthen its American operation, bought out Princess Cruises and transferred the SPIRIT OF LONDON (renamed SUN PRINCESS) to the company, later purchasing the ISLAND PRINCESS and her sister the SEA VENTURE (renamed PACIFIC PRINCESS). The popularity of American cruising undoubtedly received a boost in the mid-1970's when the PACIFIC PRINCESS starred in the US television series 'The Love Boat'. The first new ship for the growing Princess company was the 1984-built ROYAL PRINCESS, and two years later the SEA PRINCESS (formerly Swedish America Line's KUNGSHOLM) joined the fleet following a downturn in UK cruising, thus giving Princess five relatively modern ships. By 1988, however, it was apparent that the P&O Group was once again falling behind the market leaders as the US cruise market boomed. P&O had no new ships on order for Princess, and its largest ship, the ROYAL PRINCESS, was only 44,000 tons compared with the 70,000 ton ships that other lines were preparing to take into their fleets. Sitmar Line, facing various difficulties became available and P&O quickly snapped up this business for $210 million in September 1988, taking into the Princess fleet a mixed bag of older, but popular tonnage, but more importantly contracts for three large ships due for imminent delivery.

Sitmar Line had commenced trading just after the Second World War using two surplus US ships converted to carry around 800 passengers in fairly basic accommodation. Initially the company sailed in the migrant trades between the Mediterranean and Central America and the Caribbean. A little later the company acquired its third ship and entered the emigrant trade from the United Kingdom to Australia. By 1963, the star of the fleet was the former Bibby Line troopship OXFORDSHIRE, then running as the FAIRSTAR. With the acquisition in the late 1960's and the conversion for luxury cruising in 1970/71 of the former Cunard liners CARINTHIA (FAIRSEA) and SYLVANIA (FAIRWIND), the company quickly established itself at the luxury end of the US cruise market. The first new ship for the company was the FAIRSKY (latterly P&O Australia's PACIFIC SKY and now Pullmantur's SKY WONDER), delivered in 1984, and in 1986 the company ordered its largest ship to date, the SITMAR FAIRMAJESTY. However, that ship, along with two slightly larger ships ordered a little later, were to be delivered to the P&O Group, following the takeover.

The Princess story subsequently has been one of rapid expansion, keeping the company at the forefront of the premium US cruise market. The company commissioned two series of new ships in the 1990's. The SUN PRINCESS was the lead ship in a class of four vessels, but the GRAND PRINCESS was the forerunner of a much larger class of similar ships of around 110,000 gross tons. Princess Cruises became part of the new P&O Princess Cruises in 2000, when the cruise operations of the Peninsular & Oriental Steam Navigation Company were de-merged to form a new publicly listed company. Following talks on a possible merger with Royal Caribbean, the shareholders chose instead a merger with Carnival Corporation, which took place in 2003. SEA PRINCESS and OCEAN PRINCESS were sent, with little change to their interiors, to the P&O Cruises fleet in 2003, with the latter company relinquishing its Grand Class ship order to Princess. The transfer back to Princess of the former of this pair may indicate that it's not that easy to quickly adapt large ships from one market to another. With the transfer of ROYAL PRINCESS to P&O Cruises in 2005, and the REGAL PRINCESS to P&O Cruises in Australia during 2007, the oldest ship in this fleet is the 1995-built SUN PRINCESS. For 2010 Princess Cruises plan to base at least five ships in Europe for the summer.

President and Chief Executive Officer Alan Buckelew

Address 24844 Avenue Rockefeller, Santa Clarita, California 91355, United States of America

Telephone + 1 310 553 1770 **Fax** +1 310 832 0728

Website www.princesscruises.com

Areas operated North and South America, Caribbean, Mediterranean, Scandinavia, Pacific Islands and the Far East

| CARIBBEAN PRINCESS | 112894gt | 2004 | 22.5k | DE2 | 3114p | 3796p | 1200c | 289.0m | 36.0m | 8.0m | BM |

Princess Cruises' **Coral Princess** at San Francisco *(Andrew Kilk)*

Princess Cruises' **Crown Princess** in Halifax, NS *(William Mayes)*

Princess Cruises' **Golden Princess** at Quebec *(William Mayes)*

CORAL PRINCESS	91627gt	2002	24.0k	GDE2	1974p	2590p	900c	294.0m	32.2m	8.0m	BM
CROWN PRINCESS	113651gt	2006	22.5k	DE2	3064p	3842p	1200c	288.6m	36.0m	8.5m	BM
DAWN PRINCESS	77441gt	1997	21.4k	DE2	1950p	2250p	900c	261.3m	32.3m	8.1m	GB
DIAMOND PRINCESS	115875gt	2004	22.1k	DE2	2674p	3290p	1100c	290.0m	37.5m	8.0m	BM
EMERALD PRINCESS	113651gt	2007	22.5k	DE2	3064p	3825p	1200c	288.6m	36.0m	8.5m	BM
GOLDEN PRINCESS	108865gt	2001	22.5k	DE2	2600p	3209p	1100c	289.5m	40.2m	8.5m	BM
GRAND PRINCESS	108806gt	1998	22.5k	DE2	2600p	3209p	1100c	289.5m	40.2m	8.5m	BM
ISLAND PRINCESS	91627gt	2003	24.0k	GDE2	1974p	2590p	900c	294.0m	32.2m	8.0m	BM
OCEAN PRINCESS	30277gt	1999	18.0k	DE2	668p	800p	373c	181.0m	25.5m	5.8m	BM
PACIFIC PRINCESS	30277gt	1999	18.0k	DE2	668p	800p	373c	181.0m	25.5m	5.8m	BM
ROYAL PRINCESS	30277gt	2001	18.0k	DE2	710p	801p	381c	181.0m	25.5m	5.8m	BM
RUBY PRINCESS	113561gt	2008	22.5k	DEP2	3080p	3861p	1225c	290.0m	36.0m	8.5m	BM
SAPPHIRE PRINCESS	115875gt	2004	22.1k	DE2	2674p	3290p	1100c	290.0m	37.5m	8.0m	BM
SEA PRINCESS	77499gt	1998	21.4k	DE2	1950p	2250p	900c	261.3m	32.3m	8.1m	BM
STAR PRINCESS	108977gt	2002	22.5k	DE2	2602p	3211p	1105c	289.5m	40.2m	8.5m	BM
SUN PRINCESS	77441gt	1995	21.5k	DE2	1950p	2250p	900c	261.3m	32.3m	8.1m	BM

CARIBBEAN PRINCESS, ordered from the Monfalcone, Italy, yard of Fincantieri (yard number 6067) was destined for P&O Cruises for service in the growing British cruise market. Following a cascading of ships from Princess to P&O, this vessel was switched to Princess Cruises for service in the Caribbean Sea as the CARIBBEAN PRINCESS. She is currently operating itineraries to Canada and New England and the Caribbean. IMO 9215490

CORAL PRINCESS was built by Chantiers de l'Atlantique (yard number C32) at St Nazaire, France for Princess Cruises as the company's first gas turbine powered ship. She cruises to Canada and New England, through the Panama Canal and to Alaska and the Mexican Riviera. IMO 9229659

CROWN PRINCESS cruises in the Caribbean, but in summer relocates to Canada and New England. She was ordered from Fincantieri (yard number 6100) in April 2003 in place of the sixth ship in the Holland America Vista class. The forward section of her hull was actually built in Fincantieri's Sestri shipyard at Genoa and bears the yard number 1100. Her godmother is Martha Stewart, the American home decorating tycoon, and this is the second ship of this name. For 2009 she operates in Europe in the summer, followed by Canada and New England en route to the Caribbean. IMO 9293399

DAWN PRINCESS is the second ship in the SUN PRINCESS class and was built by Fincantieri (yard number 5955) at Monfalcone, Italy. For 2009 she cruises in the Pacific Ocean, based for most of the year in Australia. IMO 9103996

DIAMOND PRINCESS was laid down by Mitsubishi Heavy Industries (yard number 2181) in Japan as the SAPPHIRE PRINCESS, but following a major fire on board the DIAMOND PRINCESS while fitting out, the two ships exchanged names. She spends the summer in Alaska, and for the remainder of the year cruises to South East Asia and Australia. IMO 9228198

EMERALD PRINCESS debuted in the Mediterranean before moving to the Caribbean in autumn of 2007. She was built by Fincantieri (yard number 6131) at Monfalcone, and now spends the summer in Europe and the winter in the Caribbean. IMO 9333151

GOLDEN PRINCESS was built by Fincantieri (yard number 6050) at Monfalcone, Italy as the second of the GRAND PRINCESS Class. She is the second ship in the Princess fleet to bear this name, the first being the former ROYAL VIKING SKY chartered in the 1990's, now the BOUDICCA of Fred. Olsen Cruise Lines. In 2009 the GOLDEN PRINCESS performs Alaska, South Pacific, Canada and New England itineraries. IMO 9192351

GRAND PRINCESS was built as the first 100,000+ ton cruise ship for the P&O Group by Fincantieri (yard number 6956) at Monfalcone, Italy. One of a class of three ships, she is scheduled for a 2009 season in the Caribbean and the Mediterranean Seas. IMO 9104005

ISLAND PRINCESS is the second of a pair of ships built for the company by Chantiers de l'Atlantique (yard number D32) at St Nazaire, France, and a sister to the CORAL PRINCESS. She takes the name of one of the pair of ships upon which the long success of Princess Cruises was founded. Her summer 2009 itineraries centre on the splendours of Alaska, while later in the year she cruises to the Mexican Riviera, California, Canada and New England. IMO 9230402

OCEAN PRINCESS was built by Chantiers de l'Atlantique (yard number O31) at St Nazaire, France for Renaissance Cruises as the R FOUR. Renaissance Cruises filed for bankruptcy in the autumn of 2001

Princess Cruises' **Pacific Princess** in Southampton *(Richard Mayes)*

Princess Cruises' **Sea Princess** in Bridgetown *(William Mayes)*

Princess Cruises' **Star Princess** *(Rick Frendt)*

and the ship was laid up. P&O Princess Cruises acquired the R FOUR in 2002 and renamed her TAHITIAN PRINCESS. She is used for year round cruising based at Tahiti. This appears to be a condition of acquisition of the ship, which received French Government subsidies when built, on the basis that she would be operated for a number of years in French Polynesia. The TAHITIAN PRINCESS will be renamed OCEAN PRINCESS in late 2009. She currently spends much of the year in South East Asia. IMO 9187899

PACIFIC PRINCESS was built as the R THREE for Renaissance Cruises by Chantiers de l'Atlantique (yard number N31) at St Nazaire, France for year round service in French Polynesia. Renaissance Cruises filed for bankruptcy in the autumn of 2001 and the ship was laid up. P&O Princess Cruises acquired the R THREE in 2002, and renamed her PACIFIC PRINCESS. Her time is shared between P&O Cruises Australia (southern summer cruising in the Pacific Islands) and Princess Cruises, based in the Far East. She revives the name of one of the company's early ships. IMO 9187887

ROYAL PRINCESS was built by Chantiers de l'Atlantique (yard number Z31) at St Nazaire, France as the R EIGHT for Renaissance Cruises. Following the failure of that company in the autumn of 2001 she was laid up at Gibraltar. During 2002 it was announced that Swan Hellenic had taken her on a seven-year charter, to commence service in April 2003 following a major re-fit, as the MINERVA II, replacing the smaller MINERVA. In 2006 Carnival Corporation purchased the ship and from spring 2007 was transferred to Princess Cruises as the ROYAL PRINCESS, the second ship to bear this name. Her Princess cruises began in the Mediterranean, after which she moved to South America, a destination that she still serves, along with Alaska and Europe. IMO 9210220

RUBY PRINCESS was built by Fincantieri (yard number 6150) at Monfalcone, Italy, and was named by Trista and Ryan Sutter at Fort Lauderdale on 6 November 2008. She serves the Caribbean and Mediterranean markets. IMO 9378462

SAPPHIRE PRINCESS was laid down as the DIAMOND PRINCESS by Mitsubishi Heavy Industries (yard number 2180) in Japan, but following a major fire and consequent delay in delivery, she exchanged names with her sister under construction at the same yard. She spends summer 2009 in Alaska, and much of the remainder of the year cruising the Mexican Riviera. IMO 9228186

SEA PRINCESS was built by Fincantieri (yard number 5998) at Monfalcone, Italy as the SEA PRINCESS for Princess Cruises. As the second ship to bear this name, she subsequently cruised in the Caribbean and to Alaska before being transferred to P&O Cruises as the ADONIA for operation from Southampton in the spring of 2003. With P&O Cruises she operated as an adult-only ship, and in addition to her UK based itineraries undertook a half-world cruise in 2004. The ADONIA transferred back to Princess Cruises in April 2005, reverting to the name SEA PRINCESS and was christened by English actress Joanna Lumley. The SEA PRINCESS spent the summer of that year based at Southampton before sailing to New York for a series of cruises to Quebec. She now cruises in the Caribbean, the Mexican Riviera and to Alaska. IMO 9150913

STAR PRINCESS is the third of the GRAND PRINCESS class to be built by Fincantieri (yard number 6051) at Monfalcone, Italy. Her 2003/2004 itineraries included Mexico, Alaska, Australia, Japan, China and the Far East, and a positioning voyage from Bangkok to Venice to commence a summer 2004 season in the Mediterranean. For 2005 she spent the summer season in the Baltic, based in Copenhagen, Denmark before repositioning via the US East Coast to the Caribbean Sea. She is the second ship in the Princess fleet to bear this name. In March 2006 she suffered a major fire, which started on a balcony, damaging more than 100 cabins and putting the ship out of service for some time. In 2009 she cruises to Australia, Mexico, Alaska and South America. IMO 9192363

SUN PRINCESS was built by Fincantieri (yard number 5909) at Monfalcone, Italy, as the lead ship in what was eventually to become a series of four. She cruises in South East Asia, the Pacific Ocean and from Australia. IMO 9000259

TAHITIAN PRINCESS see OCEAN PRINCESS

SEABOURN CRUISE LINE

The Company Seabourn Cruise Line was founded in 1987 by the Norwegian industrialist Atle Brynestad, now owner of Seadream Yacht Club, with the aim of providing the highest level of personal service to its passengers. In 1991 25% of the company was acquired by Carnival. A further 25% passed to Carnival in 1996, and the remaining stock was acquired in 1998, at which time Seabourn was put under the management of Cunard, Carnival's premium brands division. Cunard's yacht-like SEA GODDESS I and II and the ROYAL VIKING SUN were transferred to the Seabourn operation and appropriately renamed. The SEA GODDESSES subsequently passed to Seadream Yacht Club. The Seabourn operation was separated from Cunard in 2005, when the latter company came under the wing of Princess Cruises, and it was thought then that Carnival Corporation was preparing to dispose of Seabourn, so it came as something of a surprise when the company announced the order for two new ships in late 2006.

President and Chief Executive Officer Pamela Conover

Address Suite 400, 6100 Blue Lagoon Drive, Miami, FL 33126, United States of America

Telephone +1 305 4633000 **Fax** +1 305 4633010

Website www.seabourn.com

Areas operated Worldwide

SEABOURN LEGEND	9961gt	1992	19.0k	D2	208p	212p	150c	135.0m	19.0m	5.2m	BS
SEABOURN ODYSSEY	32200gt	2009	19.0k	DE2	450p	450p	330c	198.0m	25.6m	6.4m	BS
SEABOURN PRIDE	9975gt	1988	19.0k	D2	208p	212p	150c	133.8m	19.0m	5.2m	BS
SEABOURN SPIRIT	9975gt	1989	19.0k	D2	208p	212p	150c	133.8m	19.0m	5.2m	BS

SEABOURN LEGEND was to have been the third ship of the series for Seabourn Cruise Line. However, the company did not exercise the option, although Royal Viking Line effectively later took it up. She was delivered to that company by Schichau Seebeckwerft (yard number 1071), Bremerhaven as the ROYAL VIKING QUEEN in 1992. By this time the three original Royal Viking ships had left the company, so the fleet consisted of only this ship and the ROYAL VIKING SUN. She was renamed QUEEN ODYSSEY in 1994 and passed to Seabourn in 1996, becoming the SEABOURN LEGEND. IMO 9008598

SEABOURN ODYSSEY was built by Mariotti (yard number 62). The hull was constructed at San Giorgio di Nogaro, in the gulf of Venice and towed to Genoa where the superstructure was added and the ship fitted out. Uniquely, all of the passengers on the maiden voyage were designated as the ship's godparents. The SEABOURN ODYSSEY is scheduled to undertake Seabourn's first world cruise, in 2010. IMO 9417086

SEABOURN PRIDE was ordered from Schichau Seebeckwerft (yard number 1065) at Bremerhaven in Germany as the first of two luxurious mega-yachts by the newly formed Seabourn Cruise Line. She was christened by Shirley Temple Black. IMO 8707343

SEABOURN SPIRIT was the second ship to be delivered to Seabourn by Schichau Seebeckwerft (yard number 1070) at Bremerhaven in Germany, and christened by Aagot Brynestad. In November 2005 the SEABOURN SPIRIT became the first cruise ship to be attacked by pirates off the coast of Somalia. IMO 8807997

Cruise ships on order

SEABOURN SOJOURN	32200gt	2010	19.0k	DE2	450p	450p	330c	198.0m	25.6m	6.4m	BS
NEWBUILDING 2	32200gt	2011	19.0k	DE2	450p	450p	330c	198.0m	25.6m	6.4m	BS

SEABOURN SOJOURN and **NEWBUILDING 2** are on order with the Mariotti shipyard (yard number 63) in Genoa. The keels these were laid on 1 July 2008. The SEABOURN SOJOURN will be named Greenwich in June 2010. IMO 9417098 and 9483126

CASPI CRUISES

The Company Caspi Cruises commenced trading in the cruise sector in the spring of 1999. The DREAM PRINCESS joined the fleet in spring 2005 with a series of short cruises from Ashdod and Haifa on what appeared to be a franchise arrangement. The ship was marketed in both Israel and Russia. Following a number of problems the charter was terminated. However, it appears that the ship has been chartered again. The company also owns a number of cargo ships.

Chief Executive Officer Yuval Caspi

Address 1 Ben Yehuda Street, Tel Aviv, Israel

Telephone +972 3 510 7424 **Fax** +972 3 516 0989

Website www.caspi-cruise.co.il

Area operated Eastern Mediterranean and Black Sea from Israel

Seabourn Cruise Line's **Seabourn Spirit** *(Theodore W Scull)*

Caspi Cruises' **Mirage 1** off Rhodes *(Rick Frendt)*

Classic International Cruises' **Arion** at Nice *(Richard Mayes)*

FESTIVAL	22945gt	1970	20.5k	D2	1140p	1400p	325c	194.3m	24.0m	6.7m	MH
MIRAGE I	14264gt	1973	21.0k	D2	554p	750p	c	141.5m	21.9m	5.7m	BS

FESTIVAL was built by Wartsila (yard number 392) at Helsinki, Finland as the SONG OF NORWAY for the new Royal Caribbean Cruise Line, one of an initial series of three revolutionary new ships. Two of the three ships, including the SONG OF NORWAY, were lengthened in 1978-1980. She was sold to Sun Cruises (Airtours) in 1997 and renamed as the SUNDREAM for cruises in the Mediterranean, the Caribbean and around the Atlantic Isles. Sun Cruises withdrew from cruising in 2004 and she was sold to Lance Shipping subsidiary, Tumaco Shipping, taking the new name DREAM PRINCESS. She was franchised to Caspi Cruises in April 2005 to undertake short cruises from Israel to Turkey, Greece and Cyprus. In early 2006 the ship was renamed DREAM. In November 2006 she was chartered by her owners to Gulf Dream Cruise to operate a cruise service between Karachi and Dubai. It is thought that only the first five-day voyage was completed before the venture collapsed. She ran for a while in 2007 for Israeli Caspi Cruises, but that came to an abrupt end with the ship almost sinking in the harbour at Rhodes following the failure of a ballast pump. She was acquired by the Danish Clipper Group and renamed CLIPPER PEARL. She was chartered to the Peaceboat Organisation from about June 2008 and renamed CLIPPER PACIFIC, but her first circumnavigation was something of a disaster, as she was holed and had to put into New York, following which she was detained by the US Coastguard due to a number of safety issues. She eventually continued her voyage, but on arrival in Piraeus, still with mechanical problems, the passengers were loaded on to the hastily chartered MONA LISA to complete their journey. With the Peaceboat charter ended she was returned to Clipper Group in late spring, 2009. In early June she was renamed FESTIVAL, and following a major overhaul in Bulgaria, she is believed to have returned to Caspi Cruises. IMO 7005190

MIRAGE I was built by Dubigeon-Normandie (yard number 133) at Nantes, France as the BOLERO for Fred. Olsen Line, initially for service between Travemunde, Germany and Sodertalje, Sweden. In the event she was, instead, chartered to Prinz Linien for North Sea service. She soon travelled west for charters to Commodore Cruise Line in winter for Caribbean cruising, and Prince of Fundy Line in summer for the ferry service between Portland, Maine and Yarmouth, Nova Scotia. She moved back to Europe in 1976 and sailed between Bergen, Norway and Newcastle, England. From 1978 to 1981 she was on Stena Line's Gothenburg, Sweden to Kiel, Germany service as the SCANDINAVICA while that company was awaiting the very late delivery of some new ships. A planned charter to Brittany Ferries in 1981 didn't materialise, so the ship underwent a major refit to resume Olsen service. Her final days with the Norwegian company were spent on the Newcastle to Bergen service, which was sold, along with the BOLERO, to Norway's Color Line in 1991. She was renamed as the JUPITER and continued on the same route until 1994. After a short charter to Baltic Sea operator Viking Line, she moved to Central America for a service between Cristobal and Cartagena on charter to Promotora de Navigation as the CRUCERO EXPRESS. In 1997 she began operating from St Petersburg, Florida as the SEMINOLE EXPRESS. The following year she returned to Europe and after another refit became the MAGIC 1 of Magic Cruise Lines. She later served as a Haifa-based cruise ship before returning to the Caribbean to operate for Ocean Club Cruises, a business which failed after only one season. ISRAMCO purchased the ship in March 2004. She had been reported as chartered to a subsidiary of Israeli travel company EGGED for summer 2005. She appears to be in operation under the marketing name of MAGIC. IMO 7221433

CASPIAN CRUISE LINE

The Company Caspian Cruise Line is a trading name of Azerbaijani tour operator Tintour. It is planned to operate a fleet of up to six ships in the Caspian and Black Sea, the first of which is the MARIYA YERMOLOVA, formerly owned by Novoships. The company was expected to begin operating in the spring of 2009.

Address Astrakahn 414000, Russia

Telephone +7 8512 395665 **Fax** +7 8512 395315

Website www.caspianline.ru

Area operated The Caspian Sea

MARIYA YERMOLOVA	4364gt	1974	14.0k	D2	220p	262p	62c	100.0m	16.2m	4.7m	RU

MARIYA YERMOLOVA was one of a series of eight ships built by Brodogradiliste Titovo (yard number 406) at Kraljevica, in what was then Yugoslavia, for the Murmansk Shipping Company. Other vessels were delivered to other Russian operating companies. Latterly the ship operated for Novoships in the Black Sea, but is reported to be the start up ship for new operator Caspian Cruises. Mariya Yermolova was a Russian actress. IMO 7367524

CELEBRATION CRUISE LINE

The Company Celebration Cruise Line is a subsidiary of Imperial Majesty Cruise Line, a company formed in 1999 to operate the OCEAN BREEZE (formerly the SOUTHERN CROSS of 1955). In 2003 the REGAL EMPRESS was acquired as a replacement for the OCEAN BREEZE, but with the SOLAS regulation changes looming in 2010 it was decided to retire the REGAL EMPRESS and begin again with a very different type of ship. At $33 million, the BAHAMAS CELEBRATION represents a very significant investment.

Address 4161 NW 5th Street, Suite 200, Plantation, Florida 33317, United States of America

Telephone +1 954 449 9080

Website www.bahamascelebration.com

Area operated Fort Lauderdale to The Bahamas

BAHAMAS CELEBRATION	35855gt	1981	21.8k	D2	1500p	1500p	c	205.3m	24.0m	5.8m	BS

BAHAMAS CELEBRATION was built by Howaldtswerke-Deutsche Werft (yard number 164) at Kiel in Germany as the PRINSESSE RAGNHILD for Norwegian ferry operator Jahre Line's Kiel to Oslo service. The Company merged with Norway Line in 1991 and was restyled as Color Line. During the following year, the ship underwent a significant rebuild in Spain, including lengthening and the addition of extra decks. In 2005 she was displaced by the new COLOR FANTASY and began a new service linking Bergen and Stavanger in Norway with Hirtshals in Denmark. In January 2008 the route closed and she transferred to the Oslo to Hirtshals service. That service closed in May 2008 and the ship was laid up. She was subsequently acquired for Celebration Cruise Line's service and refitted in the Bahamas. IMO 7904891

CLASSIC CRUISES OF NEWPORT

The Company Classic Cruises of Newport is a US company, part of Atlantic Stars Hotels and Cruises, operating small sailing vessels from Newport, Rhode Island.

Address Christies Landing, Newport, Rhode Island 02840-3455, United States of America

Telephone +1 409 849 3033 **Fax** +1 409 849 3023

Website www.cruisearabella.com.

Area operated Summer - New England, winter – Virgin Islands

ARABELLA	208gt	1983	10.0k	SD1	40p	49p	9c	47.7m	7.4m	3.8m	US

ARABELLA was built by Palmer Johnson (yard number 186) at Sturgeon Bay, Wisconsin, USA as the research vessel CENTURION. She was acquired by Altantic Star Lines in 2001, converted to a three-masted sailing yacht and renamed ARABELLA. She is marketed by Classic Cruises of Newport. IMO 8201272

CLASSIC INTERNATIONAL CRUISES

The Company Classic International Cruises is a trading name of Arcalia Shipping Company Limited of Cyprus, owned by George Potamianos, a Greek entrepreneur living in Lisbon. The FUNCHAL was the first ship to be acquired, in 1985. The company has been supplying ships for British cruisers for many years, either directly or through charters of ships to tour operators. For 2009 it appears that all of the ships are chartered to other operators for part of the year.

Chairman George Potamianos

Address   5 piso, Avenue 24 de Julho 126-128, 1350-346 Lisbon, Portugal

UK Office PO Box 278. Ormskirk, L40 3WU, England

Telephone   +351 213 953264 **Fax** +351 213 953198

UK +44 0845 8727494 **Fax** +44 0845 8727557

Website www.cic-cruises.com

Area operated Worldwide, often under charter

ARION	5888gt	1965	16.0k	D2	328p	350p	150c	116.8m	16.5m	5.3m	PT
ATHENA	16144gt	1948	16.5k	D2	550p	638p	185c	160.0m	21.0m	7.6m	PT
FUNCHAL	9563gt	1961	16.0k	D2	439p	571p	155c	152.7m	19.0m	6.3m	PT
PRINCESS DANAE	16531gt	1955	16.0k	D2	560p	670p	240c	162.4m	21.3m	7.6m	PT
PRINCESS DAPHNE	15833gt	1955	17.0k	D2	422p	526p	210c	162.4m	21.3m	7.5m	PT

ARION was built by Brodogradiliste Uljanik (yard number 248) at Pula, in what was then Yugoslavia, as the ISTRA for Jadrolinija. She operated initially on a 14-day itinerary from Venice to the far Eastern Mediterranean. She was sold to Caravella Shipping of the Ukraine in 1991 and renamed as the ASTRA. In 1996 she passed to Goring Shipping, another Ukraine owner, who renamed her ASTRA I. Constellation Cruise Holdings, a company within the Arcalia Shipping group, acquired her in 1999 and renamed her ARION for use by Classic International Cruises. She underwent a major reconstruction in Lisbon in 2000, costing some $15 million. In 2009 she operates in the Adriatic during the summer before repositioning for a series of Red Sea cruises lasting until the spring of 2010. Arion was a famous musician who dwelt at the court of Periander, King of Corinth. IMO 6419057

ATHENA was built as the transatlantic liner STOCKHOLM for Swedish America Line by the Gotaverken shipyard (yard number 611) in Gothenburg, Sweden. In 1956, while on her regular service between Gothenburg and New York, she famously collided with and sank the Italia Line flagship ANDREA DORIA. After repair by the Bethlehem Steel shipyard in Brooklyn the STOCKHOLM re-entered service on her Atlantic route. In 1960 Swedish America Line sold her to VEB Deutsche Seereederei for use by the East German Free Trades Union organisation, which renamed her VOLKERFREUNDSCHAFT. She operated cruises for East German workers until sold on in 1985 to Neptunus Rex Enterprises of Panama. She was renamed VOLKER and laid up at Southampton. She became the FRIDTJOF NANSEN in late 1986 and was moved to Oslo for use as a refugee accommodation ship. Star Lauro acquired the ship in 1989 and intended to have her refurbished and renamed SURRIENTO. In the event, she was laid up in Genoa, renamed ITALIA I and later sold to Nina Compagnia di Navigazione for whom the refit was eventually completed, transforming her appearance. She was then renamed ITALIA PRIMA and later operated cruises from Havana, Cuba as the VALTUR PRIMA. From 2001 she was laid up at Havana, until chartered by Festival Cruises in late 2003 and renamed CARIBE, but Festival collapsed shortly afterwards and the ship remained unused until taken on a ten-year bareboat charter by Classic International Cruises in 2004 and renamed ATHENA after a refit in Lisbon. She was to have replaced the PRINCESS DANAE, allowing that ship to go for an extended overhaul, but the amount of work required to bring her up to standard was greater than expected, thus delaying her entry into service. Following her refit she operated two cruises under charter in the German market. She then operated for part of the year for British travel company, Travelscope, until that arrangement was abruptly terminated in March 2007. Travelscope subsequently collapsed in early 2008. The ATHENA was due to spend the summer of 2009 with Mediterranean Classic Cruises in the Eastern Mediterranean, but she has instead been chartered to Phoenix Reisen as a temporary replacement for the ALEXANDER VON HUMBOLDT. The ATHENA then heads back to Australia for another season based there for Classic International. Athena, the Greek goddess of wisdom, was the favourite daughter of Zeus. IMO 5383304

FUNCHAL was the last of the Portuguese liners, and arguably the most attractive. She was built in Denmark, at the Helsingor Shipyard (yard number 353) for Empressa Insulana de Navegacao of Lisbon, a mini liner, for the almost local service from Lisbon to Madeira, the Azores and the Canary Islands. As built she had two Parsons steam turbines, which gave her a service speed of 20 knots. She was occasionally used as the Portuguese Presidential Yacht, and undertook voyages in that role as far afield as Brazil. She suffered recurring engine problems and in 1972 her machinery was replaced by diesel engines during a major refit in Amsterdam. Her owner, along with the other Portuguese liner operators, faced severe financial crisis and was merged in 1974 with Companhia Colonial to form Companhia Portuguesa de Transportes Maritimos. By now, the FUNCHAL was used almost exclusively for cruising and undertook a number of charters. Her owner was wound up in 1985 and the FUNCHAL was sold to Great Warwick of Panama, now managed by Arcalia Shipping. She has subsequently been operated by Arcalia Shipping under its own name, but is now marketed by Classic International Cruises. In late 2007 and early 2009 the ship underwent a phased major refit in order to enable her to carry on sailing beyond 2010. The FUNCHAL cruises for Classic International in the spring and autumn of 2009, mainly from Lisbon. Funchal is the capital of the Portuguese island of Madeira. IMO 5124162

PRINCESS DANAE began life as the Port Line cargo ship, PORT MELBOURNE, built by Harland & Wolff (yard number 1483) at Belfast, Northern Ireland, for the company's liner service from London to Australia. By 1971 Port Line was owned by Cunard Line, so when the latter company was acquired by Trafalgar House Investments, the less profitable routes, including that operated by the PORT MELBOURNE, were discontinued. She was sold along with her sister ship the PORT SYDNEY (now the OCEAN MONARCH of Monarch Classic Cruises), to Greek ship owner J C Karras. The PORT MELBOURNE was renamed THERISOS EXPRESS and was earmarked for conversion into a car ferry. That project never materialised and she was eventually renamed DANAE and converted into a luxury cruise ship. She began her new career in 1977, and two years later was chartered to Costa Line, along with her sister, now named DAPHNE. In 1984 Costa Line purchased the ships. In 1990 the sisters were transferred to a joint venture company Prestige Cruises, in which Costa had a 50% stake. Costa later regained full control, but in 1991, while undergoing a refit the ship caught fire and was subsequently declared a constructive total loss due to the damage caused by smoke, and water from the ship's sprinklers. Renamed ANAR, she was towed to Piraeus, where she was fully refurbished under the name STARLIGHT PRINCESS. She did not operate under that name, but was chartered to the Swedish Baltic Line as the BALTICA. She subsequently undertook further charters to Northern European operators before being sold to Waybell Cruises in 1996 for use by Classic International Cruises as the PRINCESS DANAE. She was completely refitted at that time. During 2006 the ship went through a major refurbishment. She operated a series of cruises for Travelscope in the summer of 2007. In Greek mythology Danae was the daughter of Acrisius and the mother of Perseus by Zeus. IMO 5282483

PRINCESS DAPHNE was built by Swan, Hunter and Wigham Richardson (yard number 1827) at Wallsend on Tyne in England for Port Line as the passenger and cargo ship PORT SYDNEY. In 1972 she was sold to Greek owners for conversion to a passenger and car ferry, but although commenced, this conversion was never completed. While undergoing work she was renamed AKROTIRI EXPRESS. She was later rebuilt as a cruise ship, taking the name DAPHNE, and was operated unsuccessfully for a while and eventually chartered to Costa Line, along with her sister (the DANAE, similarly converted and now the PRINCESS DANAE). Costa later purchased the ships and in the late 1980's marketed them under the Prestige Cruises banner. In 1996 she was renamed SWITZERLAND after sale to Leisure Cruises, a Swiss based but Monaco controlled company. In 2000 she passed to Dreamline Cruises, a company under the same control, without a change of name. She was acquired by Majestic International Cruises of Greece in spring 2002 and briefly renamed OCEAN ODYSSEY before adopting the name OCEAN MONARCH. Hansa Kreuzfahrten chartered her in 2005, and in 2006 she ran for Golden Star Cruises in place of the arrested AEGEAN I. The OCEAN MONARCH was scheduled to operate for Monarch in 2007, but following the collapse of Holiday Kreuzfahrten and the unexpected availability of the OCEAN COUNTESS, she was dropped from the company's programme and was laid up. However, she operates for Hansa Kreuzfahrten from 2008 to 2010 during the summer season. She was acquired by Classic International Cruises in 2008 and underwent a major refurbishment in Lisbon, from which emerged as the PRINCESS DAPHNE. Her summer charter to Hansa Kreuzfahrten remains in place. Daphne was the daughter of the River God Peneus. In Greek Mythology Daphne turns into a laurel tree to escape the unwelcome advances of Apollo. IMO 5282627

CLIPPER GROUP

The Company Clipper Group is a Danish ship owner that controls around 250 vessels, of which about 100 are owned. The origins of this company are in Armada Shipping, formed in 1972 by Torben Jensen and Jorgen Dannesboe. In 1991 the partnership broke up and Torben Jensen took the ships with a Clipper prefix name and started Clipper Group. Jensen stayed in Houston, from where he had been operating since 1980, but set up a head office in Switzerland. In 1997 the head office moved to Nassau, and two years later Clipper Group entered into a joint venture with two Danish banks. In 2005 the company moved its headquarters to Denmark. During 2008 the company acquired 50% of Miami-based International Shipping Partners. However, in early 2009 that shareholding was sold back to ISP's management. Clipper Group owns 15% of Danish ferry operator DFDS, has a major share in a number of Danish domestic routes and owns SeaTruck Ferries, operating between England, Ireland and Northern Ireland.

Chairman Torben Jensen

Address Harbour House, Sundkrogsgade 21. DK2100, Copenhagen, Denmark

Telephone +45 4911 8000 **Fax** +45 4911 8001

Classic International Cruises' **Athena** at Villefranche *(Richard Mayes)*

Classic International Cruises' **Funchal** in Lisbon *(Andrew Kilk)*

Classic International Cruises' **Princess Danae** in Venice *(Martin Grant)*

Classic International Cruises **Princess Daphne**, as the **Ocean Monarch** in Istanbul *(William Mayes)*

Club Cruise's **Astoria** under arrest in Barcelona *(William Mayes)*

Area operated Does not operate for its own account. Ships are chartered out.

CLIPPER ADVENTURER	4376gt	1975	14.0k	D2	122p	122p	79c	100.0m	16.2m	4.7m	BS
CLIPPER DISCOVERER	4954gt	2007	10.0k	DP2	226p	226p	74c	91.4m	15.2m	3.8m	US
CLIPPER ODYSSEY	5218gt	1989	18.0k	D2	120p	120p	70c	103.0m	15.4m	4.3m	BS
CLIPPER VOYAGER	4954gt	2001	10.0k	DP2	226p	226p	74c	91.4m	15.2m	3.8m	US
CORINTHIAN II	4200gt	1991	15.5k	D2	114p	114p	70c	90.3m	15.3m	4.0m	MT
FESTIVAL	22945gt	1970	20.5k	D2	1140p	1400p	325c	194.3m	24.0m	6.7m	MH
GEMINI	19093gt	1992	18.4k	D2	819p	916p	470c	163.8m	22.5m	5.4m	MT
ISLAND SKY	4200gt	1992	15.5k	D2	114p	114p	72c	90.6m	15.3m	4.1m	BS
QUEST	1268gt	1992	13.0k	D1	52p	60p	20c	49.6m	11.0m	3.4m	BS

CLIPPER ADVENTURER For details see under Quark Expeditions (TUI).

CLIPPER DISCOVERER was built by Atlantic Marine (yard number 4243) at Jacksonville, Florida, USA for American Classic Voyages as the CAPE COD LIGHT. That group declared bankruptcy in 2001 and the ship may never have actually been completed. She was laid up at Green Cove Spring, Florida. In early 2007 Hornblower Marine Services purported to have acquired her and her sister. That transaction was never completed. She was renamed COASTAL QUEEN 2 in late 2007. In 2008 she was purchased by Clipper Group and is to be or has been renamed CLIPPER DISCOVERER. She appears to remain laid up. IMO 9213131

CLIPPER ODYSSEY For details see under Zegrahm Expeditions (TUI).

CLIPPER VOYAGER was built as the CAPE MAY LIGHT by Atlantic Marine (yard number 4242) at Jacksonville, Florida, USA for American Classic Voyages. In 2001 she made three cruises in each direction between Buffalo and Quebec City, and was to have commenced a series of New England cruises from Providence, Rhode Island. It is not certain if these took place before the company filed for bankruptcy. Hornblower Marine Services was thought to have acquired the ship in 2007, but that transaction was never completed. She was reported to have been renamed COASTAL QUEEN 1 in 2007. In 2008 she was purchased by Clipper Group and is to be or has been renamed CLIPPER VOYAGER. She remains laid up. IMO 9213129

CORINTHIAN II For details see under Travel Dynamics.

FESTIVAL For details see under Caspi Cruises.

GEMINI For details see under Quail Cruises.

ISLAND SKY For details see under Noble Caledonia.

QUEST For details see under Polar Quest.

CLUB CRUISE

The Company Club Cruise Entertainment and Travelling Services Europe NV was formed in 1999 and acquired its first ship, the former GRUZIYA, which was renamed CLUB 1. The company initially ran cruises for the Dutch market but this was not successful and the ship was chartered out, eventually being renamed VAN GOGH. Club Cruise purchased the ALBATROS from V-Ships on the back of a charter to Phoenix Reisen in 2006. Phoenix also had the ALEXANDER VON HUMBOLDT on charter from Club Cruise, and both of these ships were permitted to continue trading after Phoenix Reisen posted guarantee bonds after the failure of the owner in November 2008. At the same time it had been agreed that the ASTORIA would be sold to Saga, but the collapse of Club Cruise has put that transaction in doubt. In November 2007 Club Cruise acquired the FINNJET for conversion into a cruise ship. The economic downturn struck and the project abandoned, with the ship sold for scrap at a significant loss. The company's other ships, the FLAMENCO 1 and the VAN GOGH were recently sold at auction.

Area operated Does not normally operate for its own account. Currently undergoing bankruptcy procedure.

ALBATROS	28518gt	1973	18.5k	D2	884p	1100p	340c	205.5m	25.2m	7.5m	BS
ALEXANDER VON HUMBOLDT	15396gt	1990	18.8k	D2	520p	556p	214c	150.7m	19.8m	5.7m	BS
ASTORIA	18591gt	1981	18.0k	D2	500p	518p	220c	164.3m	22.6m	6.1m	BS

ALBATROS For details see under Phoenix Reisen. At the time of writing the ship is operating normally.

ALEXANDER VON HUMBOLDT For details see under Phoenix Reisen. At the time of writing the ship is under arrest at Bremerhaven.

ASTORIA was built by Howaldtswerke-Deutsche Werft (yard number 165) at Hamburg, Germany as the ASTOR (laid down as the HAMMONIA) for Hadag Cruise Line. In 1984 she was acquired by the South African Marine Corporation of Cape Town for a new liner service between Southampton and Cape Town and for off-season cruising. It became apparent very early that the ship's engines were not powerful enough to maintain the required liner schedule and she was sold in August 1985 to VEB Deutfracht Seereederei of East Germany. She was refitted in Hamburg and as the ARKONA became the replacement for the VOLKERFREUNDSCHAFT (now Classic International Cruises' ATHENA). She was on a 10-year charter from Astoria Shipping to Transocean Tours, thought to be due to expire in 2012, as the ASTORIA. Club Cruise of The Netherlands acquired her in March 2007, but the charter remained in place. It would appear that Transocean Tours had agreed to an early termination of the charter as the ASTORIA was to be sold to Saga Group at the end of her 2008/9 world cruise. In the event, just a week before that cruise was due to start, during a routine overhaul, serious machinery problems were noticed, thus forcing the cancellation of the cruise. Within a week Club Cruise was in administration. At the time of writing the ASTORIA is under arrest in Barcelona. IMO 8000214

CLUB MED CRUISES

The Company Club Med Cruises is a division of the French travel company Club Med.

Address 11 Rue de Cambrai, 75957 Paris Cedex 19, France

Telephone +33 153 353553 **Fax** +33 153 353616

Website www.clubmed.com

Area operated Summer in the Mediterranean Sea and winter in the Caribbean Sea

| CLUB MED 2 | 14983gt | 1992 | 15.0k | SD2 | 392p | 419p | 181c | 187.0m | 20.0m | 5.1m | WF |

CLUB MED 2 was built by Societe Nouvelle des Ateliers et Chantiers du Havre (yard number 282) at Le Havre, France, as one of a pair of sister ships for Club Med. The other of this duo was sold to Windstar Cruises. CLUB MED 2 is managed by V-Ships. IMO 9007491

COMPAGNIE DES ILES DU PONANT

The Company Compagnie des Iles du Ponant was established in 1988 by Phillipe Videau and others, and raised the required capital by subscription to purchase and operate the luxury yacht LE PONANT. The company also became a tour agency, but later bought out the other investors to own the ship outright. The purchase of LE LEVANT was financed in the same way and that ship currently has 280 shareholders. In 2003, in conjunction with French tour operator Tapis Rouge Croisieres, the SONG OF FLOWER was acquired from Radisson Seven Seas Cruises and renamed LE DIAMANT. She is operated by Compagnie des Iles du Diamant, a joint venture between 'Ponant' and Tapis Rouge. French container shipping line CMA-CGM is currently the majority shareholder in the company, holding 70% of the stock. The Iles du Ponant are a group of islands off the northern and western coasts of Brittany, France.

Chief Executive Officer Jean Emmanuel Sauvee

Address 408 Avenue du Prado, F13008 Marseilles, France

Telephone +33 488 666564

Website www.ponant.com

Area operated Worldwide

LE DIAMANT	8282gt	1974	16.0k	D2	172p	226p	144c	124.2m	16.0m	4.9m	WF
LE LEVANT	3504gt	1998	16.0k	D2	90p	90p	49c	100.3m	13.1m	3.0m	WF
LE PONANT	1189gt	1991	14.0k	SD1	56p	64p	30c	84.3m	11.9m	4.0m	WF

LE DIAMANT was built by Kristiansands Mekaniske Verksted (yard number 220) at Kristiansand, Norway as one of a pair of ro-ro freighters, the BEGONIA (although she was launched as the FERNHILL) for Oslo ship owners, Fearney & Eger. These ships were immediately transferred to an associated Dutch company. Fearney & Eger reacquired the BEGONIA in 1985 and sent her to the Lloyd Werft yard at Bremerhaven; here she was converted into the exploration cruise ship EXPLORER

Club Med 2 approaching Bridgetown *(William Mayes)*

Iles du Ponant's **Le Diamant** in Istanbul *(William Mayes)*

Iles du Ponant's **Le Levant** in Venice *(William Mayes)*

STARSHIP. On completion she was chartered to Exploration Cruise Line and served initially in the Caribbean and later on the US West Coast and in Alaska. Exploration Cruise Line filed for bankruptcy in 1988 and eventually Fearney & Eger were able to recover their ship. She was soon sold to Seven Seas Cruise Line, a new company set up by the Japanese Kawasaki Kisen Kaisha Line and the Norwegian Skaugen concern. Following a refit that converted her to a luxury 214-passenger ship, she entered service from Singapore as the SONG OF FLOWER in February 1990. During the next five years she cruised in most of the then popular cruising areas, but in 1995 the operation was merged with Radisson Diamond Cruises, although her owners retained the ship for a further two years before she was sold to the new Radisson Seven Seas Cruises. No longer in keeping with the remainder of the fleet, she passed to her current operator in 2003 and following a major refit emerged as LE DIAMANT. Diamant translates from French as diamond. This ship operates worldwide, including Antarctica. IMO 7325629

LE LEVANT, the sleek, yacht-like luxury cruise ship was built by Alstom Leroux Naval (yard number 625) at St Malo, France for the company. She has undertaken a number of charters, including one to Classical Cruises International. The ship is named after one of the islands off the coast of Provence, France and spends the summer of 2009 in the Mediterranean Sea. IMO 9159830

LE PONANT was built by Societe Francaise Construction Navales (yard number 863) at Villeneuv-la-Garenne, France. In early April 2008 the ship and its crew of 30 were seized by pirates off the coast of Somalia as the vessel was re-positioning to the Mediterranean Sea without passengers. The ship and crew were released a week later after a ransom was thought to have been paid. The ship's usual areas of operation are the Mediterranean Sea and the Indian Ocean. IMO 8914219

Cruise ships on order

L'AUSTRAL	10600gt	2010	16.0k	DE2	264p	264p	130c	142.0m	18.0m	4.6m	FR
LE BOREAL	10600gt	2010	16.0k	DE2	264p	264p	130c	142.0m	18.0m	4.6m	FR

L'AUSTRAL and LE BOREAL are under construction by Fincantieri (yard numbers 6193 and 6192) at Ancona, Italy, with delivery dates of October and June 2010 respectively. In June 2009 it was reported that the company was seeking to delay delivery of the second ship. IMO 9502518 and 9502506

COMPAGNIE DU FLEUVE

The Company Compagnie du Fleuve is a Senegalese company, recently formed to restore and operate the BOU EL MOGDAD.

Address BP 266, Saint-Louis, Senegal

Telephone +221 961 5689 **Fax** +221 961 8320

Website www.compagniedufleuve.com

Area operated Senegal

BOU EL MOGDAD	650gt	1954	7.0 k	D2	56p	56p	22c	52.0m	10.0m	2.5m	SN

BOU EL MOGDAD is a former river boat from French colonial days in West Africa, that operated on the Senegal River from 1954 until about 1968. She was built in The Netherlands for Messageries du Senegal and plied between the northern coastal town of Saint-Loius and Kayes in Mali, to link the first capital of Senegal with the many inland trading posts. Abandoned by the company around 1968, the ship was used for humanitarian missions for a number of years, and later as a local cruise ship before again falling into disuse. Acquired by her current owner in 2005 and now fully restored, she operates as far as the border with Mauritania, but also undertakes coastal trips along the Atlantic shores of Senegal and Mauritania. The ship's name recalls that of El Hadj Boa El Mogdad Seck, the Mauritanian diplomat and explorer, the first African to receive France's Legion d'Honneur.

CORAL PRINCESS CRUISES

The Company Coral Princess Cruises is an Australian company, founded by Captain Tony Briggs, which pioneered Great Barrier Reef cruising in 1984 with a converted Second World War Fairmile class submarine chaser. The company commissioned its first purpose built vessel, the CORAL PRINCESS, in 1988.

Managing Director Tony Briggs

Address PO Box 2093, Cairns, Queensland 4870, Australia

Telephone +61 7 4040 9999 **Fax** +61 7 4035 5995

Website www.coralprincesscruises.com

Area operated Australia's Great Barrier Reef, New Zealand, Papua New Guinea and Melanesia

CORAL PRINCESS	730gt	1988	10.0k	D2	50p	54p	12c	35.0m	13.3m	2.4m	AU
CORAL PRINCESS II	729gt	1985	10.0k	D2	46p	48p	12c	37.3m	12.0m	2.4m	AU
OCEANIC DISCOVERER	1779gt	2005	14.0k	D2	72p	72p	20c	63.1m	13.0m	3.0m	AU

CORAL PRINCESS was built by Carrington Slipways (yard number 204) at Newcastle, New South Wales, Australia. IMO 8804696

CORAL PRINCESS II was built by North Queensland Engineers & Agents (yard number 121) at Cairns, Queensland, Australia as the catamaran CORAL CAT. In 1990 she was renamed SPICE ISLANDER and took her current name in 1996 when acquired by Coral Princess Cruises. IMO 8409240

OCEANIC DISCOVERER was built as the OCEANIC PRINCESS by North Queensland Engineers & Agents (yard number 220) at Cairns, Queensland, Australia for the company. She was renamed as the OCEANIC DISCOVERER in October 2006. IMO 9292747

CROISIEUROPE

The Company CroisiEurope is a French family-owned operator of river cruise ships, established in 1976 by Gerard Schmitter as Alsace Croisieres. The company adopted its current name in 1997 and operates a number of river cruise ships, including LA BELLE DE CADIX, which also ventures out into the Atlantic Ocean on its Spanish coastal itineraries.

Address 12 Rue de la Division Leclerc, 67000 Strasbourg, France

Telephone +33 3 8876 4444 **Fax** +33 3 8832 4996

Website www.croisieurope.com

Area operated The Spanish rivers and Atlantic coast

LA BELLE DE CADIX	2038gt	2005	12.0k	D3	178p	178p	45c	110.0m	11.4m	3.0m	BE

LA BELLE DE CADIX was built by Meuse & Sambre Chantier Naval (yard number 24) at Beez sur Meuse in Belgium. IMO 9068938

CROISIMER

The Company CroisiMer is the newly created coastal cruise division of the French river cruise operator CroisiEurope, which was established in 1976. A further two sisters to the 'Adriatic' were ordered from the same shipyard, but all records of these have disappeared, so it is likely the orders for LA BELLE DU BOSPHORE and LA BELLE DES CYCLADES were cancelled.

Address 12 Rue de la Division Leclerc, 67000 Strasbourg, France

Telephone +33 3 8876 4444 **Fax** +33 3 8832 4996

Website www.croisieurope.com

Area operated The Adriatic Sea and the Canary Islands

LA BELLE DE L'ADRIATIQUE	2995gt	2007	12.0k	D3	200p	200p	43c	110.0m	12.5m	3.0m	BE

LA BELLE DE L'ADRIATIQUE was built by Meuse & Sambre Chantier Naval (yard number 30) at Beez sur Meuse in Belgium. It is thought that she was originally going to be named MARCO POLO. She operates on the Dalmacian coast in summer and moves to Egypt, Jordan and the Red Sea in winter. IMO 9432799

CRUCEROS AUSTRALIS

The Company Cruceros Australis is a Chilean company, founded in 1990 to operate short cruises in and around Patagonia.

Address Avenida El Bosque Norte 0440 Piso 11, Las Condes, Santiago 6780235, Chile

Telephone +56 2 442 3110 **Fax** +56 2 203 5173

Coral Princess Cruises' **Oceanic Discoverer** in Auckland *(Andrew Kilk)*

Croisimer's **La Belle de l'Adriatique** at Alexandria *(William Mayes)*

Website www.australis.com

Area operated Patagonia, Tierra del Fuego and Cape Horn

MARE AUSTRALIS	2664gt	2002	12.0k	D2	126p	126p	40c	71.8m	13.4m	3.2m	CL
VIA AUSTRALIS	2716gt	2005	12.0k	D2	128p	128p	40c	72.3m	13.4m	3.3m	CL

MARE AUSTRALIS and **VIA AUSTRALIS** were built by Astilleros y Servicios Navales (yard numbers 132 and 145) at Valdivia, Chile for Nisa Navegacion, a Chilean operator of ferries and cargo ships within the same corporate grouping as Cruceros Australis. IMO 9265677 and 9334088

Cruise ship on order

STELLA AUSTRALIS	4500gt	2010	12.0k	D2	p	p	c	m	m	m	CL

STELLA AUSTRALIS is on order at the Asenav Shipyard in Valdivia, Chile.

CRUISE NORTH EXPEDITIONS

The Company Cruise North Expeditions is part of the Inuit-owned Makivik Corporation, based in Canada. The company previously operated the USHUAIA, now operated by Antarctica Travels.

Address 1920 Avenue Road, Toronto, Ontario, Canada

Telephone +1 416 789 3752 **Fax** +1 416 789 1974

Website www.cruisenorthexpeditions.com

Area operated Northeast Canada and Greenland

LYUBOV ORLOVA	4251gt	1976	17.2k	D2	110p	110p	70c	100.0m	16.4m	4.7m	CK

LYUBOV ORLOVA For details of this ship see under Quark Expeditions

CRUISE WEST

The Company The origins of Cruise West go back to 1946, when Chuck West founded Alaska Arctic Travel Service in Fairbanks. The company soon branched out to offer the first small ship tours of Alaska and in 1971 the business, now named Westours, was sold to Holland America Line. Two years later, West founded what is today Cruise West, offering space on the ships of Alaska State Ferries and others. In 1990 the company acquired its first ship, the SPIRIT OF GLACIER BAY (now the PACIFIC MONARCH), and began to run two-night cruises from Juneau. During the following year, the newly purchased SPIRIT OF ALASKA began cruising from Seattle to Alaska. Founder Chuck West died in 2005. In early 2006 Cruise West acquired the NANTUCKET CLIPPER and the YORKTOWN CLIPPER from Clipper Cruise Line. With the economic downturn three ships were withdrawn from the Alaska trade, and two of them were laid up.

President Dietmar Wertanzi **Chairman and Chief Executive Officer** Richard D West

Address 2301 Fifth Avenue, Suite 401, Seattle, Washington, WA98121-1856, United States of America

Telephone +1 888 851 8133 **Fax** +1 206 441 4757

Website www.cruisewest.com

Area operated Alaska (all ships except PACIFIC EXPLORER), Costa Rica and Panama (PACIFIC EXPLORER), Mexico and California (SPIRIT OF ENDEAVOUR), Japan and South Pacific (SPIRIT OF OCEANUS), British Columbia (SPIRIT OF COLUMBIA)

PACIFIC EXPLORER	1716gt	1970	12.0k	D2	100p	100p	33c	54.9m	11.6m	4.2m	HN
SPIRIT OF '98	1472gt	1984	13.0k	D1	96p	99p	26c	58.5m	12.2m	2.9m	US
SPIRIT OF ALASKA	c500gt	1980	12.0k	D1	78p	82p	21c	43.5m	8.5m	2.0m	US
SPIRIT OF COLUMBIA	514gt	1979	10.0k	D1	78p	80p	21c	43.5m	8.5m	2.0m	US
SPIRIT OF DISCOVERY	910gt	1976	13.0k	D2	84p	84p	21c	51.8m	11.0m	2.1m	US
SPIRIT OF ENDEAVOUR	1425gt	1983	13.0k	D2	102p	107p	28c	66.1m	11.3m	2.6m	US
SPIRIT OF GLACIER BAY	1471gt	1984	7.0k	D2	102p	102p	36c	63.1m	11.3m	2.6m	US
SPIRIT OF OCEANUS	4200gt	1991	14.5k	D2	114p	129p	64c	90.4m	15.3m	4.0m	BS
SPIRIT OF YORKTOWN	2354gt	1988	10.0k	D2	138p	138p	42c	78.3m	12.2m	3.8m	US

PACIFIC EXPLORER was built by American Marine Corporation (yard number 1052) at New Orleans, Louisiana, USA as the FORCE TIDE. She was renamed NORPAC II in 1987, PACIFIC WARRIOR in 1992

Cruise West's **Spirit of Oceanus** off Port Hardy, BC *(Bruce Peter)*

Cruceros Australis' **Mare Australis** off Ushuiaia *(Rick Frendt)*

Cruise West's **Spirit of 98** *(Ben Lyons)*

Cruise West's **Spirit of Discovery** at Sitka *(Rick Frendt)*

Cruise West's **Spirit of Yorktown** at Almedia, CA *(Andrew Kilk)*

Delphin Kreuzfahrten's **Delphin Voyager** in Sydney *(Alf Sims)*

Deniz Cruise and Ferry Lines' **Ankara** in Istanbul *(William Mayes)*

and on transfer to Cruceros de Sur (Temptress Voyages) in 1995, TEMPTRESS EXPLORER. In 2001 ownership passed to Transamerica Ship Holding, and in May of the following year she was renamed PACIFIC EXPLORER. Cruise West had previously been marketing voyages on the TEMPTRESS EXPLORER. IMO 7047136

SPIRIT OF '98 was built by Bender Shipbuilding & Repair Company (yard number 140) at Mobile, Alabama, USA as the PILGRIM BELLE. On sale to Cruise West (West Travel) in 1984 she became the COLONIAL EXPLORER, and in 1988 was renamed again as VICTORIAN EMPRESS. In 1993 she became SPIRIT OF 98. With the demise of Majestic America Line, the SPIRIT OF 98 is employed on the Columbia and Snake Rivers. IMO 8963703

SPIRIT OF ALASKA was built by Blount Marine Corporation (yard number 234) at Warren, Rhode Island, USA as the PACIFIC NORTHWEST EXPLORER. She became the SPIRIT OF ALASKA in 1988. She is laid up in 2009. IMO 8963715

SPIRIT OF COLUMBIA was built by Blount Marine Corporation (yard number 225) at Warren, Rhode Island, USA as the NEW SHOREHAM II. She was renamed SPIRIT OF COLUMBIA in 1993. IMO 8963727

SPIRIT OF DISCOVERY was built by the Eastern Shipbuilding Corporation (yard number 1) at Boothbay Harbor, Maine, USA as the COLUMBIA. However, when launched she had the name INDEPENDENCE. She was operated by American Cruise Lines until acquired by Cruise West in 2000 and renamed as the SPIRIT OF DISCOVERY. IMO 7641413

SPIRIT OF ENDEAVOUR was built by Jeffboat Inc (yard number 82-2542) at Jeffersonville, Indiana, USA as the NEWPORT CLIPPER. She later became SEASPIRIT and took her current name in 1993. IMO 8963698

SPIRIT OF GLACIER BAY was built in 1984 by Jeffboat Inc, at Jeffersonville, Indiana, USA as the NANTUCKET CLIPPER for Clipper Cruise Line. She was acquired in early 2006 by Cruise West and later renamed as the SPIRIT OF NANTUCKET. In 2008 she was renamed as the SPIRIT OF GLACIER BAY, and is one of two ships laid up in 2009. IMO 8883563

SPIRIT OF OCEANUS was built at the Italian Marina di Carrara yard of Nuovi Cantieri Apuania (yard number 1144) as the RENAISSANCE FIVE for Renaissance Cruises. Sold in 1997 to Sun Viva, she was renamed as the SUN VIVA. When Star Cruises acquired that company in 2000 she became the MEGASTAR SAGITTARIUS, but was quickly sold to Cruise West and renamed SPIRIT OF OCEANUS. In 2010 this ship will undertake a unique world cruise lasting for 335 days. IMO 8802868

SPIRIT OF YORKTOWN was built in 1988 by First Coast Shipbuilding Inc, at Green Cove Springs, Florida, USA as the YORKTOWN CLIPPER for Clipper Cruise Line. Cruise West acquired her in 2006 and later renamed her as the SPIRIT OF YORKTOWN. IMO 8949472

DELPHIN KREUZFAHRTEN

The Company Delphin Kreuzfahrten is a German company providing cruises for German speaking passengers. The company began operating in 1981 and in the early years chartered such ships as the KAZAKHSTAN and the KAZAKHSTAN II, the latter ship eventually operating as the DELPHIN. The charter of the DELPHIN RENAISSANCE commenced in 2003. In late 2005, Cruiseinvest, owners of the ship, cancelled the charter agreement and sold the ship to Pullmantur Cruises of Spain. For the summer of 2007 the company chartered the former ORIENT VENUS. However, shipyard delays meant that an alternative vessel was required for the company's world cruise, leading to the charter of Louis Cruise's recently acquired ORIENT QUEEN. The company has reportedly signed a letter of intent with an un-named German shipyard for the construction of a 34,000-gross ton ship, although there is no confirmation of this at the time of writing. Heinz-Herbert Hey owns both this company and Hansa Kreuzfahrten.

Managing Director Heinz-Herbert Hey

Address Deichstrasse 9, D 20459 Hamburg, Germany

Telephone +49 40 3785 7826 **Fax** +49 40 374739

Website www.delphinvoyager.de

Area operated Worldwide

| DELPHIN VOYAGER | ‡21884gt | 1990 | 16.0k | D2 | 650p | 650p | 250c | 174.0m | 24.0m | 6.5m | BS |

Disney Magic at Port Canaveral *(Rick Frendt)*

Easycruise Life in Piraeus *(Mark Amielanczyk)*

DELPHIN VOYAGER was built by Ishikawajima – Harima Heavy Industries (yard number 2987) at the Tokyo shipyard in Japan as the ORIENT VENUS for Japan Cruise Line. She operated mainly in the charter cruise trades but had been laid up for several years. In 2005 she became the CRUISE ONE of First Cruise Group, but it is not thought that she saw active service under that name. Delphin Kreuzfahrten chartered her for operation commencing in December 2006, but an over-running refit delayed her entry into service until spring 2007. She now sails as the DELPHIN VOYAGER. IMO 8902333

DENIZ CRUISE AND FERRY LINES

The Company Deniz Cruise and Ferry Lines is a Turkish operator formed in 2004 to acquire and operate these two former Turkish Maritime Lines passenger and car ferries. The Istanbul Chamber of Shipping has a lead role in the owning consortium.

Address Kemankes Mah., Gumruk Sok, Hasif Han No 20, Karakoy, Istanbul, Turkey

Telephone +90 212 292 1600 **Fax** +90 212 292 1835

Website www.denizline.com.tr

Area operated Greek Islands cruises from Istanbul and charters (and ferry services)

ANKARA	10870gt	1983	18.5k	D2	268p	564p	90c	127.6m	19.4m	5.4m	TR
SAMSUN	10870gt	1985	18.5k	D2	274p	564p	90c	127.6m	19.4m	5.4m	TR

ANKARA was built by Stocznia Szczecinska im. A Warskiego (yard number B490/03) at Szczecin, Poland. She was to have been the MAZOWIA for Polska Zeluga Baltycka, but was completed as the ANKARA and delivered to Turkish Maritime Lines as part of a debt repayment programme. She generally operated between Turkey and Italy, sometimes through the Corinth Canal. Turkish Maritime Lines was privatized in a piecemeal fashion between 2003 and 2005 and this ship was taken up by her current owner. She was extensively refurbished in 2005/6. Ankara, known as Ancyra in classical times, became the capital of the new Turkish Republic in 1923. IMO 7615672

SAMSUN was built as a sister to the ANKARA by Stocznia Szczecinska im. A Warskiego (yard number B490/04) at Szczecin, Poland for Turkish Maritime Lines. She was renovated in 2005/6 when acquired as part of the Turkish privatisation programme. Samsun is a port city on Turkey's Black Sea coast. IMO 7615684

DESERT ISLAND CRUISING

The Company Desert Island Cruising Ltd is an associated company of Leisure Park Management Ltd, a UK operator of camp and caravan sites and holiday letting properties.

Address Lodge Farm, New Hedges, Tenby, SA70 8TN, United Kingdom

Telephone +44 1834 842420

Website www.desert-island-cruising.com

Area operated The Maldives

YASAWA PRINCESS	917gt	1985	11.0k	D2	66p	66p	25c	55.0m	11.0m	2.5m	FJ

YASAWA PRINCESS was built by the Fiji Marine Shipyard & Slipways (yard number 81) at Suva, Fiji for Blue Lagoon Cruises. Yasawa is the main island in the western Fiji Yasawa group of islands. She was acquired by her current operator in December 2007 without a change of name. IMO 8325638

DISNEY CRUISE LINE

The Company Disney Cruise Line is part of the Disney Corporation leisure group.

President Karl Holz

Address PO Box 10238, Lake Buena Vista, Florida 32830-0238 United States of America

Telephone +1 407 566 3500 **Fax** +1 407 566 3541

Website www.disneycruise.com

Area operated Caribbean Sea, Mexican Riviera and Europe

| DISNEY MAGIC | 83338gt | 1998 | 21.5k | DE2 | 1750p | 2834p | 945c | 294.1m | 32.3m | 8.0m | BS |
| DISNEY WONDER | 83308gt | 1999 | 21.5k | DE2 | 1750p | 2834p | 945c | 294.1m | 32.3m | 8.0m | BS |

DISNEY MAGIC was built by Fincantieri (yard number 5989) at the Breda shipyard, Venice, Italy. The forward section of the ship was built at the company's Ancona shipyard and towed to Venice to be completed and joined to the after section. The ship's godmother was Patty Disney, wife of Roy Disney. IMO 9126807

DISNEY WONDER was built by Fincantieri (yard number 5990) at Breda, Italy for Disney Cruise Line. It is thought that this was the first ship to be christened by a cartoon character, the honour going to Tinkerbell. IMO 9126819

Cruise ships on order

| DISNEY FANTASY | c124000gt | 2011 | k | DEP2 | 2500p | 4000p | 1200c | 339.8m | 37.0m | 8.3m | BS |
| DISNEY DREAM | c124000gt | 2012 | k | DEP2 | 2500p | 4000p | 1200c | 339.8m | 37.0m | 8.3m | BS |

DISNEY FANTASY and **DISNEY DREAM** were ordered from Jos. L. Meyer (yard numbers 687 and 688) at Papenburg, Germany in February 2007. IMO 9434254 and 9445590

EASYCRUISE

The Company Easycruise is a new and radically different operator, established in 2004, which commenced sailings in May 2005. It remains to be seen whether the 'no frills' concept, so successful in the airline industry, will transform the bottom end of the cruise market in a similar way. The ship offers basic, tiny cabins, which will be serviced at an extra charge. Food is not included, but is available from a number of outlets. Passengers are able to book for any length of stay on board from two nights upwards and the ship is scheduled to sail overnight between ports allowing much of the day ashore. The company appears to have signed a letter of intent with Neorion Holdings in Greece for the construction of a pair of 500-passenger vessels, with options on a further pair. A franchise agreement with Louis Cruise Lines is thought to increase the total number of orders and options to six. However, at the time of writing, none of these orders were confirmed. Easycruise is part of Easygroup. The company's first ship, the EASYCRUISEONE was sold in 2008 and replaced by a larger vessel.

Chief Executive Officer Stelios Haji-Ioannou

Address 362 Syngrou Avenue, 17674 Kallithea, Athens, Greece

Telephone +30 211 211 6211

Website www.easycruise.com

Area operated Mediterranean in summer, Caribbean in winter

| EASYCRUISE LIFE | 12711gt | 1981 | 15.5k | D2 | 462p | 574p | 150c | 137.1m | 21.0m | 5.8m | MT |

EASYCRUISE LIFE was built by Stocznia Szczecinska (yard number B492/02) at Szczecin, Poland as the LEV TOLSTOY, the second in a series of six ships for the Black Sea Shipping Company of the USSR. In 1986 she underwent a major reconstruction at Lloydwerft, Bremerhaven, Germany. By 1991, with the break-up of the Soviet Union, she was flying the flag of Ukraine, and was chartered to Transocean Tours for a period of four years. She was subsequently laid up in Haifa, Israel, before being sold in 1998 to Columbus Leisure Cruises and renamed NATASHA. Later that year she was renamed PALMIRA and then undertook charters to two German travel companies. In 2001 she was sold to Zenith Cruises for operation by Mano cruises as THE JASMINE. In 2006 she passed to Arab Ship Management and was renamed FARAH for operation as a ferry in the Red Sea. In 2008 she was acquired by Easycruise and after refit entered service as the EASYCRUISE LIFE. IMO 7625809

ELEGANT CRUISE LINE

The Company Elegant Cruise Line was founded by US based Croatian Captain Mato Stanovic in 1989. Elegant Cruises market these ships in the USA. A number of other tour companies also sell space on these ships including Noble Caledonia in the UK. Elegant Cruise Line is a Croatian owned company.

President Mato Stanovik

Address 24 Vanderventer Avenue, Port Washington, New York, 11050, United States of America

Telephone +1 516 767 9302 **Fax** +1 516 767 9303

Elegant Cruise Line's **Andrea** in Cadiz *(William Mayes)*

Elegant Cruise Line's **Monet** in Venice *(William Mayes)*

Emeraude Classic Cruises' **Emeraude** in Halong Bay, Vietnam *(Theodore W Scull)*

Website www.elegantcruises.com

Area operated Adriatic and Mediterranean Seas, The Amazon and Antarctica

| ANDREA | 2549gt | 1960 | 16.0k | D1 | 104p | 117p | 48p | 87.4m | 13.3m | 4.6m | LR |
| MONET | 1453gt | 1970 | 13.3k | D2 | 62p | 62p | 30c | 68.0m | 10.1m | 3.3m | VC |

ANDREA was built by AS Trondheims Mek. Verksted (yard number 244) at Trondheim, Norway as the HARALD JARL for Det Nordenfjeldske Dampskibsselskab (NFDS) for service on the Norwegian Coastal Express (Hurtigruten). In 1989 she passed to another Hurtigruten operator, TFDS. She continued to operate in this service until sold in 2002 to Elegant Cruises and refitted for use as a luxury expedition cruise ship. She was renamed ANDREA, after the granddaughter of the company's president. IMO 5142657

MONET was built as the YUSHAR for Northern Shipping by the Georgi Dimitrov Shipyard (yard number 903) in Varna, Bulgaria. She became the STELLA DALMATIAE in 1997 for Dalmacija Cruise Line and was renamed as the MONET in 1998 for Danaco, following a conversion by the Brodoremont Shipyard in Croatia. She subsequently passed to Ocean Winds in 2001 and Westwind Enterprises in 2003. She is operated by Jadropov International and marketed by Elegant Cruises. The 2009 season is the ninth season that the MONET has operated on the Dalmatian Coast for Elegant Cruises. Frenchman Claude Monet was one of the greatest impressionist painters. IMO 7045803

EMERAUDE CLASSIC CRUISES

The Company Emeraude Classic Cruises is a member company of the Apple Tree Group, a tourism, land, development, import and distribution business based in French Indo-China, Myanmar, Thailand and India.

Address c/o Press Club, 59A Ly Thai To Street, Hanoi, Vietnam

Telephone +84 4 934 0888 Fax +84 4 825 5342

Website www.emeraude-cruises.com

Area operated Halong Bay, Vietnam

| EMERAUDE | 700gt | 2003 | 10.0k | D2 | 78p | 78p | 35c | 56.0m | 10.0m | 2.6m | VN |

EMERAUDE was built by the Song Cam Shipyard in Vietnam as a replica 1910 French colonial steamer. She now operates overnight cruises in Halong Bay.

FANTASEA ADVENTURE CRUISING

The Company Fantasea Cruises, trading as Fantasea Adventure Cruises, is an Australian company, founded in 2006 as part of Riverside Maritime Group, owned by the Campbell family, whose history in the Brisbane area goes back to 1861 when Peter Morrison Campbell arrived in Australia from Scotland.

Address PO Box 2399, Fortitude Valley, Queensland, Australia 4006

Telephone +61 7 3852 0900 Fax +61 7 3426 2511

Website www.fantaseaammari.com

Area operated The Whitsunday Islands

| FANTASEA AMMARI | 1520gt | 1999 | 15.0k | D2 | 68p | 76p | 20c | 60.0m | 15.0m | 2.1m | AU |

FANTASEA AMMARI was built by Austal Ships (yard number 92) at Fremantle, Australia as the RIVAGE ST MARTIN for Rivages Croisieres. In 2005 she was acquired by Italian ferry operator Ustica Lines for cruising in the islands off Sicily as the AMMARI. She was sold on within a year and in early 2007 was renamed FANTASEA AMMARI. She now operates in the Whitsunday Islands. IMO 9202429

Fred. Olsen Cruise Lines' **Balmoral** at Cozumel *(Rick Frendt)*

Fred. Olsen Cruise Lines' **Black Prince** at Cobh *(Rick Frendt)*

Fred. Olsen Cruise Lines' **Black Watch** in Dover *(William Mayes)*

FRED. OLSEN CRUISE LINES

The Company The business we know today as Fred. Olsen Cruise Lines has its origins in the ship owning firm founded in 1886 by Frederik Olsen. By the early 1900's the business had expanded to embrace routes between Norway and Europe, Britain and the Mediterranean. The latter was a particularly important development as it introduced the company to the fruit trades from the region. The Canary Islands later became the focus of this trade, and the Olsen family still have significant investments in that area including a ferry operation. In 1906 the company began to carry passengers between Norway and the River Tyne, in northeast England, and Fred. Olsen developed the North Sea business, which probably peaked with the introduction of the BRAEMAR on the route from Harwich to Oslo in 1985. Olsen first started to offer what might now be regarded as proper cruises in 1966 with the arrival of the dual purpose BLACK WATCH and BLACK PRINCE. The first of these was jointly ordered by Fred. Olsen and the Bergen Line to serve the latter company's North Sea trades in the summer under the name JUPITER and to begin a new era for the Olsen's by offering cruises to the Canary Islands from London in the winter as the BLACK WATCH. The impressive vehicle deck space was occupied on the northbound leg by Canary Islands fruit, destined for the tables of Northern Europe. The second ship was ordered by Olsen for its own account, but in 1970 the company entered into a similar arrangement with the Bergen Line and she became the VENUS in summer and the BLACK PRINCE in winter. The BLENHEIM, a larger version of the twins was delivered to the company in 1970.

The arrangement between Olsen and the Bergen Line came to an end in 1986 and the BLACK WATCH became the property of the latter. Fred. Olsen retained the BLACK PRINCE and had her converted for full cruise ship operation by Wartsila at Turku in Finland, principally by means of the installation of 125 cabins on her vehicle deck. A second cruise ship, a new BLACK WATCH joined the fleet in 1996. The third ship for this gently expanding company appeared in 2001 in the form of the BRAEMAR and a fourth ship (BOUDICCA) arrived in 2006, closely followed by the announcement of a fifth (BALMORAL). The BLACK PRINCE will be withdrawn from service in the autumn of 2009, and is unlikely to be replaced until there are signs of an upturn in the UK economy. Fred. Olsen Cruise Lines specialises in cruises for British passengers.

Managing Director Mike Rodwell **Marketing Director** Nigel Lingard

Address Fred Olsen House, White House Road, Ipswich, Suffolk, IP1 5LL England

Telephone +44 1473 292200 **Fax** +44 1473 292201

Website www.fredolsencruises.com

Area operated Ex-UK to Scandinavia, the Mediterranean and North Atlantic; Caribbean and Grand Voyages

BALMORAL	43537gt	1988	19.0k	D2	1400p	1400p	500c	217.9m	28.2m	6.8m	BS
BLACK PRINCE	11209gt	1966	18.5k	D2	412p	451p	200c	141.6m	20.0m	6.4m	BS
BLACK WATCH	28613gt	1972	18.5k	D2	761p	902p	330c	205.5m	25.2m	7.5m	BS
BOUDICCA	28372gt	1973	20.0k	D2	755p	900p	350c	205.5m	25.2m	7.6m	BS
BRAEMAR	24344gt	1993	18.5k	D2	820p	977p	304c	195.1m	22.5m	5.4m	BS

BALMORAL was built for the Greek owned Royal Cruise Line by Jos. L. Meyer (yard number 616) at Papenburg, Germany as the CROWN ODYSSEY. She was to have been one of a pair of ships, but in the event the second vessel was either never ordered or cancelled before work began. Royal Cruise Line became part of the Kloster group around 1990, but the company retained its identity until 1996 when it was absorbed into Norwegian Cruise Line and the ship was renamed NORWEGIAN CROWN. In May 2000 the ship was transferred to Orient Lines and reverted to her original name for 'exploration cruising' worldwide. In early 2003 it was announced that the ship would be returned to Norwegian Cruise Line as the NORWEGIAN CROWN, following a downturn in Orient Lines' business, reverting to her previous NCL name. She operated to Bermuda, and handled the longer South American itineraries for NCL before being sold to Fred. Olsen Cruise Lines in 2006, for delivery in late 2007. When handed over to the company in November 2007, the ship went immediately to the Blohm & Voss shipyard in Hamburg to be refitted and to have a new 30-metre mid section fitted. That structure had already been completed by Schichau Seebeckwerft in Bremerhaven, and towed to Hamburg in October. Unfortunately, the ship's delivery back to Fred. Olsen Cruise Lines was delayed and with work still to be completed the BALMORAL missed her maiden voyage. In the spring of 2008 the company experimented with a first season of Mediterranean fly cruises with the BALMORAL before

Fred. Olsen Cruise Lines' **Boudicca** off Rosyth *(Bruce Peter)*

Fred. Olsen Cruise Lines' **Braemar** in Venice *(Rick Frendt)*

repositioning to Dover for a series of UK based cruises. Balmoral Castle and Estate is Queen Elizabeth II's private residence in Scotland, purchased by Queen Victoria in 1848. IMO 8506294

BLACK PRINCE, as noted above, was built for both dual purpose and dual ownership by Lubecker Flender-Werke (yard number 561) at Lubeck, Germany. She initially served Olsen's services between Harwich and Kristiansand and Amsterdam and Kristiansand in summer and joined her sister on the Canary Islands service in winter. She became jointly owned with the Bergen Line in 1970 and continued her dual role until the ending of the agreement in 1986. Following her refit she was equipped with a retractable 'marina' that could be put out from the stern when at anchor for the provision of a number of sporting activities. Her refit had been designed to attract a younger and more active passenger. She was not very successful, and was withdrawn from cruise service. An attempt to employ her on a new ferry service between Copenhagen and Gothenburg, was spectacularly unsuccessful, primarily because her Philippine registry and international crew had caused trouble with local trades unions. She was re-fitted again, but for a British middle-aged market this time and has been an enormous success, with a fiercely loyal following. The days of this 40-year-old ship are now numbered, as she will be taken out of service in October 2009. Her sale to Servicios Acuaticos de Venezuela was confirmed in May 2009. Edward, Prince of Wales (1330-1376), famous for leading the victories at the battles of Crecy and Poitiers, became known as the Black Prince due to his wearing of black armour. IMO 6613328

BLACK WATCH was built as the first of a trio of ships for the new Royal Viking Line consortium, one of the first purpose-built luxury cruise ships, for worldwide service. When delivered by the Helsinki shipyard of Wartsila (yard number 395) as the ROYAL VIKING STAR she introduced a new and impressive profile. As built she was 21,847 gross tons and carried a mere 539 passengers in luxurious surroundings. She was lengthened by Schichau Seebeckwerft in Bremerhaven in 1981, giving her an increased passenger capacity of 829. In 1988 she was transferred to Kloster Cruise (owners of the Royal Viking Line since 1984) and three years later was given the name WESTWARD. She was transferred within the group to Royal Cruise Line in 1994 and renamed as the STAR ODYSSEY. Olsen purchased her in 1996 through an intermediary (Olsen and Kloster were both Oslo shipping families and there was a certain amount of rivalry between the two) and following a refit she entered service on ex-UK cruises as the BLACK WATCH. In 2005 she underwent a major refit, including the replacement of her engines. The Scottish army regiment, the Black Watch, was established in 1725 and until recent years only drew its recruits from Perthshire, Angus and Fife. The Black Watch was incorporated into a larger Scottish Regiment in 2006. IMO 7108930

BOUDICCA was built by Wartsila (yard number 396) at Helsinki, Finland as the ROYAL VIKING SKY for the new Royal Viking Line of Oslo. She was 21,891 gross tons as built. During 1982 Schichau Seebeckwerft at Bremerhaven lengthened her by 28m. In 1987 she was transferred to the fleet of Norwegian Caribbean Line (Kloster Cruise), the parent company (Klosters had acquired Royal Viking Line in 1984) and was renamed SUNWARD. In 1992 she passed to Birka Line, an Aland Island based shipping company, and was renamed BIRKA QUEEN for the company's short Baltic cruises. This venture was unsuccessful and the ship was chartered back to Klosters from October 1992 to May 1993. She was then chartered to Princess Cruises as the GOLDEN PRINCESS for Alaska cruising for three years, before passing to Star Cruises in 1996 as the SUPERSTAR CAPRICORN for Asian cruising. Surplus to requirements, in 1998 she was chartered to Hyundai Merchant Marine Co as the HYUNDAI KUMGANG for cruises from Korea. At the end of the charter in 2001 she reverted to the name SUPERSTAR CAPRICORN and was laid up. In 2004 she operated as the GRAND LATINO for Spanish operator Iberojet, but was sold in early 2005 to Fred. Olsen Cruise Lines, to enter service at the end of 2005 as the BOADICEA. This name was later revised to the less gentle, alternative spelling BOUDICCA. Boadicea, Queen of the Iceni, led her people in battle against the Romans in Britain around 60 A.D., and remains one of Britain's greatest heroines. IMO 7218395

BRAEMAR is the third ship in a series ordered by Commodore Cruise Line from the Valencia shipyard of Union Naval de Levante (yard number 198). She was delivered in 1993 as the CROWN DYNASTY. At the end of the following year Commodore Cruise Line entered into an arrangement with Cunard that involved the latter company in the marketing of Commodore's ships. She became the CROWN MAJESTY for a charter to Majesty Cruise Line in 1997, and later that year was renamed as the NORWEGIAN DYNASTY for Norwegian Cruise Line. She reverted to her original name for Commodore again in 1999. Fred. Olsen Cruise Lines acquired the ship as their third vessel in 2001 and following a refit by Blohm & Voss in Hamburg; she entered service in August of that year under the name BRAEMAR. In May 2008 she was sent to the Blohm & Voss shipyard in Hamburg, where she was lengthened by 31 metres. She re-entered service in July 2008, and takes her name from the site on Royal Deeside in Scotland, home to the Braemar Gathering and Highland Games since 1813. IMO 9000699

GALA TRAVEL

The Company Gala Travel is a Galapagos Island tour operator.

Address Avenida de los Shyris 1000, y Holanda, Quito, Ecuador

Telephone +593 2 243 0345 **Fax** +593 2 245 0775

Area operated Galapagos Islands

TROPIC SUN	‡790gt	1967	12.5k	D2	48p	48p	25c	51.8m	10.1m	3.0m	EC

TROPIC SUN was built by R Dunston (yard number S850) at Hessle in England as the HUMBER GUARDIAN for the British Transport Docks Board, which later became Associated British Ports. She passed through a number of owners, only changing name once, in 1993 to TROPIC SUN, before arriving with her current owner in 2002. IMO 6726826

GAP ADVENTURES

The Company GAP Adventures was founded in Toronto by Trinidadian Bruce Poon Tip in 1990, pioneering land tours to Ecuador, Belize and Peru. In September 2004 the company acquired the EXPLORER (see Recent Departures section for details), but that ship was lost on a cruise in November 2007 after striking ice off Antarctica. All of her passengers were rescued. As a stopgap measure the company chartered the Murmansk Shipping Company's POLARIS. The company acquired its current ship in early 2008 and following extensive refit she entered service in April 2009. GAP Adventures also markets space on other vessels in the Greek Islands and the Galapagos Islands.

President and Chief Executive Officer Bruce Poon Tip

Address 19 Charlotte Street, Toronto, Canada M5V 2H5

Telephone +1 416 260 0999 **Fax** +1 416 260 1888

Website www.gapadventures.com

Area operated Antarctica, Amazon, Norway, North Atlantic and the Arctic

EXPEDITION	6334gt	1972	17.0k	D2	120p	120p	c	105.2m	18.6m	4.6m	LR

EXPEDITION was built by Helsingor Skips & Maskinbygg (yard number 398) at Helsingor, Denmark as the car ferry KATTEGAT for Jydsk Faergefart of Denmark for the domestic Grenaa – Hundested service. In 1978 she was sold to P&O Ferries and renamed N F TIGER (the N F referring to the P&O Ferries subsidiary Normandy Ferries), for use on the Dover to Boulogne route. The Normandy Ferries operation along with the ship was sold to European Ferries (Townsend Thoresen) in 1985, when she was renamed TIGER. She was withdrawn from service in June 1986 and later that year was sold to Finlandshammen AB of Sweden for use on the summer service of Viking Line between Mariehamn and Kapellskar, and renamed ALANDSFARJAN. She continued in this role until May 2008, when replaced by the ROSELLA. She was immediately acquired by GAP Adventures and sent to what is now the STX shipyard at Rauma, Finland for conversion into an expedition cruise ship. During her first summer with GAP Adventures she has been chartered by Hurtigruten Group for three months. IMO 7211074

GLACIER BAY CRUISELINE

The Company Glacier Bay Tours and Cruises is a United States of America registered company, owned by Doug Simplot and Doug Toms, who also own Great American Journeys. In late 2005 the company filed for bankruptcy and the ships were laid up at Salmon Bay near Seattle. It was hoped to reorganize the company and begin trading again in 2007, but at the time of writing, two years later, there was still no sign that this was likely to happen.

Area operated South East Alaska, Prince William Sound and the Columbia River but not currently operating

WILDERNESS ADVENTURER	c500gt	1983	10.0k	D1	68p	76p	20c	47.5m	11.6m	m	US
WILDERNESS DISCOVERER	‡683gt	1992	10.0k	D2	84p	98p	22c	51.5m	11.9m	m	US
WILDERNESS EXPLORER	c300gt	1969	9.0k	D1	31p	31p	16c	31.6m	6.4m	m	US

Glacier Bay Explorer *(Andrew Kilk)*

Hansa Kreuzfahrten's **Delphin** off Rosyth *(Bruce Peter)*

WILDERNESS ADVENTURER was built by Blount Marine Corporation (yard number 250) at Warren, Rhode Island, USA as the CARIBBEAN PRINCE for American Canadian Caribbean Line. Glacier Bay Cruiseline purchased her in 1997 and she was renamed WILDERNESS ADVENTURER. IMO 8978667

WILDERNESS DISCOVERER was built by Blount Marine Corporation (yard number 280) at Warren, Rhode Island, USA as the MAYAN PRINCE for American Canadian Caribbean Line. She was acquired by Glacier Bay Cruiseline in 1998 and renamed WILDERNESS DISCOVERER. IMO 8859689

WILDERNESS EXPLORER was built by Blount Marine Corporation, Warren, Rhode Island, USA as the WILDERNESS EXPLORER. She is recorded as being acquired by her present owner in 2003. IMO 8978655

GOLDEN STAR CRUISES

The Company Golden Star Cruises is a trading name of Dolphin Hellas Shipping, a privately owned Greek company. Following an ownership dispute that ended in court, the company's ship AEGEAN I was arrested and the company chartered the OCEAN MONARCH for the 2006 season. However, for 2007 the company used Louis Cruise Lines' IVORY, renamed AEGEAN TWO, and in 2008 the same company provided the PERLA, renamed as THE AEGEAN PEARL. In 2009 the company advertised sailings on the VISION STAR (now GEMINI – see Clipper Group) but these did not take place. The company does not appear to have its own ship in 2009, but is advertising cruises on Mediterranean Classic Cruises' ship, ATHENA, even though MCC will not have that ship.

Address 85 Akti Miaouli, Piraeus, 18538, Greece

Telephone +30 210 4290650 **Fax** +30 310 4290660

Website www.goldenstarcruises.com

Area operated The Greek Islands of the Aegean Sea but not thought to be operating.

GOTA CANAL STEAMSHIP COMPANY

The Company The Gota Canal Steamship Company (Rederi AB Gota Kanal) was founded on February 27, 1869. The JUNO was the second of the company's ships, and still remains in service after more than 130 years. The company is now part of the Stromma Turism & Sjofart Group.

Address Pusterviksgaten 13, SE41301 Gothenburg, Sweden

Telephone +46 31 806315 **Fax** +46 31 158311

Website www.gotacanal.se

Area operated The Gota Canal between Gothenburg and Stockholm, Sweden

DIANA	269gt	1931	10.0k	D1	56p	56p	12c	31.6m	6.8m	2.7m	SE
JUNO	254gt	1874	10.0k	D2	58p	58p	12c	31.5m	6.7m	2.7m	SE
WILHELM THAM	268gt	1912	10.0k	D1	50p	50p	12c	31.5m	6.7m	2.7m	SE

DIANA was built at the Finnboda Shipyard in Stockholm, Sweden. Built as a steamship, she was the last of that type in regular Swedish canal service when her steam engine was replaced by diesel in 1969. Diana was the Roman goddess of the hunt and of chastity.

JUNO was built by Motala Werkstad, at Motala in Sweden. She was to have been named DARWIN, but after shareholder objection she took the name JUNO. Her steam plant was replaced by diesel engines in 1956. Her name is that of the Roman goddess of marriage and motherhood. She is the oldest registered ship with overnight cabins.

WILHELM THAM was built by Motala Werkstad, at Motala, Sweden and is named after the Swedish industrialist and director of the Husqvarna Weapons Factory from 1876 to 1911. Her steam engine was replaced by diesel in 1965.

HANSA KREUZFAHRTEN

The Company Hansa Kreuzfahrten GmbH is a German company providing cruises for German speaking passengers. The company is associated with and markets the cruises of Delphin Kreuzfahrten (both companies are owned by Heinz- Herbert Hey). Until October 2006 the company also operated the PALOMA 1, now serving as a gambling ship in Singapore. In 2007 the company took the DALMACIJA on charter for a summer season. For 2008 – 2010 the company secured the charter of

Majestic International Cruises' OCEAN MONARCH, now renamed PRINCESS DAPHNE and owned by Classic International Cruises. Heinz-Herbert Hey owns both this company and Delphin Kreuzfahrten.

Owner Heinz-Herbert Hey

Address Contrescarpe 36, D28203 Bremen, Germany

Telephone +49 421 33466 0 **Fax** +49 421 33466 25

Website www.hansakreuzfahrten.de

Areas operated Caribbean, Atlantic Isles, Mediterranean, Northern Europe, Scandinavia

DELPHIN	16214gt	1975	21.0k	D2	472p	500p	200c	156.3m	21.8m	6.2m	BS
PRINCESS DAPHNE	15833gt	1955	17.0k	D2	422p	526p	210c	162.4m	21.3m	7.5m	PT

DELPHIN was built by the Wartsila Shipyard (yard number 1212) at Turku in Finland as the BYELORUSSIYA for the Black Sea Shipping Company of the Soviet Union. On the break-up of the Eastern Bloc the company became Ukrainian. In 1993 she was renamed KAZAKHSTAN II, but her operators faced severe financial difficulties resulting in the arrest of ships and the eventual collapse of the company. In 1995 she was sold to Lady Lou Shipping, a Cypriot registered but German controlled company. Her ownership was passed to Dolphin Maritime in 1998, another company within the same group and she was renamed DELPHIN. She operates for Hansa Kreuzfahrten on year round charter, in the Caribbean in winter, the Mediterranean and Atlantic Isles in the shoulder seasons and in Northern Europe and Scandinavia in summer. The ship was reported to have been sold to an unknown Caribbean based owner (possibly Royal Zante Cruises) in late 2006, but this never happened. IMO 7347536

PRINCESS DAPHNE – for details see under Classic International Cruises

HAUMANA CRUISES

The Company Haumana Cruises is a trading name of Tahiti Cruises, a French Polynesian company.

Chairman Eugene Degage

Address BP 9254, Motu Uta, 98713 Papeete, Tahiti

Telephone +689 500674 **Fax** +689 500672

Website www.tahiti-haumana-cruises.com

Areas operated Tahiti

HAUMANA	511gt	1986	10.0k	D2	24p	24p	16c	36.5m	13.7m	1.8m	FR

HAUMANA was built by Precision Marine Holding (yard number 735) at Fremantle, Western Australia as the passenger ferry MOTIVE EXPLORER. In 1987 she became the KIMBERLEY EXPLORER and six years later took the name REEF TREK. She was converted to a cruise vessel in 1997 for Tahiti Cruises and renamed HAUMANA. Haumana translates as magical spirit. IMO 8611001

HERITAGE EXPEDITIONS

The Company Heritage Expeditions was founded in 1985 by biologist Rodney Russ.

Address 53B Montreal Street, PO Box 7218, Christchurch, New Zealand

Telephone +64 3 365 3500 **Fax** +64 3 365 1300

Website www.heritage-expeditions.com

Areas operated Antarctica

SPIRIT OF ENDERBY	1764gt	1983	12.0k	D2	48p	48p	c	71.6m	12.8m	4.7m	RU

SPIRIT OF ENDERBY is a marketing name used by Heritage Expeditions for the Far Eastern Hydrometeorological Research Institute of Vladivostok owned PROFESSOR KHROMOV. She was built by Oy Laivateollisuus Ab (yard number 345) at Turku, Finland. She operates for Heritage Expeditions in the southern summer. Enderby Land is an Antarctic landmass extending from Shinnan Glacier to William Scoresby Bay, discovered in 1831 by John Briscoe and named by him after the owners of his ship (the TULA), the Enderby Brothers of London. IMO 8010350

HERITAGE LINE

The Company Heritage Line is a Vietnamese organisation providing cruises from Ho Chi Minh City into the Mekong River and on to Cambodia.

Managing Director Thomas Peter

Address 77 Hung Thai 1, Phu My Hung, District 7, Ho Chi Minh City, Vietnam

Telephone +84 8 541 01439 **Fax** +84 8 541 01914

Website www.heritage-line.com

Areas operated Vietnam and Cambodia

JAYAVARMAN		700gt	2009	10.0k	D2	54p	65p	40c	58.0m	11.0m	1.6m	VN

JAYAVARMAN The name Jayavarman was that of several kings of Cambodia from about the ninth century. The ship is being built in the Ho Chi Minh City shipyard and is expected in service in the autumn of 2009. The ship was originally to have been named MEKONG EXPLORER, and it is thought that there will be a second ship in 2010.

HURTIGRUTEN GROUP (Norwegian Coastal Voyage)

The Company The Hurtigruten, the Norwegian Coastal Express, covers the 1,300 or so nautical miles from Bergen to Kirkenes, just ten miles from the Russian border in the far north of Norway, in a twelve-day round trip making 34 port calls. Most of the ships carry cars and other vehicles on decks accessed through side doors. All of the vessels perform a year-round lifeline service linking communities who have no other means of transport to the outside world. The Hurtigruten commenced in 1893 at which time the Norwegian Government entered into a four-year agreement with Vesteraalens Dampskibsselskab, providing the subsidy for a weekly service from Trondheim to Hammerfest in summer and to Tromso in winter. However, the story of the coastal service really begins around 1838, when the Norwegian Government paid for the construction and running costs of the steamer PRINS GUSTAV to trade between Trondheim and Hammerfest in the far north. The service only ran for about seven months each year, and then only sailed during daylight due to the lack of navigation markers north of Trondheim. Initially the service was monthly, but as new ships arrived it was extended south to Kristiansand and increased in frequency. The prime purpose of these early ships was the carriage of passengers and mail; most goods were still travelling in sailing vessels. During the 1860's the route passed in its entirety into the hands of private companies. The failure of the fish harvest in 1875/6 had the eventual result of reducing the lifeline service, as the various operating companies switched their investment to the more lucrative tourist trade. The outcome was the tendering of the service and the awarding of the agreement referred to above. In 1894 two further companies were licensed to operate the Coastal Express, Bergenske Dampskibsselskab and Nordenfjeldske Dampskibsselskab. Today the route is in the hands of just a single company, following the merger in 2006 of OVDS and TFDS, and as Government subsidies are again under scrutiny the service is once more turning to tourism as the main source of income on what has often been described as 'The World's Most Beautiful Voyage'.

OVDS or Ofotens og Vesteraalens Dampskibsselskab ASA can trace its origins back to 1881 when Captain Richard With established the Vesteraalens Dampskibsselskab. Ofotens Dampskibsselskab joined the Hurtigruten service in 1936 and in 1987 the two companies merged to form OVDS.

TFDS or Troms Fylkes Dampskibsselskab ASA was a major Norwegian ship owner at the time of the merger, with around 34 vessels. The company was founded in 1866 as Tromso Amts D/S, but assumed its current name in 1925. TFDS joined the Hurtigruten in 1979, when it purchased four ships from the Bergen Line. In 2003 the company became the major shareholder in Fjord Line, the ferry company that links Norway with Denmark and, until recently, England.

Until recently, in addition to the ships listed here, the Hurtigruten Group operated more than 50 ferries along the coasts of Norway and was a major Norwegian bus operator, employing more than 3,400 people. However, recent financial difficulties have led to the sale of most of the company's assets that were not directly associated with the Hurtigruten service. The Coastal Express was also in need of a further bail-out by the Norwegian Government and has sold one ship and laid up another.

Address PO Box 43, Havnegata 2, N8501 Narvik, Norway
UK Office 3 Shortlands, London W6 8NE, England

Telephone +47 76 96 76 00 **Fax** +47 76 96 76 01

Hurtigruten's **Fram** in London *(Matthew Sudders)*

Hurtigruten's **Lofoten** at Flam *(Matthew Davies)*

Website www.hurtigruten.com and www.hurtigruten.co.uk

Area operated Norwegian coast, Spitzbergen, the Lofoten Islands, Greenland, Chile and Antarctica

FINNMARKEN	15690gt	2002	18.0k	D2	639b	361d	85c	135.8m	21.5m	4.9m	NO
FRAM	11647gt	2007	16.0k	DEP2	348p	152d	70c	113.9m	20.2m	5.1m	NI
KONG HARALD	11204gt	1993	15.0k	D2	483b	208d	59c	121.8m	19.2m	4.7m	NO
LOFOTEN	2621gt	1964	15.0k	D1	155b	245d	40c	87.4m	13.3m	4.6m	NO
MIDNATSOL	16151gt	2003	15.0k	D2	650b	350d	74c	135.8m	21.5m	4.9m	NO
NORDKAPP	11386gt	1996	15.0k	D2	464b	227d	59c	123.3m	19.2m	4.7m	NO
NORDLYS	11204gt	1994	15.0k	D2	482b	209d	60c	121.7m	19.2m	4.7m	NO
NORDNORGE	11384gt	1997	15.0k	D2	455b	236d	57c	123.3m	19.2m	4.7m	NO
NORDSTJERNEN	2191gt	1956	14.0k	D1	114b	271d	42c	80.8m	12.6m	4.5m	NO
POLARLYS	11341gt	1996	15.0k	D2	479b	258d	63c	123.0m	19.2m	4.5m	NO
RICHARD WITH	11205gt	1993	15.0k	D2	483b	208d	57c	121.8m	19.2m	4.7m	NO
TROLLFJORD	16140gt	2002	15.0k	D2	656b	344d	74c	135.8m	21.5m	4.9m	NO
VESTERALEN	6261gt	1983	15.0k	D2	314b	236d	34c	108.6m	16.5m	4.6m	NO

FINNMARKEN was built by Kleven Verft (yard number 292) at Ulsteinvik in Norway. Finnmark is Norway's most northerly region, bordering Finland. The first FINNMARKEN served the coastal route from 1912. IMO 9231951

FRAM was built by Fincantieri (yard number 6144) at Monfalcone, Italy. She is used mainly for cruising, particularly around Greenland, during the summer and then heads south to the Antarctic during the winter. She was named by HRH Crown Princess Mette Marit in Oslo on 19 May 2007. The ship is named in honour of the polar expedition ship Fram, now housed in the Oslo Maritime Museum, which took Fridtjof Nansen across the Arctic Ocean, Roald Amundsen on his race to the South Pole, and Otto Sverdruo on many Arctic voyages of discovery. In late 2007, following a blackout, the FRAM collided with an iceberg in Antarctica, but was not seriously damaged. IMO 9370018

KONG HARALD is named in honour of the King of Norway, who succeeded to the throne in 1991. She was built in Germany at the Stralsund shipyard of Volkswerft (yard number 101). IMO 9039119

LOFOTEN is the last surviving traditional Hurtigruten ship still in regular service. She was built by AS Akers Mekanik Verksted (yard number 547) at Oslo, Norway for Vesteraalens Dampskibsselskab (VDS). From 1988 she operated for Finnmark Fklkesrederi og Ruteselskap, who sold her to OVDS in 1996. She now only operates on the Hurtigruten during the winter, when the NORDNORGE goes south to Antarctica. In the summer she operates cruises to the Lofoten Islands, off the coast of central Norway, from which she takes her name. IMO 5424562

MIDNATSOL had her hull built at Bruce's Shipyard, Landskrona, Sweden, but was completed by the Fosen Yard (yard number 73) in Norway. Her name means Midnight Sun. IMO 9247728

NORDKAPP was built by Kvaerner Kleven Ulsteinvik (yard number 265) at Ulsteinvik in Norway. She is one of two ships that travelled to South America and Antarctica in the winter, but she no longer does so. Her name translates as North Cape, the most northerly point of mainland Norway. IMO 9107772

NORDLYS takes her name from the Northern Lights, in Latin the Aurora Borealis, or Red Dawn of the North. She was built in Germany at the Stralsund shipyard of Volksverft (yard number 102). This ship is currently laid up. IMO 9048914

NORDNORGE was built by the Kvaerner Kleven Ulsteinvik shipyard (yard number 266) at Ulsteinvik in Norway. She sailed south to Antarctica in the winter for several seasons before being replaced by the FRAM. Her name simply means North Norway. For the winter of 2008/9 she was laid up due to the continuing financial woes of her owner. She was then chartered from December 2008 to April 2009 as an accommodation ship in the Mediterranean. IMO 9107784

NORDSTJERNEN was built by Blohm & Voss (yard number 787) in Hamburg, Germany as a replacement for a pre-war vessel of the same name for the Bergen Line. From 1994 she has operated the summer run from Tromso to Spitzbergen, acting as a relief Hurtigruten ship as required. In more recent years she has been based in Spitzbergen. Her name translates as North Star. IMO 5255777

POLARLYS is a product of the Ulstein Verft yard (yard number 223) at Ulsteinvik, Norway. Her name translates as Polar Lights. IMO 9107796

RICHARD WITH was the name of the founder of the Vesteralens company, with which Ofotens later merged. This ship was built at Stralsund in Germany by Volkswerft (yard number 103). IMO 9040429

Hurtigruten's **Nordkapp** arriving in Bergen *(William Mayes)*

Hurtigruten's **Nordnorge** in Travemunde *(Oliver Sesemann)*

TROLLFJORD's hull was built by Bruce's Shipyard (yard number 246) at Landskrona, Sweden but the ship was completed by the Fosen Yard in Norway, where she acquired the build number 72. Trollfjord is one of the many fjords in the Vesteralen and Lofoten district of Norway. IMO 9233258

VESTERALEN was built by Kaarbos Mek. Verksted (yard number 101) at Harstad, Norway. The very first of the coastal express ships carried the name VESTERALEN, in honour of the Vesteralen Islands, a little to the north of the Lofoten Islands. VESTERALEN was also the name of the first coastal express ship. IMO 8019368

Hurtigruten also has summer 2009 charters on the EXPEDITION (GAP Adventures) and the POLAR STAR (Polar Star Expeditions) for Spitsbergen cruises

ILIADA TOURISM

The Company Iliada Tourism (Il Tur Ileri Turizm ve Yat Isletmeleri) is a Turkish operator and organiser of exclusive tours in and around Turkey.

Address Haci IzzetPasa Sok, Cam Palas 24/5, 34427 Gumussuyu, Istanbul, Turkey

Telephone +90 212 243 2164 **Fax** +90 212 243 2658

Website www.iliadatourism.com

Area operated Bosphorus and Gulf of Fethiye, Turkey

HALAS	584gt	1915	12.0k	D2	28p	28p	26c	52.0m	8.5m	3.2m	TR

HALAS is now owned by Il-Tur Isletmeleri of Istanbul and operates on the Turkish coast as a very luxurious cruise vessel. She was built by Fairfield Shipbuilding and Engineering Company (yard number 502) at Govan on the River Clyde in Scotland, as one of the numerous steam ferries for service around Constantinople (now Istanbul) and the Bosphorus. Although completed in 1915, she was requisitioned by the Royal Navy and served as the dispatch steamer HMS WATERWITCH, and is one of only two surviving vessels to have been present at the Gallipoli Campaign. She eventually reached her intended owner in 1923, taking the name HALAS instead of her intended name RESIT PASA. She survived in her original role until the mid 1980's and after a period in lay-up she was rebuilt as the rather splendid ship she is today. IMO 5140697

INDIAN OCEAN CRUISES

The Company Indian Ocean Cruises is a British-owned company, part of the London-based Foresight Group, originally based in Goa, which started operating in 2006. Ravi Mehrotra and cruise veteran Les Royle founded the company. For 2009 the company has moved its base to Mauritius.

Owner Ravi Mehrotra

Address IOC Holidays, 5B1 Fifth Floor, Wing B, Cyber Tower, Ebne Cyber Centre, Mauritius

Telephone +44 800 032 7020

Website www.indianoceancruises.net

Area operated South India, Sri Lanka and the Lakshadweek Islands, Mauritius and Madagascar

OCEAN ODYSSEY	4561gt	1965	15.0k	D2	250p	325p	120c	97.2m	16.0m	4.5m	PA

OCEAN ODYSSEY was built by Cantieri Riunite dell'Adriatico (yard number 1882) at Monfalcone, Italy as the EROS for the Greek Government as part of the Second World War reparations scheme. She was one of three similar ships owned by the Hellenic Tourism Organisation, although each ship was operated by one of the Greek passenger shipping companies. The EROS was allocated to Typaldos Lines, but that company became bankrupt so she went to Epirotiki in 1966 and was renamed JASON. Her name was later restyled as IASON. During 2004 she operated on charter to the French tour operator Rivages. After almost 40 years with Epirotiki she was sold in December 2005 to Derwent Ocean Ltd of Panama and after renaming as the OCEAN ODYSSEY began operating for Indian Ocean Cruises. IMO 6415489

JAPAN CRUISE LINE

The Company Japan Cruise Line is part of SHK Group, a Japanese joint venture between the Shin Nohonkai, Hankyu and Kanpu ferry companies. The PACIFIC VENUS is marketed as Venus Cruise. A

Hurtigruten's **Trollfjord** in Bergen *(Rick Frendt)*

Japan Cruise Line's **Pacific Venus** in San Francisco *(Andrew Kilk)*

Kristina Cruises' **Kristina Brahe** at Lappeeranta *(Rick Frendt)*

second ship, the ORIENT VENUS, was sold to Greek investors in 2005 and is now operating as DELPHIN VOYAGER for Delphin Kreuzfahrten.

President Yasuo Iritani

Address Herbis Osaka Building 15F, 25-35 Umeda, Kita-ku, JP 530 0001 Osaka, Japan

Telephone +81 6 6347 7521 **Fax** +81 6 6341 8980

Website www.venus-cruise.co.jp

Area operated Asia and worldwide

PACIFIC VENUS	26594gt	1998	20.8k	D2	532p	720p	180c	183.4m	25.0m	6.5m	JP

PACIFIC VENUS was built by IHHI (yard number 3095) in Tokyo. She operates cruises ranging in length from a few days along the Japanese coast, to several months around the world. IMO 9160011

JUPITER CRUISES

The Company Jupiter Cruises is a new operator, owned by the Royal group of Singapore, which commenced operation in late 2008.

Address 34D North Canal Road, 059290 Singapore

Telephone +65 6338 2551 **Fax** +65 6338 1818

Website www.jupitercruises.com

Area operated Vietnam and China

JUPITER	20804gt	1975	22.0k	D2	800p	1122p	400c	175.3m	22.0m	5.9m	PA

JUPITER was built by Dubigeon-Normandie (yard number 142) at Nantes, France for Silja Line's Sweden to Finland ferry services as the WELLAMO. Replaced by a larger ship in 1981 she was sold to DFDS, becoming the DANA GLORIA for operation between Copenhagen and Oslo, a role that she performed for many years. In 1984 she was chartered back to Silja Line as the SVEA CORONA for a few months. In 1988 she was lengthened by 22 metres by Jos. L. Meyer at Papenburg, Germany, returning to service between Copenhagen and Oslo as the KING OF SCANDINAVIA. In 1994 she formed part of a ship swap when exchanged with Color Line for the VENUS and some cash. She then operated as the JUPITER between Newcastle and various Norwegian ports until the route and ship were sold to Fjord Line in 1998.She was replaced by a larger ship in 2006 and spent some time as an accommodation ship before being sold in 2008 for use in South East Asia. IMO 7360186

KLEINTOURS

The Company Kleintours is a Galapagos Islands based tour and cruise operator, which was established in 1983.

Address Av. Eloy Alfaro N 34-151 & Catalina, Aldaz, Quito, Ecuador

Telephone +593 2 2267 000 **Fax** +593 2 2442 389

Website www.galapagosecuador.com

Area operated Galapagos Islands

CORAL I	359gt	1980	10.0k	D2	36p	36p	10c	39.7m	8.4m	m	EC
CORAL II	208gt	1963	10.0k	D1	20p	26p	10c	33.5m	7.5m	2.4m	EC
GALAPAGOS LEGEND	2890gt	1963	15.0k	D2	110p	110p	60c	91.5m	14.3m	4.2m	EC

CORAL I was built by KG Norderwerft in Hamburg, Germany as the TROPIC BIRD. She was acquired by Kleintours in 2002 and extended in 2005. IMO 8978875

CORAL II was built in The Netherlands by NV Scheepswerf Alphen as the AVANTE. She was acquired by Kleintours in 2002. IMO 8978887

GALAPAGOS LEGEND was built by Howaldtswerke (yard number 943) at Hamburg, Germany as the HELGOLAND for local services on the North Sea and Baltic coasts of Germany. She had been ordered from the Hanseatische Werft yard in Hamburg, but that yard was declared bankrupt so the order was transferred. She was chartered out from 1964 to 1966 under the name LARVIKSPILEN, but reverted to her original name at the end of that period. From 1966 to 1971 she served as a hospital ship in

Vietnamese waters before returning to Europe. In 1972 she was purchased by Stena Reederei of Germany and became the STENA FINLANDICA. Three years later she was renamed BALTIC STAR for Seetouristik (later Forde Reederei) day cruises in the Baltic Sea. She was sold to her current owner in 2001, renamed the GALAPAGOS LEGEND and refitted as an overnight cruise ship. IMO 5404964

KRISTINA CRUISES

The Company Kristina Cruises is a Finnish family-owned company, founded in 1985 as Rannikkolinjat, which acquired its first ship, the KRISTINA BRAHE later that year from Fagerlines. In 1987 the former BORE joined the fleet. Unusually, cruises are operated on a bed and breakfast basis with other meals available at an extra charge.

Address Kirkkokatu 16, 48100 Kotka, Finland

Telephone +358 5 211 44 **Fax** +358 5 211 4500

Website www.kristinacruises.com

Area operated Scandinavia, Mediterranean and Red Sea (KRISTINA REGINA) Finnish lakes and coast (KRISTINA BRAHE)

KRISTINA BRAHE	1105gt	1943	12.0k	D2	80p	176p	24c	56.5m	10.1m	2.8m	FI
KRISTINA REGINA	4295gt	1960	14.5k	D1	238p	381p	55c	99.8m	15.3m	5.5m	FI

KRISTINA BRAHE was built in 1943 by the Pullman Standard Car Manufacturing Company of Chicago, Illinois, USA as the US warship PCE 830, later BEC 4. Subsequently she became the British naval ship HMS KILCHERNAN. She was sold to Norwegian owners and rebuilt as the coastal passenger ferry SUNNHORDLAND. She began cruising as the KRISTINA BRAHE for Fagerlines on the coasts and lakes of Finland in 1975, passing to her current owner in 1985. She is named after the wife of the one time Regent of Finland, Peter Brahe. IMO 5345065

KRISTINA REGINA was built by AB Oskarshamns Varv (yard number 353) at Oskarshamn in Sweden as the steamship BORE for Bore Line's Baltic Sea services. She was the last steamship to be built for service in Scandinavia. Bore Line was part of the Silja Line consortium. In 1977 she began a summer ferry service across the top of the Gulf of Bothnia as the BOREA for Bore Line subsidiary, Jakob Line. In 1984 she was sold to Ab Helsingfors Steamship Company of Helsinki and chartered to Oy Aura Line Ab of Turku for ferry service between Turku and Stockholm. Aura Line failed in the same year and the ship was laid up. In the following year she was sold to the Vanderbilt Steamship Company of Vancouver and was to have been renamed VANDERBILT. However, the sale fell through and she continued in lay-up. Her current owner acquired her in 1987 and she was immediately re-engined with diesels and following refurbishment was set to work cruising in the Baltic Sea as the KRISTINA REGINA. She later had two very substantial interior refits to bring her up to her current high standard. The ship is named after the 17th century Queen Kristina of Sweden and Finland. IMO 5048485

LINDBLAD EXPEDITIONS

The Company Lindblad Expeditions was founded in 1979 by Sven-Olof Lindblad, as a development from Lindblad Travel, which had been established some twenty years earlier by his father. From the spring of 2005 Lindblad teamed up with National Geographic in the marketing and operation of the company's expedition ships. At that time the ENDEAVOUR, was renamed as the NATIONAL GEOGRAPHIC ENDEAVOUR, and subsequently the other ships have taken the National Geographic prefix.

President Sven Lindblad

Address 96 Morton Street, 9th Floor, New York, NY 10014, United States of America

Telephone +1 212 765 7740

Website www.expeditions.com

Area operated Arctic, Northern Europe, the Americas and Antarctica (ENDEAVOUR), Galapagos Islands (POLARIS and ISLANDER), Alaska and Baja California (SEA BIRD and SEA LION)

NATIONAL GEOGRAPHIC ENDEAVOUR	3132gt	1966	15.0k	D1	124p	138p	63c	89.1m	14.0m	6.6m	BS
NATIONAL GEOGRAPHIC EXPLORER	6471gt	1982	17.5k	D2	148p	148p	34c	108.6m	16.5m	4.6m	BS

Kristina Cruises' **Kristina Regina** at Naples *(Bill Lawes)*

Lindblad Expeditions' **National Geographic Endeavour** *(Ben Lyons)*

NATIONAL GEOGRAPHIC ISLANDER	1065gt	1995	14.0k	D2	48p	48p	20c	49.9m	13.5m	1.9m	EC
NATIONAL GEOGRAPHIC POLARIS	2138gt	1960	14.0k	D2	82p	82p	32c	72.1m	13.0m	4.3m	EC
NATIONAL GEOGRAPHIC SEA BIRD	630gt	1982	12.0k	D1	62p	70p	41c	46.3m	9.4m	2.4m	US
NATIONAL GEOGRAPHIC SEA LION	630gt	1982	12.0k	D1	62p	70p	41c	46.3m	9.4m	2.4m	US
SEA VOYAGER	1195gt	1982	12.0k	D2	63p	63p	21c	51.9m	11.0m	m	HN

NATIONAL GEOGRAPHIC ENDEAVOUR was once a fishing trawler, built by AG Weser (yard number 917) at Bremerhaven, Germany as the MARBURG for German owners. In 1982 she became the LINDMAR and during the following year was converted at Gothenburg into the cruise ship NORTH STAR for Fearney & Eger of Oslo. She entered service for North Star Line in 1983 on Scandinavian cruises, switching to the Mediterranean in the winter. In 1986 she was chartered to Exploration Cruises and Holidays of Seattle, USA for service on the Alaskan coast. Three years later, her charterers were in financial trouble and the NORTH STAR was sold to the Caledonian Steamship Company, renamed CALEDONIAN STAR and chartered to Salen-Lindblad. From 1993 the ship was marketed in the UK by Noble Caledonia and in the USA by Special Expeditions. The latter company acquired the CALEDONIAN STAR in 1997, and in 2000 became Lindblad Expeditions, renaming the ship as ENDEAVOUR during the following year. In March 2005 she was renamed NATIONAL GEOGRAPHIC ENDEAVOUR. In November 2007 she assisted in the rescue operation for the sinking EXPLORER of GAP Adventures. The most famous ENDEAVOUR was that of Captain James Cook, whose epic voyages of discovery took place between 1768 and 1771. IMO 6611863

NATIONAL GEOGRAPHIC EXPLORER was built by Ulstein Hatlo (yard number 176) at Ulsteinvik in Norway, as the MIDNATSOL. She was renamed MIDNATSOL II and laid up in 2003, following the delivery of the new MIDNATSOL. Her proposed sale to Canadian owners in 2005 fell through, and she returned to service on the Hurtigruten as the LYNGEN in the winter of 2005/2006. She has also operated on the coastal voyage over the winter of 2006/2007. She was acquired by Lindblad for US$8.6m in October 2007 and after a major refit was renamed NATIONAL GEOGRAPHIC EXPLORER and entered service in the summer of 2008. IMO 8019356

NATIONAL GEOGRAPHIC ISLANDER is operated by Ecoventura and chartered to Lindblad for specific cruises. She was built by Chantiers Navale de Marseille (yard number B210) at Marseilles, France as the RIVAGES GUADELOUPE. Between 2002 and 2004 she was cruising in and around Scotland as the LORD OF THE HIGHLANDS (she is a near sister to LORD OF THE GLENS) for Highland Lord Steamship Company, but entered service in the Galapagos Islands as the ISLANDER in early 2005 for ETICA, by whom she is still owned. She took the National Geographic prefix in 2008. IMO 9139878

NATIONAL GEOGRAPHIC POLARIS was built by Solvesborgs Varv (yard number 55) at Solvesborg Sweden as the ORESUND, a passenger car ferry for service between Copenhagen, Denmark and Malmo, Sweden. In 1981 she was purchased by Salen Lines and chartered to Lindblad as the expedition ship LINDBLAD POLARIS. She was sold to Lindblad in 1987 and renamed POLARIS. Her name was lengthened in late 2007. IMO 5264704

NATIONAL GEOGRAPHIC SEA BIRD was owned by Majestic Alaska Boat Co and operated under charter to Lindblad. That company acquired the vessel in 2007. She was built by Nichols Bros (yard number S62) at Freeland, Washington State, USA as the MAJESTIC EXPLORER, but renamed as the SEA BIRD within nine months. Her NATIONAL GEOGRAPHIC prefix appeared late in 2007. IMO 8966444

NATIONAL GEOGRAPHIC SEA LION is registered under the ownership of SPEX Sea Lion (now a Lindblad group company). She was built by Nichols Bros (yard number S63) at Freeland, Washington State, USA as the GREAT RIVERS EXPLORER, but became the SEA LION in 1989. Her prefix was added in 2008. IMO 8966456

SEA VOYAGER was built by the Chesapeake Marine Railway Company in Baltimore, USA as the AMERICA. She later became the TEMPTRESS VOYAGER and took her current name in 2002 when acquired by Voyager Holdings. She is currently operating for Lindblad in Baja California, Costa Rica and Nicaragua. IMO 8963753

Lindblad Expeditions' **National Geographic Sea Bird** at San Francisco *(Andrew Kilk)*

Lord Nelson Seereisen's **Mona Lisa** at Piraeus *(Ben Lyons)*

Louis Cruise Lines' **Aquamarine** *(Richard Seville)*

LORD NELSON SEEREISEN

The Company Lord Nelson Seereisen is the successor to Holiday Kreuzfahrten, the former charterer of the MONA LISA that was declared bankrupt in 2006.

Managing Director Herbert Fervers

Address Brusseler Allee 12, 41812 Erkelenz, Germany

Telephone +49 2431 94330 **Fax** +49 2431 9433299

Website www.lord-nelson-seereisen.de

Area operated Baltic Sea and Norway, round Great Britain

MONA LISA	28891gt	1966	21.5k	D2	728p	782p	336c	201.2m	26.5m	8.6m	BS

MONA LISA was built by John Brown & Co (Clydebank) Ltd (yard number 728) on the River Clyde in Scotland, as the immensely elegant KUNGSHOLM for Swedish America Line's service from Gothenburg to New York. As that trade declined she switched to cruising and was subsequently sold to Flagship Cruises. In 1978 she was acquired by the Peninsular and Oriental Steam Navigation Company and after a drastic conversion, which included the loss of most of the forward funnel, entered service as the SEA PRINCESS. She initially replaced the ARCADIA in February 1979 in the Australian market, where she remained until 1982. She was then transferred to the British market, where she remained until 1986, operating alongside the CANBERRA. She then served Princess Cruises for five years before returning to the United Kingdom in 1991. She was renamed VICTORIA in March 1995, and at the end of 2002 was sold to the Greek controlled Leonardo Shipping and renamed MONA LISA for long-term charter to Holiday Kreuzfahrten to serve the growing German cruise demand. In September 2006 the operator was declared bankrupt and the MONA LISA was returned to her owner. Subsequently she was chartered for use as an accommodation ship at the 2006 Asian Games in Doha. She is currently registered as owned by Leonardo Shipping, a subsidiary of Kyma Ship Management. In early 2007 she was taken on a two x eight-month charter (with an option for a third term) as THE SCHOLAR SHIP, a university at sea, supported by Royal Caribbean Cruise Line. It therefore seemed logical the she should use the remainder of the year with Pullmantur Cruises, for which service she was renamed OCEANIC II. Following the loss of the SEA DIAMOND, the OCEANIC II was chartered to Louis Cruise Lines for one or two cruises, prior to taking up her Pullmantur duties. The OCEANIC II, under the guise THE SHCOLAR SHIP, completed her first two voyages, but due to lack of funding was unable to take the second year's programme. During the summer of 2008 she was chartered to Lord Nelson Seereisen, reviving the name MONA LISA, and is employed in a similar way in 2009. However, while laid up for the winter 2008/9 she was hastily reactivated to take over the role of The Peaceboat, following a string of mechanical problems with the CLIPPER PACIFIC. Although moves are afoot to preserve her in Gothenburg, as with so many of these proposed rescues, it is likely that nothing will come of it and the ship will go for scrap in 2010. IMO 6512354

LOUIS CRUISE LINES

The Company Louis began chartering passenger ships soon after the end of the Second World War, but did not actually begin owning its own vessels until the PRINCESSA MARISSA was acquired in 1987. The company also offers management services and is involved in the leisure industry. Louis was a major shareholder in the recently defunct Royal Olympic Cruises, but stepped in to fill the breach with Louis Hellenic Cruises. Louis Hellenic Cruises was a Greek-registered company set up by Louis Cruise Lines principally to operate cruises calling at Turkish ports, a destination not available to Greek Cypriot flagged vessels. The company suffered a major setback on 5 April 2007 when the Group's newest ship, the SEA DIAMOND, hit rocks on the approach to Santorini and after evacuation of passengers and crew, sank 15 hours later, close to the island's ferry port. In order to continue to provide the SEA DIAMOND's itineraries, the THOMSON SPIRIT was used for the first half of April, followed by THE EMERALD and finally the OCEANIC II (formerly the MONA LISA) on charter for most of May. That was followed by the RUBY (OCEAN COUNTESS) and eventually the permanent replacement was the CRISTAL. Louis Hellenic Cruises appears to have been disbanded and the ships have been incorporated into the Louis Cruise Lines fleet. Louis Cruise Lines is a subsidiary of the Cypriot-quoted Louis plc.

Chairman and CEO Costakis Loizou

Louis Cruise Lines' **Coral** sailing from Palma *(William Mayes)*

Louis Cruise Lines' **Cristal** in Istanbul *(William Mayes)*

Louis Cruise Lines' **Ivory** *(Bruce Peter)*

Address Louis House, 20 Amphipoleos Street, 2025 Strovolos, Nicosia TT 21301, 1506 Nicosia, Cyprus

Telephone +357 255 88168 **Fax** +357 224 42949

Website www.louiscruises.com

Area operated Mediterranean Sea and charters, Greek Islands and Turkey from Piraeus

AQUAMARINE	23149gt	1971	21.0k	D2	1056p	1160p	400c	193.3m	24.0m	6.7m	GR
CORAL	14194gt	1971	21.0k	D2	676p	912p	285c	148.1m	21.5m	5.9m	CY
CRISTAL	25611gt	1980	21.0k	D2	1096p	1452p	180c	158.9m	25.2m	5.6m	GR
IVORY	12549gt	1957	20.7k	ST2	505p	750p	210c	159.3m	21.2m	6.9m	MH
LOUIS MAJESTY	40876gt	1992	21.0k	D2	1460p	1790p	550c	207.3m	27.6m	5.8m	BS
ORIENT QUEEN	15781gt	1968	20.0k	D2	728p	912p	315c	160.1m	22.8m	6.7m	MH
SAPPHIRE	12263gt	1967	16.0k	D2	563p	650p	240c	149.0m	20.7m	6.4m	MH
THE AEGEAN PEARL	16710gt	1971	21.5k	D2	790p	1095p	326c	163.3m	22.8m	6.5m	GR
THE CALYPSO	11162gt	1967	18.5k	D2	486p	594p	240c	135.4m	19.2m	6.1m	GR
THE EMERALD	26428gt	1958	20.0k	ST2	960p	1198p	412c	177.9m	25.6m	8.3m	MT
THOMSON DESTINY	37773gt	1982	19.0k	D2	1450p	1595p	540c	214.5m	28.4m	7.0m	CY
THOMSON SPIRIT	33930gt	1983	18.0k	D2	1254p	1374p	209c	214.7m	27.2m	7.5m	CY

AQUAMARINE was the second ship in the founding fleet of the new Royal Caribbean Cruise Line when delivered. She was built by Wartsila (yard number 393) in Helsinki, Finland as the NORDIC PRINCE for year-round service in the Caribbean Sea. In 1980 she returned to her builder to have a new 26m mid section inserted, increasing her passenger capacity from 714 to 1194. By 1994 she had served out her useful life with Royal Caribbean and was sold to Airtours, one of the UK's largest package holiday operators. She was placed into service as the CAROUSEL under the Sun Cruises banner. Airtours pulled out of cruising in late 2004 and Louis Cruise Lines acquired the ship and renamed her AQUAMARINE. In 2007 she was chartered to Transocean Tours and operated as the ARIELLE. Transocean Tours used this ship to operate a number of cruises from the UK in 2007. In 2008 Transocean Tours had the use of the MARCO POLO so did not need the ARIELLE, which returned to Louis and reverted to her previous name, AQUAMARINE. She currently runs on short cruises from Piraeus. IMO 7027411

CORAL was built by the Rotterdam Drydock Company (yard number 329) at Rotterdam in The Netherlands as the CUNARD ADVENTURER for Cunard Line's new venture into Caribbean cruising in purpose built ships. She was replaced by a larger ship and sold to Kloster's Norwegian Caribbean Cruise Line in 1977 when she was renamed SUNWARD II. In 1991 she was acquired by Epirotiki Lines and renamed TRITON for cruising in the Eastern Mediterranean. On the merger with Sun Cruises she became part of the new Royal Olympic fleet, but on the final demise of that business was sold at auction in April 2005 to Louis Cruise Lines. In May 2005 she was renamed CORAL. In 2009 she operates from Genoa and Marseilles. IMO 7046936

CRISTAL as we see her now was completed in 1992 by the Rauma Yard at Rauma, Finland as the SALLY ALBATROSS, using the lower hull parts of the previous SALLY ALBATROSS destroyed by fire in 1991 while refitting in Stockholm. That ship had been built in 1980 by Wartsila (yard number 309) at Turku, Finland as the VIKING SAGA for Rederi AB Sally, then part of the Viking Line consortium. She served the Stockholm to Helsinki overnight route until replaced by the OLYMPIA in 1986, then switching to a new role, cruising mainly from Helsinki. She was later rebuilt with a rather more streamlined forward superstructure. In her current incarnation, she cruised in the Baltic Sea for Sally Line until March 1994, when she ran aground on the approach to Helsinki. She went to La Spezia for repairs and while there her after decks were rebuilt. She was then chartered to Norwegian Cruise Line and renamed LEEWARD for Caribbean service; her first cruise departed in July 1995. At the end of that charter she was taken up by Star Cruises in 2000 and as the SUPERSTAR TAURUS operated for a while in the Far East. She moved to Silja Cruise in 2002 and offered short cruises in the Baltic as the SILJA OPERA. With the sale of Silja Line in 2006 to Tallink, the SILJA OPERA was surplus to requirements and was retained by Sea Containers. She subsequently moved to Tilbury, England for lay up and was renamed OPERA. After the loss of the SEA DIAMOND, Louis needed a new ship quickly and the OPERA was just about all that was available. She was refitted and renamed CRISTAL, entering service in the summer of 2007. IMO 7827213

IVORY was the last ship in the post-war rebuilding programme of the major Italian operator, Adriatica of Venice. She was delivered by Cantieri Riuniti dell'Adriatico (yard number 1821) at Monfalcone, Italy

Louis Cruise Lines' **Orient Queen** arriving at Rhodes *(William Mayes)*

Louis Cruise Lines' **Sapphire** at Civitavecchia *(Rick Frendt)*

Louis Cruise Lines' **The Aegean Pearl** at Piraeus *(Richard Seville)*

as the AUSONIA and was immediately placed in service between Trieste, Venice, Brindisi, Alexandria and Beirut. She accommodated passengers in three classes and was the first large Italian passenger ship to be fitted with Denny Brown stabilisers. In 1978 she was converted for cruising and placed under the management of Italia Crociere Internazionali. Sicula Oceanica later operated her. She was acquired by Louis Cruise Lines in 1998 and initially chartered to UK tour operator First Choice. Louis subsequently used her for its own account. It was suggested that she was to be renamed ITHACA for the 2005 season, but that did not happen. In May 2006 she was renamed THE AUSONIA, but changed her name again a month later to IVORY. She operated for Golden Star cruises in 2007 as the AEGEAN TWO, but returned to the Louis fleet in 2008. She is currently laid up and is expected to go for breaking in 2010. IMO 5031078

LOUIS MAJESTY was laid down for Birka Line of Mariehamn, Aland Islands by Wartsila (yard number 1312) at Turku, Finland. She was to have been named BIRKA QUEEN. Following the failure of Wartsila, the ship was completed by Kvaerner Masa Yards for Majesty Cruise Line as the ROYAL MAJESTY and made her maiden voyage from Southampton to New York in July 1992. She was 32,396 tons and 173.5 metres long as built and subsequently operated for Dolphin Cruise Line. She passed to Norwegian Cruise Line in 1997 and was renamed NORWEGIAN MAJESTY. In 1999 she was lengthened by 33.8 metres by Lloydwerft at Bremerhaven, Germany by means of a new mid-section constructed by Aker MTW at Wismar, Germany. She was sold to Louis Cruise Lines in 2008, but continues to operate on Caribbean itineraries for NCL until delivered to Louis in late 2009, at which time she will be renamed LOUIS MAJESTY for Western Mediterranean itineraries. IMO 8814744

ORIENT QUEEN was built by AG Weser Werk Seebeck (yard number 935) at Bremerhaven, Germany as the STARWARD for Kloster's Norwegian Caribbean Cruise Line. She spent the bulk of her career with NCCL cruising in the Caribbean. In 1995 she became the BOLERO following her sale to Festival Cruises. For Festival she initially cruised in the Mediterranean but was later chartered out to other operators, including Britain's First Choice in 2000 and the now defunct Spanish Cruise Line in 2001. Following the collapse of Festival Cruises in early 2004 she was laid up at Gibraltar. She was registered under the ownership of Cruise Elenora in February 2004 and renamed as the ORIENT QUEEN in November 2004 She commenced service in the Eastern Mediterranean in the summer of 2005 for Abou Merhi Lines. In late 2005 she was positioned to Dubai but her programme there was unsuccessful. She was to have cruised from Beirut again in 2006, but further troubles in the area may have curtailed or prevented this programme in its entirety. In 2006 Abou Merhi Lines pulled out of the cruising market and chartered the ORIENT QUEEN to Louis Cruise lines for five years with an option to purchase. She was quickly chartered to the United States Military Sealift Command for the purpose of rescuing Americans stranded in Beirut. Subsequently she was chartered to Delphin Kreuzfarhten for a world cruise in place of the delayed DELPHIN VOYAGER. For 2009 she operates from Piraeus. IMO 6821080

SAPPHIRE has had a long and interesting history, as she spends what are likely to be her final years cruising in the Eastern Mediterranean. She was built by Cantieri Navale Felszegi (yard number 76) at Trieste, Italy as the ITALIA for Crociere d'Oltremare of Cagliari, Sicily. She was almost immediately chartered to the newly established Princess Cruises. She was marketed as PRINCESS ITALIA, but not renamed. In 1973 she was chartered to Costa Line for Caribbean cruising, and later that year Costa bought the ship. Seven years later she was sold to Ocean Cruise Lines and renamed OCEAN PRINCESS. In 1990 she was acquired by Croisieres Paquet for whom she operated until sold in 1993 to Ellis Marine of Greece, following a partial sinking after striking a wreck at the mouth of the Amazon, which rendered her a constructive total loss. She was refurbished in Piraeus and later renamed SEA PRINCE. Later she carried the name SEA PRINCE V, but reverted to SEA PRINCE before being sold to Louis Cruise Lines who renamed her PRINCESA OCEANICA. In 1996 she was chartered to UK tour operator Thomson Holidays for whom she was renamed SAPPHIRE. In 1999 France Croisieres chartered her and she has subsequently operated on other charters and for Louis' own account. For 2009 the SAPPHIRE cruises from Cyprus. Sapphire is a coloured gemstone, usually bright blue. IMO 6313994

THE AEGEAN PEARL was one of the first generation of purpose-built cruise ships, delivered by Cantieri Naval dell Tirreno e Riuniti (yard number 288) at Riva Trigoso in Italy as the SOUTHWARD for Kloster's Norwegian Caribbean Cruise Line. She served her owner well for almost 25 years before passing to UK tour operator Airtours, whose cruise operation later became Sun Cruises. In her new role she was renamed as the SEAWING. Ownership passed to the Louis group and she continued to operate for Airtours. When Airtours, by now renamed as My Travel, pulled out of cruising in 2004 she was earmarked for further use with Louis Cruise Lines, but was then switched to Louis Hellenic

Cruises, as the PERLA. Following a charter to Golden Star Cruises in 2008 she was renamed THE AEGEAN PEARL, a name that she has retained now that she is back with Louis Cruises. THE AEGEAN PEARL now operates short cruises from Piraeus. IMO 7111078

THE CALYPSO was built by Navalmeccanica (yard number 645) at Castellammare di Stabia, Italy as the car ferry CANGURO VERDE for Italian operator Traghetti Sardi. She sailed between Genoa and Sardinia in competition with Italian state owned operator, Tirrenia, and along with her sisters was eventually chartered to that company. In 1981 she was sold to a Saudi owner, renamed DURR and set to work as a pilgrim carrier. She was sold to Greek ferry operator Strintzis Lines in 1989, along with her sister, the YUM (previously CANGURO BRUNO) and was renamed as the IONIAN HARMONY. She spent two seasons on Adriatic Sea services before being sold again, this time to Danish Cruise Line. She was renamed SUN FIESTA for Caribbean cruising, but it is thought that she never actually entered service. In 1992 she was auctioned by the US Admiralty Marshall, acquired by the owner of Regency Cruise Line and towed to Greece. She was substantially rebuilt and emerged as the cruise ship REGENT JEWEL. She never actually entered service under that name and by the autumn of 1994 she was the CALYPSO, on charter to Germany's Transocean Tours. Her owners eventually collapsed and the National Bank of Greece seized the ship in 1999. Louis Cruise Lines purchased her in 2000, and she continued to operate short cruises in the Eastern Mediterranean. In April 2005 she was renamed as THE CALYPSO and in the following year, a season of cruising from Tilbury, England was severely curtailed following an engine room fire. From 2007 she has been chartered to Thomson for part of the year for cruises in the Eastern Mediterranean and the Black Sea. Calypso was the daughter of Atlas, who in Homer's Odyssey entertained Odysseus for seven years. The Thomson charter finishes in 2009 and THE CALYPSO is expected to be used on a new itinerary for Louis that involves a Corinth Canal transit. IMO 6715372

THE EMERALD, built as the SANTA ROSA by Newport News Shipbuilding and Dry Dock Company (yard number 521) at Newport News, USA for Grace Line of New York, served the company's New York to Central America service for 13 years before being laid up at Hampton Roads. She remained there for 18 years until she was acquired by Coral Cruise Lines in 1989 and towed to Greece for rebuilding. She was renamed PACIFIC SUN, then DIAMOND ISLAND before finally coming back into service as the RAINBOW in 1992 for a Caribbean cruise programme. In 1993 she passed to Regency Cruises as the REGENT RAINBOW, but following the failure of that company she was laid up again. Louis Cruise Lines acquired her in 1996 and she was renamed THE EMERALD, and the following year began a long-term seasonal charter to Thomson Cruises. In the spring she usually operated for Louis Cruise Lines on short itineraries from Piraeus, but for Thomson's season she was based in Corfu for Aegean and Adriatic Sea itineraries. For the winter of 2007/2008 she was chartered to an Australian tour operator. Her 11-year seasonal charter to Thomson finished in 2008 and she has returned to the Louis fleet. In 2009 she cruises from Cyprus. IMO 5312824

THOMSON DESTINY This ship was purchased by Louis in 2008 having previously been chartered in and out. See under Thomson Cruises (TUI).

THOMSON SPIRIT This ship was purchased by Louis in 2008 having previously been chartered in and out. See under Thomson Cruises (TUI).

MAGNA CARTA STEAMSHIP COMPANY

The Company Magna Carta Steamship Company is a British registered operator of coastal, canal and lake cruises around Scotland, formed in 1999.

Address 136 Hamilton Terrace, London NW6 9UX

Telephone +44 207 328 1123 **Fax** +44 207 604 3634

Website www.magnacarta.bz

Area operated Scotland

LORD OF THE GLENS	729gt	1985	18.0k	D2	54p	54p	18c	45.0m	10.5m	3.2m	GB

LORD OF THE GLENS was built in Greece as the VICTORIA. She was renamed VICTORIA II in 1999 and took her current name in 2000, following a major refit. She is a near sister to the NATIONAL GEOGRAPHIC ISLANDER. IMO 8966470

MAJESTIC CRUISE LINES

The Company Majestic Cruise Lines is an American owned company operating the FREEWINDS on behalf of the International Association of Scientologists.

Address 118 North Fort Harrison Avenue, Clearwater, Florida 33755-4040, United States of America

Telephone +1 727 445 4309 **Fax** +1 727 445 4339

Website www.scientology.org/en_US/religion/groups/pg011.html

Area operated Caribbean

| FREEWINDS | 9780gt | 1968 | 20.0k | D2 | 468p | 500p | 170c | 134.3m | 19.9m | 5.5m | PA |

FREEWINDS was built by Wartsila (yard number 1161) at Turku, Finland as the BOHEME for Wallenius Lines for charter to Commodore Cruise Lines for Caribbean cruising. She was sold to Sally Shipping in 1981 and passed to Sally subsidiary Hanseatic Caribbean Shipping later that year. In 1986 she was acquired by the International Association of Scientologists and registered under the ownership of San Donato Properties Corporation and renamed FREEWINDS. She is operated by Majestic Cruises for scientologist members. IMO 6810811

MAJESTIC INTERNATIONAL CRUISES

The Company Majestic International Cruises is a cruise ship-owning company that does not appear to operate ships for its own account.

President Michael Lambros

Address 87 Akti Miaouli, 18538 Piraeus, Greece

Telephone +30 211 1002020 **Fax** +30 211 1002029

Website www.mccruises.gr

Area operated Aegean Islands and Turkey

| OCEAN COUNTESS | 16795gt | 1976 | 18.5k | D2 | 814p | 950p | 350c | 163.6m | 22.8m | 5.8m | PT |
| OCEAN MAJESTY | 10417gt | 1966 | 20.0k | D2 | 500p | 613p | 235c | 130.6m | 19.2m | 5.4m | PT |

OCEAN COUNTESS started life as one of a pair of second-generation Caribbean cruise ships for Cunard Line. She was built by Burmeister & Wain (yard number 858) at Copenhagen, Denmark as the CUNARD COUNTESS. She served the company for twenty years before being sold for service in the Far East as the AWANI DREAM 2. In 1998 she was acquired by Royal Olympic Cruises and renamed OLYMPIC COUNTESS for service mainly in the Mediterranean. In 2002, under pressure from the International Olympic Committee, the company changed its name to Royal Olympia Cruises and the ship followed suit, becoming the OLYMPIA COUNTESS. Following the collapse of that company she passed to Majestic International Cruises in 2004, and was chartered to Globalia for the summer of 2005 as the OCEAN COUNTESS. She was then chartered to Holiday Kreuzfahrten as their second ship and renamed as the LILI MARLEEN. That company ran into financial difficulties and ceased trading in the summer of 2006. In 2007 she was returned to her owners and was chartered to Louis Cruise Lines as the RUBY, as part of that company's replacement programme for the SEA DIAMOND. In summer 2009 she is on charter to Quail Cruises as the NEW PACIFIC, her eighth name. IMO 7358561

OCEAN MAJESTY was built by Union Naval de Levante (yard number 93) in Valencia, Spain as the car ferry JUAN MARCH for Spain's state carrier, Compania Trasmediterranea. She was one of a series of four ships designed for both the overnight Barcelona to Palma, Majorca run and the longer route from Barcelona to the Canary Islands. She was sold in 1985 to Sol Maritime Services of Limassol, Cyprus and renamed SOL CHRISTIANA and placed on a new service linking Piraeus with Crete, Rhodes, Cyprus and Israel. The service was not a success and she was sold to another Cypriot operator, renamed KYPROS STAR and set to work as a ferry serving Rhodes, Cyprus and Egypt from Piraeus. In 1988 she operated for Italy's Adriatica and sailed between Brindisi in Italy and Patras in Greece. Between 1989 and 1994 the ship underwent a total transformation, emerging as the cruise ship OCEAN MAJESTY. She was initially chartered to Epirotiki Line as the OLYMPIC and again for the following year as the HOMERIC. For 1995 the ship was sub-chartered to Page & Moy Holidays for a number of cruises. Subsequently she has made regular appearances in the Page & Moy cruise programme, but 2009 will be her last season. She is now owned by Majestic International Cruises. IMO 6602898

Louis Cruise Lines' **The Emerald** passing through the Bosphorus *(William Mayes)*

Majestic Cruise Line's **Freewinds** at Barbados *(Rick Frendt)*

Majestic International Cruises' **Ocean Countess** as the **Ruby** in Piraeus *(William Mayes)*

MEDITERRANEAN CLASSIC CRUISES

The Company Mediterranean Classic Cruises, the successor to Monarch Classic Cruises is the cruise ship-operating subsidiary of Majestic International Cruises, a Greek passenger ship owning company was established in 2006. The company advertised cruises on the ATHENA for 2009 and was also advertising cruises on Golden Star Cruises' VISION STAR. However neither charter materialised and for 2009 the company has entered into an arrangement with EasyCruise to sell space on the EASYCRUISE LIFE.

Address 87 Akti Miaouli, 18538 Piraeus, Greece

Telephone +30 211 1002020 **Fax** +30 211 1002029

Website www.mccruises.gr

Area operated Eastern Mediterranean on the EASYCRUISE LIFE (see Easycruise)

MANO MARITIME

The Company Mano Maritime is a company within the Mano Holdings Group, an Israeli private company in the maritime and leisure sectors. Mordechai Mano founded Mano Maritime in 1945. The company's third passenger ship, THE JASMINE, was sold for service as a ferry in the Red Sea in 2006. That ship is now with EasyCruise as the EASYCRUISE LIFE. In 2009 the company acquired MSC's RHAPSODY.

President Moshe Mano

Address 2 Pal-Yam Avenue, PO Box 1400, Haifa 33031 Israel

Telephone +972 4 860 6666 **Fax** +972 4 866 7666

Website www.mano.co.il

Area operated Eastern Mediterranean and Black Seas, passenger service between Haifa and Odessa in association with Vival Marine

GOLDEN IRIS	17095gt	1977	18.5k	D2	800p	1000p	350c	163.6m	22.8m	6.0m	PA
ROYAL IRIS	14717gt	1971	18.0k	D2	720p	1000p	330c	142.1m	21.9m	5.5m	PA
THE IRIS	12825gt	1982	17.5k	D2	500p	650p	170c	137.1m	21.0m	5.8m	MT

GOLDEN IRIS was built for Cunard as the CUNARD PRINCESS (launched as the CUNARD CONQUEST) by Burmeister & Wain (yard number 859) in Copenhagen, Denmark for service in the Caribbean Sea. She was acquired by Mediterranean Shipping Cruises in 1995 and renamed RHAPSODY. In 2006 her registry was changed from Italy to Panama on transfer from MSC Crociere to fellow MSC subsidiary, Gramerco International. Following her return from South Africa in the spring of 2009, she was sold to Mano Maritime and renamed GOLDEN IRIS. IMO 7358573

ROYAL IRIS began life as the EAGLE for Southern Ferries, a company owned by the Peninsular and Oriental Steam Navigation Company. She was built by Dubigeon-Normandie (yard number 123) at Nantes, France as a car ferry for service between Southampton, Lisbon and Tangiers. In December 1975 she was sold to Nouvelle Compagnie de Paquebots, Marseilles for service in the Mediterranean Sea as the AZUR. In early 1982 she underwent conversion to become a pure cruise ship and she continued to serve her owners until sold to Chandris Lines in 1987, at which time she was renamed as THE AZUR. In 1995 she became the first ship in the new fleet of Festival Cruises, but was not officially renamed, although she carried the name AZUR for some time. When Festival Cruises failed in early 2004, she was laid up at Gibraltar and briefly renamed ELOISE prior to being acquired by Golden Cruises for operation by Mano Maritime. She was renamed ROYAL IRIS in late 2004, and underwent a refit at the Perama shipyard in Greece. IMO 7032997

THE IRIS was built by Stocznia Szczecinska (yard number B492/03) in Szczecin, Poland as the KONSTANTIN SIMONOV, the third of a series of seven ships for the Baltic Shipping Company. She operated as a ferry, serving the ports of Leningrad, Riga and Helsinki. From 1992 she ran for Baltic Shipping Company subsidiary, Baltic Line. In 1996 she passed to Pakartin Shipping and was renamed FRANCESCA. Her Australian employment failed and she was eventually laid up in Wilhelmshaven, Germany. In 2000 she was acquired by Silver Cruises and renamed THE IRIS for operation by Mano Maritime. IMO 7625811

Mano Maritime's **Royal Iris** *(Richard Seville)*

Mano Maritime's **The Iris** off Piraeus *(Rick Frendt)*

Mitsui OSK's **Nippon Maru** at San Francisco *(Andrew Kilk)*

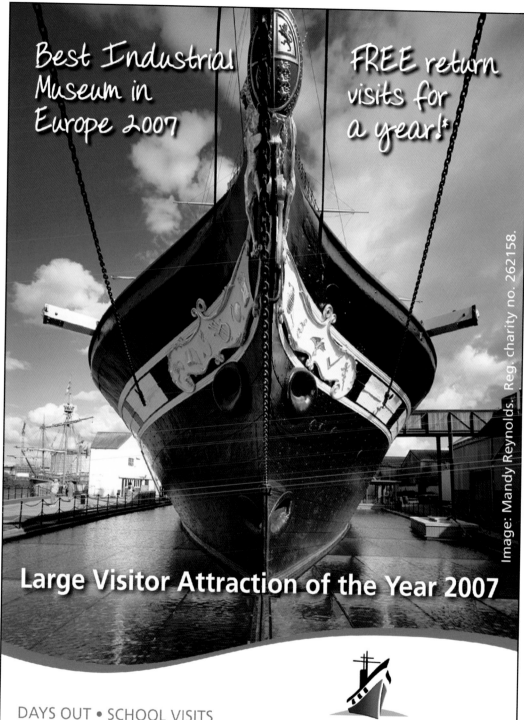

Best Industrial Museum in Europe 2007

FREE return visits for a year!*

Image: Mandy Reynolds. Reg. charity no. 262158.

Large Visitor Attraction of the Year 2007

DAYS OUT • SCHOOL VISITS
VENUE HIRE • WEDDINGS
www.ssgreatbritain.org

*Excludes groups and venue hire

BRUNEL'S
ss GREAT BRITAIN
THE WORLD'S FIRST GREAT OCEAN LINER

METROPOLIS TUR

The Company Metropolis Tur is a Russian tour operator, operating cruises for Russian passengers. The company has operated the DALMACIJA, the ASSEDO and the OLVIA in recent years. In 2005 the ORANGE MELODY, formerly the BERLIN and latterly the SPIRIT OF ADVENTURE operated for the company for a season. In 2006 it was expected that the ENCHANTED CAPRI would be chartered, but in the event the ship used was the GRAND VICTORIA (now the BLUE MONARCH of Monarch Classic Cruises). For 2008, the unexpectedly available VAN GOGH ran for the season.

Address Moscow, Russia

Telephone +7 095 788 0979 **Fax** +7 095 292 9447

Website www.mkruiz.ru

Area operated Black and Mediterranean Seas but schedules and ship information not available at time of going to press.

METROPOLITAN TOURING (ETICA)

The Company Metropolitan Touring, founded in 1953, is one of Ecuador's leading travel companies and operator of expedition cruise ships within the Galapagos Islands. Space on most sailings is block-booked by various US and European tour operators.

President Roque Sevilla

Address De Las Palmeras Avenue N45-74 and De Las Orquideas, PO Box 17-17-1649, Quito, Ecuador

Telephone +593 2 298 8200 **Fax** +593 2 334 1250

Website www.galapagosvoyages.com

Area operated Galapagos Islands

ISABELA II	‡1025gt	1979	12.0k	D2	40p	40p	24c	53.7m	11.6m	3.4m	EC
LA PINTA	1438gt	1983	12.0k	D2	32p	48p	24c	63.0m	12.0m	3.2m	EC
SANTA CRUZ	1602gt	1979	13.0k	D2	90p	90p	50c	72.3m	11.8m	3.2m	EC

ISABELA II was built by Halter Marine (yard number 848) at Patterson, Louisiana, USA as the offshore supply ship CINDY BRILEY. In 1985 she became the CARL B DOWNS and took her present name in 1988 when she passed to ETICA. She was converted in the same year for use as a cruise ship in the Galapagos Islands. IMO 7914535

LA PINTA was built by Astilleros Construcciones (yard number 175) at Vigo, Spain as the ferry CITANIA for local service around Vigo. She subsequently became the SEA TRAVELLER II, then the SEA LINER before reverting to her original name in 1992. Three years later she was the SUN JO 1, for an Israeli controlled Florida based company. She became ETICA's PINTA I in 2007 following a major reconstruction in Peru, and was renamed as LA PINTA in 2009. IMO 8112897

SANTA CRUZ was built by Astilleros y Talleres Celaya (yard number 178) at Bilbao, Spain as the SANTA CRUZ for ETICA. She underwent a major reconstruction in Chile in 1998. IMO 7811721

MITSUI OSK PASSENGER LINES

The Company Mitsui OSK Lines is one of the world's largest shipping companies, with a fleet of more than 500 ships under the control of its group companies. The cruise business is operated by Mitsui OSK Passenger Lines, or MOPAS for short and also by Nippon Charter Cruise, a joint venture between Mitsui OSK and Japan Cruise Line. Nippon Charter Cruise is recorded as the registered owner of the FUJI MARU. Mitsui OSK was formed in 1964 with the merger of Mitsui Steamship Company (de-merged from its parent in 1942) and the long-established (1884) OSK Line. A further reorganisation took place in 1999 when Navix Line was absorbed into the group. The various elements that make up Mitsui OSK today have been carrying passengers since 1868.

Chairman Kunio Suzuki **President** Akimitsu Ashida

Address 9-13 Akasaka 1-Chome, Minato-ku, Sankaido Building, 107 8532 Tokyo, Japan

Telephone +81 3 5114 5247 **Fax** +81 3 5114 5270

Website www.mopas.co.jp

Area operated Asia and worldwide for Japanese speaking passengers

FUJI MARU	23235gt	1989	20.0k	D2	364p	603p	135c	167.0m	24.0m	6.6m	JP
NIPPON MARU	21903gt	1990	18.0k	D2	368p	607p	160c	166.6m	23.6m	6.6m	JP

FUJI MARU was Japan's largest cruise ship when completed in 1989 by Mitsubishi Heavy Industries (yard number 1177) at Kobe, Japan. She has operated mainly on charter cruises, under the Nippon Charter Cruises organisation, within Asia and the Pacific Ocean. IMO 8700474

NIPPON MARU is also a product of the Kobe, Japan shipyard of Mitsubishi Heavy Industries (yard number 1188), and carries one of the most prestigious names in Japanese passenger shipping. The ship operates a mixture of cruises ranging from short domestic voyages of a few days to three-month round the world cruises. In December 2009 she is expected to undergo a major refit, during which 18 new cabins will be added. IMO 8817631

MSC CROCIERE

The Company MSC Crociere is an Italian subsidiary of the Mediterranean Shipping Company of Geneva, Switzerland; the world's largest privately owned shipping business. MSC was established in 1970, with an entry into the cruise market eighteen years later with the acquisition of what was left of Lauro Line. The business was restyled as Star Lauro, but following the loss of the ACHILLE LAURO in 1994, the cruise operation was renamed during the following year as Mediterranean Shipping Cruises. The company's oldest ship, the MONTEREY, was withdrawn from service and sold for breaking in 2006. In spring 2009, following her return from South Africa, the RHAPSODY was sold to Mano Cruises. MSC also operates one of the largest fleets of containerships worldwide and local ferries in Italy; a total of more than 420 ships, owned and chartered.

President Nicola Coccia **Managing Director** Antonia de Rosa

Address Via A Depretis 31, Naples 80133, Italy

Telephone +39 081 794 2111 **Fax** +39 081 794 2707

Website www.msccrociere.com and www.msccruises.co.uk

Area operated Mediterranean and Caribbean Seas and South America

MELODY	35143gt	1982	23.5k	D2	1064p	1250p	535c	204.8m	27.4m	7.8m	PA
MSC ARMONIA	58625gt	2001	21.0k	DEP2	1566p	2065p	711c	251.2m	28.8m	6.9m	PA
MSC FANTASIA	137936gt	2008	23.0k	DE2	3274p	3959p	1325c	333.3m	37.9m	8.7m	PA
MSC LIRICA	59058gt	2003	20.8k	DEP2	1560p	2065p	760c	251.0m	28.8m	6.6m	PA
MSC MUSICA	92409gt	2006	22.0k	DEP2	2550p	3013p	987c	293.0m	32.2m	7.9m	PA
MSC OPERA	59058gt	2004	20.8k	DEP2	1756p	2199p	760c	251.2m	28.8m	6.8m	PA
MSC ORCHESTRA	92409gt	2007	22.0k	DEP2	2550p	3013p	987c	293.0m	32.2m	7.9m	PA
MSC POESIA	92627gt	2008	22.0k	DEP2	2550p	3013p	987c	293.0m	32.2m	7.9m	PA
MSC SINFONIA	58625gt	2002	21.0k	DEP2	1566p	2065p	711c	251.0m	28.8m	6.8m	PA
MSC SPLENDIDA	137936gt	2009	23.0k	DE2	3320p	3882c	1330c	333.3m	37.9m	8.7m	PA

MELODY, formerly Home Lines' second new ship, the ATLANTIC, was built by Construction Navales & Industrielles de la Mediterranee (yard number 1432) at La Seyne, France and initially operated between New York and Bermuda. Home Lines was sold to Holland America Line in 1988, but the ATLANTIC was not included in the deal. She went instead to Premier Cruise Line, and after a refit in Bremerhaven she emerged as the Caribbean cruise ship STARSHIP ATLANTIC. In 1997 she was sold to Mediterranean Shipping Company and renamed MELODY. Following summer 2008 service in the Mediterranean, she moved to South Africa for the winter, where she is marketed by Starlight Cruises. Her 2009 Mediterranean itinerary is a one-week Western Mediterranean cruise from Genoa. IMO 7902295

MSC ARMONIA began as the second new building for Festival Cruises as the EUROPEAN VISION. She was built by Chantiers de l'Atlantique (yard number V31) at St Nazaire, France. Festival Cruises failed in early 2004 and Mediterranean Shipping Cruises quickly snapped up the ship, renaming her MSC ARMONIA. She operates in the Mediterranean in summer, based in Venice in 2009, before repositioning to South America for the winter. IMO 9210141

MSC FANTASIA is the first of a pair of massive ships for MSC, built by Aker Yards (yard number A33) at St Nazaire France. Sophia Loren christened the ship in Naples in December 2008. For the summer

MSC Crociere's **Melody** in Genoa *(Rick Frendt)*

MSC Crociere's **MSC Armonia** sailing from Venice *(William Mayes)*

MSC Crociere's **MSC Fantasia** in Rhodes *(Matthew Sudders)*

MSC Crociere's **MSC Lirica** at Genoa *(Matthew Davies)*

of 2009 the MSC FANTASIA operates a weekly Mediterranean circuit with boarding in both Genoa and Barcelona. IMO 9359791

MSC LIRICA was built by Chantiers de l'Atlantique (yard number K32) at St Nazaire, France for Mediterranean Shipping Cruises. She was named by Sophia Loren. Her current operation includes Northern Europe in summer, Mediterranean Sea in autumn and the Caribbean Sea in winter. IMO 9246102

MSC MUSICA is the first of a trio of ships built by Chantiers de l'Atlantique (yard number Q32), and delivered in 2006. She is another of the company's ships to have been named by Sophia Loren. She will spend summer 2009 in the Mediterranean, based in Venice and is expected to return to South America in the winter. IMO 9320087

MSC OPERA, a sister to MSC LIRICA, was delivered by Chantiers de l'Atlantique (yard number L32) in 2004 and named by Sophia Loren. After returning from South America she spends the summer of 2009 based in Copenhagen before moving to the Mediterranean Sea in the autumn. IMO 9250464

MSC ORCHESTRA, a sister to the MSC MUSICA was built by Chantiers de l'Atlantique (yard number R32), named by Sophia Loren and delivered in 2007. She will be in Northern Europe for the summer of 2009. IMO 9320099

MSC POESIA is the third in a series of six ships, built by Aker Yards (yard number S32) at St Nazaire, France. Based in Venice for summer 2009, she was named in Dover by Sophia Loren. IMO 9387073

MSC SINFONIA was built by Chantiers de l'Atlantique (yard number X31) at St Nazaire, France as the EUROPEAN STARS for Festival Cruises. She was originally advertised to carry the name EUROPEAN DREAM. When Festival Cruises failed, the ship was laid up for some time before being acquired by Mediterranean Shipping Cruises and refitted as the MSC SINFONIA for service beginning in the spring of 2005. MSC SINFONIA is based in the Mediterranean in summer 2009. IMO 9210153

MSC SPLENDIDA was built by STX Europe (yard number B33) at St Nazaire. She was named by Sophia Loren in Barcelona in July 2009 and remains based there for the remainder of the year. IMO 9359806

Cruise Ships on Order

MSC FAVOLOSA	92409gt	2012	22.0k	DEP2	2550p	3013p	987c	293.0m	32.2m	7.9m	PA
MSC MAGNIFICA	92409gt	2010	22.0k	DEP2	2550p	3013p	987c	293.0m	32.2m	7.9m	PA
MSC MERAVIGLIA	92409gt	2011	22.0k	DEP2	2550p	3013p	987c	293.0m	32.2m	7.9m	PA

MSC FAVOLOSA, **MSC MAGNIFICA** and **MSC MERAVIGLIA** are on order from STX Europe (formerly Aker Yards and before that Chantiers de l'Atlantique), (yard numbers V32, T32 and U32) at St Nazaire, France. However in May 2009 MSC Cruises advised that the MSC FAVOLOSA and MSC MERAVIGLIA orders were being re-negotiated and would be for larger ships. IMO 9534705, 9387085 and 9534690

NOBLE CALEDONIA

The Company Noble Caledonia is a British operator of exploration, expedition and educational tours and cruises. The company was founded in 1991 and now operates the ISLAND SKY on long-term seasonal charter. The company also sells space on other ships, both ocean and river, worldwide and operates extensive programmes on the CLIPPER ADVENTURER and the CLIPPER ODYSSEY.

Address 2 Chester Close, Belgravia, London SW1X 7BE, England

Telephone +44 207 752 0000 **Fax** +44 207 245 0388

Website www.noble-caledonia.co.uk

Area operated Baltic, Black and Mediterranean Seas and the Indian Ocean

CLIPPER ADVENTURER	4376gt	1975	14.0k	D2	122p	122p	79c	100.0m	16.2m	4.7m	BS
CLIPPER ODYSSEY	5218gt	1989	18.0k	D2	120p	120p	70c	103.0m	15.4m	4.3m	BS
ISLAND SKY	4200gt	1992	15.5k	D2	114p	114p	72c	90.6m	15.3m	4.1m	BS

CLIPPER ADVENTURER For details see under Quark Expeditions (TUI).

CLIPPER ODYSSEY For details see under Zegrahm Expeditions (TUI).

ISLAND SKY was built by Nuovi Cantieri Apuania (yard number 1147) at Marina di Carrara in Italy as the RENAISSANCE EIGHT for Renaissance Cruises. She remained with the company until it filed for

MSC Crociere's **MSC Poesia** in Istanbul *(William Mayes)*

Noble Caledonia's **Island Sky** (Bill Lawes)

NYK's **Asuka II** at San Francisco *(Andrew Kilk)*

bankruptcy in the autumn of 2001, following which she was renamed as the RENAI II and laid up. She became the SKY in 2003 and was renamed ISLAND SKY in 2004 when acquired by Mauritius Island Cruises. ISLAND SKY and her sister the ISLAND SUN (now the CORINTHIAN II of Travel Dynamics International) were acquired by Danish container operator Clipper Group from Mauritius Island Cruises, which has now ceased trading. Noble Caledonia has chartered the ISLAND SKY since 2004. She is currently owned by Clipper Group of Denmark and managed by ISP. IMO 8802894

NOMADE YACHTING BORA BORA

The Company Nomade Yachting Bora Bora is a privately owned Tahitian company, founded in 2002 as Bora Bora Cruises and operating two luxury yachts, and several smaller day vessels in the islands of French Polynesia.

Address PO Box 40186, Fare Tony-Vaiete, 98713 Papeete, Tahiti, French Polynesia

Telephone +689 544505 **Fax** +689 451065

Website www.boraboracruises.com

Area operated Tahiti and the Leeward Islands

TI'A MOANA	2728gt	2003	14.0k	D2	50p	50p	38c	69.1m	13.8m	2.1m	PF
TU MOANA	2728gt	2003	14.0k	D2	50p	50p	38c	69.1m	13.8m	2.1m	PF

TI'A MOANA and **TU MOANA** were built by Austal Ships (yard numbers 173 and 172) at Fremantle, Western Australia for the company. The names both mean 'to stand upright in the sea' and come from the Polynesian dialect of Tahiti. IMO 9267522 and 9267510

NOMADS OF THE SEAS

The Company Nomads of the Seas is a Chilean company, founded in 2006 by Andres Ergas, offering luxury fishing cruises.

Address 5A Piso, 4446, Las Condes, Chile

Telephone +56 2 414 4600 **Fax** +56 2 206 1450

Website www.nomadsoftheseas.com

Area operated

ATMOSPHERE	695gt	2006	k	D2	28p	28p	32c	45.7m	10.0m	2.8m	CL

ATMOSPHERE was built by Astilleros y Servicios Navales (yard number 147) at Valdivia, Chile. IMO 9401001

NORTH STAR CRUISES

The Company North Star Cruises was established in 1987. The new ship TRUE NORTH replaced a 1999-built ship of the same name, and is equipped with a Bell 407 helicopter.

Owner Craig Howson

Address PO Box 654, Broome 6725, Western Australia

Telephone +61 8 9192 1829 **Fax** +61 8 9192 1830

Website www.northstarcruises.com.au

Area operated Australia North West coast, and to Papua New Guinea

TRUE NORTH	730gt	2005	13.0k	D2	36p	36p	20c	49.9m	10.0m	2.2m	AU

TRUE NORTH was built by Image Marine Pty Ltd (yard number 287) in Fremantle, Western Australia. IMO 9308651

Nomade Yachting's **Ti'a Moana** at Raiatea *(Rick Frendt)*

Crystal Cruises' **Crystal Symphony** at Dover *(Martin Grant)*

NYK CRUISES

The Company Nippon Yusen Kaisha (NYK) was formed in 1885 with the merger of the Mitsubishi Mail Steamship Company and Kyodo Unyu Kaisha, creating a fleet of 58 ships. Over the ensuing years the company developed an impressive network of liner services that eventually encompassed the whole world. It was not until 1929, however, that the now familiar twin red stripes on a white background was adopted as the company's new funnel marking. NYK emerged from the Second World War with 37 ships and gradually began to re-establish itself, initially in Japanese domestic service, and from 1950 in international trades, although now in freight rather than passengers. The merger in 1964 with Mitsubishi Shipping Company, created a new NYK Group, owning a total of 87 ships. Four years later the company began to containerise its cargo services, and in 1969 NYK disposed of its coastal and domestic operations to concentrate on its liner shipping business. In 1989 Crystal Cruises was established, and in the same year NYK began operating the expedition ship FRONTIER SPIRIT. NYK today operates a fleet of around 800 ships around the world. The company operates a single ship in the Japanese domestic market.

Address 2-3-2 Marunouchi Chiyoda-ku, 100-0005 Tokyo, Japan

Telephone +81 3 3284 5665 **Fax** +81 3 3284 6334

Website www.asukacruise.co.jp

Area operated Japan and worldwide

ASUKA II		50142gt	1990	22.0k	DE2	960p	960p	530c	240.9m	29.6m	8.0m	JP

ASUKA II was the first ship for the newly formed Crystal Cruises. She was built by Mitsubishi Heavy Industries (yard number 2100) at Nagasaki, Japan, as the CRYSTAL HARMONY and was christened by Mary Tyler Moore. She was transferred to parent company NYK in December 2005 as the ASUKA II, to replace the ASUKA, which had been sold. Asuka was the capital city of Japan in the 6th century. IMO 8806204

CRYSTAL CRUISES

The Company Crystal Cruises was established by NYK in 1989 as a luxury cruise operator geared to the US market. It would appear that the increase in capacity created with the arrival of the CRYSTAL SERENITY in 2003 has not been matched by the increase in passengers, as the company's first ship, the CRYSTAL HARMONY, was transferred to Crystal's parent company at the end of 2005.

Chairman Mitsuhiko Takahashi **President** Gregg Michel

Address 2049 Century Park East, Suite 1400, Los Angeles, California 90067, United States of America

Telephone +1 866 446 6625

Website www.crystalcruises.com

Area operated Worldwide

CRYSTAL SERENITY	68870gt	2003	22.0k	DEP2	1080p	1140p	635c	250.0m	32.2m	7.6m	BS
CRYSTAL SYMPHONY	51044gt	1995	22.0k	DE2	940p	940p	545c	238.0m	30.2m	7.6m	BS

CRYSTAL SERENITY was built by Chantiers de l'Atlantique (yard number H32) at St Nazaire, France, and christened by Dame Julie Andrews in Southampton.. IMO 9243667

CRYSTAL SYMPHONY was built by Kvaerner Masa Yards (yard number1323) at Turku, Finland. Her godmother was Angela Lansbury. IMO 9066667

OCEAN ADVENTURES

The Company Ocean Adventures SA is an Ecuador registered company, established in 2001.

Address Avenida Republica de El Salvador N36-84 Naciones Unidas, Edificio Quilate 9th Floor, Quito, Ecuador

Telephone +593 2 2466301 **Fax** +593 2 2463681

Website www.oceanadventures.com.ec

Area operated Galapagos Islands

Oceanwide Expeditions' **Grigory Mikheyev** at Ushuaia *(Rick Frendt)*

Orion Expedition Cruises' **Orion** *(Theodore W Scull)*

ECLIPSE		1610gt	1998	14.5k	D2	48p	48p	31c	64.0m	12.5m	3.3m	EC

ECLIPSE was built by Astilleros Construcciones at Vigo, Spain as the ferry CAMELIA. The hull was launched in 1982 but spent many years uncompleted at the shipyard. Later she is thought to have become the AGEAN SEA II and was acquired by Ocean Adventures in 1998, following which she was converted for cruising and renamed ECLIPSE. IMO 8978954

OCEANWIDE EXPEDITIONS

The Company Oceanwide Expeditions is a Netherlands based operator of expedition cruises to the Polar Regions. The company also markets space on other ships.

Address Bellamypark 9, 4381 CG Vlissingen, The Netherlands

Telephone +31 118 410 410 **Fax** +31 118 410 417

Website www.oceanwide-expeditions.com

Area operated Arctic and Antarctic regions and the Atlantic islands

ALEKSEY MARYSHEV	1698gt	1990	12.5k	D1	46p	46p	20c	66.0m	12.8m	3.5m	RU
GRIGORIY MIKHEYEV	1729gt	1990	12.5k	D1	46p	46p	20c	66.0m	12.8m	3.5m	RU
PLANCIUS	3175gt	1976	10.0k	DE3	112p	112p	30c	84.5m	14.4m	4.8m	NL

ALEKSEY MARYSHEV was built by the Holming Shipyard (yard number 287) at Rauma, Finland for the Hydrographic Research Institute of St Petersburg. Her name commemorates the former Captain of the Soviet High Fleet and hydrographer, Aleksey Vasiljevitsj Maryshev (1906-1981). IMO 8909329

GRIGORIY MIKHEYEV is owned by the Hydrographic Research Institute of St Petersburg, Russia and was built by the Hollming Shipyard (yard number 288) at Rauma in Finland. IMO 8909331

PLANCIUS was built as the TYDEMAN, an oceanographic research vessel for the Royal Dutch Navy by the De Mervede shipyard (yard number 612) at Hardinxveld, in the Netherlands. She was decommissioned in 2004, purchased by Oceanwide Expeditions in 2006 and converted for adventure cruising. Her transformation will be completed by October 2009. She is the only ship to be owned by the company. IMO 7432044

ORIENT LINES

The Company Orient Lines was the trading name of a British based company (Shipping and General Services Ltd) formed in 1991 by Gerry Herrod to acquire and operate one of the quintet of Russian liners built in the mid-1960's on exclusive expedition type cruises. The MARCO POLO entered service in 1994 and four years later Orient Lines was sold to Norwegian Cruise Line. Orient Lines has continued to operate with its own identity and the fleet briefly expanded to two ships (with the expectation of a third) before contracting back to a single vessel. NCL later sold the MARCO POLO, which currently operates for Transocean Tours. In 2008 NCL sold the ship-less Orient Lines to US travel Agent Wayne Heller. It was intended to recommence trading with the MARCO POLO II, formerly the MAXIM GORKIY, but the economic downturn hit before the deal had been concluded. Orient Lines is not currently trading.

Address 1170 Celebration Boulevard, Suite 200, Celebration, FL34747, United States of America

Telephone +1 407 566 7100 **Fax** +1 407 566 7162

Website www.orientlines.com

Areas operated Not currently operating

ORION EXPEDITION CRUISES

The Company Orion Expedition Cruises Pty Ltd was established in 2003 by Sarina Bratton, founder of Norwegian Capricorn Line, as a new Australian entrant to the expanding world of expedition cruise operators. In May 2008 the company was sold to US private equity firm KSL Capital Partners.

Managing Director Sarina Bratton

Address Level 2, 26 Ridge Street, North Sydney, New South Wales 2060, Australia

Telephone +61 2 9033 8700 **Fax** +61 2 9033 8799

Overseas Adventure Travel's **Arethusa** at Aqaba (William Mayes)

Page & Moy's **Ocean Majesty** in Southampton Water *(Alan Ryszka-Onions)*

Patricia Voyages' **Patricia** at Harwich *(William Mayes)*

Website www.orioncruises.com.au

Area operated Australia, Papua New Guinea and Antarctica

ORION	3984gt	2003	16.0k	D1	106p	130p	70c	102.7m	14.0m	3.8m	BS

ORION was built by Schiffswerft u Maschinenfabrik Cassens (yard number 236) at Emden, Germany as the ORION for Explorer Maritime Ltd of Greece. It is believed that she was laid down as the SUN EXPLORER. She began a long-term charter to Orion Expedition Cruises at the beginning of 2005, having previously operated for Travel Dynamics. IMO 9273076

OVERSEAS ADVENTURE TRAVEL

The Company Overseas Adventure Travel was established in 1978 and is part of the Grand Circle Travel Group.

Chairman Alan Lewis

Address Suite 200 North, 124 Mount Auburn Street, Cambridge, MA 02138, United States of America

Website www.oattravel.com

Area operated Dalmacia and the Mediterranean and Red Seas

ARETHUSA	1206gt	2008	13.6k	D2	52p	52p	21c	59.0m	10.7m	2.9m	MT
ARTEMIS	1206gt	2007	13.6k	D2	52p	52p	21c	59.0m	10.7m	2.9m	MT
ATHENA	1206gt	2007	12.5k	D2	52p	52p	21c	59.0m	10.7m	2.9m	MT

ARETHUSA, ARTEMIS and **ATHENA** were built by Brodosplit (yard numbers 509, 508 and 507) at the Split shipyard in Croatia. IMO 9398022, 9398010, 9398008

Grand Circle Travel also owns the PAUL GAUGUIN (see Regent Seven Seas Cruises).

PAGE & MOY HOLIDAYS

The Company Page & Moy was established in 1961, although the company began offering its own cruise products somewhat later, and today is not only one of the United Kingdom's leading travel agents, but also an important tour operator. In 1979 London Weekend Television acquired a controlling interest. Nine years later the company was wholly acquired by Barclays plc, whose subsidiary Barclaycard was Page & Moy's largest client. In 2004 UK rival, Travelsphere Holdings, acquired the business, but both companies have retained their identity for the time being. The Travelsphere Group itself was sold to venture capitalists Electra in 2006. The OCEAN MAJESTY finishes her service with Page & Moy in the autumn of 2009, but it has not yet been announced which ship will operate the 2010 cruise programme.

Address Compass House, Rockingham Road, Market Harborough, LE16 7QD, England

Telephone +44 870 010 6430 **Fax** +44 1858 461956

Website www.cruisecollection.com

Area operated Europe, from UK ports

OCEAN MAJESTY	10417gt	1966	20.0k	D2	500p	613p	235c	130.6m	19.2m	5.4m	PT

OCEAN MAJESTY was built by Union Naval de Levante (yard number 93) in Valencia, Spain as the car ferry JUAN MARCH for Spain's state carrier, Compania Trasmediterranea. She was one of a series of four ships designed for both the overnight Barcelona to Palma, Majorca run and the longer route from Barcelona to the Canary Islands. She was sold in 1985 to Sol Maritime Services of Limassol, Cyprus. She was renamed SOL CHRISTIANA and placed on a new service linking Piraeus with Crete, Rhodes, Cyprus and Israel. The service was not a success and she was sold to another Cypriot operator, renamed KYPROS STAR and set to work as a ferry serving Rhodes, Cyprus and Egypt from Piraeus. In 1988 she operated for Italy's Adriatica and sailed between Brindisi in Italy and Patras in Greece. Between 1989 and 1994 the ship underwent a total transformation, emerging as the cruise ship OCEAN MAJESTY. She was initially chartered to Epirotiki Line as the OLYMPIC and again for the following year as the HOMERIC. For 1995 the ship was sub-chartered to Page & Moy Holidays for a number of cruises. Subsequently she has made regular appearances in the Page & Moy cruise programme, but 2009 will be her last season. She is now owned by Majestic International Cruises. IMO 6602898

PAQUET CROISIERES

The Company Paquet Croisieres is a new French company, reviving the Paquet name (owned by Costa), set up by Marseilles travel company TMR and Jean Maurice Ravon. The company will charter the COSTA ALLEGRA from 2010.

PATRICIA VOYAGES

The Company Patricia Voyages is a marketing name of Trinity House, the General Lighthouse Authority for England, Wales and the Channel Islands. The PATRICIA is bookable though Strand Travel, www.strandtravel.co.uk.

Address The Quay, Harwich, Essex, CO12 3JW, England

Telephone +44 1255 245034

Website www.trinityhouse.co.uk

Area operated Around the coasts of England and Wales

PATRICIA	2639gt	1982	14.0k	D2	12p	12p	c	86.3m	13.8m	4.4m	GB

PATRICIA was built by Henry Robb (yard number 530) at Leith, Scotland as the lighthouse and buoy tender PATRICIA for Trinity House. In recent years she has carried a small number of passengers on operational voyages. IMO 8003632

PETER DEILMANN CRUISES

The Company Peter Deilmann set up his cargo handling business Deilmann Reederei in 1972, and within a year had established Peter Deilmann Cruises as a company offering cruises in the premium sector. He withdrew from the cargo business in 1979 to concentrate on cruising. Until 2004 the company also operated the small cruise ship BERLIN, but this has now been returned to her owners. Peter Deilmann died in 2004 and the company is now in the hands of his daughters. The company also operated a fleet of river cruise ships on the waterways of Europe until June 2009, when that part of the business filed for bankruptcy.

Owners Gisa and Hedda Deilmann **Managing Directors** Norbert Becker, Traute Hallmann-Schulze

Address Am Holm 25, 23730 Neustadt in Holstein, Germany

Telephone +49 4561 3960 **Fax** +49 4561 8207

Website www.deilmann-cruises.com, www.deilmann.de and www.deilman.co.uk

Area operated Worldwide

DEUTSCHLAND	22496gt	1998	20.0k	D2	513p	576p	260c	175.3m	23.0m	5.8m	DE

DEUTSCHLAND was built by Howaldtswerke Deutsche Werft (yard number 328) at Kiel, Germany for grand style cruising for Peter Deilmann Cruises. Initially she was marketed only to German-speaking passengers, but has recently become a bi-lingual German and English ship. IMO 9141807

PHOENIX REISEN

The Company Phoenix Reisen is a German privately owned tour and travel company, founded by Johannes Zurnieden. Until withdrawn in November 2008, the company's longest serving ship was the MAXIM GORKIY.

Address Pfalzer Strasse 14, 53111 Bonn, Germany

Telephone +49 228 9260 0 **Fax** +49 228 9260 999

Website www.phoenixreisen.com

Area operated Europe and South America

ALBATROS	28518gt	1973	18.5k	D2	884p	1100p	340c	205.5m	25.2m	7.5m	BS
ALEXANDER VON HUMBOLDT	15396gt	1990	18.8k	D2	520p	556p	214c	150.7m	19.8m	5.7m	BS
AMADEA	28856gt	1991	21.0k	D2	584p	604p	243c	192.8m	24.7m	6.6m	BS
ATHENA	16144gt	1948	16.5k	D2	512p	638p	250c	160.0m	21.0m	7.6m	PT

ALBATROS has had a long and varied career. She was built by Wartsila (yard number 397) at Helsinki, Finland as the ROYAL VIKING SEA, the final member of the trio of luxurious first generation vessels for the new Royal Viking Line. She was lengthened in 1983 in Bremerhaven, but just a year later both she and her owners were acquired by Kloster Cruise (Norwegian Cruise Line). Royal Viking Line continued to operate as a separate entity for some time. In 1991 the ship was transferred within the group to Royal Cruise Line and renamed ROYAL ODYSSEY. Later, while NCL was experiencing financial difficulties, the ship was sold to Actinor and chartered back. In 1997 she was renamed NORWEGIAN STAR and chartered to a new company, Norwegian Capricorn Line, in which Norwegian Cruise Line had an interest. Norwegian Capricorn Line used the ship for cruises from Australia, but was not entirely successful. She passed to Star Holdings in 1999, and in 2001 she was operated by Star Cruises as the NORWEGIAN STAR 1, but did not stay in the Far East for long as, following a charter to Crown Investments for cruising on the Chinese coast, she moved to the Mediterranean Sea as the CROWN, serving the Spanish market. By now Club Cruise of the Netherlands owned her. Phoenix Reisen managed to charter the ship at relatively short notice in 2004 to replace the previous ALBATROS, which had suffered mechanical failure and was considered beyond economic repair. From spring 2004 she has sailed as the ALBATROS. She was acquired by Club Cruise of The Netherlands in 2006, on the strength of the Phoenix Reisen charter. Club Cruise went into administration in late 2008, but Phoenix Reisen appears to have been able to keep the ship operating by means of posting deposit bonds. IMO 7304314

ALEXANDER VON HUMBOLDT was built by Union Naval de Levante (yard number 185) at Valencia, Spain as the CROWN MONARCH for Crown Cruise Lines, a subsidiary of Effjohn Intl. The ship operated cruises in the Caribbean and South Pacific until being chartered to Singaporean interests for use as the casino cruise ship NAUTICAN in 1995. The Singaporean authorities banished the ship from its waters a few months later, and it moved up to Hong Kong, where it operated as the WALRUS until replaced by the CT NEPTUNE in April 2005. The ship was returned to Sea Containers, the then owners of former Effjohn company Silja Line, and was laid up awaiting new employment. In 2006 she was sold to Dutch operator Club Cruise for US$21 million and was chartered by new Spanish operator, Vision Cruceros, for whom she operated as the JULES VERNE. From spring 2008 she has operated as the ALEXANDER VON HUMBOLDT, although for the first two months she was named ALEXANDER VON HUMBOLDT II. She replaced a previous ship of the same name, now Swan Hellenic's MINERVA. Alexander von Humboldt, born in 1769, was described by Charles Darwin as the greatest scientific traveller who ever lived. He was the author of the five-volume Kosmos, the last volume of which was published in 1862, three years after his death. Following the ship's owner going into administration the ship was arrested in Bremerhaven, and remained in that position at the time of writing. Phoenix Reisen were expecting to have the ship operational again by late spring 2009, but in view of likely delays has chartered the ATHENA as a temporary replacement. IMO 8709573

AMADEA was built by Mitsubishi Heavy Industries (yard number 2050) at Nagasaki, Japan as the ASUKA for operation by NYK in the deluxe sector of the Japanese cruise market. The ASUKA became Phoenix Reisen's fourth ship, AMADEA in March 2006 when she was replaced in the NYK fleet by the CRYSTAL HARMONY (renamed ASUKA II) in December 2005. The AMADEA is managed by V-Ships. IMO 8913162

ATHENA For details see under Classic international Cruises. However for Phoenix Reisen the passenger and crew numbers are different.

PLANTOURS & PARTNER

The Company Plantours and Partner GmbH is a German cruise operator, long-term charterer of the VISTAMAR, and operator of European river cruises. In late 2006 Venice-based Ligabue acquired the company.

Managing Director Oliver Steuber

Address Obernstrasse 76, D28195 Bremen, Germany

Telephone +49 421 173690 **Fax** +49 421 1736935

Website www.plantours-partner.de

Area operated Amazon, Western Europe, Scandinavia, Mediterranean, round Africa

VISTAMAR	7478gt	1989	16.5k	D2	300p	340p	110c	117.4m	16.8m	4.5m	IT

Peter Deilmann Cruises' **Deutschland** at Greenwich *(Martin Grant)*

Phoenix Reisen's **Albatros** in the Kiel Canal *(Oliver Sesemann)*

Phoenix Reisen's **Amadea** in Hamburg *(William Mayes)*

Plantours & Partner's **Vistamar** at Kiel *(Andrew Kilk)*

Plein Cap Croisieres' **Adriana III** *(Richard Seville)*

Polar Quest Expeditions' **Quest** at Tobermoray *(Bruce Peter)*

VISTAMAR was built by Union Naval de Levant SA (yard number 175) at Valencia, Spain as the VISTAMAR for Mar Line Universal Shipping, a subsidiary of Hoteles Marinos. In 2000 she was transferred to Vistamar Canarias and two months later to Servicios Maritimos Litoral, based in The Netherlands, both without change of name. IMO 8701193

PLEIN CAP CROISIERES

The Company Plein Cap Croisieres is a trading style of French company, Marina Cruises, founded in 1997.

Address 251 route de La Colle, 06270 Villeneuve Loubet, France

Telephone +33 4 9320 2120 **Fax** +33 4 9373 7001

Website www.plein-cap.com

Area operated Mediterranean, Red Sea, Indian Ocean, Black Sea and Scandinavia

| ADRIANA III | 4490gt | 1972 | 15.0k | D2 | 240p | 298p | 100c | 103.7m | 14.0m | 4.5m | VU |

ADRIANA III was built by the United Shipyard (yard number 54) at Perama, Greece for Hellenic Mediterranean Lines as the AQUARIUS. She was both the first cruise ship for that company and the first such vessel to be built in Greece. With her long raked bow she was a very elegant ship, and made an attractive sight on her Greek Island cruises during the summer. She did spend a few winters in the Caribbean, but served mostly in the Mediterranean. The ACHILLE LAURO hijacking in 1985 had a particularly bad effect on the business of Hellenic Mediterranean Lines, and in 1986 her mortgagees seized the AQUARIUS. She was sold to Adriatic General Shipping, part of the Yugoslav Jadrolinija company and began operating in the Adriatic Sea as the ADRIANA. She often ran cruises on charter to German tour operators. In 1997 she passed to Marina Cruises of Nice and in February of the following year commenced cruising under the Plein Cap banner. In 2008 she was renamed ADRIANA III. The V Ships Group owns the ship. IMO 7118404

POLAR QUEST EXPEDITIONS

The Company Polar Quest is a Swedish operator of expedition cruises. In addition to the ships listed here, the company markets space on a large number of major polar exploration ships.

Address Slussgaten 1, PO Box 180, 40123 Gothenburg, Sweden

Telephone +46 31 333 1730 **Fax** +46 31 333 1731

Website www.polar-quest.com

Area operated with these ships, Spitzbergen

ORIGO	368gt	1955	10.5k	D1	24p	24p	10c	39.9m	8.8m	3.2m	SE
QUEST	1268gt	1992	13.0k	D1	52p	60p	20c	49.6m	11.0m	3.4m	BS
STOCKHOLM	383gt	1953	10.5k	D1	12p	12p	c	37.8m	8.8m	3.2m	SE

ORIGO was bult for the Swedish National Maritime Administration as the lighthouse tender KALMAR by AB Finnboda Varf (yard number 360) in Stockholm, Sweden. In 1970 she became the VIRGO. She was renamed ORIGO in 1983 when acquired by Rederi AB Origo, and converted for use as a passenger ship in 1991. Most cabins have shared facilities. IMO 5180295

QUEST was built as the SAQQIT ITTUK for Greenland Government owner KNI Piilersvisoq as a coastal passenger liner for 150 passengers by the Orskov Shipyard (yard number 157) at Frederikshavn, Denmark. She was renamed as DISKO II in 2004 and converted into an expedition cruise ship by Hotell and Fartyginredning of Gothenburg, Sweden, although the work took place in Tallinn, Estonia. The works included the installation of 26 new outside cabins, and a new observation lounge. When she re-entered service, it was under charter to the German tour operator, Norden Tours, for whom she undertook summer Greenland coastal cruises. She was acquired by Clipper Group in 2007,further refurbished, and renamed QUEST. She operates for a variety of expedition cruise companies. IMO 8913904

STOCKHOLM was built by Helsingborgs Varf AB at Helsingborg, also for SNMA as the STOCKHOLM. She was renamed STOCKHOLM AV GOTEBORG in 1997 and converted for cruising in 1999 with just six cabins, all with private facilities. She is marketed as the STOCKHOLM. IMO 8226612

POLAR STAR EXPEDITIONS

The Company Polar Star Expeditions, although Canadian based, is a Norwegian owned company, part of the Karlsen Shipping Company. Karlsen was founded more than 100 years ago, and first expanded into Canada in 1940. Polar Star Expeditions was formed in 2000. It was expected that tenders would be issued for a new 200-passenger vessel to replace the POLAR STAR, but to date that has not happened.

President Martin Karlsen

Address 55 Crane Lake Drive, Halifax, Nova Scotia, B3S 1B5, Canada

Telephone +1 902 423 7389 **Fax** +1 902 420 9222

Website www.polarstarexpeditions.com

Area operated Antarctic, Arctic, Greenland and long connecting voyages

POLAR STAR		4998gt	1969	11.5k	DE3	90p	105p	30c	86.5m	21.2m	9.8m	BB

POLAR STAR was built by Wartsila (yard number 389) at Helsinki, Finland as the icebreaker NJORD for the Swedish Maritime Administration. Karlsen Shipping acquired her in 2000, converted her for use as an expedition ship and renamed her POLAR STAR. IMO 6905745

POSEIDON ARCTIC VOYAGES

The Company Poseidon Arctic Voyages is a British expedition cruise company. The company also sells space on other major expedition ships.

Address 9 Perseverance Works, Kingsland Road, London E2 8DD

Telephone +44 870 068 9142 **Fax** +44 870 068 8265

Website www.northpolevoyages.com

Area operated Antarctic and Arctic, Kamchatka and Sakhalin

50 LET POBEDY	23439gt	2007	21.4k	NST3	128p	128p	140c	159.6m	28.0m	11.0m	RU
MARINA TSVETAYEVA	4575gt	1989	14.3k	D1	94p	100p	c	90.0m	17.2m	5.3m	RU

50 LET POBEDY For details see under Quark Expeditions (TUI).

MARINA TSVETAYEVA was built by Stocznia im. Komuny Paryskiej (yard number B961/03) at Gdynia, Poland for Glavmorneft, as one of six similar vessels. The MARINA TSVETAYEVA is owned by Morskaya Kompaniya Sakhalin-Kurily, and is thought to operate for that company when not in service with Poseidon, for whom she is marketed as the MARINA SVETAEVA. Marina Tsvetayeva (1892-1941) was a Russian poet, born in Moscow. IMO 8509181

QUAIL CRUISES

The Company Quail Cruises is an offshoot of the Spanish Quail Travel Group. The company began its cruise operation in 2008 using a former Pullmantur ship, the PACIFIC. In 2009 Clipper Group's GEMINI operated a series of spring cruises following mechanical problems with the PACIFIC. The PACIFIC was later reported to be under arrest in Genoa, so her replacement was the renamed OCEAN COUNTESS.

President Javier Gomez-Navarro

Address 2 planta, Calle Caleruega 79, 28033 Madrid, Spain

Telephone +34 91 7663252

Website www.quailcruises.com

Area operated Mediterranean from Valencia

GEMINI	19093gt	1992	18.4k	D2	819p	916p	470c	163.8m	22.5m	5.4m	MT
NEW PACIFIC	16795gt	1976	18.5k	D2	814p	950p	350c	163.6m	22.8m	5.8m	PT
PACIFIC	20186gt	1971	19.0k	D2	648p	723p	300c	168.7m	24.6m	7.7m	BS

GEMINI was built by Union Naval de Levante (yard number 197) at Valencia, Spain for Effjohn Group's Crown Cruise Line as the CROWN JEWEL. Cunard marketed her from 1993 as the CUNARD CROWN

Polar Star Expeditions' **Polar Star** *(Ben Lyons)*

The World of Residensea at Monte Carlo *(Rick Frendt)*

Azamara Cruises' **Azamara Quest** at Coco Cay *(Rick Frendt)*

JEWEL before passing to Star Cruises in 1995 when she was renamed as the SUPERSTAR GEMINI. She operated cruises to Japan from her Taiwan base, but in the autumn of 2005 moved back to Singapore to cruise in the Straits of Malacca and the Andaman Sea. She was sold to Clipper Group of Denmark in 2007, and remained under charter to Star Cruises. In 2009 she was to have operated for Spanish company, Vision Cruises, in place of the JULES VERNE (now ALEXANDER VON HUMBOLDT) but that company apparently sub-chartered the vessel to Golden Star Cruises and pulled out of cruising. Although Golden Star Cruises was advertising this ship at the time of writing as the VISION STAR, she was renamed GEMINI in March 2009 and was then chartered to Quail Cruises for six months. For her first three months she operated from Valencia, before taking a series of Eastern Mediterranean cruises. IMO 9000687

NEW PACIFIC started life as one of a pair of second-generation Caribbean cruise ships for Cunard Line. She was built by Burmeister & Wain (yard number 858) at Copenhagen, Denmark as the CUNARD COUNTESS. She served the company for twenty years before being sold for service in the Far East as the AWANI DREAM 2. In 1998 she was acquired by Royal Olympic Cruises and renamed OLYMPIC COUNTESS for service mainly in the Mediterranean. In 2002, under pressure from the International Olympic Committee, the company changed its name to Royal Olympia Cruises and the ship followed suit, becoming the OLYMPIA COUNTESS. Following the collapse of that company she passed to Majestic International Cruises in 2004, and was chartered to Globalia for the summer of 2005 as the OCEAN COUNTESS. She was then chartered to Holiday Kreuzfahrten as their second ship and renamed as the LILI MARLEEN. That company ran into financial difficulties and ceased trading in the summer of 2006. In 2007 she was returned to her owners and was chartered to Louis Cruise Lines, as the RUBY, as part of that company's replacement programme for the SEA DIAMOND. In 2009 she has been chartered to Quail Cruises as a replacement for the PACIFIC, under the name NEW PACIFIC. IMO 7358561

PACIFIC was built by Rheinstahl Nordseewerke (yard number 411) at Emden, Germany as the SEA VENTURE for Norwegian Cruiseships of Oslo. She was initially operated by Flagship Cruises between New York and Bermuda, but was soon sold to a joint venture between Oivind Lorentzen and Fearney & Eger. She was sold on to the Peninsular and Oriental Steam Navigation Company in 1975, becoming the PACIFIC PRINCESS for P&O subsidiary Princess Cruises. She was sold to Pullmantur in 2002 and renamed PACIFIC. The ship was operated in conjunction with CVC of Brazil on Brazilian coastal cruises until 2007. Summer cruises included the Fernando de Noronha Islands, while winter itineraries took in the River Amazon. From the summer of 2007 she returned to the Mediterranean Sea for a season based in Valencia, Spain. Subsequently the ship was sold to CVC, but chartered to Quail Cruises for the European summer. She is now owned by Quail Cruises and has operated for CVC during the northern winter as the NEW PACIFIC. IMO 7018563

QUASAR NAUTICA EXPEDITIONS

The Company Quasar Nautica has been operating cruise yachts in the Galapagos Islands since the mid 1980's. The company also operates the 16-passenger GRACE and ALTA.

President Eduado Diez

Address Jose Jusseiu N41-28y, Alonso de Torres, Quito, Ecuador

Telephone +593 2 244 6996 **Fax** +593 2 225 9305

Website www.quasarnautica.com

Area operated Galapagos Islands

EVOLUTION	654gt	1970	10.0k	D1	28p	32p	18c	58.5m	8.9m	3.2m	EC

EVOLUTION was built by KK Kanasashi Kosen (yard number 986) at Shimitzu, Japan as the fishing vessel WAKACHIBA MARU. In 1980 she became the YUWA MARU and was converted into the cruise ship EVOLUTION in 2004. IMO 7122326

REAL JOURNEYS

The Company Real Journeys is a New Zealand tour operator and cruise ship owner, founded in the early 1950's by Les and Olive Hutchins. Real journeys also owns and operates the 1912-built coal-fired steamer TSS EARNSHAW on Lake Wakapitu, and the 12-berth FRIENDSHIP. The ships listed here were previously operated by Fiordland Travel, a business acquired by Real Journeys in 1966.

Address PO Box 1, Corner Town Centre and Mokonui Streets, Te Anua, New Zealand

Telephone +64 3 249 7416 **Fax** +64 3 249 7022

Website www.realjourneys.co.nz

Area operated The fjords of New Zealand

FIORDLAND NAVIGATOR	693gt	2001	11.0k	D1	52p	68p	9c	38.2m	10.0m	m	NZ
MILFORD MARINER	693gt	2000	11.0k	D2	60p	60p	10c	38.2m	10.0m	m	NZ
MILFORD WANDERER	258gt	1992	9.5k	D1	61p	61p	5c	28.5m	8.4m	m	NZ

All three ships were built by J K Stevenson Ltd at Invercargill, New Zealand. IMO 8975641, 8975653 and 8975665

RESIDENSEA

The Company Residensea is the company formed to operate THE WORLD. The concept for THE WORLD, the first luxury apartment ship, was that of Knut Kloster Jr, son of the founder of Kloster Cruise (now Norwegian Cruise Line). The original plans were for a ship of twice the size of THE WORLD, but these were scaled back before construction once it became apparent that it would be difficult to sell on the scale originally envisaged. Some apartments are available for rent on a cruise basis.

Address 14471 Miramar Parkway, Suite 401, Miramar, Florida 33027, United States of America

Telephone +1 954 538 8400 **Fax** +1 954 431 7443

Website www.residensea.com

Area operated Worldwide

THE WORLD	43188gt	2002	19.0k	D2	330p	657p	250c	196.4m	29.2m	6.9m	BS

THE WORLD is one of that select number of ships where the hull was built in one yard and the ship completed elsewhere. The hull was constructed at Bruce's Shipyard (yard number 247) in Landskrona, Sweden and towed to the Fosen Yard at Rissa, Norway for completion. The ship was originally to have been about 80,000 tons, but insufficient interest had been generated by a crucial stage in the planning, so the size was scaled back. The ship features 106 two- and three-bedroom apartments, 19 one- and two-bedroom studio apartments and 40 studios. IMO 9219331

ROYAL CARIBBEAN CRUISES LIMITED

The Company The early history of Royal Caribbean Cruises Limited (RCCL) can be found under Royal Caribbean International. The cruise ship operator within the group was renamed as Royal Caribbean International in 1997, the same year that the Celebrity Cruises business was acquired, with the new Royal Caribbean Cruise Lines becoming the holding company for the operating entities. In late 2001 a proposed joint venture operation with P&O Princess Cruises was close to becoming a reality before Carnival Corporation stepped in with its own bid for the P&O companies. During the following year the Island Cruises joint venture with British tour operator, First Choice was established. That venture closed in 2009. In summer 2006 Royal Caribbean Cruises' bid for Pullmantur, Spain's largest cruise operator and a major player in that country's tour industry, was accepted by owners, Marsans Group, and the European interest has further expended with the introduction of Croisieres de France in 2008. The Pullmantur acquisition also allowed the extraction of the mis-placed former Renaissance ships from the Spanish company and the establishment of Azamara Cruises. Royal Caribbean will enter the German market through the joint venture TUI Cruises, established in conjunction with Germany's TUI AG. These developments, coupled with RCI ships based in the UK and the Mediterranean give RCCL a very strong, and easily expandable base in four of Europe's most important markets. Royal Caribbean is the second largest of the world's cruise ship groups. Royal Caribbean group ships carried a little over 4 million passengers in 2008.

Chairman and Chief Executive Officer Richard Fain

AZAMARA CRUISES

The Company Azamara Cruises was created on May 4, 2007. Originally intended for Celebrity Cruises' Xpeditions brand, the two former Renaissance Cruises ships, transferred from Pullmantur Cruises, started the new venture, which is positioned between Premium and Luxury. Royal Caribbean Cruises

Limited had previously been interested in acquiring Oceania Cruises (the operator of three similar ships), but that particular avenue of expansion was not encouraged. Azamara Cruises is operated as a subsidiary of Celebrity Cruises. In 2009/10 the ships operate in the Caribbean and Mediterranean and Baltic Seas, and in Asia. Azamara roughly translates from Latin as blue sea.

President and Chief Executive Officer Larry Pimentel

Address 1050 Caribbean Way, Miami, Florida 33132-2096, United States of America

Telephone +1 305 539 6000

Website www.azamaracruises.com

Areas operated Caribbean Sea, Europe, South America and Antarctica, Asia and world cruises

AZAMARA JOURNEY	30277gt	2000	20.0k	DE2	694p	694p	376c	181.0m	25.5m	6.0m	MT
AZAMARA QUEST	30277gt	2000	18.0k	DE2	694p	694p	376c	181.0m	25.5m	6.0m	MT

AZAMARA JOURNEY was marketed while under charter to Pullmantur Cruises in 2003-4 as the BLUE STAR, but not officially renamed from R SIX. She was built by Ateliers et Chantiers de l'Atlantique (yard number Q31) at St Nazaire, France as the R SIX, one of a series of eight elegantly furnished ships for Renaissance Cruises. Following the collapse of that company in 2001 she, along with many of her sisters, was laid up in Gibraltar. The ships were auctioned and acquired by Cruiseinvest, an offshoot of her builders, who still had a significant financial interest in the ships. Pullmantur eventually chartered her. In 2005 she was acquired by Pullmantur and renamed BLUE DREAM. She spent her first winter operating on the Brazilian coast for tour operator CVC, before returning to Europe for the summer. Pullmantur was acquired by Royal Caribbean in 2006 and one of the first moves was to take this ship for the Celebrity Expeditions brand, in an exchange with Celebrity's ZENITH. She was intended to take the name CELEBRITY JOURNEY for her new owner, but just before she entered service following a major refit she was switched to new brand Azamara Cruises as the AZAMARA JOURNEY. IMO 9200940

AZAMARA QUEST was built as the R SEVEN by Chantiers de l'Atlantique (yard number X31) at St Nazaire, France for Renaissance Cruises. Following the failure of that company she was laid up off Gibraltar before being sold to Cruiseinvest, a company associated with her builders, part of the Alstom Group. She was subsequently chartered by Delphin Seereisen and renamed DELPHIN RENAISSANCE. In 2006 she was purchased by Pullmantur and renamed BLUE MOON. In October 2007 she transferred to Azamara Cruises as the second ship for this new company and was named the AMAZARA QUEST. It was originally intended that this ship would join her sister (above) as the CELEBRITY QUEST in the Celebrity Expeditions fleet. IMO 9210218

CELEBRITY CRUISES

The Company Celebrity Cruises was founded in 1989 as a joint venture between Greek shipping company Chandris Group and bulk shipping company Overseas Shipholding Group, as an up market cruise operation to complement its existing passenger operations, which were generally at the lower end of the market. Chandris gradually disposed of its own fleet and concentrated on a small number of high quality ships within the Celebrity brand. The first ship was the former Italian transatlantic liner GALILEO GALILEI, which entered service after a massive refit in 1990 as the MERIDIAN. The second ship (HORIZON, now ISLAND STAR) was also the first new-build for the company, and began a relationship with the shipbuilder Jos. L. Meyer which would produce another four ships over the next seven years. Celebrity Cruises became part of the Royal Caribbean Cruises Limited group in 1997, although at the time Carnival Corporation had also made an offer for the company. In 2004 the company acquired the small expedition ship XPEDITION to expand its range of cruises to include the Galapagos Islands. For 2005, in a further expansion, Celebrity teamed up with Quark Expeditions to offer a cruise from Ottawa to the Arctic, and in 2006 the Antarctic from Ushuaia aboard the Russian icebreaker KAPITAN KHLEBNIKOV. In 2007 the Celebrity Expeditions sub-brand was going to be further expanded with the transfer of two of the former Renaissance ships from fellow subsidiary Pullmantur Cruises. However, in a change of plan these ships became the start-up vessels for Azamara cruises. Unfortunately, Celebrity Cruises seems to be the latest in a long line of cruise companies that thinks it necessary to put its corporate name into its ships' names.

President Daniel Hanranhan

Address 1050 Caribbean Way, Miami, Florida 33132-2096, United States of America

Celebrity Cruises' **Celebrity Century** at Villefranche *(Richard Mayes)*

Celebrity Cruises' **Celebrity Constellation** at Dover *(John Hendy)*

Celebrity Cruises' **Celebrity Solstice** at Papenburg *(Bruce Peter)*

Telephone +1 305 539 6000 **Fax** +1 305 406 8630

Website www.celebritycruises.com

Areas operated Caribbean Sea, Alaska, Mexican Riviera, East Coast USA, Europe

CELEBRITY CENTURY	72458gt	1995	21.5k	D2	1808p	2156p	858c	246.5m	32.2m	7.8m	MT
CELEBRITY CONSTELLATION	90280gt	2002	24.0k	GEP2	2034p	2449p	999c	294.0m	32.2m	8.2m	MT
CELEBRITY EQUINOX	121878gt	2009	22.0k	DEP2	2850p	3000p	1250c	315.0m	36.8m	8.3m	MT
CELEBRITY INFINITY	90280gt	2001	24.0k	GEP2	2046p	2449p	999c	294.0m	32.2m	8.2m	MT
CELEBRITY MERCURY	76522gt	1997	21.5k	D2	1886p	2229p	908c	263.9m	32.2m	7.7m	MT
CELEBRITY MILLENNIUM	90228gt	2000	24.0k	GEP2	2034p	2449p	999c	263.9m	32.2m	7.7m	MT
CELEBRITY SOLSTICE	121878gt	2008	22.0k	DEP2	2850p	3000p	1250c	315.0m	36.8m	8.3m	MT
CELEBRITY SUMMIT	90280gt	2001	24.0k	GEP2	2034p	2449p	999c	294.0m	32.2m	8.2m	MT
XPEDITION	2842gt	2001	13.5k	D1	98p	98p	56c	88.5m	14.0m	3.6m	EC

CELEBRITY CENTURY is the lead ship of a trio of ships built by Jos. L. Meyer (yard number 637) at Papenburg, Germany as the CENTURY. Her maiden voyage in 1995 was from Southampton to New York. Her refit in 2006 included the addition of three decks of balconies, resulting in an increase in gross tonnage from 70,606 to 72,458. She was renamed two years later. She is based in Europe in the summer of 2009 before repositioning to the Caribbean. IMO 9072446

CELEBRITY CONSTELLATION was built by Chantiers de l'Atlantique (yard number U31) at St Nazaire, France as the CONSTELLATION. She was renamed in 2007, and will operate in Northern Europe in 2010 following a Caribbean season. IMO 9192399

CELEBRITY EQUINOX was built by Jos. L. Meyer (yard number 676) at Papenburg, Germany. She operates in the Mediterranean in the summer of 2009 and 2010, and spends winter in the Caribbean. She was named in Southampton by Nina Barough, founder of the British breast cancer charity Walk The Walk. IMO 9372456

CELEBRITY INFINITY, built as the INFINITY is the second of the Millennium class ships to come from Chantiers de l'Atlantique (yard number S31) at St Nazaire, France. She had the Celebrity prefix added to her name in 2007. Her itineraries include Alaska, West Coast USA, South America and the Caribbean. IMO 9189421

CELEBRITY MERCURY is the third and final member of the trio of ships built by Jos. L. Meyer (yard number 639) at Papenburg, Germany. She entered service in 1997 as the MERCURY and was renamed in 2008. She operates on the East and West coasts of the USA and in the Caribbean. IMO 9106302

CELEBRITY MILLENNIUM is the lead ship in a series of four built by Chantiers de l'Atlantique (yard number R31) at St Nazaire, France. She suffered serious problems with her pod propulsion system before delivery, as the MILLENNIUM, and has had to be dry-docked for repairs subsequently. The MILLENNIUM's speciality restaurant has some of the original walnut panels from the White Star Line's Atlantic liner OLYMPIC, built in 1911. She was renamed CELEBRITY MILLENIUM in 2008 and currently operates Alaska and Caribbean cruises. IMO 9189419

CELEBRITY SOLSTICE was built by Jos. L. Meyer (yard number 675) at Papenburg, Germany as the lead ship in the Solstice class. She was named in Fort Lauderdale by ocean scientist, Professor Sharon Smith. After completing her summer 2009 European season she moves to the Caribbean. IMO 9362530

CELEBRITY SUMMIT was built by Chantiers de l'Atlantique (yard number T31) at St Nazaire, France as the SUMMIT. She was renamed with the Celebrity prefix in 2008. She is in Southern Europe in summer 2009 and then moves to the US East Coat and the Caribbean. IMO 9192387

XPEDITION was built by Schiffswerft U Maschinenfabrik Cassens (yard number 228) at Emden in Germany as the SUN BAY for Sun Bay Shipping, by whom she is still owned. Celebrity chartered her in 2004 to commence a programme of cruises in the Galapagos Islands. She is marketed as the CELEBRITY XPEDITION. IMO 9228368

Cruise ships on order

CELEBRITY ECLIPSE	c122000gt	2010	22.0k	DEP2	2850p	3000p	1250c	315.0m	36.8m	8.3m	BS
SOLSTICE 4	c122000gt	2011	22.0k	DEP2	2850p	3000p	1250c	315.0m	36.8m	8.3m	BS
SOLSTICE 5	c122000gt	2012	22.0k	DEP2	2850p	3000p	1250c	315.0m	36.8m	8.3m	BS

CELEBRITY ECLIPSE, SOLSTICE 4 and SOLSTICE 5 are under construction by Jos. L. Meyer at Papenburg, Germany (yard numbers 677, 679 and 691). The CELEBRITY ECLIPSE will be based in Southampton for the summer of 2010. IMO 9404314, 9451094 and 9506459

CROISIERES DE FRANCE

The Company Croisieres de France is a new subsidiary of Royal Caribbean Cruise Lines aimed at developing the French cruise market, and was established in August 2007, although cruises did not commence until May 2008. The company is expected to be operating a second ship (possibly Pullmantur's PACIFIC DREAM) by 2010.

Managing Director Brigitte Tissier

Address 8 rue du Dahomy, 75011 Paris, France

Telephone +33 173 775920 **Fax** +33 140 091298

Website www.cdfcroisieresdefrance.com

Area operated Mediterranean Sea in summer and Caribbean Sea in winter

| BLEU DE FRANCE | 37301gt | 1981 | 21.0K | D2 | 752p | 752p | 406c | 199.6m | 28.5m | 8.4m | MT |

BLEU DE FRANCE was built by Bremer Vulkan (yard number 1001) at Vegesack, Germany for Hapag-Lloyd of Bremen as the EUROPA. She was widely acclaimed as the most luxurious ship afloat, but after 17 years of worldwide cruising she was sold to Star Cruises, but retained for a further year until the new EUROPA was delivered. She was possibly renamed MEGASTAR ASIA for a very short time, but soon had the name SUPERSTAR EUROPE for cruising the waters of Southeast Asia. In February 2000 she became the SUPERSTAR ARIES and was due to transfer to the Orient Lines fleet in the spring of 2003, but following a general downturn in business, was retained within the Star Cruises fleet. She was sold to Pullmantur in 2003 and renamed HOLIDAY DREAM in March 2004. Her Caribbean winter cruises were also marketed by Brazilian tour operator CVC, but with the acquisition of Pullmantur by American based Royal Caribbean, her Cuba calls ceased. In early 2008 she was transferred from Pullmantur to Croisieres de France and after refit in Barcelona was renamed BLUE DE FRANCE. IMO 7822457

ISLAND CRUISES

The Company Island Cruises was a joint venture between Royal Caribbean Cruises Limited and British tour operator First Choice Holidays plc that began operating in spring 2002 with a single ship (the ISLAND ESCAPE) based at Palma de Majorca. In 2005, Celebrity Cruises' HORIZON joined the fleet as the ISLAND STAR. The joint venture was terminated after the 2008/9 Caribbean season and the ISLAND ESCAPE went to First Choice for future use by Thomson Cruises, which may retain the Island Cruises brand. The ISLAND STAR was transferred to Pullmantur as the PACIFIC DREAM. The company is no longer trading.

PULLMANTUR CRUISES

The Company Pullmantur, formerly part of the Marsans Group, is a large Spanish tour company operating its own small airline, cruise line and tour business. The company was established in 1971, but only entered the cruise business with the establishment of Pullmantur Cruises in 2000. Pullmantur has a total staff of more than 2,000, and in the few years since the cruise division was formed, has taken almost 50% of the Spanish cruise market. During the early part of 2006 the entire fleet, with the exception of PACIFIC was re-flagged to Malta. The company passed to Royal Caribbean Cruises Limited in 2006. Following the takeover Royal Caribbean took the two R ships for Celebrity Expeditions and replaced them by transferring the ZENITH and, in 2008, the EMPRESS OF THE SEAS. Two ships have been acquired from P&O Cruises Australia, and with the departure of HOLIDAY DREAM to Bleu de France, the company's largest ship to date, the SOVEREIGN arrived. In a surprise move the OCEANIC was sold at short notice to Panamanian Interests for onward charter to the Peaceboat Organisation.

President Alfonso Perez

Address Calle de Orense 16, 28020 Madrid, Spain

Telephone +34 91556 1114 **Fax** +34 91 555 1319

Croisieres de France's **Bleu de France** in Palma *(Matthew Davies)*

Pullmantur's **Ocean Dream** arriving at Civitavecchia *(Matthew Davies)*

Pullmantur's **Sovereign** in Barcelona *(William Mayes)*

Pullmantur's **Zenith** at Dubrovnik *(Rick Frendt)*

Royal Caribbean's **Brilliance of the Seas** in Barcelona *(William Mayes)*

Website www.pullmanturcruises.com

Area operated Mediterranean and South America

ATLANTIC STAR	46087gt	1984	21.5k	ST2	1184p	1550p	608c	240.4m	27.8m	8.2m	MT
EMPRESS	48563gt	1990	19.0k	D2	1602p	2020p	668c	210.8m	30.7m	7.1m	MT
OCEAN DREAM	36265gt	1981	21.0k	D2	1022p	1350p	550c	204.0m	26.3m	7.0m	MT
PACIFIC DREAM	47427gt	1990	19.5k	D2	1506p	1874p	573c	208.0m	29.0m	7.4m	BS
SOVEREIGN	73529gt	1987	21.0k	D2	2292p	2852p	840c	268.3m	32.2m	7.5m	MT
ZENITH	47413gt	1992	18.0k	D2	1376p	1776p	643c	208.0m	29.0m	7.2m	MT

ATLANTIC STAR was ordered by Sitmar Line from Chantiers du Nord et de la Mediterranee (yard number 1436) at La Seyne, France as the FAIRSKY, as an alternative to converting the former Portuguese liner PRINCIPE PERFEITO into a luxury cruise ship. The FAIRSKY was the last major passenger vessel to be built with steam turbine machinery. Delivered in 1984, she was used on west coast USA cruises. Following the takeover by P&O in 1988 she was integrated into the Princess Cruises fleet and renamed SKY PRINCESS, although still under the ownership of P&O Lines. Ownership was transferred to Princess Cruises in 1994, and in 2000 the ship was transferred to P&O Cruises (Australia) and renamed PACIFIC SKY for cruising from Australia. In 2006 she was acquired by Pullmantur Cruises and repositioned to the Adriatic Sea for summer cruising under the new name, SKY WONDER. In June 2007 she was replaced on her Adriatic itineraries by the newly introduced ZENITH. She then moved to Barcelona to begin a series of one-week cruises, but by 2008 was back in the Eastern Mediterranean. She was withdrawn from service and laid up in December 2008, and it was widely thought that it was the end of her. However, in 2009, as the ATLANTIC STAR she will become Pullmantur's first dedicated Portuguese cruise ship, based in Funchal and Lisbon. IMO 8024026

EMPRESS was ordered from Chantiers de l'Atlantique (yard number G29) at St Nazaire in France in 1987 by Admiral Cruises as their FUTURE SEAS. Admiral Cruises was merged with Royal Caribbean the following year and the ship was delivered as the NORDIC EMPRESS and employed on shorter Caribbean cruises. In 2004 she was refitted and subsequently renamed EMPRESS OF THE SEAS by Gloria Estefan. In 2007 she operated Caribbean cruises as well as a new series of Bermuda cruises from Philadelphia. In spring 2008, the ship was transferred to Pullmantur Cruises as the EMPRESS. For 2009 she is based in the Adriatic and Eastern Mediterranean Seas. IMO 8716899

OCEAN DREAM was the first new cruise ship to be ordered by Carnival Cruise Lines. She was built by Aalborg Vaerft (yard number 234) of Aalborg, Denmark and delivered in December 1980 for service in the Caribbean as the TROPICALE. As the smallest unit in Carnival Cruise Lines' fleet in 2001, she was transferred to Costa Crociere and renamed the COSTA TROPICALE for service in the Mediterranean. In the autumn of 2005 she took up a new role within the group, being transferred to P&O Cruises (Australia) and renamed PACIFIC STAR by Sarah Davies, Miss World Australia 2004. For 2008 the PACIFIC STAR was due to spend a season home-ported in Singapore, but in the event was sold to Pullmantur Cruises and renamed OCEAN DREAM. She is expected to remain in the Caribbean Sea, based at Aruba. IMO 7915096

PACIFIC DREAM was Celebrity's first new ship and was built by Jos. L. Meyer (yard number 619) at Papenburg, Germany. When delivered in 1990 as the HORIZON, she was the largest ship to have been completely built in a building hall. She generally operated in the Caribbean and on the East Coast of the USA and Canada in her last years with Celebrity. In autumn 2005 she transferred within the group to Island Cruises with the new name ISLAND STAR. For her first winter with her new owner she operated in Brazil and in summer 2006 moved to the Mediterranean to serve the UK market. Island Cruises was closed in spring 2009 and the ship transferred to Pullmantur. From early summer 2009 she has taken up a new service and is expected to be based in Acapulco year-round as the PACIFIC DREAM. IMO 8807088

SOVEREIGN is the lead ship of a trio built by Chantiers de l'Atlantique (yard number A29) at St Nazaire, France. When delivered to Royal Caribbean Cruise Lines, as the SOVEREIGN OF THE SEAS, she was the world's largest cruise ship. She was named by Rosalynn Carter, wife of former US president, Jimmy Carter. She was transferred to Pullmantur Cruises in November 2008, and, as the SOVEREIGN, for 2009 takes over the weekly Mediterranean Breezes itinerary based at Barcelona, made popular by the OCEANIC. IMO 8512281

ZENITH was delivered to Celebrity Cruises two years after the HORIZON (now PACIFIC DREAM) by the Papenburg yard of Jos. L. Meyer (yard number 620). In 2007 she was transferred from Celebrity Cruises to fellow Royal Caribbean subsidiary Pullmantur Cruises in a ship swap involving the BLUE

Royal Caribbean's **Enchantment of the Seas** at Fort Lauderdale *(Andrew Kilk)*

Royal Caribbean's **Grandeur of the Seas** (Rick Frendt)

Royal Caribbean's **Independence of the Seas** leaving Southampton *(William Mayes)*

DREAM. She began her service with Pullmantur on Adriatic itineraries. In 2009 she spends the summer in the Baltic Sea and later moves to Lisbon for a series of Canary Island cruises. IMO8918136

ROYAL CARIBBEAN INTERNATIONAL

The Company Royal Caribbean Cruise Line was founded by Anders Wilhelmsen & Co and I M Skaugen & Co in 1969 (and later joined by Gotaas Larsen) to take a part of the fledgling Caribbean cruise trade. The first ship, the SONG OF NORWAY (now with Clipper Group as the FESTIVAL), was delivered during the following year. During the next two years, two further new ships were introduced. By the end of the 1970's the ships were too small for the market they were serving, and two of them were stretched by means of a new mid-section approximately 26 metres in length. A fourth ship, the 37,000-ton SONG OF AMERICA was introduced in 1982. By 1988 Anders Wilhelmsen & Co had bought out the other partners, but later entered into a new agreement with other parties in order to raise finance for new-buildings. In the same year, Royal Caribbean merged with Admiral Cruise Line. When delivered in 1988, the 73,000-ton SOVEREIGN OF THE SEAS was the world's largest cruise ship. In 1993 Royal Caribbean became a public company, with a listing on the New York Stock Exchange, although a major block of stock was retained by Anders Wilhelmsen & Co. The company became Royal Caribbean International in 1997, to better reflect its global operations. By 1998 the three original ships with which the company had laid its foundations had found new homes, and Royal Caribbean was in the middle of a massive building programme. With the entry into service in 1999 of the VOYAGER OF THE SEAS (137,000 tons), the company once again operated the largest cruise ship in the world. This class of ship has subsequently been eclipsed by the massive ships of the 'Freedom' class, which in turn will be dwarfed by the 220,000 gross ton OASIS OF THE SEAS and ALLURE OF THE SEAS currently under construction.

President Adam Goldstein **Chief Executive Officer** Richard Fain

Address 1050 Caribbean Way, Miami, Florida 33132-2096, United States of America

Telephone +1 305 539 6000 **Fax** +1 305 372 0441

Website www.royalcaribbean.com

Areas operated Caribbean Sea, East Coast North America, Alaska, and Europe

ADVENTURE OF THE SEAS	137276gt	2001	23.7k	DEP3	3114p	3835p	1185c	311.0m	38.6m	8.6m	BS
BRILLIANCE OF THE SEAS	90090gt	2002	24.0k	GEP2	2112p	2501p	848c	293.2m	32.2m	8.1m	BS
ENCHANTMENT OF THE SEAS	82910gt	1997	22.0k	DE2	2252p	2730p	840c	301.4m	32.2m	7.8m	BS
EXPLORER OF THE SEAS	137308gt	2000	23.7k	DEP3	3114p	3835p	1185c	311.0m	38.6m	8.6m	BS
FREEDOM OF THE SEAS	154407gt	2006	22.5k	DEP3	3634p	4375p	1360c	338.8m	38.6m	8.8m	BS
GRANDEUR OF THE SEAS	73817gt	1996	22.0k	DE2	1950p	2446p	760c	279.1m	32.2m	7.6m	BS
INDEPENDENCE OF THE SEAS	154407gt	2008	22.0k	DEP3	3600p	4375p	1360c	339.0m	38.6m	8.5m	BS
JEWEL OF THE SEAS	90090gt	2004	24.0k	GEP2	2112p	2501p	859c	293.2m	32.2m	8.1m	BS
LEGEND OF THE SEAS	69130gt	1995	24.0k	DE2	1804p	2074p	726c	264.3m	32.0m	7.3m	BS
LIBERTY OF THE SEAS	154407gt	2007	22.5k	DEP3	3600p	4328p	1365c	338.8m	38.6m	8.8m	BS
MAJESTY OF THE SEAS	74077gt	1992	21.0k	D2	2356p	2744p	812c	268.3m	32.2m	7.5m	BS
MARINER OF THE SEAS	138279gt	2003	23.7k	DEP3	3114p	3835p	1185c	311.0m	38.6m	8.6m	BS
MONARCH OF THE SEAS	73937gt	1991	21.0k	D2	2390p	2744p	856c	268.3m	32.2m	7.5m	BS
NAVIGATOR OF THE SEAS	138279gt	2002	23.7k	DEP3	3114p	3835p	1185c	311.0m	38.6m	8.6m	BS
RADIANCE OF THE SEAS	90090gt	2001	24.0k	GEP2	2112p	2501p	857c	293.2m	32.2m	8.1m	BS
RHAPSODY OF THE SEAS	78491gt	1997	22.0k	DE2	1998p	2435p	765c	279.0m	32.2m	7.8m	BS
SERENADE OF THE SEAS	90090gt	2003	24.0k	GEP2	2110p	2490p	891c	293.2m	32.2m	8.1m	BS
SPLENDOUR OF THE SEAS	69130gt	1996	24.0k	DE2	1804p	2074p	720c	264.3m	32.0m	7.3m	BS
VISION OF THE SEAS	78340gt	1998	22.0k	DE2	1998p	2441p	765c	279.0m	32.2m	7.8m	BS
VOYAGER OF THE SEAS	137276gt	1999	23.7k	DEP3	3114p	3838p	1176c	311.1m	38.6m	8.6m	BS

ADVENTURE OF THE SEAS was built by Kvaerner Masa Yards (yard number 1346) at Turku, Finland as the third and final unit of the original requirement for three Eagle Class ships. Subsequently two further ships were ordered. ADVENTURE OF THE SEAS generally operates Southern Caribbean cruises, but will spend summer 2010 in the Mediterranean. Her godparents were four members of the New York Fire Department - Tara Stackpole, Kevin Hannafin, Margaret McDonnell and Richard Lucas. IMO 9167227

Royal Caribbean's **Monarch of the Seas** *(Rick Frendt)*

Royal Caribbean's **Navigator of the Seas** in Southampton *(William Mayes)*

BRILLIANCE OF THE SEAS is the second ship in a four ship series under construction by Jos. L. Meyer (yard number 656) at Papenburg, Germany. She was named by Marilyn Ofer. The BRILLIANCE OF THE SEAS is based in the Mediterranean in 2009 and the summer of 2010 and will spend Spring 2010 and 2011 sailing from Dubai. IMO 9195200

ENCHANTMENT OF THE SEAS is one of a pair of ships built by Kvaerner Masa Yards (yard number 493) at Helsinki, Finland. She currently operates Caribbean and East Coast USA programmes. During 2005 she was lengthened by the Keppel Verolme Shipyard in Rotterdam by means of the insertion of a 22-metre mid section, increasing her tonnage to 80,700 and adding a further 151 cabins. Her godmother is Coleen Fain, wife of the CEO. IMO 9111802

EXPLORER OF THE SEAS, named by Jackie Joyner-Kersee, is the second of the Eagle Class ships built by Kvaerner Masa Yards (yard number 1345) at Turku, Finland. She currently operates predominantly on cruises to Bermuda, Canada and the Caribbean from Cape Liberty Cruise Port, New Jersey. IMO 9161728

FREEDOM OF THE SEAS is the first of the Ultra-Voyager class ships, and when delivered in 2006, took the title of the world's largest passenger ship. She was built by Aker Finnyards at Turku, Finland (yard number 1352). Her godmother was Katherine Louise Calder, foster mother to over 400 children. The FREEDOM OF THE SEAS currently operates Eastern and Western Caribbean cruises from Port Canaveral, Florida. IMO 9304033

GRANDEUR OF THE SEAS is one of a pair of ships built by Kvaerner Masa Yards (yard number 492) at Helsinki, Finland. Named by Aviva Ofer, she operates in the Caribbean, with a series of cruises to Bermuda and the Caribbean Sea from Baltimore. IMO 9102978

INDEPENDENCE OF THE SEAS is the last of the so-called Ultra-Voyager class ships under construction by Aker Finnyards (yard number 1354) at Turku, Finland. She was named at Southampton on 30 April 2008 by Sir Steven Redgrave and spent her first two seasons based at Southampton. She returns for the summers of 2010 and 2011, but spends the winters in the Caribbean. IMO 9349681

JEWEL OF THE SEAS was built by Jos. L. Meyer (yard number 658) at Papenburg, Germany. Kathy Mellor, 2004 National Teacher of the Year, was her godmother. Her current areas of operation are Northern Europe in summer and the East coast of the USA and the Caribbean Sea at other times. IMO 9228356

LEGEND OF THE SEAS is the lead ship of a pair built by Chantiers de l'Atlantique (yard number A31) at St Nazaire, France. Cindy Pritzker, wife of board member Jay Pritzker, named her. When she completes her 2009 Mediterranean season she will head for the Far East, where she is expected to remain until the end of 2010. IMO 9070620.

LIBERTY OF THE SEAS was built by Aker Finnyards at Turku, Finland (yard number 1353). Based in Miami, she operates to the Eastern and Western Caribbean. IMO 9330032

MAJESTY OF THE SEAS is the final member of a trio built by Chantiers de l'Atlantique (yard number B30) at St Nazaire, France. She was named by Her Majesty Queen Sonja of Norway. She operates short Bahamas and Caribbean cruises from Miami, Florida. IMO 8819512

MARINER OF THE SEAS is the fifth and (for the time being) final unit in the Eagle Class and was built by Kvaerner Masa Yards (yard number 1348) at Turku, Finland. The MARINER OF THE SEAS was named by Jean Driscoll, Olympian and Paralympian, and serves the Mexican Riviera market from her base in Los Angeles. IMO 9227510

MONARCH OF THE SEAS is one of a trio of ships built by Chantiers de l'Atlantique (yard number A30) at St Nazaire, France, and was named by actress Lauren Bacall. She operates cruises to the Bahamas from Port Canaveral, Florida. IMO 8819500

NAVIGATOR OF THE SEAS was laid down by Kvaerner Masa Yards (yard number 1347) at Turku, Finland as the JOURNEY OF THE SEAS, but was renamed during construction. Her godmother is tennis player Steffi Graf. Her programme of Western Caribbean Sea cruises is based in Miami, Florida, but she spends the summers in the Mediterranean. IMO 9227508

RADIANCE OF THE SEAS is the company's first gas turbine powered ship and was built by Jos. L. Meyer (yard number 655) at Papenburg, Germany. She is the lead ship in a series of four Panamax vessels and was named by Margot Pritzker, wife of board member Thomas Pritzker. She operates in the Caribbean, Mexican Riviera and Alaska with positioning voyages via the Panama Canal. IMO 9195195

RHAPSODY OF THE SEAS was built by Chantiers de l'Atlantique (yard number E31) at St Nazaire, France as the first ship of another pair (the other one being VISION OF THE SEAS). Named by Bodil Wilhelmsen, she is based at Seattle for a series of Alaska cruises for part of the year and transfers to the Australia for a season of cruises from Sydney. IMO 9116864

SERENADE OF THE SEAS was built by Jos. L. Meyer (yard number 657) at Papenburg, Germany. Her sphere of operation takes in Alaska, Hawaii and the Caribbean Sea. She was named by Whoopi Goldberg. IMO 9228344

SPLENDOUR OF THE SEAS is the second ship of the first pair built by Chantiers de l'Atlantique (yard number B31) at St Nazaire, France. Her godmother is Lise Wilhelmsen. The SPLENDOUR OF THE SEAS operates in the Mediterranean and South America. IMO 9070632

VISION OF THE SEAS was built as the second ship of the second pair by Chantiers de l'Atlantique (yard number F31) at St Nazaire, France. She is one of the company's more widely travelled ships as she operates in Northern Europe and South America. She was named by Helen Stephan, wife of Royal Caribbean's founder and vice-chairman, Edwin Stephan. IMO 9116876

VOYAGER OF THE SEAS was built by Kvaerner Masa Yards (yard number 1344) at Turku, Finland as the lead ship in the Eagle Class of (initially three and later five) massive vessels. The VOYAGER OF THE SEAS became the largest passenger ship ever built when she entered service in the autumn of 1999. Her godmother is Katarina Witt, and the ship is employed on Caribbean and Mediterranean itineraries. IMO 9161716

Cruise ships on order

OASIS OF THE SEAS	c225000gt	2009	22.0k	DEP3	5400p	p		c	360.0m	47.0m		m	BS
ALLURE OF THE SEAS	c225000gt	2010	22.0k	DEP3	5400p	p		c	360.0m	47.0m		m	BS
NEWBUILDING 3	c154000gt	2012	22.0k	DEP3	3600p	4328p	1365c		338.8m	38.6m	8.5m		BS

OASIS OF THE SEAS and **ALLURE OF THE SEAS** are under construction by STX (yard number 1363 and unknown) at Turku, Finland under the name Project Genesis. They will be the most expensive passenger ships ever built, with an estimated price tag of $1.1 billion each, and are expected to be the largest passenger ships in service for some years. When delivered in late 2009 the OASIS OF THE SEAS will be based in Fort Lauderdale. IMO 9383936 and 9383948

NEWBUILDING 3 will be a further unit of the 'Freedom' class, although not yet confirmed. IMO 9506083

TUI CRUISES

The Company See under TUI AG.

SAGA GROUP

The Company Saga Holidays and Saga Shipping are subsidiaries of the British financial services and holiday group Saga Group Limited. The company, established in the 1950's by Sidney De Haan, was sold by its founding family in October 2004 to private equity firm Charterhouse. Although the company had been selling cruises on other operators' ships for many years, it was not until 1997 that the company acquired its first ship, the SAGA ROSE. Prior to that, however, the company had undertaken many whole ship charters from as early as 1978, when Epirotiki Lines' ATLAS was used. Other vessels were used from time to time, including the RUSS in 1992. Saga cruises are only sold to the over 50's, and are not generally sold through travel agents. Saga Shipping Ltd and its subsidiaries own the ships. A temporary replacement for the SAGA ROSE was to have been the SAGA PEARL II (originally intended to be QUEST FOR ADVENTURE), but the ship was caught up in the bankruptcy of Club Cruise and at the time of writing the transaction had not been completed.

Address The Saga Building, Enbrook Park, Folkestone, Kent, CT20 3SE, England

Telephone +44 1303 771964 **Fax** +44 1303 771243

Website www.saga.co.uk

Area operated Europe, North Atlantic, Caribbean and World Cruises

SAGA PEARL II	18591gt	1981	18.0k	D2	446p	446p	252c	164.3m	22.6m	6.1m	BS
SAGA ROSE	24528gt	1965	18.0k	D2	574p	574p	350c	188.9m	24.5m	8.3m	BS
SAGA RUBY	24492gt	1973	18.0k	D2	661p	661p	380c	191.1m	25.0m	8.2m	GB

Royal Caribbean's **Vision of the Seas** at Vancouver *(Andrew Kilk)*

Saga Group's **Saga Rose** in the Bay of Biscay *(William Mayes)*

Saga Group's **Spirit of Adventure** *(Bill Lawes)*

SAGA PEARL II For full details see under Club Cruise (ASTORIA) and late news

SAGA ROSE was built by Forges et Chantiers de La Mediterranee (yard number 1366) at La Seyne in France as the SAGAFJORD for Den Norske Amerikalinje A/S (Norwegian America Line) for service between Oslo and New York, but with cruising in mind, too. Her liner role had ceased by 1980, and three years later she was sold to Cunard Line Ltd without a change of name. She continued to operate under Norwegian America Cruises for some years, but was later marketed as a Cunard Line ship, although retaining her original name. In 1996 she was chartered to Transocean Tours as the GRIPSHOLM, but suffered damage due to grounding and was withdrawn from service. She was acquired by Saga Shipping in 1997 and refitted to become the SAGA ROSE. In late 2006 the ship underwent her final major internal refit. During the summer of 2008 Saga announced the retirement of the Saga Rose. She completes her service with Saga in December 2009, and is expected to become a floating hotel, possibly in London's Docklands. IMO 6416043

SAGA RUBY was delivered in 1973 by Swan Hunter (yard number 39) at Wallsend on Tyne, England as the VISTAFJORD for Den Norske Amerikalinje A/S (Norwegian America Line) and was thus the last passenger liner to be built in the United Kingdom. She was initially employed on line voyages between Oslo and New York, and worldwide cruising. By 1980 she was used exclusively for cruising and was transferred along with her sister the SAGAFJORD to Norwegian American Cruises A/S, but retained her Oslo registry. In 1983 the two ships, together with the Norwegian American Cruises name, were sold to Cunard Line and continued to trade under their existing names. Already by then in Cunard colours, the VISTAFJORD was renamed CARONIA following a major refit in 1999. She was the third Cunarder to carry this name, in a short-lived revival of the 'names ending in 'ia' theme'. CARONIA was based in Southampton for cruises from the United Kingdom to Europe and further afield, but in 2004 was sold to Saga Shipping with delivery in November of that year. Following a major refit in Malta, costing some £17 million, she took up service as the SAGA RUBY with her new owner early in 2005. IMO 7214715

SPIRIT OF ADVENTURE

The Company Spirit of Adventure is a subsidiary of Saga Group specialising in cultural cruises of the Swan Hellenic type. This operation is marketed separately from Saga Cruises as SPIRIT OF ADVENTURE and is not restricted to passengers over the age of 50. During 2008 the company announced that it had acquired the ASTORIA from Club Cruise and that she was to become the QUEST FOR ADVENTURE. However, within a few months this planned expansion was put on hold with the ship being diverted to the Saga Cruises fleet as the SAGA PEARL II. However, that ship has still not been acquired at the time of writing.

Address Spirit of Adventure, Enbrook Park, Folkestone, Kent, CT20 3SE, England

Telephone +44 1303 771964 **Fax** +44 1303 771243

Website www.spiritofadventure.co.uk

Area operated Europe, round Africa, South America, the Caribbean and Antarctica

SPIRIT OF ADVENTURE	9570gt	1980	17.0k	D2	352p	352p	170c	139.3m	17.5m	4.8m	BS

SPIRIT OF ADVENTURE was the ship by which Peter Deilmann entered the ocean cruise market. She was built by Howaldtswerke-Deutsche Werft (yard number 163) at Kiel, Germany as the BERLIN for a consortium of German investors in which Deilmann held a small share. Late in 1982 she was chartered to Blue Funnel Cruises of Singapore, an associated business of the Straits Steamship Company, as a replacement for the CENTAUR, which had in turn been chartered to St Helena Shipping. She was renamed PRINCESS MAHSURI. Blue Funnel's Far East and Australian operation was already in decline and she was returned to her owners a year early in 1984, when she reverted to her original name. She was lengthened by 17 metres in 1986 at Rendsburg, Germany and continued to operate for Deilmann until that company terminated her charter at the end of 2004, following which she was laid up until purchased by Saga, with delivery at the end of 2005. In the meantime she secured a charter for a Metropolis Tur, for whom she operated as the ORANGE MELODY. For her new service with Saga she was renamed as the SPIRIT OF ADVENTURE, although it was originally thought that she would be named SAGA OPAL. IMO 7904889

Saga Group's **Saga Ruby** in Dover *(John Hendy)*

Salamis Cruise Lines' **Salamis Glory** in Limassol *(William Mayes)*

SALAMIS CRUISE LINES

The Company Salamis Cruise Lines is a Cypriot private sector company within the Salamis Tours (Holdings) Group (established in 1959), which is publicly quoted on the Cyprus Stock Exchange. The company previously operated the most regular service on long ferry routes in the Eastern Mediterranean. However, the political violence in the state of Israel and the occupied territories of Palestine caused this service to cease in 2002. The company's ro-ro passenger ferry has been variously laid up and chartered to other Mediterranean operators. Salamis Lines has operated short cruises from Cyprus for a number of years, and also owns a small ro-ro freighter that is chartered out.

Managing Director Panagiota Gripeou

Address Salamis House, 1 G. Katsounotos Street, PO Box 50531, 3607 Lemesos, Cyprus

Telephone +357 2586 0000 **Fax** +357 2537 4437

Website www.salamisinternational.com

Area operated Short cruises from Cyprus to Egypt and Israel

SALAMIS GLORY	10392gt	1962	17.5k	D2	444p	600p	190c	150.0m	19.0m	5.6m	CY
VAN GOGH	15402gt	1975	22.0k	D2	428p	640p	216c	156.3m	21.8m	5.9m	CY

SALAMIS GLORY was built by Brodogradiliste Uljanik (yard number 237) at Pula in what was then Yugoslavia as the ANNA NERY for Companhia Nacional de Navegacao Costeira Autarquia of Brazil for the coastal passenger trades. She also operated cruises both in South America and to Europe. She was transferred to Lloyd Brasiliero in 1966, who used her until 1977, when she was laid up. In 1978 she was acquired by the Greek ship owner Kavounides and renamed as the DANAOS. She entered service later that year for Kavounides (Hellenic Cruises) as the CONSTELLATION. Her owners failed in 1987 and the ship was seized by the Greek Development Bank, subsequently being laid up for four years. In 1992 she operated briefly in the Far East as the MORNING STAR, before becoming the REGENT SPIRIT of Regency Cruises. That company, too, was declared bankrupt in 1995 and the ship was arrested in Nice, France. She was sold at auction to a company within the Salamis Shipping Group and has operated since 1996 as the SALAMIS GLORY on short cruises from Limassol, Cyprus. IMO 5018698

VAN GOGH was owned by Club Cruise of The Netherlands' subsidiary Maritime & Leasing Ltd and operated on year-round charter for Travelscope until the beginning of 2008. She was built by Wartsila (yard number 1213) at Turku, Finland as the GRUZIYA, one of a series of five ro-ro passenger vessels for the Black Sea Shipping Company of Odessa, and was immediately chartered to the German tour operator, TUI. She subsequently operated for a number of charterers until the early 1990's when, following the break-up of the Soviet Union, the Black Sea Shipping Company was in financial difficulties. In 1994 the ship was chartered to the United States Military Sealift Command. In the following year BLASCO, as her owners had become, renamed her as the ODESSA SKY. In 1998 she was converted at Bremerhaven for use as the casino ship CLUB CRUISE 1, and was later renamed simply as CLUB 1. She was acquired by Club Cruise in 1999, converted back to a normal cruise ship and renamed as the VAN GOGH. Her first charter in 2000 was to Nouvelles Frontieres, but in recent years she became a regular with Travelscope. On the failure of Travelscope, Club Cruise tried to operate the ship under the trading name of Van Gogh Cruises, but this was unsuccessful and the ship eventually operated under charter to Metropolis Tur of Russia in 2008. She was laid up at Piraeus until sold at auction to Salamis Lines. She is expected to replace the SALAMIS GLORY. Vincent van Gogh (1853-1890) is possibly the most famous Dutch painter. IMO 7359400

SAVECA

The Company Servicios Acuaticos de Venezuela CA is a shipbroker, re-designer and operator of ships, founded in 2000. The use of these vessels is unclear, as the company appears to operate in the offshore industry in an accommodation supply role. However, the company's website also indicates an interest in the operation of cruise ships for Venezuelan passengers.

Address Av. Francisco de Miranda, Esq. Plaza Francia-Edif. Humboldt, Piso 8, Off 35, Altamira, Caracas, Venezuela

Telephone +58 212 266 8616 **Fax** +58 212 267 1753

Website www.savecaonline.com

Area operated Possibly cruises to the Caribbean islands from Venezuela

Saveca's **Amazing Grace** *(Mark Amielanczyk)*

Sea Cloud Cruises' **Sea Cloud** at Kusadasi *(Rick Frendt)*

AMAZING GRACE	1585gt	1955	14.0k	D2	92p	92p	44c	78.3m	12.2m	3.8m	TT
BLACK PRINCE	11209gt	1966	18.5k	D2	412p	451p	200c	141.6m	20.0m	6.4m	BS

AMAZING GRACE was built as the buoy and lighthouse tender PHAROS by the Caledon Shipbuilding and Engineering Company (yard number 507) at Dundee in Scotland. Unconfirmed reports suggest that for a short time in 1988 she was given the name ORIENT EXPRESS. She started operating for Windjammer Barefoot Cruises as the AMAZING GRACE in 1988 and until recently offered cruises on her supply voyages servicing the company's sailing ships. She was laid up in the company's shipyard in Port of Spain awaiting renovation. It would appear that she has been acquired by SAVECA without a change of name. IMO 5276874

BLACK PRINCE For details see under Fred. Olsen Cruise Lines.

SEA CLOUD CRUISES

The Company Sea Cloud Cruises, founded in 1979, is a subsidiary of the German Hansa Truehand Group, a business with interests in ship management, engineering and consultancy. The company also operates two river cruise ships on the waterways of Europe.

Chairman Hermann Ebel

Address Ballindamm 17, D 20095 Hamburg, Germany

Telephone +49 4030 9592 0 **Fax** +49 4030 959 222

Website www.seacloud.com

Area operated Worldwide

SEA CLOUD	2532gt	1931	12.0k	SD2	64p	64p	60c	109.7m	14.6m	4.9m	MT
SEA CLOUD II	3849gt	2000	14.0k	SD2	94p	94p	58c	117.0m	16.0m	5.3m	MT

SEA CLOUD was built by the Krupp Shipyard in Kiel, Germany as the HUSSAR, the largest sailing yacht ever built, for E F Hutton, a wealthy New York businessman. After their divorce in 1935, Hutton handed the ship over to his former wife (who had actually designed the vessel) and she renamed her SEA CLOUD. Following the entry of the United States into the Second World War, the SEA CLOUD was taken up for military service, principally around the Azores and Southern Greenland. She was equipped with weaponry and also served as a weather station under the name IX-99. The ship was returned to her owners at the end of the war, and after a refit lasting four years she re-emerged as good as new. The SEA CLOUD was sold in 1955, becoming the presidential yacht of the Dominican Republic, and renamed ANGELITA. Following the assassination of the president in 1961, she was renamed again, becoming the PATRIA. Five years later, she was back in American hands as the ANTARNA for Operation Sea Cruises. She was subsequently laid up at Colon for eight years before being bought by her German owners and renamed again as the SEA CLOUD. She was refitted in Kiel, and entered service as a sail cruise ship in 1979. Her current owners acquired her in 1994. IMO 8843446

SEA CLOUD II was built by Astilleros Gondan (yard number 405) at Castropol, Spain for operation by Sea Cloud Cruises. IMO 9171292

Cruise ship on order

SEA CLOUD HUSSAR	4228gt	2010	14.0k	SDE2	136p	136p	90c	135.7m	17.2m	5.6m	MT

SEA CLOUD HUSSAR is under construction by Factoria de Naval Marin (yard number 158) at Marin, near Vigo, Spain and is expected to become the largest full-rigged passenger tall ship ever built when she enters service in spring 2010. IMO 9483712

SEADREAM YACHT CLUB

The Company Seadream Yacht Club, a Norwegian registered company, was founded in August 2001 by Atle Brynestad (the founder of Seabourn) and Larry Pimentel (former President of Cunard-Seabourn). Pimentel retired in January 2009. The company operates two luxury yacht-type vessels.

Chairman and Chief Executive Officer Atle Brynestad **President** Robert Lepisto

Address 601 Brickell Key Drive, Suite 150, Miami, Florida 33131, United States of America

Telephone +1 305 631 6100 **Fax** +1 305 631 6110

Sea Cloud Cruises' **Sea Cloud II** at Fowey *(Andrew Kilk)*

Seadream Yacht Club's **Seadream II** at San Juan *(Andrew Kilk)*

Website www.seadreamyachtclub.com

Area operated Mediterranean Sea in summer, Caribbean Sea in winter

SEADREAM I	4333gt	1984	17.5k	D2	110p	110p	95c	104.8m	14.5m	4.3m	BS
SEADREAM II	4333gt	1985	17.5k	D2	110p	110p	95c	104.8m	14.5m	4.3m	BS

SEADREAM I and **SEADREAM II** were built as the SEA GODDESS I and SEA GODDESS II by Wartsila (yard numbers 466 and 467) at Helsinki, Finland for Sea Goddess Cruises of Norway (Norske Cruise) as luxury yacht style vessels. Following a disastrous year for the company in 1986, Cunard Line took the two ships on a twelve-year charter. Cunard continued to market the ships as Sea Goddesses. Following the acquisition of Cunard by Carnival Corporation in 1998, the ships were transferred to Carnival's luxury cruise line, Seabourn, and renamed as SEABOURN GODDESS I and II. In 2001 they were both sold to a new company, Seadream Yacht Club and renamed SEADREAM I and SEADREAM II. IMO 8203438 and 8203440

SILVERSEA CRUISES

The Company Silversea Cruises, created by the Lefebvre family of Rome débuted in 1994 with its first ship, the SILVER CLOUD. A recent innovation has been to provide personalised voyages allowing embarkation and disembarkation at almost any port, providing a minimum of five nights is spent aboard. In a diversification, the company entered the soft expedition market in 2008 with the introduction of the PRINCE ALBERT II.

President Amerigo Perasso

Address   Head Office Gildo Pastor Centre, 7 rue de Gabian, 98000 Monte Carlo, Monaco

European office: 77/79 Great Eastern Street, London, EC2A 3HU, England

Telephone +377 9770 2424 **Fax** +377 9770 2428

+44 844 770 9030 **Fax** +44 844 770 9040

Website www.silversea.com

Areas operated Worldwide

PRINCE ALBERT II	6130gt	1989	15.0k	D2	132p	132p	66c	108.1m	15.6m	4.4m	BS
SILVER CLOUD	16927gt	1994	20.0k	D2	296p	296p	185c	155.8m	21.4m	5.3m	BS
SILVER SHADOW	28258gt	2000	20.5k	D2	382p	382p	295c	182.0m	24.8m	6.0m	BS
SILVER SPIRIT	c36000gt	2009	20.3k	D2	540p	540p	378c	195.8m	26.6m	6.3m	BS
SILVER WHISPER	28258gt	2001	20.5k	D2	382p	382p	295c	182.0m	24.8m	6.0m	BS
SILVER WIND	16927gt	1995	20.0k	D2	298p	298p	185c	155.8m	21.4m	5.3m	BS

PRINCE ALBERT II was built by Rauma Repola (yard number 304) at Rauma, Finland as the DELFIN CLIPPER for Delfin Cruises. Following the failure of Delfin she was repossessed by her builder and later renamed SALLY CLIPPER in 1990 for a charter to Sally Line for Baltic cruising. In 1992 she became the BALTIC CLIPPER and later that year was renamed again, becoming the DELFIN STAR for gambling cruises from Hong Kong and Singapore. She was sold to the Samsung Shipyard in South Korea in 1997 and renamed DREAM 21. She was subsequently renamed WORLD DISCOVERER in 2002 when sold to Discoverer Reederei (the owner of Society Expeditions). Society Expeditions ceased trading in June 2004. She was subsequently repossessed by the Sembawang Shipyard, which was owed substantial sums in respect of her conversion, and remained laid up in Singapore. She was reported to have been sold to Chikara Shipping early in 2007, but that transaction was never completed. Subsequently she was acquired by Silversea and after a major refit has emerged as the soft expedition ship PRINCE ALBERT II. She was renamed in Monte Carlo in the presence of HSH Prince Albert II. IMO 8806747

SILVER CLOUD and **SILVER WIND** were built by Cantieri Navali Visentini (yard numbers 775 and 776) at Donada, Italy and completed by Esercizio at Viareggio, Italy. The SILVER WIND underwent a major refurbishment in the autumn of 2008. IMO 8903923 and 8903935

SILVER SHADOW and **SILVER WHISPER** were built by Cantieri Navali Visentini (yard numbers 981 and 982) at Donada, Italy and completed by T. Mariotti at Genoa, Italy. IMO 9192167 and 9192179

SILVER SPIRIT was ordered from Fincantieri (yard number 6178) in March 2007 and was completed at the Ancona yard. IMO 9437866

Silversea's **Silver Cloud** in London *(David Trevor-Jones)*

Silversea's **Silver Shadow** in Vancouver *(Andrew Kilk)*

Cruise ship on order

NEWBUILDING 1		c36000gt	2010	20.3k	D2	540p	540p	378c	195.8m	26.6m	6.3m	BS

NEWBUILDING 1 is currently an option, and if built will be cnstructed by Fincantieri. IMO 9437878

SKORPIOS TOURS

The Company Naviera & Turismo Skorpios is a Chilean private sector business, founded in 1976 by Constantino Kochifas Caracamo, a businessman and shipowner from Southern Chile. The first cruises to the San Rafael Glacier utilized the small cargo ship MIMI, with a capacity for 12 passengers.

Chief Executive Officer Constantino Kochifas Caracarno

Address Augusto Leguia Norte 118, Las Condes, Santiago, Chile

Telephone +56 2 477 1900 **Fax** +56 2 232 2269

Website www.skorpios.cl

Area operated Chilean Patagonia

SKORPIOS I	337gt	1978	12.0k	D1	66p	74p	24c	50.0m	8.4m	3.0m	CL
SKORPIOS II	1263gt	1988	12.0k	D1	130p	160p	34c	70.0m	10.0m	2.9m	CL
SKORPIOS III	1597gt	1995	14.0k	D1	100p	125p	34c	69.0m	10.0m	3.3m	CL

SKORPIOS I No further details available.

SKORPIOS II was built by Kochifas (yard number 1) at Puerto Montt in Chile. She was launched in 1981, but not completed until 1988. IMO 8006397

SKORPIOS III was built by Kochifas Shipyard (yard number 2) at Puerto Montt, Chile. IMO 9143908

SOCIETA ITALIANA DI NAVIGAZIONE

The Company Societa Italiana di Navigazione is an Italian company.

Address Via Saverio Mercadante 32, 00198 Rome, Italy

Telephone +39 06 84 17000 **Fax** +39 06 85 344959

Website www.signoradelvento.com

Area operated Italian West coast, Sardinia and Corsica

SIGNORA DEL VENTO	818gt	1962	12.0k	D1	66p	74p	24c	50.0m	8.4m	3.0m	IT

SIGNORA DEL VENTO was built by Stocznia im Komuny Paryskiej (yard number B20/13) at Gdynia, Poland as the trawler GOPLO. She was acquired by Kings Lake Shipping in 1993 and renamed PEACE. At some stage she was converted for use as a training ship, but in 2006 she was acquired by her current owner and converted for use as a cruise ship under the name SIGNORA DEL VENTO, entering service in 2008. IMO 5133589

ST LAWRENCE CRUISE LINES

The Company St Lawrence Cruise Lines, a Canadian business, was founded by Robert Clark in 1981.

Chief Executive Officer Robert Clark

Address Suite 200, 253 Ontario Street, Kingston, Ontario, K7L 2Z4 Canada

Telephone +1 613 549 8091 **Fax** +1 613 549 8410

Website www.stlawrencecruiselines.com

Area operated The St Lawrence and Ottawa Rivers in Canada

CANADIAN EMPRESS	463gt	1981	10.0k	DE2	64p	66p	13c	32.9m	9.2m	1.5m	CA

CANADIAN EMPRESS was built for the company in Canada.

Star Clippers' **Royal Clipper** off Dubrovnik *(Rick Frendt)*

Star Clippers' **Star Clipper** *(Ben Lyons)*

STAR CLIPPERS

The Company Star Clippers was founded by Swedish entrepreneur Mikael Krafft in 1991. Fred. Olsen Travel is the United Kingdom agent for Star Clippers. Until the recent economic downturn, the company was planning to build a new ship for delivery in 2010. However, the 7,400 gross ton, 296-passenger ship has been deferred for the time being.

President and Chief Executive Officer Mikael Krafft

Address Clipper Palace, 4 rue de la Turbie, 98000 Monte Carlo, Monaco

Telephone +377 9797 8400 **Fax** +377 9797 8401

Website www.starclippers.com

Area operated Caribbean Sea, French Polynesia and the Far East, all three ships operate in the Mediterranean Sea in summer

ROYAL CLIPPER	4425gt	2000	13.5k	SD1	227p	227p	106c	132.7m	16.0m	5.7m	LU
STAR CLIPPER	2298gt	1992	12.0k	SD1	170p	170p	72c	111.6m	15.0m	5.5m	LU
STAR FLYER	2298gt	1991	12.0k	SD1	170p	170p	72c	111.6m	15.0m	5.5m	LU

ROYAL CLIPPER, inspired by the legendary tall ship, PREUSSEN of 1902, is the only 5-masted full-rigged ship built since that time. Her 42 sails require a crew of 20 just to handle the canvas. She was built by Stocznia Gdansk (yard number B811/01) at Gdansk, Poland, and was launched as the GWAREK in 1991 for Zaglebie Gdanska S A. Her hull lay incomplete at Gdansk until purchased by White Star Clippers in 1998. At that time her owners contracted with Cenal Shipyard to lengthen the hull by 23 metres, and this hull was then delivered to the de Merwede shipyard in The Netherlands for fitting out in April 1999. She had originally been fitted with Sulzer-Cegielski engines, but these were replaced with Caterpillar diesels. She was completed and delivered as the ROYAL CLIPPER in July 2000. For 2009/2010 she cruises in the Caribbean and Western Mediterranean. IMO 8712178

STAR CLIPPER and **STAR FLYER** were built by Scheepswerf van Langerbrugge (yard numbers 2184 and 2183) at Ghent, Belgium. The STAR FLYER was actually launched as the STAR CLIPPER, but following a complaint by American owner Clipper Cruise Line, the name was changed. Star Clippers subsequently won the US court case and called the second ship STAR CLIPPER. For 2009/2010 the STAR CLIPPER cruises in the Far East and Eastern Mediterranean, while the STAR FLYER operates in French Polynesia. IMO 8915445 and 8915433

STAR CRUISES GROUP

The Group Star Cruises was established in 1993 by Malaysia's Genting Group, controlled by Lim Goh Tong. The company revolutionized the Asian cruise industry by operating large, modern cruise ships at internationally accepted levels of service and entertainment. In 2000 Star bought out Norwegian Cruise Lines in a deal that propelled it to the position of the third largest cruise line in the world. The Genting Group has its origins in the Genting Highlands Resort, which commenced in 1965. The group is now involved in the oil, power generation, property, paper and leisure industries. Lim Goh Tong passed away in October 2007.

In 2008 an agreement was reached with Apollo Management under which that organisation took 50% of the equity, and control of NCL. Subsequently, the Cruise Ferries business was closed when its sole ship, the WASA QUEEN, was sold for use as a ferry in the Adriatic Sea.

NORWEGIAN CRUISE LINE

The Company Norwegian Cruise Line is 50% owned by Star Cruises, but as it is controlled by Apollo Management it is listed under that group.

STAR CRUISES

The Company From its early foundations in 1993 to the present day, the development of Star Cruises has not been without difficulty, due to a number of regional factors. The company acquired its first ships, the former Viking Line Baltic ferries ATHENA (the previous STAR AQUARIUS) and KALYPSO (STAR PISCES) in the spring of 1994, and these were followed by other good quality second-hand tonnage. It was not until 1998 that the first purpose built ship for the company's South East Asian itineraries entered the fleet, and the story subsequently has been one of alternate expansion and cut

Star Cruises' **Megastar Aries** and **Superstar Libra** in Singapore *(Jonathan Boonzaier)*

Star Cruises' **Star Pisces** in Hong Hong *(Theodore W Scull)*

back as new markets in the region have been explored and either developed or abandoned. Star Cruises recently sold the WASA QUEEN, thereby effectively closing down subsidiary Cruise Ferries.

Chairman, President and Chief Executive Officer Tan Sri Lim Kok Thay

Address Star Cruises Terminal, Pulau Indah, Pelabuhan Barat, 42009 Klang, Selangor, Malaysia

Telephone +60 3 3101 1313 **Fax** +60 3 3101 1406

Website www.starcruises.com

Areas operated South East Asia, India

MEGASTAR ARIES	3341gt	1989	16.0k	D2	72p	72p	80c	82.2m	14.0m	3.4m	PA
MEGASTAR TAURUS	3341gt	1989	16.0k	D2	72p	72p	80c	82.2m	14.0m	3.4m	PA
STAR PISCES	40053gt	1990	21.3k	D2	1378p	1900p	750c	176.6m	29.0m	6.0m	PA
SUPERSTAR AQUARIUS	51309gt	1993	20.3k	D2	1726p	2016p	614c	229.9m	28.5m	7.0m	BS
SUPERSTAR LIBRA	42285gt	1988	21.5k	D2	1494p	1796p	609c	216.2m	28.4m	7.0m	BS
SUPERSTAR VIRGO	75338gt	1999	24.0k	DE2	1964p	2975p	1125c	268.6m	32.2m	7.9m	PA

MEGASTAR ARIES was built by Flender Werft (yard number 648), Lubeck, Germany for the Windsor Cruise Line as the LADY SARAH. She was renamed AURORA II in 1991 when operating for New Frontier Cruises of Hamburg, and passed to Star Cruises in 1995, becoming the MEGASTAR ARIES. IMO 8705278

MEGASTAR TAURUS was built by Flender Werft (yard number 647) at Lubeck, Germany for the Windsor Cruise Line as the LADY DIANA, later renamed the LADY DI, before transferring to New Frontier Cruises of Hamburg as the AURORA I. She became the MEGASTAR TAURUS on acquisition by Star Cruises in 1995. IMO 8705266

STAR PISCES was built by Masa Yards (yard number 1298) at Turku, Finland as the car ferry KALYPSO for the Swedish partner in the Viking Line consortium, Rederi AB Slite. Following the financial difficulties encountered by that company, receivers were appointed and in 1994 the ship was sold together with her sister, the ATHENA (now DFDS Seaways' PEARL OF SCANDINAVIA) to Star Cruises. She was rebuilt as the cruise ship STAR PISCES and has since been based in Hong Kong. In recent years she has operated overnight cruises out of Hong Kong. While these are geared mainly for gamblers, unlike the rest of the Hong Kong casino cruise fleet, she still offered a full range of cruise-type activities as well. The STAR PISCES is currently laid up. IMO 8710857

SUPERSTAR AQUARIUS was built as the WINDWARD for Kloster Cruise of Nassau (Norwegian Caribbean Line) by Chantiers de l'Atlantique (yard number D30) at St Nazaire, France. When built, the ship was 39,217 gross tons and had a length of 190 metres. In 1998 she went to Lloydwerft at Bremerhaven, Germany to have a new 40 metre mid section inserted and was renamed NORWEGIAN WIND for the now re-styled Norwegian Cruise Line. In 2007 she was transferred to Star Cruises for short cruises based in Hong Kong for which she was renamed SUPERSTAR AQUARIUS. IMO 9008421

SUPERSTAR LIBRA was built as the SEAWARD for Kloster's Norwegian Caribbean Cruise Line by Wartsila (yard number 1294) at Turku, Finland and following her naming ceremony in New York she commenced cruising in the Caribbean. In 1997 she was renamed NORWEGIAN SEA. In September 2005 she was transferred within the group to Star Cruises and was renamed SUPERSTAR LIBRA to start a new cruise venture, operating from Mumbai, India. That service finished after the Indian Government extended the territorial limits for gambling to 200 miles. She was laid up for a while but has now resumed her Taiwan programme. IMO 8612134

SUPERSTAR VIRGO was built by Meyer Werft (yard number 647) at Papenburg, Germany for Star Cruises. She is the current flagship of the Star Cruises fleet and is a sister to the NORWEGIAN SPIRIT. She currently operates short cruises from Singapore. IMO 9141077

TRANSOCEAN TOURS

The Company Transocean Tours Touristik is a German tour company, established in 1954, operating ocean cruises and river cruises on the waterways of Europe for German-speaking passengers. In a move away from its core market, the company positioned the ARIELLE (Louis Cruise Lines' AQUAMARINE) for a number of ex-UK cruises for British passengers in 2007, and the MARCO POLO performed a similar programme in 2008 and 2009.

Address   Stavendamm 22, 28195 Bremen, Germany

Star Cruises' **Superstar Aquarius** in Hong Kong *(Andrew Kilk)*

Star Cruises' **Superstar Virgo** *(Jonathan Boonzaier)*

UK Cruise and Maritime Services, 274 Main Road, Sutton-at-Hone, Dartford, Kent, DA4 9HJ, England

Telephone +49 421 33360 **Fax** +49 421 3326 100

UK +44 1322 863928 **Fax** +44 8715 602074

Website www.transocean.de and www.transoceancruises.co.uk

Area operated Northern Europe, Mediterranean Sea and South America

ASTOR	20606gt	1987	18.0k	D2	590p	590p	260c	176.3m	22.6m	6.1m	BS
MARCO POLO	22080gt	1965	19.5k	D2	850p	850p	350c	176.3m	23.6m	8.2m	BS

ASTOR was ordered by the South African Marine Corporation as a replacement for the 1981-built ASTOR, from Howaldtswerke-Deutsche Werft (yard number 218) at Kiel, Germany. During construction however, the company decided to abandon its plans to re-start the Cape Town to Southampton liner service and in a complicated series of moves the ship was delivered as the ASTOR to Ireland Blyth and registered in Mauritius. After only eighteen months she was sold to the Black Sea Shipping Company of Odessa as the FEDOR DOSTOEVSKIY. In 1991 she was registered under the ownership of a SOVCOMFLOT group company. She subsequently performed a number of charters was then chartered to Transocean Tours as the ASTOR under long-term arrangement. In 2006 she was acquired by German-based Premicon, but remains on charter to Transocean. IMO 8506373

MARCO POLO was built in what was then East Germany by Mathias-Thesen-Werft (yard number 126) at Wismar, Germany as one of a series of five liners for the Black Sea Shipping Company and the Baltic Shipping Company. The ALEKSANDR PUSHKIN entered service for the Baltic Shipping Company in the summer of 1965 with a series of cruises before taking up her intended employment on the service from Leningrad to Montreal during the following spring. From 1975 she was mainly used for cruising and from 1979 was on a five-year charter to Transocean. In 1985 she was transferred to the Far Eastern Shipping Company of Vladivostok and over the next few years she undertook charters to CTC Lines for cruising from Sydney, Australia. Following a brief lay-up in Singapore she was sold in 1991 to Shipping and General (Orient Lines) and sent to Greece for a major refit that took almost three years to complete. As the MARCO POLO she proved to be both popular and successful with her out of the way itineraries. Norwegian Cruise Line subsequently acquired Orient Lines in 1998, but the operation retained its own identity. NCL closed Orient Lines in 2007 and sold the ship to Global Maritime of Greece, from whom she is chartered by Transocean Tours. Marco Polo, the great Italian traveller, was born in 1254 on the Dalmatian island of Korcula, which at that time belonged to Venice. His epic journey along the Silk Road through Asia lasted 24 years and resulted in the production of the greatest travelogue ever written. IMO 6417097

TRAVEL DYNAMICS INTERNATIONAL

The Company Travel Dynamics International, formerly known as Classical Cruises, is an operator of high calibre educational programmes on small ships and was founded in the 1970's.

Address 132 East 70th Street, New York, NY 10021, United States of America

Telephone +1 212 517 7555 **Fax** +1 212 774 1560

Website www.traveldynamicsinternational.com

Area operated Mediterranean Sea, South America and Australia

CALLISTO	430gt	1963	12.0k	D2	34p	34p	16c	46.8m	8.0m	2.3m	GR
CLELIA II	4077gt	1990	15.0k	D2	84p	84p	65c	88.3m	15.3m	3.3m	MT
CORINTHIAN II	4200gt	1991	15.5k	D2	114p	114p	70c	90.3m	15.3m	4.0m	MT

CALLISTO was the daughter of Lycaon, and associated with Artemis, the goddess of the hunt in Greek Mythology. The ship was built as the MARINA by D W Kremer Sohn (yard number 1104) at Elmshorn in Germany. She became the ILLYRIA II in 1985 and was renamed CALLISTO in 2000 by Blue Sea Shipping Line. She is operated under charter. IMO 5416533

CLELIA II was built by Cantieri Navale Ferrari (yard number 46) at La Spezia, Italy as the RENAISSANCE FOUR for Renaissance Cruises. She became the CLELIA II for Lindos Maritime in 1996. She is currently owned by Goodwin Sands Marine as a private yacht, although she has recently operated for Travel Dynamics from time to time, and appears in the current programme. IMO 8708672

Transocean Tours' **Astor** in Auckland *(Andrew Kilk)*

Travel Dynamics' **Clelia II** at Valletta *(Rick Frendt)*

CORINTHIAN II was built as the RENAISSANCE SEVEN by Nuovi Cantieri Apuania (yard number 1146) at Marina di Carrara, Italy for Renaissance Cruises. She became the REGINA RENAISSANCE in 1992, reverting to her original name in 1998. Sold in 2001 she was renamed as the RENAI I. In 2003 she became the SUN, and in the following year was renamed as the ISLAND SUN. She was then owned by Mauritius Island Cruises, but was sold in 2005 along with her sister the ISLAND SKY (now operated by Noble Caledonia) to the Danish Clipper Group. Mauritius Island Cruises has now ceased to trade. The ship was renamed CORINTHIAN II and following a refit in Piraeus was chartered to Travel Dynamics for service in the Mediterranean Sea. IMO 8802882

TUI AG

The Group TUI AG, of Germany, is the largest tourism and service group in the world, employing more than 80,000 people in over 500 companies throughout the world. TUI AG also still owns 43% of Container ship owner Hapag Lloyd. TUI and Carnival Corporation agreed to set up a joint venture company in Germany, of which Aida Cruises would be a building block. However the proposed deal failed to get regulatory approval and instead TUI has formed a joint venture with Royal Caribbean Cruise Lines, which will be known as TUI Cruises. The first ship will be Celebrity Cruises' GALAXY. TUI AG merged with UK based First Choice Holidays in 2007 to form TUI Travel plc, in which TUI has a 51% stake. At that time Thomson Cruises was transferred from TUI AG to the new UK business, bringing the English speaking brands together.

Chairman Michael Frenzel

Address Karl-Weichert-Allee 4, 30625 Hanover, Germany

Telephone +49 511 56600 **Fax** +49 511 5661901

Website www.tui-group.com

HAPAG LLOYD CRUISES

The Company Hapag-Lloyd Cruises is part of the giant German shipping group Hapag-Lloyd, itself part of the travel and leisure group TUI. Hapag-Lloyd was formed in 1970 on the amalgamation of Hamburg America Line and Norddeutscher Lloyd. The former had been established in 1847 by a group of Hamburg ship owners and businessmen. The North German Lloyd company was formed ten years later. At the outbreak of the First World War, Hamburg America Line (Hapag) was one of the world's largest shipping companies, with a fleet of 175 ships, including some magnificent transatlantic liners. NDL had 135 ships at this time, and both companies effectively lost all of them. Hapag re-entered the passenger shipping market in 1923 with the liner ALBERT BALLIN, and during the following year NDL introduced the COLUMBUS, the largest and fastest ship in the German fleet. By 1926, Hapag was once again a major ship owner with a fleet of 118 vessels. NDL's BREMEN took the Blue Riband of the North Atlantic in 1929. The Second World War saw the loss of both fleets for the second time, following which NDL concentrated on passenger trades and Hapag on cargo services. The Preussag Group acquired a controlling interest in Hapag-Lloyd in 1997, and five years later acquired the minority interests to become the sole shareholder. In 1998 Hapag-Lloyd acquired a majority shareholding in the major German travel group Touristik Union International. In 2001 Preussag re-branded its tourist businesses as World of TUI. Until 2009 Hapag-Lloyd operated an impressive fleet of large containerships, but then disposed of a majority interest in that business.

Managing Director Gunther Brauer

Address Ballindamm 25, 20095 Hamburg, Germany

Telephone +49 40 3001 4600 **Fax** +49 40 3001 4601

Website www.hl-cruises.com

Area operated Worldwide

BREMEN	6752gt	1990	15.0k	D2	164p	164p	100c	111.5m	17.0m	4.6m	BS
C. COLUMBUS	15067gt	1997	18.5k	D2	420p	420p	170c	145.0m	21.5m	5.1m	BS
EUROPA	28890gt	1999	21.0k	DEP2	408p	408p	280c	198.6m	24.0m	6.1m	BS
HANSEATIC	8378gt	1991	14.0k	D2	184p	184p	125c	122.7m	18.0m	4.8m	BS

BREMEN began life as the FRONTIER SPIRIT, an expedition ship for Japan's NYK Line. She was built by Mitsubishi Heavy Industries (yard Number 1182) at Kobe in Japan. She has been used by Hapag-Lloyd as the expedition cruise ship BREMEN since 1993. In 2005 she was to have been chartered to

Travel Dynamics' **Corinthian II** in the Dardanelles *(Rick Frendt)*

Hapag Lloyd's **C. Columbus** at Duluth *(Rick Frendt)*

a new business under the name Expedition Leaders in order to promote dual language (German and English) cruises, but that arrangement never materialised. Her 2007 programme includes Antarctica, Greenland and Northern Europe. The city of Bremen in Germany, after which this ship is named, has a history going back more than 1,200 years, and played a major role in the Hanseatic League. IMO 8907424

C. COLUMBUS was built at the Wismar, Germany yard of MTW Schiffswerft (yard number 451) for operation by Hapag-Lloyd. She cruises in Northern Europe, the Great Lakes and Round the World in 2007. Her name commemorates one of the greatest of the European discoverers, Genoa-born Christopher Columbus (1451-1506). IMO 9138329

EUROPA was built by Kvaerner Masa Yards (yard number 495) in Helsinki, Finland as a replacement for an earlier, and unusually, larger ship of the same name. Her current itineraries include the Mediterranean, Northern Europe, South America and Round the World. IMO 9183855

HANSEATIC was built by Rauma Yards (yard number 306) at Rauma in Finland in 1991 as the SOCIETY ADVENTURER for Society Expeditions. However, once completed she was laid up in the shipyard until March 1993, when she was chartered by Hanseatic Tours and given the name HANSEATIC. Hanseatic Tours was acquired by Hapag-Lloyd in 1996. The HANSEATIC operates in Antarctica and Greenland, with positioning and other voyages in between. The Hanseatic League was a mercantile league of German and Baltic cities, which began to emerge in the 1240's and which seems to have ceased to have importance in 1669, although never officially dissolved. Hamburg, Lubeck and Bremen are still known as Hanseatic Cities. IMO 9000168

TUI CRUISES

The Company TUI Cruises is a German Joint Venture between Royal Caribbean Cruise Lines and TUI AG, established in 2008. The company commenced operating in spring 2009.

Chief Executive Officer Richard Vogel

Address Anckelmannsplatz 1, 20537 Hamburg, Germany

Telephone +49 40 286 677168 **Fax** +49 40 286 677103

Website www.tuicruises.com

Area Operated Caribbean, Baltic and Mediterranean Seas and Norway

MEIN SCHIFF	76998gt	1996	21.5k	D2	1948p	2232p	780c	263.9m	32.2m	7.7m	MT

MEIN SCHIFF is the second member of a trio of ships built by Jos. L. Meyer (yard number 638) at Papenburg, Germany as the GALAXY. Renamed CELEBRITY GALAXY in 2008, in spring 2009 she was transferred to TUI Cruises, the new Royal Caribbean/TUI German joint venture, to become the company's first ship and after a refit in Bremerhaven was renamed MEIN SCHIFF. IMO 9106297

TUI TRAVEL

The Company TUI Travel plc was formed in 2007 on the merger of TUI AG's tourism business and UK travel Group First Choice.

Website www.tuitravelplc.com

THE ADVENTURE FLEET

The Company The Adventure Fleet, formerly First Choice Expedition Cruising, is part of First Choice Holidays, a leading British-based international leisure travel group. First Choice was, until the spring of 2009, a partner with Royal Caribbean Cruises Limited in Island Cruises (see under RCCL). In 2007 First Choice holidays merged with TUI AG to form TUI Travel plc. TUI AG holds 51% of the new company, with the remainder in the hands of the former shareholders of First Choice. First Choice Expedition Cruising was formed in 2006 by the amalgamation of Peregrine Adventures and Intrav's Clipper Cruise Line. In May 2007 the company acquired Quark Expeditions, and during the spring of 2008 reorganised the expedition cruise business under the name The Adventure Fleet. The Clipper Cruise Line name was discontinued and the Clipper Odyssey returned to her owner.

Address First Choice House, London Road, Crawley, RH10 9GX, England

Website www.adventurefleet.com

Hapag Lloyd's **Europa** in Sydney *(Alf Sims)*

TUI Cruises' **Mein Schiff** in Hamburg *(William Mayes)*

Quark Expeditions' **Clipper Adventurer** in the Kiel Canal *(Oliver Sesemann)*

PEREGRINE ADVENTURES

The Company Peregrine Adventures, part of The Adventure Fleet, is a British and Australian based operator of adventure and exploration tours, including cruises to Antarctica and the Arctic using two chartered ships. The company began operating in 1977.

Address First Floor, 8 Clerewater Place, Lower Way, Thatcham, Berkshire, RG19 3RF, England

Telephone +44 844 736 0170 **Fax** +44 1635 872758

Website www.peregrineadventures.com

Area operated Antarctica and the Arctic

AKADEMIK IOFFE	6450gt	1989	16.0k	D2	110p	118p	53c	117.0m	18.3m	6.1m	RU
AKADEMIK SERGEY VAVILOV	6344gt	1988	16.0k	D2	105p	118p	53c	117.0m	18.3m	6.1m	RU

AKADEMIK IOFFE is operated by Peregrine Adventures under the marketing name PEREGRINE MARINER. She is owned by the Shirskov Oceanological Institute of Kaliningrad, and was built by the Hollming Shipyard (yard number 266) at Rauma, Finland for the Russian Academy of Sciences. The ship was designed for research into long distance submarine acoustics, along with her sister ship (below). She was transferred to her current owner in 1993. In 1995 she operated for Marine Expeditions under the marketing name MARINE ADVENTURER, but was not officially renamed. Abraham Ioffe (1880-1960) was a nuclear physicist with the Russian Academy of Sciences. IMO 8507731

AKADEMIK SERGEY VAVILOV was built by the Hollming Shipyard (yard number 265) at Rauma, Finland for the Russian Academy of Sciences. She is operated by Peregrine Tours under the marketing name PEREGRINE VOYAGER, although not officially renamed. She was transferred to the Shirskov Oceanological Institute of Kaliningrad in 1993. Her owners, under the trading style Poseidon Arctic Expeditions, may also operate the ship. Sergey Vavilov was a Russian botanist who lived from 1887 to 1943. IMO 8507729

QUARK EXPEDITIONS

The Company Founded by Lars Wikander and Mike McDowell, Quark Expeditions began taking travellers to far-flung destinations in 1991 with a voyage aboard the SOVIETSKIY SOYUZ to the North Pole. The KAPITAN KHLEBNIKOV was first used in the following year, and has remained a favourite ever since. Quark Expeditions became part of TUI in 2007. Other expedition operators also market many of the ships.

President Patrick Shaw

Address 47 Water Street, Norwalk. Connecticut 06854, United States of America

Telephone +1 203 803 2888 **Fax** +1 203 857 0427

Website www.quarkexpeditions.com

Area operated Arctic (July and August), Antarctic (November to March)

50 LET POBEDY	23439gt	2007	21.4k	NST3	128p	128p	140c	159.6m	28.0m	11.0m	RU
AKADEMIK SHOKALSKIY	1764gt	1982	14.0k	D2	46p	46p	23c	71.6m	12.8m	4.5m	RU
CLIPPER ADVENTURER	4376gt	1975	14.0k	D2	122p	122p	79c	100.0m	16.2m	4.7m	BS
KAPITAN KHLEBNIKOV	12288gt	1981	18.7k	DE3	108p	112p	60c	129.4m	26.5m	8.5m	RU
LYUBOV ORLOVA	4251gt	1976	17.2k	D2	110p	110p	70c	100.0m	16.2m	4.7m	MT
OCEAN NOVA	2183gt	1992	12.0k	D1	82p	98p	34c	72.8m	11.3m	3.7m	BS

50 LET POBEDY was built by the Baltijskiy Zavod shipyard (yard number 1705) in St Petersburg, Russia for the Murmansk Shipping Company. Her keel was laid in 1989 and she was launched in 1993, but not completed until 2007. She was originally to have been named URAL, and has a 5-metre wide stainless steel ice belt hull capable of breaking ice up to 2.5 metres thick. She is a nuclear powered icebreaker, whose name translates as 50 Years of Victory; this is the name under which she is marketed. IMO 9152959

AKADEMIK SHOKALSKIY was built by Oy Laivateollisuus Ab (yard number 343) at Turku, Finland for the Russian Hydrometeorological Institute. She was transferred to the Far Eastern Research Institute

Quark Expeditions' **Lyubov Orlova** *(Ben Lyons)*

Quark Expeditions' **Ocean Nova** *(Ben Lyons)*

Zegrahm Expeditions' **Clipper Odyssey** *(Theodore W Scull)*

in 1994. Her name commemorates the Russian critic and novelist who lived from 1893 to 1984. IMO 8010336

CLIPPER ADVENTURER was built by Brodogradiliste Titovo (yard number 408) at Kraljevica in what was then Yugoslavia as the ALLA TARASOVA, one of a series of eight ships for Murmansk Shipping for coastal passenger service. Among her surviving sisters are the LYUBOV ORLOVA and the MARIYA YERMOLOVA. In 1997 she was rebuilt as the cruise ship CLIPPER ADVENTURER for Clipper Cruise Line. Clipper Cruise Line was acquired by First Choice Travel and the ship was surplus to requirements so was sold to Clipper Group and chartered back on a limited basis. IMO 7391422

KAPITAN KHLEBNIKOV was constructed by Wartsila (yard number 430) at Helsinki, Finland as an icebreaker for the Far Eastern Shipping Company of Vladivostok. She was converted for use as an expedition ship by Rickmer Lloyd at Bremerhaven in 1992, and currently operates on charter to Quark Expeditions. Velimir Khlebnikov (1885-1922) was a leading member of the Russian Futurist movement. IMO 7824417

LYUBOV ORLOVA was built by Brodogradiliste Titovo (yard number 413) at Kraljevica in what was Yugoslavia for the Far Eastern Shipping Company of Vladivostok as one of a series of eight ships for various Soviet owners. She has been owned by Lyubov Orlova Shipping Company of Novorossiysk since 1996, but is marketed as the ORLOVA by Quark Expeditions. This ship operated under charter to Cruise North Expeditions of Canada for the summer of 2007. Lyubov Orlova (1902-1975) was probably the most glamorous and popular actress of the Soviet cinema. This ship also operates for Cruise North Expeditions. IMO 7391434

OCEAN NOVA was built by the Orskov Shipyard (yard number 159) in Frederikshavn, Denmark for the KNI Pilersvisoq, a Greenland Government company, as the SARPIK ITTUK, a coastal passenger liner. In February 2000 she was lengthened by 23 metres at Stocznia Remontowa, Gdansk, Poland. She was converted for use as a cruise ship in 2006, and in the following year was acquired by International Shipping Partners of Miami and chartered to Quark Expeditions under the name OCEAN NOVA. IMO 8913916

ZEGRAHM EXPEDITIONS

The Company Zegrahm Expeditions is a Seattle-based expedition cruise and holiday company, formed in 1990, that appears to have the CLIPPER ODYSSEY on a five-year charter from Clipper Group. The company also charters and sells space on other expedition ships. Zegrahm Expeditions was acquired by TUI plc in July 2009 and is likely to be incorporated into the Adventure Fleet..

Address 192 Nickerson Street, Suite 200, Seattle, Washington State, 98109, United States of America

Telephone +1 206 285 4000 **Fax** +1 206 285 5037

Website www.zeco.com

Area operated Pacific and Indian Oceans

CLIPPER ODYSSEY	5218gt	1989	18.0k	D2	120p	120p	70c	103.0m	15.4m	4.3m	BS

CLIPPER ODYSSEY was built by Nippon Kokan KK (yard number 112) at Tsu, Japan as the OCEANIC GRACE for Oceanic Cruises. In 1997 she was renamed as the OCEANIC ODYSSEY for Spice Island Cruises, but lasted less than a year with that organisation, being sold in 1998 and becoming the CLIPPER ODYSSEY for Clipper Cruise Line. When First Choice Holidays acquired Clipper Cruise Line, the CLIPPER ODYSSEY was not required and was sold to Clipper Group, from whom she is seasonally chartered by Abercrombie & Kent and Noble Caledonia, amongst others. In 2008 she was reported to have been chartered to Zegrahm for five years. In 2009 most of her itineraries are within the Pacific Ocean. IMO 8800195

THOMSON CRUISES

The Company Thomson Holidays, the long established British package holiday company began offering cruises on other companies ships in the late 1960's, but by 1973 the company was chartering ships on a long-term basis. The first such vessels were the CALYPSO, formerly Shaw Savill & Albion's SOUTHERN CROSS and the rather smaller ITHACA that had been built for Zim Israel as the ZION. Lord Thomson founded the company in 1965, with the purchase of Universal Sky Tours, Britannia Airways and Riviera Holidays. By 1974 Thomson was the largest of the UK package tour operators. Thomson withdrew from the charter market in the early 1980's, but later re-entered the market with the ISLAND

Thomson Cruises' **Island Escape** in Barcelona *(John May)*

Thomson Cruises' **The Calypso** in Istanbul *(Rick Frendt)*

Thomson Cruises' **Thomson Destiny** at Civitavecchia *(Rick Frendt)*

BREEZE, THE EMERALD and THE TOPAZ. Thomson Travel Group was floated on the London Stock Exchange by the Thomson Group in 1999, and in the following year was acquired by the German Preussag Group. In 2001 Preussag re-branded its tourist business as World of TUI, encompassing 66 brands within the group. In 2007, Thomson Travel Group became part of TUI Travel plc on the merger of TUI AG and First Choice Holidays.

Address Wigmore House, Wigmore Lane, Luton, LU2 9EX, England

Telephone +44 1582 399970

Website www.thomson.co.uk

Area operated Scandinavia, Mediterranean, Atlantic Islands, Caribbean and the Red Sea

ISLAND ESCAPE	40171gt	1982	18.0k	D2	1542p	1740p	540c	185.2m	27.0m	6.8m	BS
THE CALYPSO	11162gt	1967	18.5k	D2	486p	594p	220c	135.4m	19.2m	6.1m	CY
THOMSON CELEBRATION	33933gt	1984	18.0k	D2	1254p	1374p	520c	214.7m	27.2m	7.5m	MT
THOMSON DESTINY	37773gt	1982	19.0k	D2	1450p	1595p	540c	214.5m	28.4m	7.0m	CY
THOMSON DREAM	54763gt	1986	22.5k	D2	1494p	1773p	642c	243.2m	29.7m	6.5m	MT
THOMSON SPIRIT	33930gt	1983	18.0k	D2	1254p	1374p	209c	214.7m	27.2m	7.5m	CY

ISLAND ESCAPE was built by Dubigeon-Normandie (yard number 164) at Nantes, France for The United Steamship Company (Bahamas) Ltd, a DFDS of Copenhagen subsidiary, as the SCANDINAVIA to operate in the cruise ferry service between New York and the Bahamas for Scandinavia World Voyages. After disappointing results she was transferred to DFDS and put into service on its capital cities car ferry route between Copenhagen and Oslo in 1984. Later that year she was sold to Sundance Cruises of Nassau, Bahamas and after a refit entered service as the STARDANCER in spring 1985. In the summer months she operated from Vancouver to Alaska and in winter from Los Angeles to Puerto Vallarta. In 1990 she was sold to Royal Caribbean Cruise Line, renamed VIKING SERENADE and put into service on the West Coast of the USA. During a major refit in 1991 by Southwest Marine in San Diego, California, passenger cabins replaced her car decks. She continued to operate for Royal Caribbean until being transferred to a new joint venture with British tour operator First Choice in spring 2002. Renamed as the ISLAND ESCAPE, her itineraries for the newly formed Island Cruises included the Mediterranean in summer and South America in winter. Island Cruises ceased trading in spring 2009 and the companies ships were dispersed to the partners in the joint venture. The ISLAND ESCAPE joined the Thomson fleet and continues to offer a casual style of cruising in the western Mediterranean and around the Canary Islands. IMO 8002597

THE CALYPSO is detailed under Louis Cruise Lines. Her Thomson charter finishes in 2009.

THOMSON CELEBRATION is one of a pair of cruise ships ordered by Holland America Line from Chantiers de l'Atlantique (yard number X27) at St Nazaire, France in 1980. She was delivered as the NOORDAM in March 1984 and sailed on her maiden voyage from Le Havre, France to Tampa, Florida on 8 April. She subsequently cruised to Alaska in the summer and to Mexico in the winter. In later years she often spent the summer in Europe. In late 2004 she was chartered by Holland America Line to Thomson Cruises and renamed the THOMSON CELEBRATION. Her debut season featured ex-UK cruises in the summer, after which she was based in the Canary Islands. In 2009 she operates in the Eastern Mediterranean and the Red Sea. IMO 8027298

THOMSON DESTINY was the fourth ship to be delivered to the still relatively new Royal Caribbean Cruise Lines, as the SONG OF AMERICA. She was built by Wartsila (yard number 431) at Helsinki, Finland for service in the Caribbean Sea. Replaced by new tonnage she was sold to Airtours of the UK (marketed as Sun Cruises) and renamed as the SUNBIRD in 1999. Airtours later re-styled themselves as My Travel, but that did not stop the losses mounting in other sections of the company from almost pulling the whole business down. The cruise business was sold in 2004, with Louis Cruise Lines taking a number of ships, including the SUNBIRD. From 2005 she has been chartered to Thomson Cruises as the THOMSON DESTINY. In 2009 she operates in the Western Mediterranean and the Caribbean. IMO 7927984

THOMSON DREAM was built for Home Lines by Jos. L. Meyer (yard number 610) at Papenburg, Germany and delivered in 1986 as the HOMERIC. She operated for Home Lines on their summer service between New York and Hamilton, Bermuda, but spent her winters cruising in the Caribbean. Home Lines was acquired by Holland America Line in 1988 and on 2 November the HOMERIC was renamed WESTERDAM. Her duties were now split between the Caribbean (winter) and Alaska cruises from Vancouver (summer). In October 1989 the ship was returned to her builders to have a 39.6 metre mid section inserted, resuming service in March 1990 and subsequently being re-registered to the Dutch flag in 1996. She was transferred to Costa Crociere during 2002 and renamed COSTA EUROPA. During a refit in 2007 the area over the bridge that was previously a cinema was converted into six grand suites with oval balconies. She currently spends most of the year operating in the Mediterranean and Red Seas. From April 2010 she is chartered to Thomson Cruises as the THOMSON DREAM. IMO 8407735

THOMSON SPIRIT was built by Chantiers de l'Atlantique (yard number V27) at St Nazaire, France as the first of a pair of ships of fairly revolutionary appearance for Holland America Line. She was delivered as the NIEUW AMSTERDAM in 1983. In 2000 she was sold to American Hawaii Cruises (part of American Classic Voyages) for use in the Hawaiian Islands as the PATRIOT. Following the September 11 terrorist attacks in 2001, the company collapsed and the ship was repossessed by Holland America Line and laid up. She was chartered to Louis Cruise Lines in May 2002 and renamed SPIRIT. In May 2003 she was sub-chartered to Thomson Cruises, as the THOMSON SPIRIT, and now cruises in the Mediterranean and Scandinavia in summer. During the spring of 2007 she operated for Louis Cruise Lines as the SPIRIT, and spent a further two weeks deputizing for the ill-fated SEA DIAMOND. Louis Cruise Lines acquire the ship in 2008. In 2009 she operates in Northern Europe for Thomson, but often undertakes cruises for Louis before and after her main season. IMO 8024014

UKRRICHFLOT

The Company UKRRICHFLOT is a major Ukraine operator of river and short sea cargo services, owned by the Ukraine Ministry of Transport. The two ships shown here are principally river vessels, but also cruise from the port of Odessa into the Black Sea. The company was formed in 1992 following the break up of the Soviet Union.

President P I Podlesny

Address 51 Nizhniy Val Str, Kyiv, 04071 Ukraine

Telephone +380 44 4174233

Website www.ukrrichflot.com

Area operated Black Sea and the River Danube

| AKADEMIK VIKTOR GLUSHKOV‡ | 5475gt | 1983 | 12.0k | D3 | 314p | 332p | 98c | 129.1m | 16.0m | 2.9m | UA |
| GENERAL LAVRINENKOV | ‡5475gt | 1990 | 12.0k | D3 | 314p | 332p | 98c | 129.1m | 16.0m | 2.9m | UA |

AKADEMIK VIKTOR GLUSHKOV and **GENERAL LAVRINENKOV** were built by VEB Elbeverften Boizenburg Rosslau (yard numbers 389 and 397) at Boizenburg, Germany. IMO 8326008 and 8963595

VARIETY CRUISES formerly ZEUS GROUP

The Company Variety Cruises is an operating name for Zeus Group. The Zeus Group is a Greek company whose origins can be traced back to the founding of D Venetopoulos Travel and Tourism in 1949 by Diogenis Venetopoulos. In 1966 the company was renamed as Zeus Tours and two years later began offering small ship cruises using the chartered yacht ELEFTHERIOS. In 1973 the company's first owned vessel, the NIKI, a converted wooden cargo vessel joined the fleet. Today the Zeus Group operates under the brands Variety Cruises and Zeus Casual Cruises. In 2006 the business of Variety Yachting was established as the owner/manager of small motor yachts, too small to warrant inclusion in this book.

President and Managing Director Lakis Venetopoulos **Chief Operating Officer** Dinitris Vassilakis

Address 214-216 Syngrou Avenue, 17672 Athens, Greece

Telephone +30 210 691 9191 **Fax** +30 210 699 8484

Website www.varietycruises.com

Area operated Aegean Ionian and Red Seas

DIOGENIS V	419gt	1984	10.0k	D2	48p	50p	14c	50.4m	8.2m	3.5m	GR
H&B		2002	9.0k	SD1	43p	43p	10c	44.0m	9.0m	3.8m	GR
HARMONY G	498gt	2001	11.0k	D2	46p	46p	17c	53.9m	7.1m	3.7m	GR
HARMONY V	gt	2003	12.0k		52p	52p	16c	55.0m	8.2m	3.0m	GR
GALILEO	480gt	1995	11.0k	SD2	52p	55p	17c	51.0m	10.0m	2.9m	GR
PAN ORAMA	674gt	1991	12.5k	SD2	50p	54p	18c	53.3m	12.0m	3.0m	GR
PANTHEON	489gt	2004	10.0k	SD1	50p	55p	18c	50.0m	11.0m	4.3m	GR

PEGASUS	730gt	1990	15.0k	D2	46p	51p	17c	45.0m	11.0m	3.7m	GR
VIKING STAR	gt	1991	8.0k	SD2	48p	50p	10c	32.2m	8.7m	4.4m	GR
ZEUS II	gt	1942	12.0k	D2	32p	38p	9c	34.5m	5.8m	2.9m	GR

DIOGENIS V was built in Turkey as the TURQUAZ. She became the DIOGENIS V in 2000 and was acquired by the Zeus Group in 2003. IMO 8989654

H&B is a three-masted yacht.

HARMONY G was built by N Savvas Shipyard at Eleusis in Greece. IMO 8984989

HARMONY V Entered service for Zeus Group in spring 2008. No further details available.

GALILEO was built by Fratsis G Shipyard (yard number 470) at Perama, Greece as a three-masted yacht for the Zeus Group. IMO8986286

PAN ORAMA was built by N Kastrinos (yard number 23) at Perama, Greece as a three-masted yacht for the Zeus Group. IMO 8928260

PANTHEON is a two-masted yacht.

PEGASUS was built by L Glynos in Greece as the DOUBLE FORCE. She was renamed PEGASUS in 2002 and acquired by Zeus Group in 2006. IMO 8936841

VIKING STAR is a two-masted yacht.

ZEUS II No further details available.

VIKING LINE

The Company Today's Viking Line is the sole remaining company from the consortium that formed the original Viking Line in 1959, when the VIKING began sailing between Finland, the Aland Islands and Sweden. That company was Vikinglinjen AB, established by Aland Island sea captain Gunnar Eklund. The company joined forces with Rederi AB Slite and Alandfarjan AB (later SF Line) to form the joint marketing company Oy Viking Line AB in 1966. Vikinglinjen AB (then part of Rederi AB Sally) left the consortium in 1988 and Rederi AB Slite was put into liquidation by the banks in 1993, leaving just SF Line, which restyled itself as Viking Line in 1995. Viking Line is one of the two major ferry companies operating overnight services between Stockholm, Sweden and Helsinki and Turku, both Finland.

Chairman Ben Lundquist **Managing Director** Nils-Erik Eklund

Address Norragatan 4, 22100 Mariehamn, Aland Islands, Finland

Telephone +358 18 26211 **Fax** +358 18 26116

Website www.vikingline.fi

Area operated 24 hour cruises from Stockholm, Sweden

VIKING CINDERELLA	46398gt	1989	22.0k	D2	1828p	2766p	224c	190.9m	29.0m	6.6m	SE

VIKING CINDERELLA was built by the Wartsila shipyard (yard number 1302) in Turku, Finland as the CINDERELLA for the SF Line of Finland, part of the Viking Line consortium. She was initially employed on the overnight intercity route between Stockholm and Helsinki, providing a tandem sailing on alternate nights. She also provided some cruise sailings from Helsinki to Tallinn. From 1993 she became the principal vessel on the Stockholm to Helsinki service, running opposite the MARIELLA. With the arrival of the GABRIELLA, she switched to full time cruising, initially from Helsinki, but latterly from Stockholm. She was renamed VIKING CINDERELLA in 2003. The VIKING CINDERELLA has a large vehicle deck, which allows passengers to park their cars on the ship while on the 24-hour cruise to Mariehamn. IMO 8719188

WINDJAMMER BAREFOOT CRUISES

The Company Windjammer Barefoot Cruises was founded in 1947 by former US Navy submariner Mike Burke. The company has gone through turbulent times financially and is currently not trading. All of its interesting fleet of historic vessels are laid up. It is also thought that in 2001 the company purchased a former United States research vessel, the 1966-built DISCOVERER, with the intention of rebuilding the ship into a 5-masted cruise ship. That vessel has been laid up at Port of Spain, Trinidad

Thomson Cruises' **Thomson Spirit** at Palma *(Martin Grant)*

Viking Line's **Viking Cinderella** in the Stockholm Archipelago *(Miles Cowsill)*

Windjammer's **Legacy** at Philipsburg *(Andrew Kilk)*

since about 2002. The company also appears to own the former Northern Lighthouse Board tender, POLE STAR (now ROGUE), which may have been laid up since 1993.

President Susan Burke

Address 1759 Bay Road, Miami Beach, Florida, 33119-1413, United States of America

Telephone +1 305 672 6453 **Fax** +1 305 674 1219

Website www.windjammer.com

Area operated Not currently operating

LEGACY	1740gt	1959	12.0k	SDE2	119p	122p	43c	76.4m	12.6m	6.0m	TT
MANDALAY	420gt	1923	9.5k	SD1	72p	72p	30c	61.6m	10.0m	4.9m	GD
POLYNESIA	430gt	1939	8.0k	SD1	112p	112p	45c	63.8m	9.9m	5.0m	GD
YANKEE CLIPPER	‡327gt	1927	9.0k	SD1	64p	64p	30c	60.0m	8.6m	5.2m	GD

LEGACY started out as the meteorological research vessel FRANCE II for the French Government. She was built by Forges et Chantiers de la Mediterranee (yard number 346B) at Le Havre, France. She was acquired by Windjammer in 1989 and for a while is thought to have operated as the ABSOLUTE. Between 1997 and 1999 she was refitted as the four-masted sailing cruise vessel LEGACY. Her length including the bowsprit is 89.6 metres and her most recent programme included the Bahamas, the Virgin Islands, St Lucia and the Windward Islands. Her sister, the FRANCE I currently serves as a museum at La Rochelle, France. IMO 5119167

MANDALAY is a barquentine, which was built for E F Hutton by Burmeister & Wain (yard number 323) in Copenhagen, Denmark and named HUSSAR. She was acquired by George Vettlesen in the 1930's and renamed as the VELMA. In later life she operated as a research ship for Columbia University. Windjammer acquired her in 1983, when she was renamed MANDALAY. IMO 7738383

POLYNESIA was built by Scheepswerf de Haan & Oerlemans (yard number 206) at Heusden in The Netherlands as the ARGUS, one of the last of the fishing schooners of the Portuguese Grand Banks fleet. She moved to Windjammer in 1976 and was renamed POLYNESIA I as a four-masted sailing cruise vessel. Including her bowsprit, she is 75.5 metres long. She carried the name OISEAU DE POLYNESIA for the 1984 season, but changed to her current name in the following year. IMO 5023564

YANKEE CLIPPER was built by the Krupp shipyard in Kiel, Germany as the armour plated private yacht CRESSIDA. Later she was renamed CRIMPER. She was later acquired by the Vanderbilts and renamed PIONEER. Windjammer purchased the ship in 1965 and renamed her YANKEE CLIPPER I. She was renamed as the YANKEE CLIPPER in 1996. IMO 8845872

Windjammer's **Polynesia** *(Windjammer Barefoot Cruises)*

the **leading** *guide to the cruise industry*

section 2

Gambling cruise ships

ASIA CRUISE

The Company Asia Cruise (pte) Ltd is a Singaporean owned casino ship operator. The company had chartered the OMAR III from Conning Shipping of Hong Kong, but in June 2007 acquired the ship for its continued gambling cruise operation based in Singapore.

Address 1 Maritime Square, 09-09 Harbourfront Centre, Singapore 099253

Telephone +65 6376 4390 **Fax** +65 6376 4391

Area operated Gambling cruises from Singapore

LONG JIE	18455gt	1972	18.0k	D2	600p	600p	380c	168.4m	24.0m	6.3m	PA

LONG JIE was built as the SUN VIKING for the Wilhelmsen Group for its new joint venture, Royal Caribbean Cruise Lines, by Wartsila (yard number 394) at Helsinki, Finland as one of a trio of revolutionary new Caribbean cruise ships. She was the only one of the three ships not to be lengthened in 1978-80. Her ownership was officially transferred to Royal Caribbean in 1991. In 1994 she was sold to Star Cruises and renamed SUPERSTAR SAGITTARIUS, for a new career cruising in South East Asia. In 1998 she was purchased by Hyundai Merchant Marine of Seoul, South Korea and began offering short cruises as the HYUNDAI PONGNAE. This venture was relatively unsuccessful and after a period of lay-up and brief service in China as the PONGNAE, she was sold to Kong Way of Hong Kong. Renamed OMAR III, she was marketed under the Asia Cruiser Club banner from Hong Kong. She then moved to Asia Cruises in Singapore, initially under charter. She was acquired by the company in June 2007 and renamed LONG JIE. IMO 7125861

ASIA CRUISES

The Company Asia Cruises (formerly Asia Cruiser Club) is a Hong Kong casino cruise operator, owned by Stanley Ho, a casino magnate from Macau. The company commenced operating in 1997 with the gambling ship CAPTAIN OMAR, followed by the OMAR II (now the MACAU SUCCESS) and OMAR III (now the LONG JIE).

Address Room 3603, 36th Floor, China Merchants Tower, Shun Tak Centre, 168-200 Connaught Road Central, Hong Kong, Peoples Republic of China.

Telephone +852 2727 2729 **Fax** +852 2723 0123

Website www.asiacruiser.com

Area operated Hong Kong

ASIA STAR	20295gt	1992	12.5k	D2	354p	354p	206c	131.2m	32.0m	8.4m	BS

ASIA STAR was built by Finnyards (yard number 310) at Rauma, Finland as the RADISSON DIAMOND for Diamond Cruise Line. Conceived for a conference/seminar/incentive tours market, she has had greater success as a cruise ship. She is still the only SWATH (Small Waterplane Area Twin Hull) cruise vessel. Her owners merged later with Seven Seas Cruises to become Radisson Seven Seas Cruises. She was sold to Asia Cruiser Club in early 2005 with delivery in June, at the end of her time with Radisson Seven Seas Cruises, for use as the gambling ship OMAR STAR in the Hong Kong casino cruise trade. In October 2005 she was renamed as the ASIA STAR. IMO 9008407

Asia Cruises' **Long Jie** in Singapore *(Mark Amielanczyk)*

Asia Cruises' **Asia Star** in Hong Kong *(Theodore W Scull)*

Everis International's **Royale Star** in Singapore *(Mark Amielanczyk)*

EVERIS INTERNATIONAL

Telephone +65 6270 2282

Website www.luckystar.com.sg

Area operated Gambling cruises from Singapore

ROYALE STAR	12586gt	1980	20.0k	D2	342p	528p	170c	133.5m	21.0m	5.3m	VC

ROYALE STAR was built by Stocznia Szczecinska (yard number B492/01) at Szczecin, Poland as the DMITRIY SHOSTAKOVICH for the Black Sea Shipping Company of the Soviet Union. Following the collapse of that company she passed through a number of owners between 1996 and 2000, when she was acquired by Macro Maritime, a Liberian registered company, and renamed PALOMA I. In 2003 D&P Cruises, an Italian company, purchased her. Subsequently she has undertaken a number of charters, including that to Hansa Kreuzfahrten for whom she operated in the Mediterranean and Northern Europe. She was sold by D&P in 2007 for use as a gambling ship in Singapore and renamed ROYALE STAR. IMO 7625794

JIMEI GROUP

The Company The Jimei Group is a Hong Kong registered company that operates in the casino cruise trade.

Address 1 B Hyde Center, 221 Gloucester Road, Wan Chai, Hong Kong, Peoples Republic of China

Telephone +852 2730 2000 **Fax**: + 852 2730 2488

Website www.jimei.com.hk

Area operated Gambling cruises from Hong Kong

JI MEI	9878gt	1966	21.0k	D2	412p	614p	c	140.8m	20.0m	5.8m	PA

JI MEI was built by Kieler Howaldtswerke (yard number 1190) as the Jahre Line ferry PRINSESSE RAGNHILD for the Oslo, Norway – Kiel, Germany service. After brief stints as JALINA and AMATISTA, she was sold to Fujian Xiamen Shipping of China and renamed JIN JIANG in 1981. Used as a ferry between Hong Kong and Xiamen, her name was later changed to JI MEI. In 1998 she was withdrawn from service and chartered to the newly formed Jimei Group to operate in the casino trades. She was given an extensive internal rebuilding when the company bought her outright in 2000. She operates both day and overnight cruises from Hong Kong, as well as a monthly cruise along the Chinese coast. IMO 6604482

MAJESTIC STAR CASINO

The Company Majestic Star Casino is an Indiana casino operator, founded by Don Barden in 1993. Although this ship has never had overnight accommodation, she is included due to her size.

Address 1 Buffington Harbour Drive, Gary, Indiana 46406-3001, United States of America

Telephone +1 888 225 8259

Website www.majesticstar.com

Area operated Gambling cruises from Gary, Indiana

MAJESTIC STAR	12805gt	1997	k	DP4	400d		c	108.0m	23.1m	3.5m	US

MAJESTIC STAR was built by Atlantic Marine (yard number 234) at Jacksonville, Florida, USA. IMO 8642933

MERIDIAN SHIP MANAGERS

The Company Meridian Ship Managers is a US company that manages the former gambling ship ISLAND ADVENTURE for its subsidiary Burrell Shipping. The ship was acquired at auction in October 2008 following the bankruptcy of former owner Sea Escape Cruises. It is not known if the ship is currently operating.

Address 3301 SE 14th Avenue, Fort Lauderdale, Florida 33316, United States of America

Telephone +1 954 767 8686 **Fax** +1 954 767 9959

Area operated May not be operating

ISLAND ADVENTURE	15409gt	1976	20.0k	D2	585p	975p		c	156.3m	21.8m	5.9m	PA

ISLAND ADVENTURE was built by Wartsila (yard number 1222) at Turku, Finland as the KAZAKHSTAN, the fourth in a series of five ships for the Black Sea Shipping Company of the Soviet Union. She was renamed UKRAINA in 1994 for BLASCO UK as her owners were then styled. In 1996 she became the ROYAL SEAS for Chastnaya Kompaniya Globus of Odessa and was chartered to Royal Seas Cruise Line of Florida. She reverted to the name UKRAINA in 1997 and was subsequently chartered to Sea Escape Cruises, taking the name ISLAND ADVENTURE. She was sold in 2008 following the bankruptcy of Sea Escape Cruises. IMO 7359486

NEPTUNE CRUISES

The Company Neptune Cruises is a trading name of Hong Kong company Loyalty Merit Management Limited, operator of the NEPTUNE, and was established in 1996.

Address Unit 1101 11/F Office Tower, The Harbour Front, 18-22 Tak Fung Street, Hunghom, Kowloon, Hong Kong, Peoples Republic of China

Telephone +852 2723 0909 **Fax** +852 2723 1777

Website www.neptune.com.hk

Area operated Gambling cruises from Hong Kong

NEPTUNE	15791gt	1976	21.0k	D2	500p	500p	200c	156.3m	21.8m	5.9m	PA

NEPTUNE was built by Wartsila (yard number 1223) at Turku, Finland as the Russian cruise ferry KARELIYA. She was one of a class of five similar vessels and operated for many years under charter to London-based CTC cruises, as the KARELIYA and later under the name LEONID BREZHNEV. After the break up of the Soviet Union she was renamed as the KARELIYA by the Black Sea Shipping Company. In 1998 she was sold to Kaalbye Shipping and renamed OLVIA. She was chartered to various cruise operators, and later operated for Peaceboat. She was sold to Wide Asia in early 2005, and entered the Hong Kong casino cruise trade in September as the CT NEPTUNE. She was later renamed as the NEPTUNE and is currently owned by Walden Maritime. IMO 7359498

NEW CENTURY CRUISE LINE

The Company New Century Cruise Lines is a Singapore-based casino cruise operator, founded in 1993 by Singaporean Albert Ng. From 2004 the company has been managed by Universal Shipmanagement, part of New Century Group.

Address 50 Tanah Merah Ferry Road, 01-05 Tanah Merah Ferry Terminal, Singapore, 498833

Telephone +65 6214 2822 **Fax** +65 6542 5250

Website www.nctoursonline.com

Area operated Singapore and Malaysia

AMUSEMENT WORLD	12764gt	1967	18.0k	D2	635p	635p		c	141.2m	22.5m	5.5m	TV
LEISURE WORLD	15653gt	1969	16.0k	D2	580p	850p		c	160.3m	22.8m	6.3m	TV

NOTE: New Century ships carry a significant number of day cruise passengers who do not occupy cabins. Their numbers are not factored into above statistics. Furthermore, the ships have very large casino staffs. Some of these occupy passenger cabins, while others commute to the ships by ferry on a daily basis.

AMUSEMENT WORLD was built as Swedish Lloyd's ferry PATRICIA for service between the UK and Spain, by AB Lindholmens Varv (yard number 1095) in Gothenburg, Sweden. She was sold to Stena Line and became STENA OCEANIC in 1978. Since then she has sailed for numerous operators in a variety of roles under the names STENA SAGA, LION QUEEN, CROWN PRINCESS VICTORIA, PACIFIC STAR and SUN FIESTA. She was sold to New Century in 1997, and operated briefly as PUTRI BINTANG before becoming the casino ship AMUSEMENT WORLD. She operates mainly out of Penang in Malaysia. The ship made headlines in December 2000, when police in Singapore discovered the karaoke lounge was also being operated as a brothel. IMO 6620773

Jimei Group's **Jimei** in Hong Kong *(Bruce Peter)*

Meridian's **Island Adventure** at Port Everglades *(Andrew Kilk)*

Neptune Cruises' **Neptune** in Hong Kong *(Andrew Kilk)*

LEISURE WORLD was built by AG Weser Werk Seebeck (yard number 942) at Bremerhaven, Germany as the SKYWARD for Klosters Rederi, Oslo (Norwegian Caribbean Cruise Line) for cruising in the Caribbean Sea. She was sold for Asian cruising in 1991 as the SHANGRI-LA WORLD and during the following year became the ASEAN WORLD. Later in 1992 she was renamed as the FANTASY WORLD, then in 1993 as the CONTINENTAL WORLD. Later in 1993 she became the LEISURE WORLD for gambling cruises. She continues to operate in this trade and is usually anchored in international waters off Singapore, with gamblers shuttled to and fro by high speed ferry. IMO 6921828

OCEANS 21

The Company 21 Miami Oceans International is a Florida based casino ship operator. The company is also reported to be the co-owner, with Omega Commercial Finance Corporation, of a vessel named OMEGA ROYALE, but details have remained elusive. The ISLAND BREEZE (see ships laid up) is also linked with this company in some way.

Area operated Gambling cruises from Tampa, and St Petersburg, Florida

CASINO ROYALE	9511gt	1974	17.0k	D2	550p		132.0m	19.8m	5.3m	BS
OCEAN JEWEL OF ST PETERSBURG	12602gt	1982	18.0k	D2	1010p		136.6m	21.0m	5.6m	VC

CASINO ROYALE was built by the Kynossoura Dockyard Company (yard number 282) at Salamis, Greece as the CASTALIA for Hellenic Mediterranean Lines, a larger version of the elegant little AQUARIUS. In 1988 she became the SCANDINAVIAN SAGA and three years later the PRIDE OF SAN DIEGO for Sea Escape Cruises. She sailed as the TROPIC STAR II from 1992. In 1995 she was renamed STENA ARCADIA for Stena America Line and subsequently carried the names EMERALD EMPRESS (1997), SOFIA (1998), ENCHANTED SUN (1999), THE TALISMAN (2001) and MANISTA (2002) before becoming the ST TROPEZ of St Tropez Casino Lines in January 2005. In March 2005 she was renamed FORTUNE STAR, and was acquired for operation by Oceans 21 and renamed CASINO ROYALE in early 2006. She was arrested in October 2006 in a dispute over crew wages, but is thought to have resumed service early in 2007. IMO 7350442

OCEAN JEWEL OF ST PETERSBURG was built as the MIKHAIL SUSLOV by Stocznia Szczecinska (yard number B492/04) at Szczecin, Poland as one of a series of ships built for the Black Sea Shipping Company. She was laid down as the VASILIY SOLOVYEV SEDOY. In 1989 she was renamed PYOTR PERVVY for conversion for use as an eye hospital. In 1997 she was renamed as the PETR PERVVY. In 2000 all of the passenger cabins and some crew cabins were removed, leaving just 26 cabins for officers. In 2001 she became the OCEAN EMPRESS for Oasis Shipmanagement. She was acquired by Titan Cruise Lines in 2003 and renamed OCEAN JEWEL OF ST PETERSBURG. From February 2006 she was laid up at the naval port of Bani, close to San Domingo in the Dominican Republic, but is believed to be back in service now. IMO 7625823

PACIFIC CRUISES

The Company China Golden Development Holdings is a Hong Kong-listed cruise company that trades under the marketing name of Pacific Cruises. The company operated cruises between Hainan Island in China, and Halong Bay in Vietnam initially, but now only operates from Hong Kong.

Address Rooms 3 & 4, 25th Floor, Concordia Plaza, 1 Science Museum Road, Tsim Sha Tsui East, Kowloon, Hong Kong, Peoples Republic of China

Area operated Hong Kong

METROPOLIS	17261gt	1972	18.7k	D2	761p	1000p	130c	155.0m	22.8m	6.0m	KI

METROPOLIS was built in Shimizu, Japan by K K Kanashasi Zosensho (yard number 1008) as the car and freight ferry SHIRETOKO MARU for Nippon Enkai Ferry KK of Tokyo. She was sold to Minoan Lines of Greece in 1988 and completely rebuilt as the passenger and car ferry N KAZANTZAKIS. China Golden Development Holdings purchased her in 2001, renamed her MING FAI PRINCESS and rebuilt her into a cruise ship with numerous gambling facilities. In January 2007 she was renamed METROPOLIS, without a change of owner. IMO 7215161

New Century's **Leisure World** in Singapore *(Theodore W Scull)*

Ocean 21's **Casino Royale** at Tampa *(Andrew Kilk)*

Pacific Cruises' **Metropolis** in Hong Kong *(Richard Seville)*

Palm Beach Casino's **Palm Beach Princess** at Freeport *(Rick Frendt)*

Singapore Star Shipping has acquired the former **New Flamenco** *(William Mayes)*

Success Universal's **Macau Sucess** in Hong Kong *(Andrew Kilk)*

PALM BEACH CASINO LINE

The Company Palm Beach Casino Line is a subsidiary of International Thoroughbred Breeders. The company also operates the BIG EASY and ROYAL STAR, neither of which have ever had overnight accommodation.

President Fran Murray

Address One East 11th Street, Riviera Beach, Florida 33404, United States of America

Telephone +1 561 845 7447

Website www.pbcasino.com

Area operated Gambling cruises from Palm Beach, Florida

PALM BEACH PRINCESS	6659gt	1964	17.0k	D3	850p		190c	128.3m	16.4m	4.4m	PA

PALM BEACH PRINCESS was built by Wartsila (yard number 375) at Helsinki, Finland as the ILMATAR for Finska Angfartygs of Helsinki for its passenger and car ferry service from that city to Stockholm. From her earliest days, in addition to her ferry duties, she operated short cruises in the Baltic. In 1970, she appeared in Silja Line livery for the first time, although her owner had been trading as part of the Silja consortium for some years. For a change of route, and a greater emphasis on cruising, she was sent to Germany in 1973 for lengthening by about 20 metres, and for the installation of additional engines. She re-entered service, now trading between Helsinki and Travemunde as a three-screw vessel, and almost three knots faster than previously. Finska withdrew from the route in 1975 and the ILMATAR was used principally as a cruise ship. She was sold to Norwegian owners in 1980, but continued to offer a similar range of cruises encompassing the Baltic and Norway in summer and the Mediterranean and Atlantic Isles in winter. Her new owners were less than successful and she was laid up in 1982. Two years later she was sold to Grundstad Maritime Overseas to run gambling cruises from California, as the VIKING PRINCESS. She later moved to Florida where she continues to operate in a similar role as the PALM BEACH PRINCESS for the Palm Beach Casino Line. IMO 6402937

SHANGHAI INTER-CONTINENTS CRUISER

The Company Shanghai Inter-Continents Cruiser Management Company is a privately owned Chinese cruise operator.

Address Room 7G, JinAn Tower, 908 Daming Donglu, 200082, Shanghai, Peoples Republic of China

Telephone +86 21 6595 0776 **Fax** +86 21 6595 2707

Area operated Overnight and weekend cruises from China to Vietnam

GLOBETROT PRINCESS	7717gt	1986	16.0k	D2	400p	400p	200c	120.0m	18.8m	5.2m	SL
ORIENTAL PRINCESS	11513gt	1976	22.5k	D2	402p	750p	200c	137.9m	20.5m	5.6m	SL

GLOBETROT PRINCESS was built at the Xingang Shipyard in China as the coastal passenger/cargo vessel BAI LING. She was converted into the cruise ship JIA RI by Guangzhou Wenchong Shipyard in 1998, and has since operated short cruises in Chinese waters. Until recently she has been in use by her owner, Shanghai Wan Bang Cruise Company, which is a subsidiary of the Shenzhen Zhongda Cruise Company. She has now been chartered to Shanghai Inter-Continents Cruiser Management Company for operation between Beihai in China and Halong Bay in Vietnam as the GLOBETROT PRINCESS. IMO 9028029

ORIENTAL PRINCESS was built for the Spanish Ybarra Line as the CANGURO CABO SAN JORGE by Union Naval de Levante (yard number 131) at Valencia, Spain. When taken over by Trasmediterranea in 1981 she was renamed CIUDAD DE SANTA CRUZ DE LA PALMA, simplified during the following year to CIUDAD DE PALMA. In 2004 she was sold, and for a single season in 2005 operated as the DALMATINO for Italian Di Maio Lines between Italy and Croatia. The service ended after the summer season and the ship was later arrested and laid up in Choggia, Italy. She was sold to Horizon Corporate (Chinese owner) and was expected to be renamed as PRINCESS ANGEL. In the event she took the name OCEAN PRINCESS in 2006 for short cruises from China to Vietnam. She was renamed ORIENTAL PRINCESS in 2008. IMO 7387718

SINGAPORE STAR SHIPPING

The Company Singapore Star Shipping is a Singapore company.

Area operated Not known if currently operating

FLAMENCO I	17042gt	1972	17.0k	D2	792p	983p	350c	163.3m	22.8m	6.5m	PA

FLAMENCO I was the first new passenger ship to be bought by the Peninsular & Oriental Steam Navigation Company since the CANBERRA of 1961, and that company's first purpose built cruise ship, although she had not been ordered by P&O, but acquired off the stocks. She was laid down as one of a pair of ships for Kloster's Norwegian Caribbean Cruise Line by Cantieri Navale del Tirreno e Riuniti shipyard (yard number 290) at Riva Trigoso in Italy. Her sister was delivered as the SOUTHWARD (now Louis Cruise Lines PERLA), but due to escalating costs the order for this ship was cancelled. She was to have been named SEAWARD, but was eventually launched for P&O as the SPIRIT OF LONDON. She was initially employed on the US West Coast along with the 1954-built ARCADIA. When P&O acquired Princess Cruises in 1974, the SPIRIT OF LONDON was transferred to that operation and renamed SUN PRINCESS. By 1989 she was the baby of the fleet and no longer fitted in with the larger ships, so was sold to Premier Cruise Line who renamed her STARSHIP MAJESTIC. In 1995 she was chartered to CTC Lines for cruising from the UK and from Australia, and renamed SOUTHERN CROSS. CTC Lines ceased trading in 1997 and the ship was sold to Festival Cruises, becoming the FLAMENCO. After Festival failed in 2004, she was quickly acquired by Elysian Cruises (Ravenscroft Shipping) and renamed NEW FLAMENCO. She commenced a charter with Travelplan in the spring of 2004. In 2007 she was acquired by Club Cruise, renamed FLAMENCO I, and fixed on a charter for use as an accommodation ship for miners in New Caledonia. In November 2008 Club Cruise defaulted on its loans and subsequently the ship was sold at auction in Singapore for US$ 3.4 million, against the $ 26 million that Club Cruise paid for the ship two years earlier. Flamenco is a Spanish dance. IMO 7211517

SUCCESS UNIVERSE GROUP

The Company Success Universe Group Ltd (formerly Macau Success Ltd) is a publicly listed Hong Kong company in the travel, finance, entertainment and property sectors. The company operates in the Hong Kong casino ship trade.

Chairman Sonny Yeung Hoi Sing

Address Unit 411-413, 4th Floor Tower A, New Mandarin Plaza, 14 Science Museum Road, Tsim Sha Tsui East, Kowloon, Hong Kong, Peoples Republic of China

Telephone +852 3107 1111 **Fax** +852 2303 4489

Website www.successcruises.com

Area operated Hong Kong

MACAU SUCCESS	9848gt	1974	21.0k	D2	414p	600p	200c	130.2m	19.5m	5.3m	BS

MACAU SUCCESS was built by Helsingor Vaerft (yard number 404) at Helsingor, Denmark as the GOLDEN ODYSSEY for the new Royal Cruise Line of Greece. She initially operated cruises in the Mediterranean and later spent winter seasons in South America and the Caribbean Sea. From 1985 she began to spend her winters in South East Asia, and from the following year cruised in Alaskan waters in the summer. In 1989 Royal Cruise Line was sold to Norwegian Cruise Line and although there was little change to the operation, the GOLDEN ODYSSEY was re-flagged to the Bahamas. By 1994 she no longer fitted in with the rest of the fleet and was chartered to Mitsui-OSK Line. Later that year she was sold to Deutsche Seereederei, renamed ASTRA II and chartered to German tour operator Neckermann. She passed to Kong Wing (Asia Cruisers Club) in 2000 and was renamed as the OMAR II for gambling cruises from Hong Kong. She moved to her current operator in 2004 and was renamed MACAU SUCCESS. IMO 7346934

the **leading** *guide to the cruise industry*

section 3

Passenger ships in other transport roles

ADL HOLDINGS

The Company ADL Holdings is a Greek registered company, group owner of two large luxury charter yachts.

Address 26 Skouze Street, 18536 Piraeus, Greece

Telephone +30 210 428 0208 **Fax** +30 210 418 2136

Area operated Does not operate for its own account. Vessels available for charter.

ALYSIA	2982gt	2004	18.0k	D2	36p	36p	38c	85.2m	14.0m	3.7m	MT
LAUREN L	2942gt	2002	16.0k	D1	40p	96p	56c	88.5m	14.0m	3.6m	MT

ALYSIA was built for Mediterranean Yachts by Neorion Shipyards (yard number 1102) at Syros, Greece. She was acquired by ADL Holdings (Alysia Shipping) in 2005. IMO 9288215

LAUREN L was built as the SUN BAY II by Schiffswerft u. Maschinenfabrik Cassens (yard number 235) at Emden in Germany for Sun Bay Shipping. She was renamed CORINTHIAN in 2002 and operated for Travel Dynamics International for a while. She was renamed CONSTELLATION in 2003 when sold to Mitridat Shipping, a subsidiary of Helios Shipping. She was acquired by her current owner (Constellation Shipping) in 2007 and renamed LAUREN L in 2008. IMO 9246827

ARTIKMORNEFTEGAZRAVEDKA

The Company Artikmorneftegazravedka is a Russian state-owned oil and gas exploration company, which appears to operate two passenger vessels in conjunction with its exploration activities.

Address Kolskiy Prospekt 1, 183032 Murmansk, Russia

Telephone +7 8152 254647 **Fax** +7 8152 8115

Website www.amngr.ru

Area operated Unknown

ANNA AKHMATOVA	4575gt	1988	14.3k	D1	150p	150p	34c	90.0m	17.2m	5.3m	RU
BORIS PASTERNAK	4575gt	1989	14.3k	D1	150p	150p	34c	90.0m	17.2m	5.3m	RU

ANNA AKHMATOVA was built by Stocznia im. Komuny Paryskiej (yard number B961/01) at Gdynia, Poland. Anna Akhmatova (1889-1966) was a Ukrainian born poet who found fame with her first poetry collections in 1912 and 1914, but was condemned by the Soviet authorities after the revolution. Following the death of Stalin in 1953 she came back into favour and is now regarded as one of the greatest Russian poets. IMO 8509167

BORIS PASTERNAK was built by Stocznia im. Komuny Paryskiej (yard number B961/02) at Gdynia, Poland. Boris Pasternak (1890-1960) was the author of Doctor Zhivago, for which he won the 1958 Nobel Prize for Literature, although he was not allowed to receive it. IMO 8509179

ATLANTIC MADEIRA YACHT

The Company Alantic Madeira Yacht Management is a Madeira based owner/operator of about 15 small vessels plus the SS Delphine.

Address 56 Rua Dr. Fernao Ornelas, 9050-021, Funchal, Madeira

Telephone +351 291 224859 **Fax** +351 291 225168

Website www.ssdelphine.com

Area operated Mediterranean charters

SS DELPHINE		1961gt	1921	9.0k	SE2	26p	28p	24c	78.5m	10.8m	4.5m	PT

SS DELPHINE was built by the Great Lakes Engineering Works at River Rouge, Michigan, USA as the private yacht for Horace Dodge, one of the founders of the Dodge vehicle manufacturing business, and was named after his daughter. In 1926, while in New York, the DELPHINE caught fire and sank. She was raised and restored, and in 1942 was acquired by the US Navy, becoming the USS DAUNTLESS, flagship of Admiral Ernest King. At the end of the Second World War, the Dodge family re-acquired the yacht and restored her again. From 1955 to 1967 she was permanently moored, but in that year she was donated to the People to People Health Foundation. In the following year she became the Lundeberg Maryland Steamship School and was renamed DAUNTLESS. In 1986 she was acquired by New York-based Travel Dynamics, with the idea of a full restoration for luxury cruising. That transformation never materialised, and three years later she was sold to Sun Sea Cruises with a similar plan. She was laid up in the Mediterranean until purchased by an investor who had her towed to Bruges, Belgium. The restoration took five years to complete, and in 2003, following a renaming by Princess Stephanie of Monaco, the elegant SS DELPHINE entered service in the Mediterranean luxury yacht charter market. IMO 8971815

CHINA SHIPPING GROUP

The Company China Shipping Group was formed in 1997 with merger of Trans Shanghai, Trans Dalian, Trans Guanghzou, China Shipping International Marine and Zhong Jiao Marine Industry, all Chinese Government controlled companies. China Shipping Group operates more that 450 ships in total, including some smaller passenger vessels on which details are not available.

President Li Shaode

Address 5th Floor, Shipping Tower, 700 Daming Donglu, Shanghai 200080, Peoples Republic of China

Telephone +86 216 596 6666 **Fax** +86 216 596 6219

Website www.cnshipping.com

Area operated Unknown, but likely to be Chinese coastal

CHANG BENG	‡5926gt	1978	16.5k	D2	850b	d		c	138.0m	17.6m	6.0m	CN
CHANG HE	‡5926gt	1974	16.5k	D2	850b	d		c	138.0m	17.6m	6.0m	CN
CHANG JIN	‡5926gt	1974	16.5k	D2	850b	d		c	138.0m	17.6m	6.0m	CN
CHANG XIU	‡5926gt	1974	16.5k	D2	850b	d		c	138.0m	17.6m	6.0m	CN
TIAN YUN	‡5500gt	1984	k	D2	948b	d		c	120.0m	17.0m	5.8m	CN
TONG HU	‡6476gt	1964	18.0k	D2	576b	d		c	130.3m	17.0m	3.7m	CN
XIANG XUE LAN	16071gt	1996	20.0k	D1	244p	392p	95c		150.5m	24.0m	7.2m	PA
XIN YU JIN XIANG	12304gt	1995	20.0k	D2	190p	348p	93c		148.2m	22.7m	6.1m	CN

CHANG BENG was built in Shanghai. IMO 7741835

CHANG HE was built at the Hudong Shipyard in Shanghai. IMO 7741770

CHANG JIN is a product of the Hudong Shipyard in Shanghai. IMO 7741782

CHANG XIU was built in Shanghai by the Hudong Shipyard. IMO 7741823

TIAN YUN was built by the Xingang Shipyard (Yard number 248) at Tianjin, China. IMO 8311871

TONG HU was built by Soc Espanola de Construccion Naval (yard number 98) at Puerto Real, Spain as the CIUDAD DE BUENOS AIRES for Fluvial of Argentina. In 1979 she was renamed as the MING YI for Guangdong Province, Hong Kong and Macau Navigation Company. Later that year she became China Ocean Shipping's GU LANG. She took her current name in 1992. IMO 5074355

XIANG XUE LAN was built by MTW Schiffswerft (yard number 162) at Wismar, Germany. She operates a passenger and container service between China and South Korea. She was transferred from China Shipping Passenger Liner in 2008. IMO 9086904

XIN YU JIN XIANG was built by De Merwede (yard number 667) at Hardinxveld in the Netherlands as the YU JIN XIANG for China Shipping container Lines. She was transferred to China Shipping in 2008 and renamed. IMO 9110810

Christina Yachting's **Christina O** at Villafranche *(Rick Frendt)*

Demar's **Enchanted Capri** at Freeport *(Rick Frendt)*

The **F Diamond** in Singapore *(Martin Wright)*

CHINA SHIPPING CONTAINER LINES

The Company China Shipping Container Lines is a Chinese Government owned company operating a fleet of around 150 ships. The ships listed here have a high passenger capacity and operate short sea passenger and cargo services across the Yellow Sea.

Address 27th Floor, 450 Fushan Lu, Pudong Xinqu, Shanghai 200121, Peoples Republic of China

Telephone +86 216 596 6984 **Fax** +86 216 596 6495

Website www.cscl.com.cn

Area operated China to South Korea

ARAFURA LILY	12307gt	1996	20.0k	D2	190p	348p	95c	148.2m	22.7m	6.1m	CN
ZI YU LAN	16071gt	1995	20.0k	D2	244p	392p	95c	150.5m	24.0m	7.2m	CN

ARAFURA LILY was built by the De Merwede Shipyard (yard number 668) in Hardinxveld, The Netherlands as the ZI DING XIANG for the Shanghai Hai Xing Shipping Company. She was renamed ARAFURA LILY for a charter in 1996 and appears not to have reverted to her original name. IMO 9110822

ZI YU LAN was built by MTW Schiffswerft (yard number 161) at Wismar, Germany. She is thought to have carried the name JAOKRAN for a short time in 2007. IMO 9086899

CHINA SHIPPING PASSENGER LINER

The Company China Shipping Passenger Liner was formed in 1997 with the merger of Dalian Marine Transport and Shanghai Shipping Passenger Company. Currently around 28 vessels of varying types are in operation. The ships shown here are all cargo/passenger vessels. Unfortunately information on these vessels is rather sketchy.

Address 1 Minzhu Plaza, Zhongshonqu, 116001 Dalian, Peoples Republic of China

Telephone +86 411 8263 0160 **Fax** +86 411 8263 0160

Area operated China coastal

CHANG BAI	7670gt	1980	18.2k	D1	p	p	c	138.0m	17.6m	6.0m	CN
CHANG SHEN	‡5926gt	1979	18.2k	D2	p	850p	c	138.0m	17.6m	6.0m	CN
CHANG XIN	‡3857gt	1979	16.0k	D1	p	p	c	106.7m	15.8m	3.8m	CN
HAI HUA	13547gt	1972	18.5k	D1	p	72p	62c	161.7m	23.1m	9.9m	CN
RONG XIN	‡3857gt	1978	16.0k	D1	p	p	c	106.7m	15.8m	3.8m	CN
TIAN HE	‡5492gt	1983	k	D2	p	p	c	120.0m	17.0m	5.8m	CN
TIAN HUAI	‡5002gt	1983	k	D2	p	948p	c	120.0m	17.0m	5.8m	CN
WANG XIN	‡3858gt	1984	16.0k	D2	p	p	c	106.7m	15.8m	3.8m	CN
WU TONG SHANG	7160gt	1987	k	D2	p	p	c	120.0m	17.0m	5.8m	CN
XIN SHANG HAI YOU LUN	‡3857gt	1983	16.0k	D2	p	p	c	106.7m	15.8m	3.8m	CN

CHANG BAI and **CHANG SHEN** were built by the Hudong Shipyard in Shanghai, China. IMO 8425103 and 7741811

CHANG XIN was built by the Qiuxin Shipyard in Shanghai, China. IMO 8425177

HAI HUA was built by Cockerill (yard number 861) at Hoboken, Belgium as the FABIOLAVILLE for CMB. She passed to her current owners in 1989 when she was renamed HAI HUA. IMO 7204356

RONG XIN was built by the Qiuxin Shipyard in Shanghai, China. IMO 8426573

TIAN HE and **TIAN HUAI** were built by the Xingang Shipyard (yard numbers 239 and 238) at Tianjin, China. IMO 8311857 and 8311845

WANG XIN was built by the Qiuxin Shipyard in Shanghai, China. IMO 8833283

WU TONG SHANG was built by the Xingang Shipyard (yard number 250) at Tianjin, China as the XI QUE. She was renamed WU TONG SHANG in 2005. IMO 8705371

XIN SHANG HAI YOU LUN was built by the Qiuxin Shipyard in Shanghai, China as the ZHAN XIN. She was renamed in 1998 and converted into a cruise ship. IMO 8831962

CHRISTINA YACHTING

Website www.christina-o.com

CHRISTINA O	1802gt	1943	19.0k	D2	36p	36p	32c	99.1m	11.1m	4.1m	PA

CHRISTINA O, the Onassis yacht for more than twenty years began as the Canadian frigate STORMONT. She was acquired by Onassis in 1948, converted to a yacht and given the name CHRISTINA. In 1998 she was restored and is available for charter as the CHRISTINA O. IMO 8963818

COMPAGNIE POLYNESIENNE DE TRANSPORT MARITIME

The Company Compagnie Polynesienne de Transport Maritime is a French Polynesian registered company providing lifeline services to the Marquesas Islands. The ship listed here is the third vessel to be operated by the company, and the first one to be acquired new.

Address PO Box 220, Papeete, Tahiti

Telephone +689 426242 **Fax** +689 434889

Website www.aranui.com

Area operated Passenger cargo service between Tahiti and the Marquesas, French Polynesia

ARANUI 3	7325gt	2002	15.0k	D1	208p	208p	c	117.0m	17.6m	5.5m	PF

ARANUI 3 was built by Societatia Comerciala Severnav (yard number 170) at Drobeta, Romania for the company's inter-island service in French Polynesia. Her crew is predominantly Marquesian. In addition to her passengers, she can carry up to 3,800 tons of general cargo. The ship's name means Great Highway in Maori, and perpetuates the name of the first ship purchased for this service from a New Zealand owner in 1959. IMO 9245354

DEMAR

The Company Demar is a Mexican Industrial company involved in the off-shore oil industry.

Address Puerto Industrial Pesquero, Col Pallas, Ciudad de Carmen, COM, Mexico

Website www.demar.com.mx

Area operated Accommodation and transport ship for offshore oil-workers in Mexico

ENCHANTED CAPRI	15410gt	1975	21.2k	D2	460p	650p	250c	156.2m	21.8m	5.9m	MX

ENCHANTED CAPRI was built as one of a series of five passenger/ro-ro vessels for the Black Sea Shipping Company by Wartsila (yard number 1221) at Turku, Finland as the AZERBAYDZHAN. She was chartered to CTC for UK cruising for several years. In 1991 she moved from the Soviet flag to that of Ukraine and five years later was renamed ARKADIYA for a charter to Royal Venture Cruises. During the following year she was chartered to Sea Escape under the name ISLAND HOLIDAY. From 1998 she operated for New Commodore Cruise Line as the ENCHANTED CAPRI. That business collapsed in 2000 and the ship was arrested in New Orleans. She subsequently sailed as a gambling ship from Florida before being chartered by her owner (Faraglioni) to Demar in 2003. She was purchased by Demar in late 2007 and is currently anchored off the Mexican coast about 65 nautical miles from Ciudad del Carmen. She is managed by ISP. IMO 7359474

DESGAGNES

The Company Desgagnes is a Canadian operator of small coastal cargo ships that also operates one passenger and cargo ship. The origins of the company go back to 1866, when Captain Zepherin Desgagnes started trading with the schooner MARY-ANN. Subsidiary Relais Nordik operates the NORDIK EXPRESS.

Address 21 Marche-Champlain Street, Suite 100, Quebec, G1K 8Z8, Canada

Tel +1 418 692 5000 **Fax** +1 418 692 6044

Website www.groupsdesgagnes.com

Area operated St Lawrence, Canada

NORDIK EXPRESS	1748gt	1974	12.5k	D2	72b	196d	c	69.5m	13.4m	5.8m	CA

NORDIK EXPRESS was built by the Todd Shipyard (yard number 61) at Seattle, USA the offshore support vessel THERIOT OFFSHORE IV. She was renamed NORDIK EXPRESS in 1987 and began operating for her current owner in 1992. A replacement ship is currently on order in Croatia, but as this is ro-ro vessel it falls outside the scope of this book. IMO 7391290

ECROLIGHT

The Company Ecrolight is an Australian company specialising in diving cruises.

Address PO Box 5264 Cairns, Queensland 4870, Australia

Area operated Diving cruises on the Queensland coast

OCEAN QUEST II	628gt	1988	12.0k	D2	48p	48p	16c	34.7m	15.0m	2.0m	AU

OCEAN QUEST II was built by SBF Engineering (yard number 36) at Fremantle, Western Australia as the catamaran cruiser MTS DISCOVERER for service in Papua, New Guinea. She was acquired by her current owner late in 2006, and may be sailing under the name OCEAN QUEST. IMO 8717398

EGYPTIAN GOVERNMENT

Area operated Egypt, as a naval training ship

EL HORRIYA	4560gt	1865	15.0k	ST3			160c	128.5m	13.0m	5.3m	EG

EL HORRIYA was built by Samuda Brothers at Poplar on the River Thames, London as the paddle steamer MAHROUSSA, the Egyptian Royal Yacht. She was lengthened by about 12 metres in 1872 and again by a further 5 metres in 1905, at which time her paddle wheels were replaced by screw propulsion. She served as the Egyptian Royal Yacht until the abdication of King Farouk in 1951. She was taken over by the Egyptian Navy for use as a naval training ship, a role that she continues to play. IMO 8642816

ENKA INSAAT

The Company Enka Insaat ve Sanayi is a Turkish construction and engineering company, with a large number of major construction projects in Russia, the Caspian Sea area and Eastern Europe..

Address Enka Binasi 1, Balmumku Mah, Besiktas, 34349 Istanbul, Turkey

Telephone +90 212 376 1000 **Fax** +90 212 272 8869

Website www.enka.com

Area operated Unknown, but possibly as accommodation ships or to transport workers

DICLE	967gt	1959	12.0k	D2	76p	80p	25c	56.0m	10.7m	3.1m	VC
SAKARYA	705gt	1967	11.5k	D1	38p	38p	8c	49.9m	9.5m	3.3m	KZ

DICLE was built by Stord Verft (yard number 50) at Stord, Norway as the HARDANGERFJORD for the Norwegian coastal trade. In 1982 she was briefly renamed HARDANGERFJORD 1 to free up her previous name for a new ship. She was sold later that year becoming the FIRDA. In 1989 she passed to Brand and was renamed BRAND for expedition voyages. She was acquired by Dami Cruises and renamed DARLI in 2004, and following a major refit entered service on the beautiful Croatian coast. In April 2009, following a period of lay up, she was sold to Enka Insaat ve Sanayi of Turkey and renamed DICLE.IMO 5142750

SAKARYA was built by Cantieri Navali Felszegi (yard number 87) at Trieste, Italy as the Norwegian cargo ship TRILLINGEN. In 1971 she was renamed FLORNES and in 1992 passed to Danish owners who gave her the name SIKKER HAVN. In 2004 she was lengthened and converted for use as cruise ship. She was acquired by her present owner in 2008 and renamed SAKARYA. IMO 6726711

F SEA LINE

The Company F Sea Line is an offshoot of FTV (Fashion TV) and a new venture for that organisation. The ship appears to be being used as an event venue.

Website www.ftv.com

Area operated Mediterranean Sea

Gemi Kurtarma's **Savarona** in Istanbul *(William Mayes)*

The **Golden Prince** at Santorini *(Bill Lawes)*

The **Omega G** in Istanbul *(Douglas Cromby)*

| F. DIAMOND | 11621gt | 1967 | 21.0k | D2 | 300p | 680d | 94c | 138.0m | 21.0m | 5.8m | MT |

F. DIAMOND was built by Luebecker-Flender Werke (yard number 559) at Lubeck, Germany as the TOR HOLLANDIA for Tor Line of Gothenburg, Sweden. She inaugurated the company's new service linking Gothenburg with Amsterdam and Immingham. Replaced by a larger vessel in 1976 she was sold to Minoan Lines of Greece and renamed ARIADNE for service between Piraeus and Heraklion. She passed to Adriatic operator Fragline in 1998 and operated as the OURANOS on that company's services between Italy and Greece until sold to FTV and renamed F. DIAMOND in 2007. IMO 6704402

GEMI KURTARMA DENIZCILIK

The Company Gemi Kurtarma Denizcilik is a Turkish company, which has taken a 49-year charter on the Turkish Government-owned cruise yacht SAVARONA, expiring in 2038. The company charters the vessel out through charter brokers.

Address Tersaneler Bolgesi 23, 34944 Tuzla, Turkey

Telephone +90 216 446 3911 **Fax** +90 216 446 3919

Website www.savaronavoyage.com

Area operated Worldwide

| SAVARONA | 4701gt | 1931 | 18.0k | D2 | 34p | 34p | 55c | 136.0m | 17.5m | 6.5m | TR |

SAVARONA was built by Blohm & Voss in Hamburg, Germany for Mrs Emily Cadwallader (the grand-daughter of John Roebling, the builder of New York's Brooklyn Bridge) as the world's largest private yacht. The ship was sold to the Government of Turkey in 1938, and was briefly used as a presidential yacht for Kemal Ataturk, the by then ailing president and founder, in 1923, of the Turkish Nation. The ship was eventually converted for use as a training ship and renamed GUNES DIL. She was almost destroyed by fire in 1979, but following the placing of the charter to her current operator, was rebuilt and currently operates where required. She is named after a long-necked African black swan living in the Indian Ocean. IMO 5314810

GOLDEN PRINCE CRUISES

The Company Golden Prince Cruises is a Greek operator.

Address Plateia Peiraios Zotou & Marinelli Streets, 71202 Heraklion, Crete, Greece

Telephone +30 2810 341701 **Fax** + 30 2810 341706

Area operated Day cruises from Heraklion but currently laid up

| GOLDEN PRINCE | 7735gt | 1973 | 19.5k | D1 | 112b | 900d | 90c | 124.9m | 17.2m | 5.8m | GR |

GOLDEN PRINCE was built by KK Usuki Tekkosho (yard number 1165) at Saiki, Japan as the WAKASHIO MARU for local service in Japan. In 1979 she was renamed as the SUN FLOWER 7. She moved to Greek owners, Epirotiki, in 1991 as the APOLLON and was later converted for use as a day cruise ship. Minoan Lines acquired her in 1995, and renamed her PRINCE, later MINOAN PRINCE. She was sold to Golden Prince Cruises in 2002 and renamed GOLDEN PRINCE. IMO 7323449

GOVERNMENT OF NEWFOUNDLAND AND LABRADOR

The Company The Government of Newfoundland and Labrador runs a fleet of nine vessels, most of which are cargo carriers. The ship listed here is the sole passenger/cargo ship in the fleet that is not a ro-ro.

Address 6th Floor, Confederation Building Complex, St John's Newfoundland, A1C 5T7, Canada

Telephone +1 709 576 3278

Area operated Newfoundland and Labrador coasts

| NORTHERN RANGER | 2556gt | 1986 | 14.0k | D1 | 46b | 86d | 34c | 71.9m | 15.6m | 4.2m | CA |

NORTHERN RANGER was built by Port Weller Dry Docks (yard number 75) at St Catherine's, Ontario, Canada. IMO 8512504

GRANADA LOGISTICS

The Company Granada Logistics is an Anguilla-registered, but probably Ukrainian-owned company.

Area operated Shopping trips to Istanbul from Russia or Ukraine.

OMEGA G		1987gt	1965	14.0k	D2	160p		90c	89.7m	13.0m	4.9m	KM

OMEGA G was built by Stocznia Szczecinska im A Warskiego (yard number B850/06) at Szczecin, Poland as the research ship FADDEY BELLINGSHAUSEN. She was one of the series of eleven ships of the NIKOLAY ZUBOV class. In 1996 she was renamed OMEGA, still under the Ukrainian flag and in 2002 she became the OMEGA G. At some stage she was converted for passenger use. IMO 8927735

IDO ISTANBUL SEA BUSES

The Company IDO, Istanbul Deniz Otobusleri Sanyaii ve Ticaretas, was founded by the Municipality of Greater Istanbul in 1987 in order to reduce land-based traffic congestion by opening up new passenger routes across and along the Bosphorus, and in the Sea of Marmara. The first ten sea-buses came into service in 1987 and 1988, and the fleet has grown considerably since then. More recently the company has invested in fast car ferries. In 2005 the company took over the Istanbul City Lines services and ships from Turkish Maritime Lines and is now the main provider of water-borne transport in and around Istanbul. Turkiye Denizcilik Isletmeleri (Turkish Navigation Management), a company whose origins, through its constituent companies, can be traced as far back as 1843, is generally referred to as Turkish Maritime Lines, and was the Turkish State passenger shipping company controlling around 120 ships. Most of those were ferries operating on local services within Turkey, but with some Turkish coastal services and, until recently, international voyages. The MAVI MARMARA was acquired with the City Line services and operates in the Sea of Marmara. The company is likely to be privatised in the near future.

General Manager Dr Ahmet Paksoy

Address Kennedy Cad., Yenikapi Hizli Feribot Iskelesi, Fatih, Istanbul, Turkey

Telephone +90 212 455 6900 **Fax** +90 212 517 3958

Website www.ido.com.tr

Area operated Passenger services within the Sea of Marmara

MAVI MARMARA		4142gt	1994	15.0k	D2	150b	1500d	62c	93.0m	15.8m	3.9m	TR

MAVI MARMARA was built by Turkiye Gemi Sanayii A.S. (yard number 302) at the Halic (Golden Horn) shipyard in Istanbul, Turkey for the Turkish Maritime Lines Group and launched as the BEYDAGI. Her current name translates as Blue Marmara, a reference to the sea through which she operates. IMO 9005869

IHATAI NUI PRODUCTIONS

The Company Ihatai Nui Productions operates the passenger and cargo ship VAEANU in the islands of French Polynesia.

Address Boite Postale 9062, Papeete, Tahiti, French Polynesia

Area operated Passenger and cargo services within French Polynesia

VAEANU		1540gt	1967	13.5k	D1	50b	d	c	79.7m	11.8m	5.8m	FP

VAEANU was built by J.J.Sietas (yard number 601) in Hamburg, Germany as the cargo vessel CADIZ. She was sold to Compagnie Polynesienne de Transport Maritime in 1980 and renamed ARANUI. She was converted to carry passengers in 1984. In 1991 she became the TUHAAPAE 3, and was acquired by her current owner and renamed VAEANU in 1993. IMO 6726175

ISTANBUL TECHNICAL UNIVERSITY

AKDENIZ		7864gt	1955	17.0k	D2	444p			144.3m	18.6m	6.2m	TR

AKDENIZ is the last surviving member of a series of beautifully proportioned coastal passenger cargo ships built for Turkish Maritime Lines in 1955/56 by A G Weser at Bremen (yard number 1293) in Germany. Her initial employment took her from Istanbul to Piraeus, Naples, Genoa, Marseilles and

Barcelona. In later years she operated Turkish coastal services and cruises in the Mediterranean Sea and beyond. She was withdrawn from service in 1997 and transferred to the Technical University of Istanbul for use as a cadet ship for the Turkish Maritime Academy. IMO 5006815

KOVALEVSKIY BIOLOGICAL INSTITUTE

The Company Kovalevskiy Biological Institute is a Government of the Republic of Ukraine controlled organisation.

Address Prospekt Nakhimova 2, 99011 Sevastopol, Krym, Ukraine

Telephone +380 692 544110 **Fax** +380 692 557813

Area operated It is not known if this ship is currently carrying passengers

PROFESSOR VODYANITSKIY	1498gt	1976	14.0k	D1	32p		p	c	68.9m	11.9m 4.2m	UA

PROFESSOR VODYANITSKIY was built by Oy Lavateollisuus (yard number 312) at Turku, Finland for the Ukraine Academy of Sciences, transferring to her current owner in 1994. It is not known if she currently operates passenger sailings. IMO 7406148

LINDOS MARITIME

The Company Lindos Maritime is a Greek Company, owned by the Greek Cypriot Haji-Ioannou family.

Address 16 Atki Moutsapoulou, 18535 Piraeus, Greece

Telephone +30 210 428 0451 **Fax** +30 210 428 0454

Website www.lindos-maritime.gr

Area operated Yacht available for charter

CLELIA II	4077gt	1990	15.0k	D2	84p	84p	65c	88.3m	15.3m	3.3m	MT
ESMERELDA	1002gt	1981	12.5k	D2	22p	22p	19c	61.5m	10.0m	4.5m	BS

CLELIA II For details see Travel Dynamics International.

ESMERELDA was built by Cantieri Navale Ugo Codecasa (yard number 38) at Viareggio, Italy as the MARIA ALEKSANDRA, although laid down as the TAOUEY. She later became the LUISELLA. She was renamed in about 2003 when acquired by Lindos Maritime. IMO 8979817

LUXURY YACHT CHARTER

The Company Luxury Yacht Charter Sdn Bhd is a Singapore company owned by Brian Chang, Chairman of Raffles Yacht, Singapore.

Address 11th Floor, Menara Berjaya, K2 Plaza, 179 Jalan Bukit Bintang, 55100 Kuala Lumpur, Malaysia

Area operated Charters from Singapore

ASEAN LADY	2385gt	2004	14.0k	D2	22p	22p		c	88.1m	21.3m 3.5m	PA

ASEAN LADY was built by Yantai Raffles Shipyard (yard number YPZ97-92) at Yantai, China. Her appearance is rather unusual as she has a large outrigger on one side. IMO 9303857

MARINE GROWTH VENTURES

The Company Marine Growth Ventures is a United States based organization, operating the PACIFIC AURORA on a timeshare basis.

Address 405A Atlantis Road, Cape Canaveral, Florida 32920 United States of America

Telephone +1 321 783 1744 **Fax** +1 321 301 0202

Website www.marinegrowthventures.com

Area operated Canadian coast

PACIFIC AURORA	1135gt	1962	13.0k	D2	68p	72p	27c	57.4m	11.6m 3.8m	MT

IDO's **Mavi Marmara** in Istanbul *(William Mayes)*

Murmansk's **Professor Molchanov** at Jamestown *(Chris Mason)*

Operation Mobilization's **Doulos** in Southampton Water *(Alan Ryszka-Onions)*

PACIFIC AURORA was built by the Collingwood Shipyard (yard number 175) at Collingwood, Ontario, Canada as the passenger/cargo vessel TAVERNER for Marine Atlantic. She was acquired by British Columbia Discovery Voyages in 1997 and had been undergoing conversion for several years, before being sold on to Marine Growth Ventures. IMO 5353983

MAURITIUS SHIPPING

The Company Mauritius Shipping Corporation is part of Swiss controlled Societe de Gerance Maritime SA (SGM) and operates two cargo/passenger ships serving Mauritius, Rodriques, Reunion and Madagascar. The ships are managed and operated by MSC Coraline, a Mauritius Shipping Corporation subsidiary.

Address Suite 512, St James Court, St Denis Street, Port Louis, Mauritius

Telephone +230 208 5900 **Fax** +230 212 5176

Website www.mauritiusshipping.intnet.mu

Area operated Local services in the Indian Ocean from Mauritius

MAURITIUS PRIDE	5234gt	1990	14.5k	D2	12b	248d	52c	99.5m	17.0m	6.5m	MU
MAURITIUS TROCHETIA	5492gt	2001	14.5k	D2	112p	112p	37c	107.9m	17.5m	6.2m	MU

MAURITIUS PRIDE was built by the Husumer Shipyard (yard number 1505) at Husum, Germany for the company. IMO 8906767

MAURITIUS TROCHETIA was built by the Hudong Shipyard (yard number H1260A) at Shanghai, China for the company. IMO 9225287

MERCY SHIPS

The Company Mercy Ships, a global charity, has operated hospital ships in developing nations since 1978. In the organisation's own words 'Following the example of Jesus, Mercy Ships brings hope and healing to the poor, mobilizing people and resources worldwide'. Don and Deyon Stephens founded the organisation in 1978, with the purchase of the VICTORIA (at a cost of $1m) being completed in October of that year. The ANASTASIS, as the VICTORIA was renamed, was then the world's largest non-government hospital ship. She was joined in 1994 by the CARIBBEAN MERCY and five years later by the AFRICA MERCY, which underwent an eight year refit as a hospital ship with six operating theatres and an 84-bed ward. The AFRICA MERCY took the title of the largest non-government hospital ship when she entered service in 2007. In late 2006 the CARIBBEAN MERCY was sold. In 2007, with the entry into service of the AFRICA MERCY, the ANASTASIS was sold for scrap.

Chief Executive Officer Don Stephens

Address PO Box 2020, Garden Valley, Texas 75771-2020, United States of America

Telephone +1 903 939 7000 **Fax** +1 903 882 0336

Website www.mercyships.org

Area operated Worldwide

AFRICA MERCY	16071gt	1980	19.0k	D2		152.0m	22.8m	6.0m	MT

AFRICA MERCY was built by Helsingor Vaerft (yard number 418) at Helsingor, Denmark as one of a trio of Inter-City train ferries for Danske Statsbaner (DSB – Danish State Railways) for service between Korsor and Nyborg on the Great Belt. As the DRONNING INGRID she served until the opening of the Great Belt Bridge in 1997 and was then laid up at Nakskov, Denmark. She was purchased for Mercy Ships in 1999 and temporarily renamed INGRID. She took her current name, AFRICA MERCY, in 2000 and then underwent an 8-year conversion on the River Tyne in North East England. She entered service in April 2007, replacing the ANASTASIS. IMO 7803188

MORSKAYA KOMPANIYA SAKHALIN-KURILY

The Company Morskaya Kompaniya Sakhalin-Kurily is a Government of the Russian Federation controlled company.

Address ul Sovetskaya 111 A, Kholmsk, Sakhalinskaya Oblast, 694620 Russia

Area operated In the Sakhalin region of Eastern Russia, possibly carrying oil workers

IGOR FARKHUTDINOV	4575gt	1991	14.3k	D1	150p		p		c	90.0m	17.2m	5.3m	RU

IGOR FARKHUTDINOV was built for Yuzhmorgeologiya as the research vessel NEVA by Stocznia im. Komuny Paryskiej (yard number B961/06) at Gdynia, Poland as the last of a series of six similar research vessels. She was renamed as the ADMIRAL LAZAREV in 1996 and passed to her current owner in 2003 when she took the name IGOR FARKHUTDINOV, honouring the former Governor of the Region of Sakhalin. IMO 8714384

MURMANSK ADMINISTRATION

The Company The full title of this Russian Federation controlled organisation is the State Institution Murmansk Administration for Hydrometeorology and Environmental Monitoring. The PROFESSOR MOLCHANOV is currently operating an extensive programme of expedition cruises in the Arctic and Antarctic, but it is not known to whom (if anyone) the ship is chartered as she is being marketed by a large number of travel companies. It is likely that both ships are used for research programmes when not engaged in cruising.

Address ul Shmidta 23, Murmansk 183789, Russia

Telephone +7 8152 473726 **Fax** +7 8152 472406

Website www.kolgimet.ru

Area operated Ships chartered out

PROFESSOR MOLCHANOV	1753gt	1982	9.0k	D1	49p	49p	23c	71.6m	12.8m	4.5m	RU
VIKTOR BUYNITSKIY	693gt	1986	12.8k	D1	30p	35p	c	49.9m	10.0m	3.6m	RU

PROFESSOR MOLCHANOV was built for the Government of Russia's Hydrometeorological Institute by Oy Laivateollisuus (yard number 344) at Turku, Finland. The ship passed to the Murmansk Territorial Hydrometeorological Institute in 1994. She operated mainly on charters to Quark Expeditions until about 2008, but it is currently unclear who is the lead charterer of this ship. Pavil Alexandric Molchanov (1893-1930) was an eminent meteorologist who developed radio signals for weather balloons and was the first Soviet to captain a Zeppelin. IMO 8010348

VIKTOR BUYNITSKIY was built by the Valmet Shipyard (yard number 370) at Turku, Finland for the Murmansk Territorial Administration. Viktor Harlampievich Buynitskiy (1911-1980) was a renowned oceanographer. IMO 8422448

MURMANSK SHIPPING COMPANY

The Company The Murmansk Shipping Company operates a fleet of icebreakers in the Barents Sea and also operates some of them under charter on Arctic and Antarctic expedition cruises. Among the fleet are nine nuclear powered icebreakers, including the YAMAL, operated for Quark Expeditions. The company was founded in 1939, but one of the most significant events in the company's history was the expedition by the icebreaker ARKTIKA in 1977 to the North Pole, making that ship the first surface vessel to reach the Pole. In 1993 the company was converted from a state-owned enterprise into a joint-stock company. Murmansk Shipping Company operates a fleet of ice-strengthened cargo ships and tankers and three conventional icebreakers.

Chief Executive Alexander Medvedev

Address 15 Kominterna Street, 183038 Murmansk, Russia

Telephone +7 8152 481049 **Fax** +7 8152 481148

Website www.msco.ru

Area operated Polar regions

KLAVDIYA YELANSKAYA	4329gt	1977	13.0k	D2	206p	224p	c	100.0m	16.2m	4.6m	RU
POLARIS	2097gt	1968	13.0k	D1	76p	96p	36c	70.5m	15.5m	4.4m	RU
SOVETSKIY SOYUZ	20646gt	1989	21.0k	ST3	106p	114p	48c	150.0m	30.0m	11.0m	RU
YAMAL	20646gt	1992	21.0k	N3	100p	100p	130c	150.0m	30.0m	11.0m	RU

KLAVDIYA YELANSKAYA is a passenger and cargo vessel offering a service from Murmansk. However, she does also offer occasional cruises. She was built by Brodogradiliste (yard number 416)

The **Logos Hope** undergoing conversion *(William Mayes Collection)*

The **Kay** in Bangkok *(Martin Wright)*

Peaceboat's **Oceanic** in New York *(Theodore W Scull)*

at Kraljevica in what was then Yugoslavia. The ship was used as a vantage point for journalists and relatives during the raising of the sunken Russian submarine KURSK in 2001. IMO 7422922

POLARIS was built as the DISKO for the local services of KNI Service A/S within Greenland by Svendborg Skibsvaerft (yard number 122) at Svendborg, Denmark. Her owner was restyled as Arctic Umiaq Line in 1994. She was laid up at Nakskov, Denmark in 1999 and during the following year passed to Scandinavian Cruise Line for whom she was renamed SHEARWATER. Rebuilt at Fredericia in Denmark, she re-entered service later in 2000 cruising around Scotland and the Isles. In 2001 she was renamed as the BRAND POLARIS and two years later took the name VIKING POLARIS. She is now owned by the Murmansk Shipping Company and was renamed POLARIS at the end of 2004. IMO 6807395

SOVETSKIY SOYUZ was built by Baltiyskiy Zavod (yard number 703) at Leningrad, Russia for the Murmansk Shipping Company. Her name commemorates the Soviet Soyuz space programme. IMO 8838582

YAMAL was built by the Baltic Shipbuilding and Engineering Works (yard number 704) at St Petersburg, Russia as the nuclear powered icebreaker YAMAL for the Murmansk Shipping Company. The Yamal peninsula in Siberia is home to the Nenets, reindeer herders who have occupied the region for more than 1,000 years. She has operated charters for Quark expeditions for a number of years, but does not appear to be in passenger service in 2009. IMO 9077549

OCEAN INDEPENDENCE

The Company Ocean Independence is a Swiss registered company in the yacht management business. The company also manages a number of smaller vessels.

Address Building U81, Turbinenweg 4, 8610 Uster, Switzerland

Telephone +41 4 3399 2277 **Fax** +41 4 3399 2271

Website www.oceanindependence.com

Area operated Charter market

NOMAD	1260gt	2003	15.5k	D2	p	p	14c	69.5m	11.6m	3.0m	KY
SUNRISE	4200gt	1991	15.5k	D2	80p	80p	65c	90.6m	15.3m	3.6m	BS

NOMAD was built by Oceanfast (yard number 75) at Fremantle, Western Australia as the yacht AUSSIE RULES. She became the FLORIDIAN in 2005 and was renamed NOMAD in 2008. IMO 1007316

SUNRISE was built for Renaissance Cruises as the RENAISSANCE SIX by Nuovi Cantieri Apuania (yard number 1145) at Marina di Carrara, Italy as one of a series of eight small luxury cruise ships. She was sold to Sun Cruises of Singapore in 1998, when replaced by impressive new tonnage, and renamed as the SUN VIVA 2. Following the loss of the SUN VISTA, that company was taken over by Star Cruises and she was renamed MEGASTAR CAPRICORN in 2000. She was soon sold on, and her purchaser, Hebridean Island Cruises had her refitted, reducing her passenger capacity from 112 to 80, thus producing the exclusive and luxurious HEBRIDEAN SPIRIT in 2001. Troubled economic times forced her sale in April 2009, shortly before Hebridean International Cruises went into administration. She was renamed SUNRISE in April 2009. IMO 8802870

OGASAWARA KAIUN

The Company Ogasawara Kaiun Co Ltd is a Japanese company.

Address Asahi Building, 29-19 Shiba 5-chome, Minato-ku, Tokyo 108-0014, Japan

Telephone +81 3 3451 5171 **Fax** +81 3 3541 4522

Website www.ogasawarakaiun.co.jp

Area operated Long distance Japanese domestic service from Tokyo

OGASAWARA MARU	‡6700gt	1997	22.5k	D2	198b	833d	49c	131.0m	17.2m	5.7m	JP

OGASAWARA MARU was built by Mitsubishi Heavy Industries (yard number 1030) in Japan. She is a passenger and cargo vessel, serving the long route south from Tokyo to Bonin Island. IMO 9150353

OPERATION MOBILIZATION

The Company Operation Mobilization is a missionary organisation taking its floating bookshops to the ports of the world. The first ship, the UMANAC was purchased from the Danish Government in 1970 and became the LOGOS. The DOULOS joined the fleet in 1977 and the LOGOS II was purchased as a replacement for the LOGOS, which was lost after running onto rocks in South America in 1988. With the arrival of the newly refitted LOGOS HOPE in 2008, the LOGOS II was sold for scrap.

International Director and Founder George Verwer

Address Alte Neckarelzer Str. 2, D74821 Mosbach, Germany

Telephone +49 6261 92630

Website www.omships.org

Area operated Worldwide

DOULOS	6818gt	1914	13.0k	D1	414b		130.4m	16.5m	5.6m	MT
LOGOS HOPE	12519gt	1973	22.0k	D2	500b		129.0m	20.8m	4.9m	FO

DOULOS was built by the Newport News Shipbuilding and Dry Dock Company (yard number 176) as the cargo ship MEDINA for the US East Coast to Gulf of Mexico service of the Mallory Steamship Company. This unremarkable little ship survived both world wars and was sold in 1948 for conversion as an emigrant ship for the trade from Europe to Australia. Renamed as the ROMA she carried 287 first class passengers and almost 700 in tourist class. Costa Line purchased the ship in 1952 and she was rebuilt as that company's FRANCA C. Modern Fiat diesels replaced her coal-fired boilers and triple expansion steam engine. She ran between Italy and South America until 1959, following which she was used for cruising. Re-engined again in 1970, she cruised for a further seven years before, at the age of 63, she passed to Operation Mobilization and was renamed DOULOS for use as a Christian missionary ship and floating bookshop. Doulos is Greek for servant. IMO 5119105

LOGOS HOPE was built by Werft Nobiskrug (yard number 678) at Rendsburg, Germany as the GUSTAV VASA for Saga Line's Baltic Sea car ferry services. In 1983 Smyril Line of the Faeroes bought her and she was renamed NORRONA for her long journeys between Denmark and Torshavn and Iceland. On the delivery of a new NORRONA she was renamed NORRONA 1 and laid up in Esbjerg, Denmark. OM acquired her in 2004 and after a spell in Malta she was moved to Trogir in Croatia to be refitted as the LOGOS HOPE. Her refit was completed early in 2008. IMO 7302914

PACIFIC SEAWAYS

The Company Pacific Seaways is a subsidiary of Care Offshore.

Address L'Oujonnet. PO Box 5, 1195 Bursinel, Switzerland

Area operated Unknown

KAY	4575gt	1990		D1	150p	150p	c	90.0m	17.2m	5.3m	VC

KAY was built by Stocznia im. Komuny Paryskiej (yard number B961/05) at Gdynia, Poland as the VLADIMIR CHIVILIKHIN for Dalryba. She later passed to Vladivostok Trawling and in 1998 was registered as the KAY for Falkland Investments. Her current owner acquired her in 1999. She has spent a number of years in Singapore and Bangkok being converted into a luxury yacht. IMO 8509208

PEACEBOAT ORGANISATION

The Company Peace Boat is a Japan-based non-government and non-profit organisation, founded in 1983, that works to promote peace, human rights, equality, sustainable development and environmental protection. The Peaceboat used THE TOPAZ, for a number of years until she was replaced in 2008 by the CLIPPER PACIFIC. That ship suffered a number of mechanical problems and the charter was terminated part way through her first voyage, with the passengers being transferred to the hastily chartered MONA LISA. The OCEANIC joined in 2009 as a permanent replacement and commenced Peaceboat's 66th voyage in April 2009.

Address B1 3-13-1 Takadanobaba, Shinjuku, Tokyo 169-0075 Japan

Telephone +81 3 3363 8047 **Fax** +81 3 3363 7562

Website www.peaceboat.org

Area operated Three world cruises plus shorter Asian voyages annually

OCEANIC		38772gt	1965	27.0k	STE2	1136p	1500p	565c	238.4m	29.4m	8.8m	MT

OCEANIC was the first new ship to be built for Home Lines. She was constructed by Cantieri Riunite dell'Adriatico (yard number 1876) at Monfalcone, Italy as the OCEANIC for transatlantic service between New York and Italy. She later sailed between New York and Bermuda and was used extensively for cruising. She was sold to Premier Cruise Lines in 1985, when she became the ROYALE OCEANIC, but was renamed as the STARSHIP OCEANIC later that year. She reverted to her original name in 1998. In 2000 she was renamed BIG RED BOAT I, but reverted to her original name in December of that year, and two years later was sold to Pullmantur. She developed a loyal following on her weekly Western Mediterranean circuits from Barcelona. In 2009 she was to move to Valencia, from where she was to operate alternate 2- and 5-day itineraries. However, at short notice she was sold to Panamanian interests for charter to the Peaceboat Organisation. IMO 5260679

PEDLEY MARINE

The Company Pedley Marine is part of Pedley Furniture International, a company established in 1954.

Address Shirehill Works, Safron Walden, Essex, CB11 3AL, England

Telephone +44 1799 522461 **Fax** +44 1799 513100

Website www.pedley.com

Area operated In 2008 Mediterranean

HARMONY II		878gt	1955	12.0k	D2	12p	12p	c	57.7m	8.7m	2.7m	VC

HARMONY II was built by the Brodogradiliste Uljanik shipyard (yard number 165) at Pula in Yugoslavia as the coastal passenger and cargo vessel MOSTAR (although launched as the OSIJEK) for the Yugoslavian state ferry operator, Jadranska Linjska Plovidba, the fore-runner of today's Jadrolinija. After a little over 10 years service she was sold to a Greek operator and converted into a day cruise ship under the name MELTEMI II. In 1983 she was sold to Epirotiki Lines and renamed APOLLO I, but continued her day cruise role. In 1987 she was renamed PRINCE ALBERT and came to the UK. Her use in the early years is somewhat hazy, but she was laid up at Tilbury for a number of years before being towed to Liverpool in 1999 where her lay-up continued. Plans to convert her for use as a Russian restaurant came to nothing. In 2002 she was sold and towed to Ipswich where she has been converted to become a floating furniture showroom. The original HARMONY (a sailing boat) was built by a team, including the company's founder, Neville Pedley, consisting of four members of Shoreditch Training College's diploma year, in 1951. In a change of plan a number of Mediterranean cruises were advertised on the HARMONY II in 2008, although it unclear exactly who was operating the ship. IMO 5242627

PLATINUM YACHT MANAGEMENT

The Company Platinum Yachts is a Dubai based company that builds, converts and manages large super yachts owned by the Crown Prince of Dubai and his family. This owner appears to be creating a collection of the former Renaissance first generation ships. The company is part of Dubai World, the owner of the Peninsular and Oriental Steam Navigation Company.

Address PO Box 17215, Jebel Ali, Dubai, United Arab Emirates

Telephone +971 4 883 3323 **Fax** +971 4 883 3686

Website www.platinum.gov.ae

CRUISEONE	4077gt	1990	15.5k	D2	p	p	c	88.3m	15.3m	4.0m	MT
DUBAI	12488gt	2006	25.0k	D2	p	p	88c	162.0m	22.0m	5.0m	AE
DABAWI	4077gt	1989	14.0k	D2	44p	44p	71c	90.6m	15.3m	4.0m	AE

CRUISEONE was built by Cantieri Navale Ferrari (yard number 44) at La Spezia, Italy as the RENAISSANCE TWO, the second in a series of eight ships for the new Renaissance Cruises, a company in which the Norwegian ship owner Fearney & Eger was initially involved. She was sold in 1998 as new and larger ships were delivered, and became THE NEPTUNE for Malaysian owner Robert Tan, who chartered her to his Singaporean brother Alan Tan to operate under the Universal Cruises banner. She was briefly renamed as THE NEPTUNE 2 when sold to Owen Shipping. She was converted from her original luxury to a very basic ship carrying twice the number of passengers, in a Singapore shipyard, before entering service in the spring of 2005 for EasyCruise as the EASYCRUISEONE in the Western Mediterranean. EasyCruise replaced her with a larger ship in 2008 and she passed to the control of Platinum Yacht Management and was renamed CRUISE ONE. She is currently undergoing conversion. IMO 8708658

DUBAI had her hull constructed by Blohm & Voss (yard number 965) in Hamburg and was completed by Platinum Yachts (yard number1) in Dubai. IMO 1006324

DABAWI was built as the RENAISSANCE; eventually the first ship in what became a series of eight for Renaissance Cruises by Cantieri Navale Ferrari (yard number 43) at La Spezia, Italy. Her career with the line was short-lived as she was placed on long term charter to casino cruise operator Universal Cruise Lines of Singapore two years later. Subsequently she was renamed THE MERCURY. She was laid up when Universal went bankrupt in 2002. Ownership then passed to a Malaysian company called Viking Lines, who continued to keep the ship in lay-up until she was sold to New Century at the beginning of 2004. She operated overnight casino cruises from Singapore and ports in Malaysia as the LEISURE WORLD I until sold in March 2007 to Dubai based Platinum Yacht Management and renamed DABAWI for conversion into a luxury private yacht. IMO 8708646

PRIMA MANAGEMENT

The Company Prima Management is part of the Halim Mazmin shipping and ship agency group of Malaysia.

Address 49 The Boulevard, Mid Valley City, Lingkaran Syed Putra, 59200 Kuala Lumpur, Malaysia

Telephone +30 211 600 7000 **Fax** +30 210 984 2057

Website www.halimazmin.com

Area operated Charter yachts - Malaysia

| LILI MARLEEN | 704gt | 1994 | 8.5k | SD1 | 50p | 54p | 25c | 76.0m | 9.5m | 2.9m | MY |
| PUTERI MAHSURI | 794gt | 1990 | 11.0k | SD1 | 36p | 36p | 20c | 66.5m | 10.5m | 4.5m | MY |

LILI MARLEEN was built by Elsflether Werft (yard number 417) at Elsfleth, Germany for Peter Deilmann Cruises. She was acquired by her current owner without a change of name in 2004. IMO 9086863

PUTERI MAHSURI was built by the De Merwede Shipyard (yard number 654) at Hardinxveld, Netherlands as the KANRIN MARU. She passed to her current owner in 2003 and was renamed PUTERI MAHSURI. IMO 8900696

PRIVATE SEA YACHTING

The Company Private Sea Yachting is a Greek yacht management company, managing a number of small vessels in addition to the two ships listed here.

Address 360 Syngrou Avenue, 17674 Athens, Greece

Telephone +60 3 2730 5000 **Fax** +60 3 2730 5151

Website www.privateseayachting.com

Area operated Charter yachts

| ALEXANDER | 5933gt | 1966 | 17.0k | D2 | 54p | 54p | 60c | 122.0m | 16.9m | 5.8m | MT |
| TURAMA | 7560gt | 1990 | 15.0k | D2 | 52p | 52p | 60c | 116.4m | 17.0m | 4.4m | MT |

ALEXANDER was built by Lubecker Flender Werke (yard number 558), at Lubeck in Germany as the REGINA MARIS, a small cruise ship for Lubeck Line of Germany. As built she had a small garage for about 40 cars. In 1976 she was sold to Canadian owners, who renamed her MERCATOR ONE. She did one season of Caribbean cruises before being arrested for non-payment of debts. She was laid up until late 1979, when she was sold to Peter Deilmann, and renamed FRANKFURT, although when she entered service as an upmarket ship in 1980 she had reverted to her original name. Sun World Cruises of St Louis chartered her in 1982 and used her for a series of cruises on the St Lawrence in Canada. Deilmann again used the REGINA MARIS for a short series of cruises in 1983, following which she was laid up. In October 1983 she was acquired by John S Latsis and then underwent a two-year refit at Bremerhaven, to emerge as the luxury yacht ALEXANDER (named after Latsis' grandson). IMO 6603012

The **Alexander** at Mykonos *(Rick Frendt)*

PT Pelni's **Gunung Dempo** in the River Ems *(Meyer Wevft)*

The **Gann** at Stavanger *(William Mayes)*

TURAMA was built by Rauma (yard number 305) at Rauma in Finland for Delfin Cruises, an investor group from the Finnish Aland Islands, as the DELFIN CARAVELLE. Delivered in June 1990, the ship operated unsuccessfully until October, when the company ceased operations and the ship was returned to her builder. In 1991 she was chartered to Sally Line as the SALLY CARAVELLE to replace the burnt-out SALLY ALBATROS. At the end of 1991 she was chartered to Odessa Cruise Lines, renamed COLUMBUS CARAVELLE and sub-chartered to the German tour operator, Transocean Tours. In 1994 she moved to Singapore to become a gambling ship, marketed as the LIDO STAR, but her name was never officially changed. Following a lay-up in Singapore, she appears to have been renamed ERNEST HEMINGWAY, but was trading out of Hong Kong as the gambling ship CAPTAIN OMAR by January 2000. In 2004 she was bought by Greek owners, rebuilt as a luxury charter yacht and renamed the TURAMA. IMO 8907216

PT PELNI

The Company PT PELNI (PT Pelayaran Nasional Indonesis) was established in 1952 as a direct competitor to the Dutch Koninklijke Paketvaart Maatshaappij, and eventually as the sole operator of passenger liner services within Indonesia. The company is state owned and serves more than 100 ports in 24 provinces of this 17,000-island nation. The company also operates some smaller vessels without overnight berths, and a number of ro-ro ferries. The relationship with the Meyer shipyard began in 1959, when five traditional passenger/cargo vessels were constructed for the company. That relationship was substantially strengthened following a shipping disaster off the Indonesian coast in 1981, after which the Government began a major modernisation programme for the PT PELNI fleet.

President M Husseyn Umar

Address Lot 8, Jalan Gajah Mada 14, Kota Pos 1115, Jakarta 10130, Indonesia

Telephone +62 21 6385 7747 **Fax** +62 21 6386 4837

Website www.pelni.co.id

Area operated Indonesian local passenger services

AWU	6022gt	1991	D2	14.0k	54b	915d	84c	99.8m	18.0m	4.2m	ID
BINAIYA	6022gt	1994	D2	15.0k	54b	915d	84c	100.0m	18.0m	4.2m	ID
BUKIT RAYA	6022gt	1994	D2	14.0k	54b	915d	84c	99.8m	18.0m	4.2m	ID
BUKIT SIGUNTANG	14649gt	1996	D2	20.3k	416b	1557d	147c	146.5m	23.4m	5.9m	ID
CIREMAI	14581gt	1993	D2	20.0k	416b	1557d	145c	146.5m	23.4m	5.9m	ID
DOBONSOLO	14581gt	1993	D2	20.0k	420b	1557d	145c	146.5m	23.4m	5.9m	ID
DORO LONDA	14685gt	2001	D2	22.4k	104b	2066d	147c	146.5m	23.4m	5.9m	ID
GUNUNG DEMPO	14030gt	2008	D2	17.0k	1487b	96d	141c	146.6m	23.4m	5.9m	ID
KAMBUNA	14501gt	1984	D2	20.0k	1096b	500d	119c	144.8m	23.4m	5.9m	ID
KELIMUTU	6022gt	1986	D2	14.0k	54b	866d	84c	99.8m	18.0m	4.2m	ID
KELUD	14665gt	1998	D2	22.4k	416b	1557d	157c	146.5m	23.4m	5.9m	ID
KERINCI	14501gt	1983	D2	20.0k	1096b	500d	119c	144.8m	23.4m	5.9m	ID
LABOBAR	15136gt	2004	D2	22.4k	66b	3084d	161c	146.5m	23.4m	5.9m	ID
LAMBELU	14649gt	1997	D2	20.3k	416b	1557d	147c	146.5m	23.4m	5.9m	ID
LAWIT	6022gt	1986	D2	14.0k	54b	866d	84c	99.8m	18.0m	4.2m	ID
LEUSER	6022gt	1994	D2	15.0k	54b	915d	84c	99.8m	18.0m	4.2m	ID
NGGAPULU	14685gt	2002	D2	22.4k	104b	2102d	155c	145.6m	23.4m	5.9m	ID
RINJANI	14501gt	1984	D2	20.0k	1096b	500d	119c	144.8m	23.4m	5.9m	ID
SINABUNG	14665gt	1997	D2	20.0k	508b	1398d	147c	146.5m	23.4m	5.9m	ID
SIRIMAU	6022gt	1991	D2	15.0k	54b	915d	84c	99.8m	18.0m	4.2m	ID
TATAMAILAU	6022gt	1990	D2	15.0k	54b	915d	84c	99.8m	18.0m	4.2m	ID
TIDAR	14501gt	1988	D2	20.0k	416b	1488d	145c	144.0m	23.4m	5.9m	ID
TILONGKABILA	6022gt	1995	D2	14.0k	54b	915d	84c	99.8m	18.0m	4.2m	ID
UMSINI	14501gt	1985	D2	20.0k	1096b	500d	119c	144.0m	23.4m	5.9m	ID

All of the above ships were built by Jos. L. Meyer at Papenburg, Germany for PT Pelni.

IMO numbers and yard numbers

AWU	8915653	630	LABOBAR	9281542	663
BINAIYA	9032161	634	LAMBELU	9124548	643
BUKIT RAYA	9032173	635	LAWIT	8502353	615
BUKIT SIGUNTANG	9124536	642	LEUSER	9032159	633
CIREMAI	9032135	631	NGGAPULU	9226499	662
DOBONSOLO	9032147	632	RINJANI	8303252	611
DORO LONDA	9226487	661	SINABUNG	9139672	644
GUNUNG DEMPO	9401324	664	SIRIMAU	8915641	629
KAMBUNA	8209688	609	TATAMAILAU	8915639	628
KELIMUTU	8502341	614	TIDAR	8700292	617
KELUD	9139684	645	TILONGKABILA	9102760	641
KERINCI	8209676	608	UMSINI	8303264	612

Shipping Corporation of India's **Kavarati** *(Mark Amielanczyk)*

RAK TRAINING SHIP SINBAD

The Company RAK Training Ship Sinbad is a not for profit organization under the supervision of the Ras Al Khaimah Investment Authority of the United Arab Emirates.

Chief Executive Officer Manager Ajay Kotwal

Address PO Box 31291, Ras Al Khaimah, United Arab Emirates

Telephone +971 7236 1842 **Fax** +971 7236 1843

Website www.merchantnavyeducation.com

Area operated The Arabia Gulf

RTS SINDBAD BITIC	637gt	1949	12.0k	D1	30s	c	50.9m	8.5m	3.8m	KN

RTS SINDBAD BITIC was built by Trosvik Verksted (yard number 63) at Brevik, Norway as the coastal vessel SOROY. In 1966 she was renamed SKULE, in 1981 OSTFOLD and in 1991 GLOMMEN. She was acquired by Zambezi Shipping in 2004 and renamed as the RTS SINBAD in the following year. She passed to her current owner in 2007 and is now in service as a training ship, carrying 30 cadets. She was renamed in 2008. IMO 5334614

ROGALAND SJOASPIRANTSKOLE

The Company Rogaland Sjoaspirantskole (Rogaland Sea Recruit High School) is a maritime training institution, founded in 1949, run by the Young Seamen's Christian Society.

Address Tommerodden, N4085 Hundvag, Norway

Telephone +47 5154 7558 **Fax** +47 5186 1885

Website www.gann.no

Area operated Norway

GANN	6257gt	1982	15.0k	D2	105s		36c	108.6m	16.5m	3.7m	NO

GANN was built by Aker Trondelag AS (yard number 827) at Trondheim, Norway as the so-called mid-generation Hurtigruten (coastal express) ship NARVIK. She passed to her current owner in February 2007, and took the name GANN, as a replacement for a smaller ship of the same name. She is the sixth ship owned by the school to bear this name, which is thought to refer to the nearby Gandsfjord. IMO 8019344

ROSMORPORT

The Company Rosmorport is a Russian state controlled enterprise charged with the improvement of the management of Russia's seaports. It was set up in 2003.

Address Suschevskaya str 19, B7, 127055 Moscow, Russia

Telephone +7 495 626 1425 **Fax** +7 495 626 1239

Website www.rosmorport.ru

Area operated Not known if still in use as a passenger ship

KAPITAN DRANITSYN	12919gt	1980	19.5k	DE3	100p	116p	60c	129.4m	26.5m	8.5m	RU

KAPITAN DRANITSYN was built by Wartsila (yard number 429) at Helsinki, Finland. In 1997 she rescued 128 passengers from the cruise ship HANSEATIC, which was in danger of sinking. She has featured in a number of expedition operators' programmes, but it is difficult to tie her to any lead operator at the time of writing. IMO 7824405

SAMPO TOURS

The Company Sampo Tours operates day cruises on the icebreaker SAMPO between December and April.

Address Kauppakatu 16, 94100 Kemi, Finland

Telephone +358 16 256548 **Fax** +358 16 256361

Website www.sampotours.com

Area operated Day cruises in the Gulf of Bothnia, Finland

SAMPO	2630gt	1960	16.0k	D2	150d		16c	74.7m	17.4m	6.2m	FI

SAMPO was built by Wartsila (yard number 368) at Helsinki as an icebreaker. She was converted for use as a passenger ship in 1988 and carries 150 passengers on day cruises. IMO 5308938

SEMESTER AT SEA

The Company The Institute for Shipboard Education or Semester at Sea, founded by Hong Kong shipping magnate C Y Tung, began operating in 1977 aboard the UNIVERSE in conjunction with the University of Colorado. In 1981 the relationship with the University of Pittsburgh, which was to last 25 years, began, using the same ship. She was scrapped in India in 1996 and replaced by the UNIVERSE EXPLORER, built in 1958 as Moore McCormack Lines' BRASIL. When she was sold for scrap in 2004 a fast modern ship, the EXPLORER, was acquired to continue the tradition of the 'university at sea'. These voyages are only available to students that can meet the entry requirements. Meals are served cafeteria style and the students are responsible for most of the housekeeping, leading to a requirement for fewer crew than might be expected on a ship of this size. The University of Virginia currently Sponsors semester at Sea.

Address 2410 Old Ivory Road, Charlottesville, Virginia 22903, United States of America

Telephone +1 800 854 0195 **Fax** +1 434 243 4076

Website www.semesteratsea.com

Area operated Three annual round the world voyages

| EXPLORER | 24318gt | 2001 | 28.0k | D2 | 630s | 630s | 196c | 180.4m | 25.5m | 7.3m | BS |

EXPLORER was built by Blohm & Voss (yard number 962) in Hamburg, Germany, as the OLYMPIC EXPLORER for Royal Olympic Cruises. She was designed with a high speed to operate the company's new 'Three Continents in Seven Days' itinerary. Political unrest and worse in the Middle East caused the abandonment of that programme and the ship was used on more mundane itineraries in the Mediterranean and Caribbean Seas. Ludicrously, after pressure from the Olympic organisation in the run-up to the Athens Olympic Games, the company re-styled itself as Royal Olympia Cruises and the ship was renamed OLYMPIA EXPLORER. The company within ROC that owned the ship filed for bankruptcy in 2003, later bringing down the whole group. She was laid up and later auctioned, being purchased by Stella Maritime and becoming the EXPLORER for Semester at Sea. IMO 9183518

SHIPPING CORPORATION OF INDIA

The Company The Shipping Corporation of India, an Indian Government controlled company, was formed in 1961 with the merger of the Eastern Steamship Corporation and the Western Steamship Corporation. The company currently controls about 100 ships including a number of smaller passenger vessels and some ro-ro ferries. SCI owns the HARSHA VARDHANA, which is chartered to the Andaman and Nicobar Administration. The other ships are owned by the latter organisation and managed by the Shipping Corporation of India. Additionally, a number of small ferries and ro-ros are owned by the Administration.

Address Shipping House, 245 Madam Cama Road, Mumbai 400-021, India

Telephone +91 22 220 27346 **Fax** +91 22 220 26905

Website www.shipindia.com

Area operated Indian Ocean, Andaman and Nicobar Islands

HARSHA VARDHANA	‡8871gt	1974	17.0k	D1	753b	d	c	132.6m	21.5m	7.0m	IN
KAVARATI	8763gt	2008	17.0k	D2	702b	d	c	118.0m	19.0m	5.3m	IN
NANCOWRY	14176gt	1992	15.5k	D2	300b	900d	119c	157.0m	20.1m	6.7m	IN
NICOBAR	14195gt	1991	15.5k	D2	300b	900d	119c	157.0m	20.1m	6.7m	IN
SWARAJ DWEEP	14239gt	1999	16.0k	D2	300b	900d	119c	157.0m	20.1m	6.7m	IN

HARSHA VARDHANA was built at the Magazon Dock (yard number 272) in Mumbai, India. IMO 7219026

KAVARATI was built by the Hindustan Shipyard (yard number 11102) at Visakhapatnam, India. IMO 9238260

NANCOWRY was built in Szczecin, Poland by Stocznia Szczecinska (yard number B561/02). IMO 8606434

NICOBAR was built by Stocznia Szczecinska (yard number B561/01) in Szczecin, Poland. IMO 8606161

SWARAJ DWEEP was built by the Hindustan Shipyard (yard number 11101) at Visakhapatnam, India. IMO 9101168

Passenger/cargo ship on order

| CAMPBELL BAY | 8475gt | 2009 | 17.0k | D2 | 500p | p | c | 125.0m | 18.0m | 4.5m | IN |

CAMPBELL BAY is under construction at ABG Shipyard (yard number 205) at Surat, India. IMO 9309124

SINOKOR MERCHANT MARINE

The Company Sinokor Merchant Marine is a Korean container ship operator established in 1989, predominant in the trades between Korea, China and other countries of South East Asia. It operates a large fleet of container ships, including the GOLDEN TRADE, which previously carried passengers.

Address 301 Dongsung Building, 17-7 Namdaemun-no 4 ga, Jung-Gu, Seoul 100-094, South Korea

Telephone +82 2 774 8494 **Fax** +82 2 774 8483

Website www.sinokor.co.kr

Area operated South East Asia – but does not carry passengers

GOLDEN TRADE	19188gt	1988	18.3k	D1	104p	110p	44c	176.7m	26.0m	8.8m	KR

GOLDEN TRADE was built by Hyundai Heavy Industries (yard number 464) at Ulsa, Korea as the AMERICANA for Ivaran Lines service between New York and South America. She passed through a number of owners before arriving with Sinokor in 2004 and taking the new name GOLDEN TRADE. She has not carried passengers since 1999. IMO 8608119

SORLANDETS SEILENDE SKOLESKIBS

The Company Sorlandets Seilende Skoleskibs (Sorlandet Maritime Highschool) is the Norwegian operator of the training ship SJOKURS. The previous ship of this name has been acquired by Stavanger Municipality for preservation.

Address Tollbodgata 2, 4611 Kristiansand S, Norway

Area operated Norway as a training ship

SJOKURS	2191gt	1956	14.0k	D1				81.3m	12.6m	4.5m	NO

SJOKURS was built as the Hurtigruten ship RAGNVALD JARL by Blohm & Voss (yard number 789) in Hamburg, Germany for NFDS. That business was absorbed into TFDS in 1989 and the ship was sold six years later to Rogaland Sea Recruit Highschool to become the maritime training ship GANN, although unconfirmed reports suggest that she carried the name SOUTHERN PRIDE for a short time. In early 2007 she passed to her current owner and was renamed SJOKURS as a replacement for a ship of the same name. IMO 5289247

SOVEREIGN SEA HERMES

The Company Sovereign Sea Hermes is a Greek yacht refitting and management company.

Address 2A Areos Street,, Vouliagmeni, 16671, Athens, Greece

Telephone +30 210 896 4460

Website www.goldenport.gr

Area operated Mediterranean charter market

O'MEGA	1809gt	1985	14.0k	D2	30p	30p	21c	82.5m	11.6m	3.8m	GR

O'MEGA was built by Mitsubishi Heavy Industries (yard number 883) at Shimonoseki, Japan as the TOSHIMA. She was renamed KIMA in 2001 and took her current name in 2004 when acquired by Omega Cruises and converted into a yacht. She passed to Prestige Yachting in 2008 and is managed by the associated Sovereign Sea Hermes. IMO 8503151

ST HELENA LINE

The Company Andrew Weir Shipping is the manager and operator of the RMS St Helena on behalf of St Helena Line. The RMS ST HELENA was managed from the outset by the Cornish business, Curnow Shipping. The former company was formed in 1977 to fill the gap left when the Union Castle Mail Steamship Company ceased to operate passenger ships between the United Kingdom and South Africa (with regular calls at the island of St Helena). The first ST HELENA was a small former Canadian coastal passenger/cargo ship previously named the NORTHLAND PRINCE. She entered service in 1977 and continued until the new ST HELENA was delivered in 1990. During the Falklands War, the first ST HELENA was requisitioned for use as a mother ship for the minesweepers of the Royal Navy. Her temporary replacement was the former Blue Funnel passenger and cargo ship CENTAUR. In 2001

Semester at Sea's **Explorer** *(Theodore W Scull)*

The RMS **St Helena** at Jamestown *(Andrew Kilk)*

The **Sevastopol 1** in Istanbul *(William Mayes)*

Curnow Shipping lost the contract to manage the ST HELENA to Andrew Weir Shipping. The island of St Helena, one of 13 remaining United Kingdom Overseas Territories, is likely to have an airport built in the next 10 years.

Address Andrew Weir Shipping Ltd, Dexter House, 2 Royal Mint Court, London, EC3N 4XX, England

Telephone +44 207 575 6480 **Fax** +44 207 575 6200

Website www.rms-st-helena.com

Area operated South African and Namibian ports to St Helena, Ascension Island and occasionally to Tristan da Cunha, with two annual voyages to the UK

ST HELENA	6767gt	1990	14.5k	D2	98p	128p	56c	105.0m	19.2m	6.0m	GB

ST HELENA is the last British example of a true working passenger and cargo ship; ordered from the Aberdeen shipyard of Hall Russell (yard number 1000) in 1987, but completed by A&P Appledore in October 1990 after the collapse of the Scottish builder. She was built as a replacement for the former (smaller) ship of the same name to provide the lifeline service to the island of St Helena, once the staging post for the ships of the British East India Company. Following initial mechanical problems, she has served the Island well for the past 15 years. From 2005 her UK calls were limited to two each year with most voyages linking Cape Town to the island. The ST HELENA is the sole remaining true Royal Mail Ship. IMO 8716306

STAD AMSTERDAM

The Company Rederij Clipper Stad Amsterdam is a Dutch company.

Executive Director Frank Weermeijer

Address PO Box 12600, 1100AP Amsterdam, The Netherlands

Telephone +31 20 569 5839 **Fax** +31 20 569 1720

Website www.stadamsterdam.nl

Area operated Europe and Caribbean cruises and charters

STAD AMSTERDAM	723gt	2000	11.0k	SD1	28p	28p	30c	78.0m	10.5m	4.2m	NL

STAD AMSTERDAM is a three-masted square-rigged ship, built by Damen Oranjewerf (yard number 6900) in Amsterdam, The Netherlands. Her design is based on the AMSTERDAM of 1854. The ship was named by Mrs Rita Kok, wife of the former Prime Minister, Wim Kok, at Sail Amsterdam 2000.

STATSRAAD LEHMKUHL

The Company Stratsraad Lehmkuhl Foundation is a Norwegian organisation, founded in 1978, with the objective of preserving the working sailing ship STATSRAAD LEHMKUHL. The ship operates organized excursions and cruises and is also available for charter.

Address Skur 7, Bradbenken 2, 5003 Bergen, Norway

Telephone +47 55 30 17 00 **Fax** +47 55 30 17 01

Website www.lehmkuhl.no

Area operated Norway

STATSRAAD LEHMKUHL	1516gt	1914	10.0k	SD2			22c	84.6m	12.6m	5.2m	NO

STATSRAAD LEHMKUHL was built by Schiffswerke u Maschin Joh. C Tecklenborg (yard number 263) at Bremerhaven, Germany as the GROSSHERZOG FRIEDRICH AUGUST, a training ship for the German Merchant Marine. She was taken as reparations by the British in 1921 and two years later ended up in Bergen, where she was used as a sail training ship up to the outbreak of the Second World War. In 1940 she was seized by the Germans and between 1940 and 1945 she carried the name WESTWARTS. She can carry 350 day passengers or 150 trainees and her total length including the bowsprit is 98.0 metres. IMO 5339248

STAVANGER MUNICIPALITY

The Company Stavanger is a city on the west coast of Norway.

Address Haakon VII's Gate, N4068 Stavanger, Norway

Telephone +47 51 50 70 90 **Fax** +47 51 50 70 20

Website www.stavanger.kommune.no

Area operated Tourist attraction at Stavanger, Norway

SANDNES	1432gt	1950	14.0k	D1	60p		67.6m	11.0m	4.8m	NO

SANDNES was built by Nylands Verksted (yard number 374) at Oslo, Norway as the passenger vessel SANDNES. She was renamed VIKINGFJORD in 1974 and was acquired by the Rogaland Sjoaspirantskole who renamed her GANN. She passed to Sorlandets Seilende Skoleskibs in 1995 and was renamed SJOKURS. When she was replaced in 2007 she was acquired by the Stavanger Municipality for use in promoting the city's maritime heritage, reverting to her original name, SANDNES. IMO 5310905

SUDOSTROYENIYE

The Company Chastnoye Predpriyatiye Firma Sudostroyeniye is a Government of Ukraine owned company.

Address ul Lastovaya 3, Sevastopol, Krym, Ukraine

Area operated Shopping trips from Ukraine to Istanbul

GEROI SEVASTOPOLYA	1987gt	1965	14.0k	D2	160p		90c	89.7m	13.0m	4.9m	UA

GEROI SEVASTOPOLYA was built by Stocznia Szczecinska im A Warskiego (yard number B850/04) as the research vessel SVYATOY NIKOLAY, one of a series of eleven similar ships. She was quickly renamed as VASILIY GOLOVNIN and was probably converted for passenger use in 1999 when she was acquired by Sudostroyeniye and renamed GEROI SEVASTOPOLYA. IMO 8929393

SULPICIO LINES

The Company Sulpicio Lines was established in 1973 by Mr Go Guioc So, commonly known as Don Sulpicio Go. The company currently also operates a number of smaller passenger ferries, ro-ro ferries and cargo ships and is one of the largest inter-island shipping companies in the Philippines. Following the loss of THE PRINCESS OF THE STARS, it appears that the company's licence to carry passengers was withdrawn. These ships seem now only to carry cargo.

DIPOLOG PRINCESS	‡3786gt	1969	18.5k	D1	b	d	c	111.2m	15.2m	5.5m	PH
PRINCESS OF THE CARIBBEAN	‡3767gt	1979	20.8k	D2	316b	684d	c	110.5m	15.2m	4.8m	PH

DIPOLOG PRINCESS was built by Onomichi Zosen KK (yard number 210) at Onomichi, Japan as the TOKYO MARU. She became the DON EUSEBIO in 1978 and passed to her current owner in 1989, when she was renamed DIPOLOG PRINCESS. She is used in the domestic trades around the Philippine Archipelago. The ship has a capacity for 1,261 passengers but the mix between berthed and deck is unknown. IMO 6924765

PRINCESS OF THE CARIBBEAN was built by Mitsubishi Heavy Industries (yard number 802) at Shimonoseki, Japan as the OGASAWA MARU for Ogasawa Kaiun of Japan. She was acquired by Sulpicio Lines and renamed in 1997. IMO 7815363

SULTANATE OF OMAN ROYAL YACHTS

The Company Royal Yachts is a Sultanate of Oman Government organisation. .

Address Royal Court Affairs, PO Box 2769, Ruwi, Sultanate of Oman

Telephone +968 2473 3000 **Fax** +968 2474 0207

Website www.rca.gov.om

AL SAID	15580gt	2008	k	D2	p	p	c	155.0m	23.0m	5.5m	OM

AL SAID was built as the SUNFLOWER by Luerssen Werft (yard number 13644) in Bremen, Germany. She was delivered as the AL SAID. IMO 9463774

TALLSHIP ARTEMIS

The Company Rederij Tallship Artemis b.v. is a Dutch operator of tall ships that are available for day or longer charters.

Address Wieuwens 2, 8835 KX Easterlittens, The Netherlands

Telephone +31 517 342810 **Fax** +31 517 342808

Website www.tallship-artemis.com

Area Operated Mediterranean, North Sea and Baltic - charters

ANTIGUA	212gt	1957	k	SD1	32p	32p	c	49.5m	7.1m	2.9m	NL
ARTEMIS	321gt	1926	k	SD1	28p	35p	c	59.0m	7.0m	3.5m	NL
ATLANTIS	380gt	1905	10.0k	SD2	36p	36p	12c	42.5m	7.5m	3.8m	NL
ELIZABETH	gt	1913	k	SD1	35p	35p	c	41.0m	6.9m	1.4m	NL
MARE FRISIUM	210gt	1916	8.0k	SD1	24p	38p	c	49.5m	6.5m	2.2m	NL

ANTIGUA was built by Henry Scarr (yard number 750) at Hessle in England as the trawler ANTIGUA for Southard Trawlers. She later became a safety ship and was converted to a passenger vessel in 1997. She started operating for her current owner in 2006 and can carry up to 95 day passengers. IMO 5019800

ARTEMIS was built in 1926 by Nylands Verksted (yard number 281) in Oslo as the Danish whaling ship POLII. She was converted for use as a cargo ship in 1948 and renamed LISTER and three years later she was lengthened. In 1966 she became the ARTEMIS and in 2000 was converted to become a three mast passenger sailing ship for the Frisian Sailing Company. Her present owner acquired her in 2006. IMO 5209699

ATLANTIS had her origins in the River Elbe where she served as the lightship ELBE 2 from the time that she built by J H N Wichhorst (yard number 200) in Hamburg in 1905 until hit by the Danish freighter BANANA on 10 December 1974. She was laid up in Hamburg until 1979 and then served as a training ship for the Hamburg fire brigade from 1980 to 1983. Over the next two years she was converted into the three-masted barquentine ATLANTIS. Tallship Artemis acquired her in 2006. Her areas of operation are generally the Balearic Islands and the Cote d'Azur. She can carry up to 140 day passengers. IMO 8333635

ELIZABETH was built in 1913 as a Zeeland clipper. She can carry up to 60 day passengers when cruising in the Frisian Lakes, Waddensea and Ijsselmeer.

MARE FRISIUM was built by N V Weerter Scheepsbouw (yard number 90) at Weert in The Netherlands as the Swedish fishing lugger PETRONELLA. She was lengthened in 1952 and converted for use as a cargo ship. In 1995 she was rebuilt as a three masted passenger topsail lugger and was renamed MARE FRISIUM in 1997. She can carry 90 day passengers. IMO 5344592

UKRAINE MARINE ECOLOGY RESEARCH CENTRE

The Company The Ukraine Marine Ecology Research Centre is a Government of the Republic of Ukraine owned organisation, established in 1994.

Address Frantsuzskiy Bulvar 89, 270009 Odessa, Ukraine

Telephone +380 482 636622 **Fax** +380 482 636741

Area operated Ukraine ports to Istanbul with passengers and cargo

SEVASTOPOL-I	2996gt	1968	16.0k	D2	100p	100p	c	97.1m	13.8m	5.2m	UA

SEVASTOPOL-I was built by Stocznia Szczecinska (yard number B88/02) at Szczecin, Poland as the MUSSON for the Government of Russia's Hydrometeorological Research Institute. She passed to Ukraine Marine Ecology and appears to operate a passenger and cargo service between Ukraine and Istanbul, Turkey. Her sister ship, the PASSAT may or may not carry passengers, but appears to operate cargo sailings from time to time around the Black Sea. A third ship of this type is the BRIZ. Sevastopol is a seaport city in the Crimea, a region of southern Ukraine. IMO 6904155

UNITED STATES TRAINING SHIPS

Websites www.csum.edu www.maritime.edu www.sunymaritime.edu www.mainemarite.edu
www.tamug.edu

EMPIRE STATE	14557gt	1962	20.0k	STE1	684s		107c	172.2m	23.2m	9.6m	US
ENTERPRISE	13886gt	1967	19.0k	STE1	600s		110c	164.6m	23.2m	7.8m	US
GOLDEN BEAR	12517gt	1989	20.0k	D1	300s		50c	152.1m	21.9m	9.3m	US
STATE OF MAINE	12517gt	1990	20.0k	D1	258s		58c	152.4m	21.9m	9.1m	US
TEXAS CLIPPER	14113gt	1967	17.0k	D1	s		c	159.5m	22.0m	7.8m	US

EMPIRE STATE was built by the Newport News Shipbuilding and Drydock Company (yard number 552) at Newport News, Virginia, USA as the OREGON of States Steamship Company, for Pacific trades. In 1977 she became Moore McCormac's MORMACTIDE and in 1989 was purchased for the New York Maritime Academy, converted by Bay Shipbuilding Corporation and renamed as the sixth EMPIRE STATE. IMO 5264510

ENTERPRISE was built by Avondale Shipyards (yard number 1069) at Avondale, Louisiana, USA as the freighter VELMA LYKES for Lykes Lines. She became CAPE BON in 1986 and five years later participated in Operation Desert Storm. In 2003 she was converted for use as a training ship for the Massachusetts Maritime Academy, to replace the PATRIOT STATE, and was renamed ENTERPRISE, in honour of the Academy's first training ship, which served from 1893 to 1909. IMO 6621662

GOLDEN BEAR is a cadet training ship attached to the California Maritime Academy, Vallejo, California. She was built by Bethlehem Steel (yard number 4667) at Sparrows Point, Maryland, USA as the hydrographic survey vessel USNS MAURY. She was converted for her current use in 1996 and renamed GOLDEN BEAR, the third ship to carry this name. IMO 8834407

STATE OF MAINE is the second training ship of the Maine Maritime Academy and was built by Bethlehem Steel (yard number 4668) at Sparrows Point in Maryland as the fast oceanographic research vessel USNS TANNER. She was laid up in 1993 with engine problems and was laid up in the James River. She was converted for use as a training ship between 1996 and 1997 and joined the academy in June 1997. She does not appear to have been renamed until 2000. IMO 8835217

TEXAS CLIPPER, the third ship of the Texas Maritime Academy, was built by Swan, Hunter & Wigham Richardson (yard number 2016) at Wallsend on Tyne in the North East of England as the Royal Fleet Auxiliary's replenishment vessel LYNESS. She was acquired by the US Navy in 1980, but does not appear to have been renamed until 1997 when she was given the name SIRIUS. When decommissioned she was acquired by the Texas Maritime Academy in 2005, and refitted as a training ship. She was renamed as the TEXAS CLIPPER in 2007. IMO 6706888

VIVAL MARINE

The Company Vival Marine is a Ukraine Government controlled travel and tour operator, established in 1998. The company previously operated the car ferry PALLADA in the Black Sea and offered voyages between Odessa and Haifa in conjunction with Mano Cruises, however both of these activities appear to have ceased.

Address ul Grecheskaya 22, 65026 Odessa, Ukraine

Telephone +380 482 375037

Website www.vivaltour.com

Area operated Round trip voyages from Odessa to Istanbul

GLORIYA	5745gt	1968	16.0k	D2	158p	p	c	124.2m	m	m	UA

GLORIYA was built by VEB Mathias-Thesen-Werft (yard number 186) at Wismar in what was East Germany as the research vessel AKADEMIK VERNADSKIY for the Academy of Science at Sevastopol. She was transferred to the Marine Hydrophysics Institute of the National Academy of Sciences of the Ukraine in 1994 without a change of name. In 1999 she was transferred to Cambodian company Hullman International, but was re-acquired in 2001, when she was renamed GLORIYA. IMO 6726929

WEM LINES

The Company WEM Lines is a Greek ship owner and operator of general cargo ships and bulk carriers, founded in 1982. The RM ELEGANT is placed with brokers for charter.

Chairman N Mazarakis

Address 152 Kifisias Avenue and Sokhou Street, 11525 Athens, Greece

Telephone +30 210 672 7220 **Fax** +30 210 672 7221

Website www.wem.gr

Area operated Mediterranean Sea charters

| RM ELEGANT | 1541gt | 2005 | 17.0k | D2 | 30p | 30p | 32c | 72.4m | 12.0m | 3.4m | GR |

RM ELEGANT was built by Kanellos Bros (yard number 586) at Perama, Greece for Marinic Marine Company, a subsidiary of WEM Lines. IMO 9334442

WINDWARD ISLES SAILING SHIP COMPANY

The Company Windward Isles Sailing Ship Company, a Canadian company, operates the PICTON CASTLE on round the world itineraries for square-rigger sail trainees, with or without experience. In May 2010 the ship will set sail on another epic 14-month circumnavigation. Fares for the full voyage, in dormitory accommodation are US$ 46,000.

Address PO Box 1076, 132 Montague Street, Lunenburg, Nova Scotia, B0J 2C0, Canada

Telephone +1 902 634 9984 **Fax** +1 902 634 9985

Website www.picton-castle.com

Area operated Worldwide

| PICTON CASTLE | ‡299gt | 1928 | 10.5k | D1 | 40p | | 12c | 43.0m | 7.2m | 4.0m | CK |

PICTON CASTLE was built by Cochrane & Sons (yard number 1031) at Selby in Yorkshire, England as the Swansea trawler PICTON CASTLE. In 1939 she was requisitioned for use as a minesweeper and given the HMS prefix. In 1955 she was renamed TETYS and two years later was converted into a cargo

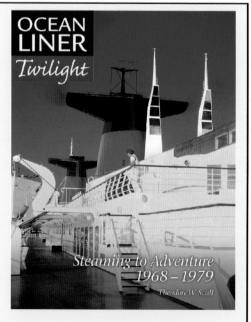

ship. In 1960 she became the UTSTRAUM, and in 1970 was renamed STEINFOREST. She became the BERGFOREST in 1973 and some years later is thought to have been converted for use as a dredger. She was given the name TURNSTEIN in 1981 and three years later was renamed as the DOLMAR. She was converted to a sail training ship in the late 1990's and renamed PICTON CASTLE. IMO 5375010

YUG-KARGO

The Company Yug-Kargo is a Russian state controlled company.

Address Pereulok Vinogradnyy 8, Sochi 354068, Russia

Area operated Black Sea ports

PRINCESSA ELENA	2964gt	1991	13.0k	D1	p	200p	c	88.5m	13.6m	3.6m	SL

PRINCESSA ELENA was built by the Yichang Shipyard in China as the METANGULA for a Mozambique owner. She is thought to have been sold at auction in 2001 and may have been renamed REGINA ELENA. Yug-Kargo acquired her in 2002 and she became the PRINTSESSA YELENA, later westernised to PRINCESSA ELENA. IMO 888824

ZANZIBAR SHIPPING

The Company Zanzibar Shipping is a Government of Tanzania owned company.

General Manager Rashid Mzee

Address Mizingani Road, PO Box 80, Zanzibar, Tanzania

Telephone +255 22 22787 **Fax** +255 22 22186

Area operated Between Zanzibar and Tanzania

MAENDELEO	‡1431gt	1980		D2	32b	422d	c	77.5m	12.2m	4.1m	TZ
MAPINDUZI	‡3999gt	1974	15.5k	D2	140b	567d	c	109.9m	16.0m	4.7m	TZ

MAENDELEO was built by Tsuneishi Shipbuilding Co (yard number OE80) at Numakuma, Japan IMO 7900974

MAPINDUZI was built by Niigata Engineering (yard number 1286) at Niigata, Japan. In January 2009 this ship was advertised for sale. IMO 7355234

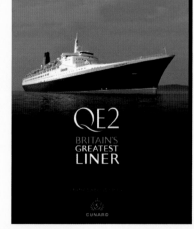

the **leading** *guide to the cruise industry*

section 4

Passenger ships in static roles

ANDAMAN CLUB

The Company Andaman Club is a Thai operator of resort hotels and casinos.

Address 25th A Floor, Lumphini Tower, 1168/71 Pharamthi Road, Yannuawa, Bangkok 10120, Thailand

Telephone +66 2 5154 7558 **Fax** +66 2 5186 1885

Website www.andamanclub.com

Area operated Possibly in use as a hotel ship at Similan Island, NW of Phuket, Thailand

KONG OLAV	2637gt	1964				87.4m	13.3m	4.6m	TH

KONG OLAV was built by AS Bergens Mek. Verksted (yard number 433) at Bergen, Norway for DSDS, an operator on the Hurtigruten. That company became part of VDS in 1978. She was sold to Thai owners in 1997 and is believed to be in static use as a hotel. IMO 6401206

CAPTAIN JOHN'S

The Company Captain John's is the local name for the JADRAN, owned and operated by Toronto restaurateur John Letnik.

Address 1 Queen's Quay West, Captain John's Pier, Toronto, Ontario, M5J 2H1, Canada

Telephone +1 416 363 6062 **Fax** +1 416 363 6065

Website www.captainjohns.ca

Area operated Static restaurant ship in Toronto, Canada

JADRAN	2564gt	1957				90.3m	13.0m	4.7m	

JADRAN was built as the second member of a trio of coastal liners for the services of Jadrolinija along the coast of Yugoslavia. She was built by Brodogradiliste at Split to carry 200 berthed and 1,000 deck passengers. She also used to cruise in the off-season. In 1975 she was sold to her current owner and converted for use as a static restaurant ship. Her surviving sister is Epirotiki's HERMES. She is marketed as CAPTAIN JOHN'S.

C-BED FLOATING HOTELS

The Company C-Bed Floating Hotels is a Dutch company operating a single ship.

Address Saturnussraat 25J, 2132 HB Hoofddorp, The Netherlands

Telephone +31 23 808 0101

Website www.c-bed.dk

Area operated Hotel ship for construction workers, currently off the coast of Lincolnshire, England

WIND SOLUTION	8893gt	1969	k	D2	300p		25c	123.5m	19.6m	5.3m	GB

WIND SOLUTION was built by Aalborgs Vaerft (yard number 180) at Aalborg Denmark as the Sessan Line car ferry PRINSESSAN CHRISTINA. Stena Line subsequently acquired Sessan Line, but the ship was not renamed and continued on her Sweden to Denmark service. She was sold to JCE Safe in 1981 and was renamed SAFE CHRISTINA. Initially she was put out on charter, but when the company set up a rival Frederikshavn to Gothenburg service, Stena bought the ship back. She was renamed STENA NORDICA in 1983 and moved to Stena subsidiary Lion Ferry in 1985 as the EUROPAFARJAN I. During the following year she became the LION PRINCE. In 1999 she was sold to an Italian operator and

C-Bed's **Wind Solution** in Esbjerg *(William Mayes)*

The **Delta Queen** in better days *(Andrew Kilk)*

renamed COMMODORE. She later moved to ENERMAR and operated from Genoa as the PALAU. She passed to her current owner in 2008 and after refit was renamed WIND SOLUTION. IMO 6918560

DELTA KING HOTEL

The Company Delta King Hotel operates the DELTA KING as a hotel in Sacramento.

Address 1000 Front Street, Old Sacramento, CA 95814, United States of America

Telephone +1 916 444 5464 **Fax** +1 916 444 5314

Website www.deltaking.com

Area operated Static hotel in Sacramento, USA

DELTA KING	‡3360gt	1927					86.9m	17.7m	m	US

DELTA KING was partially constructed in Scotland and the hull re-assembled and superstructure added at Stockton, California for the overnight service between San Francisco and Sacramento and entered service in 1927. She served as a troop carrier in San Francisco Bay during the Second World War, but was then mothballed by the US Navy. When the DELTA QUEEN was acquired for Mississippi service, the DELTA KING's engines were removed to provide spares for the former ship. Following a long period of inactivity, the derelict ship was acquired in 1984 and after a 5-year renovation opened in 1989 as the Delta King Hotel.

DELTA QUEEN HOTEL

The Company The DELTA QUEEN, withdrawn from service by Majestic America Line has been temporarily located in Chattanooga as a hotel. It is understood that if SOLAS exemption can be acquired she may return to cruise service.

Address 100 River Street, Chattanooga, TN 37405, United States of America

Telephone +1 423 468 4500

Website www.deltaqueenhotel.com

Area operated Static hotel in Chattanooga, USA

DELTA QUEEN	‡3360gt	1927	10.0k	SR1	174p	174p	80c	86.9m	17.7m	m	US

DELTA QUEEN was partially constructed in Scotland and the hull re-assembled and superstructure added at Stockton, California for the overnight service between San Francisco and Sacramento and entered service in 1927. She served as a troop carrier in San Francisco Bay during the Second World War, but was then mothballed by the US Navy. Greene Line Steamers bought the DELTA QUEEN for $47,000 and boarded her up for her long journey to the Mississippi, via the Panama Canal. Following refurbishment she entered service in 1948 and has been an attraction on the Mississippi River ever since. However, in 2008 her owner, Majestic America Line filed for bankruptcy and the DELTA QUEEN, already under threat from an inability to have her SOLAS exemption extended, became a temporary hotel. She opened for business on 5 June 2009. IMO 8643327

DIAMOND PRINCESS HOTEL

The Company Diamond Princess Hotel operates the HAKON JARL as a static hotel and nightclub in Antwerp.

Address St Laureiskaai 2, Antwerp 2000, Belgium

Telephone +32 3 227 0815 **Fax** +32 3 227 1677

Website www.diamondprincess.be

Area operated Static hotel in Antwerp, Belgium

HAKON JARL	2173gt	1952					80.8m	12.2m	4.5m

HAKON JARL was built by Aalborg Vaerft (yard number 93) at Aalborg in Denmark as the Hurtigruten ship HAKON JARL. In 1983 she was briefly renamed HAKON GAMLE, but then reverted to her original name. She was renamed CHRISTIAN V in 1992, and DIAMOND PRINCESS in 1997, before reverting again to her original name in 2004. She operated as a restaurant ship in Oslo for some time, but in 1997 opened as the Diamond Princess Hotel in Antwerp. IMO 5140300

HURTIGRUTE MUSEUM

Address Markedsgata 1, 8450 Stokmarknes, Norway

Telephone +47 7611 8190 **Fax**: +47 7611 8191

Website www.hurtigrutemuseet.no

Area operated Static museum ship at Stokmarknes, Norway

FINNMARKEN	2188gt	1956	16.0k	D1	131b	d	c	81.3m	12.6m	4.5m	NO

FINNMARKEN was built by Blohm & Voss (yard number 788) in Hamburg, Germany for Vesteraalens Dampskibsselskab. IMO 5115240

KEEWATIN MARITIME MUSEUM

The Company The Keewatin Maritime Museum was established in 1967.

Address 225 Union Street and Blue Star Highway, Douglas, Michigan 49406, United States of America

Telephone +1 269 857 2464

Website www.keewatinmaritimemuseum.com

Area operated Static museum ship at Douglas, Michigan, USA

KEEWATIN	3856gt	1907	14.0k		288p	p	86c	107.0m	13.3m	4.9m	

KEEWATIN was built in Scotland for the Canadian Pacific Railway for service on the Great Lakes. She sailed from Greenock to Montreal in September 1907 and was separated into two sections for her transit of the Welland Canal. She initially operated between Owen Sound, Port Arthur and Port William on Lake Superior. She was retired from service in 1967.

LAGOS YACHT HOTEL

The Company The Lagos Yacht Hotel is owned by the Lagos State Government, Lagos, Nigeria. Unfortunately little information was available as this edition went to press, and it does not appear to be open.

Area operated Marina, Lagos, Nigeria static hotel

LAGOS YACHT HOTEL	5756gt	1997	0.0k	-	200p			108.0m	18.4m	2.9m	FI

LAGOS YACHT HOTEL was built by Kvaerner Warnow (yard number 010) at Warnemunde, Germany for Sunborn International as the un-powered SUNBORN and was situated in London's Docklands. She was sold to her current owner in 2008 and went to Brazil for refit before taking her place on the Lagos waterfront. She is now the LAGOS YACHT HOTEL. IMO 8639950

LOGINN HOTEL

The Company Loginn Hotel is a waterfront hotel in Stockholm, Sweden.

Address Kajplats 16, Sodermalarstrand, Stockholm, Sweden

Telephone +46 8 442 4420 **Fax** +46 8 442 4421

Website www.loginn.se

Area operated Static hotel in Stockholm, Sweden

KRONPRINSESSE MARTHA	906gt	1929						58.6m	9.5m	4.2m	SE

KRONPRINSESSE MARTHA was built for Stavanger Steamships for a Norwegian domestic service between Oslo and Bergen by Danziger Werft, Danzig as the KRONPRINSESSE MARTHA. In 1934 she saved 553 people from the sinking German luxury liner DRESDEN, off the Norwegian coast. Following the German occupation of Norway she was renamed RYFYLKE, reverting to her original name in 1945. Four years later her steam engine was replaced by a second-hand diesel engine, and she was rebuilt, increasing her length by 5 metres. Following a sinking in 1956, she was completely rebuilt with a rather more modern appearance. She ceased operating along the Norwegian coast in 1974 and for a short time became a static hotel ship at Stavanger, Norway. At the end of that year she was sold for use as a hotel ship in Sweden and renamed KOSTER. Following a major refurbishment in 1979 she became the SPORT VENTURE for West Indies activity cruises. Her owners were declared bankrupt in the following year and she eventually returned to Europe and served for some years as a static casino ship in The Netherlands. In 1987 she was purchased by Magellan Cruises and went to Falmouth, England to be refitted for service in the Caribbean, for which she was to have been renamed CROWN PRINCESS MARTHA. That venture never materialised and in 1990 she reverted to her original name. In 1998 she became the EMERALD SEA but reverted to KRONPRINSESSE MARTHA in 2001 when she moved back to Sweden to become a hotel ship again. IMO 5197028

LYDIA

Address Avenue de la Grande Plage, Le Barcares, Languedoc-Roussillon 66420 France

Area operated Static spa and night club at Le Barcares on the French Mediterranean coast

| LYDIA | 2696gt | 1931 | | | | | | | 91.1m | 13.5m | 4.8m | |

LYDIA was built by Burmeister & Wain in Copenhagen, Denmark for the Adelaide Steamship Company as the MOONTA for Australian coastal work from Adelaide. She carried 140 passengers. In 1955 she was acquired by Hellenic Mediterranean Lines for service between Marseilles, Greece and the Eastern Mediterranean. For her new role she took the name LYDIA. She was sold to French owners in 1967 and following her engine removal she was permanently moored in a basin at Le Barcares for use as a hotel, nightclub and casino, as part of a larger leisure complex.

MANILA FLOATING HOTEL & RESTAURANT

The Company Manila Floating Hotel and Restaurant is owned by the Manila Hotel, itself part of the business interests of Filipino billionaire Emilio Yap.

Address 1000 Corner of San Marcelino Street & United Nations Avenue, Manila, Philippines

Area operated The PHILIPPINES is berthed by the Manila Hotel, Manila, Philippines

| PHILIPPINES | 27090gt | 1952 | 21.0k | D2 | 1000p | 1186p | 440c | 207.4m | 26.6m | 8.5m | PH |

PHILIPPINES was built by Cantieri Riunite dell'Adriatico (yard number 1757) at Trieste in Italy as the AUGUSTUS for the Italian Line. She was the second major passenger ship to be delivered to the company as part of its post-war rebuilding programme and was immediately placed on the service to South America. Following the loss of the ANDREA DORIA, the AUGUSTUS was transferred to Italia's North Atlantic service in 1957. She returned to the South Atlantic in 1961 following the delivery of the new LEONARDO DA VINCI. She had a long career as a transatlantic liner until she was sold to Emilio Yap, owner of Philippine President Lines, in 1976. The ship then went into a semi-retirement at anchor in various Far Eastern ports. During this time she has had frequent name changes including GREAT SEA, OCEAN KING, PRESIDENT, ASIAN PRINCESS and more recently, PHILIPPINES. Despite almost three decades of lay-up, the ship has always been well maintained and fully crewed. Her only voyages have been occasional private cruises for the Yap family and their friends, and trips to Subic Bay for dry-docking. In recent years the ship has been tied up at a pier next door to the Manila Hotel, where her public rooms are available for private parties. IMO 5030684

MS GEORG BUCHNER

The Company The GEORG BUCHNER is a floating hotel and youth hostel, moored in Rostock.

Address Am Stadhafen 72, 18057 Rostock, Germany

Telephone +49 381 6700 320 **Fax** +49 381 6700 321

Website www.ms-georg-buchner.m-vp.de

Area operated Rostock, Germany as a static hotel/hostel

| GEORG BUCHNER | 11060gt | 1951 | | | | | | | 153.7m | 19.6m | 8.4m | DE |

GEORG BUCHNER was built by Cockerill (yard number 743) at Hoboken, Belgium as the CHARLESVILLE for Cie Maritime Belge for service from Antwerp to the Belgian Congo and Angola. She was the last ship in a series of five passenger/cargo liners, each with accommodation for around 200 first class passengers. In 1967 she was sold to the East German Merchant Marine for use as a cadet training ship and renamed GEORG BUCHNER, but by 1991 she had become a hotel ship in Rostock.

She is named after Georg Buchner (1813-1837), the German author, playwright and academic. IMO 5068863

NYK HIKAWA MARU

The Company The Hikawa Maru is owned by NYK Line and the City of Yokohama. She has recently been given a major refurbishment.

Address Yamashita-cho, Naka-ku, Yokohama 231-0023, Japan

Area operated Museum Ship at Yokohama, Japan

HIKAWA MARU	11622gt	1930	17.0k	D2				163.3m	20.1m		m	JP

HIKAWA MARU was built by the Yokohama Dock Company (yard number 177) for NYK Line of Japan for service between Japan and the west coast of the USA. In 1941 she became a Japanese Navy hospital ship, and was the only large Japanese liner not sunk during the Second World War. She was seized by the USA in 1945 and put into service transporting US personnel between the USA and Japan. She returned to Japan in 1947 and operated more mundane sailings than those for which she had been built. However, she resumed her Pacific passenger sailings in 1954, following a full refit. She was withdrawn in 1960 and refitted as a youth hostel. She has subsequently served various static roles, including latterly that of a museum ship. The hostel closed in 1973, but she continued to operate as a museum. By 2006 the ship was owned by Hikawa Maru Marine Tower Inc, but that company folded at the end of that year and the ship passed to NYK and the City of Yokohama. NYK restored the ship and she re-opened in April 2008.

OCEAN PEARL HOTEL

The Company Ocean Pearl Hotel is operated by Texas Queen Tours, a business owned by two Trinidadian sea captains.

Address PO Box 3142 Carenage, Pier II Chaguaramas, Trinidad, West Indies

Website www.oceanpearltt.com

Area operated Hotel ship in Trinidad

WINDWARD II	5739gt	1964	k	D2				99.5m	17.7m	4.4m	VC

WINDWARD II was built by Kaldnes Mekaniske Verksted (yard number 160) at Tonsberg, Norway as the VIKING II for Thoresen Car Ferries for service from Southampton. In 1977 she became Sealink's EARL WILLIAM and when sold to Greek owners she was renamed PEARL WILLIAM. She later became the MER-JULIA and the CESME STERN before taking her current name in 2001. IMO 6417047

QE2 ENTERPRISES

The Company QE2 Enterprises is a UAE registered Government owned company, part of the Nakheel Hotels Group, formed in 2008 to operate the Nakheel-owned QUEEN ELIZABETH 2. It is intended that eventually the ship will become a hotel, conference centre and museum at Nakheel's Palm Jumierah development project, but with the global economic slowdown conversion plans appear to be on hold at present. At the time of writing the QUEEN ELIZABETH 2 was in dry dock and there is a strong possibility that she may go to Cape Town for up to 18 months.

Chief Executive Officer Manfred Ursprunger

Address PO Box 17777, Dubai, United Arab Emirates

Telephone +971 4 390 3333 **Fax** +971 4 390 3314

Website www.nakheel.com

Area operated Dubai as a static hotel and tourist attraction

QUEEN ELIZABETH 2	70327gt	1969	28.5k	DE2	1778p	1778p	921c	293.5m	32.0m	9.9m	GB

QUEEN ELIZABETH 2 was launched in 1967 by HM Queen Elizabeth II. The ship's builders, Upper Clyde Shipbuilders (yard number 736), delivered her in December 1968, but a number of problems caused the curtailment of her inaugural cruise and the ship was returned to the shipyard. She eventually commenced her maiden voyage in May 1969, sporting a revolutionary single thin black funnel with white casing. In 1982 she served as a British troopship during the Falklands War and

The **Queen Elizabeth 2** in Quebec *(William Mayes)*

Ocean Pearl Hotel's **Windward II** *(Mark Amielanczyk)*

The **Savannah** in Baltimore *(Alan Zamchick)*

following her refit she emerged with a light grey hull and traditional Cunard funnel colours. This hull colour lasted for only a short time and she soon reverted to a traditional black hull. In October 1986 she was sent to the Lloyd Werft shipyard at Bremerhaven, Germany for a six-month refit that included the replacement of her sometimes-troublesome steam turbines with a new diesel-electric propulsion system. When she was re-delivered in April 1987 she had a much more substantial funnel. During her 39 years of service with Cunard she has provided the traveller with a regular transatlantic service, has undertaken numerous cruises in Europe and from the United States of America, and has completed many round-the-world cruises. From 2004 she has been UK based, but still did annual world cruises and occasional transatlantic crossings. In September 2005, she became the longest serving Cunarder ever. Her sale for $100 million was announced in the summer of 2007 and she sailed on her final Cunard voyage on 11 November 2008. IMO 6725418

RMS QUEEN MARY HOTEL & CONVENTION CENTRE

The Company RMS Foundation is a non-profit foundation, managing the QUEEN MARY.

Address 1126 Queens Highway, Long Beach, California 90802, United States of America

Telephone +1 562 435 3511 **Fax** +1 562 437 4531

Website www.queenmary.com

Area operated Static hotel and exhibition centre at Long Beach, California, USA

QUEEN MARY	‡81237gt	1936	28.5k	ST4				310.7m	36.0m	12.0m	US

QUEEN MARY was first conceived in the late 1920's as Cunard planned its next generation of express Atlantic liners. The order was placed with John Brown & Company, Clydebank, Scotland for what was known as yard number 534 on May 28, 1930. Construction began in December of that year, but within twelve months work had stopped due to The Depression. Eventually, the British Government was prepared to make a loan to allow the completion of the ship, on condition that Cunard and White Star Line were merged. The Government held a 'Golden Share' in order to prevent the company being acquired by foreign interests. Cunard White Star Limited was formed on January 1, 1934 and work on the partially completed ship resumed in April. The QUEEN MARY was launched by Her Majesty Queen Mary on September 26, 1934 and was handed over to Cunard White Star on May 12, 1936. On her sixth round trip she won the coveted Blue Riband from the NORMANDIE, but that ship took it back in 1937. In 1938 the QUEEN MARY regained the title and then held it for fourteen years until she lost it to the UNITED STATES in 1952. She saw impressive war service as a troop transport, carrying up to 10,000 troops at a time. She returned to peacetime transatlantic service in 1946 and continued until September 1967. She was sold to the City of Long Beach for use as a hotel ship and tourist attraction. The City spent a fortune renovating the ship, but her location, some distance from the main waterfront left her somewhat isolated. In 1988 the giant Walt Disney Corporation acquired the company that then held the lease on the ship. Disney disowned the ship in 1991 and her management moved into other hands. The current leaseholder, Queen's Seaport Development, filed for Chapter 11 protection in early 2005 due to falling income. IMO 5287938

ROYAL YACHT BRITANNIA TRUST

The Company The Royal Yacht Britannia Trust was formed in 1998 to operate and preserve the last British Royal Yacht, the BRITANNIA, which was withdrawn from service soon after the Labour Government came to power in the United Kingdom in 1997.

Address Ocean Terminal, Ocean Drive, Leith, Edinburgh, EH6 6JJ, United Kingdom

Telephone +44 1315 555566 **Fax** +44 1315 558835

Website www.royalyachtbritannia.co.uk

Area operated Static exhibit at Leith

BRITANNIA	5769gt	1954	25.0k	STE2	p	p	c	125.6m	16.6m	5.2m	GB

BRITANNIA was built by John Brown (Clydebank) Ltd (yard number 691) on Clydebank, Scotland as what was probably the last British Royal Yacht. She was decommissioned at the end of 1997 and arrived in Leith in May 1998. IMO 8635306

SAVANNAH (UNITED STATES MARITIME ADMINISTRATION)

Website www.nssavannah.net (N S Savannah Association)

Ship location Pier 13 Canton Marine Terminal, 4601 Newgate Avenue, Baltimore, MD21224, United States of America

SAVANNAH	15585gt	1962	k		p	p	c	m	m	m	US

SAVANNAH was built for the United States Department of Commerce by the New York Shipbuilding Corporation (yard number 529) at Camden, New Jersey, USA as the world's first nuclear powered merchant ship. Her keel was laid in 1957 and she was launched on 21 July 1959. She cost $47 million to build, including $28 million for the nuclear reactor and fuel core. Following a series of demonstration and experimental voyages she entered commercial service in 1964 mainly between US ports and the Mediterranean. From 1965 she ceased to carry passengers. In 1972 she was laid up at Savannah. From 1981 to 1994 she was a museum ship at Charleston, South Carolina but has subsequently been laid up in the James River. The ship is currently berthed at Baltimore, Maryland and has undergone a considerable amount of maintenance. It is hoped that eventually she will become a permanent museum. IMO 5314793

SEA WORLD LTD

The Company Sea World Ltd is a Hong Kong-Chinese joint venture operating this ship as a static hotel in Shekou, China.

Area operated Static hotel ship at Shekou, near Shenzhen, Peoples Republic of China

MINGHUA	14225gt	1962	500p	168.8m	21.8m	6.6m	CN

MINGHUA was built by Chantiers de l'Atlantique (yard number M21) at St Nazaire, France as the four-class passenger liner ANCERVILLE for Paquet Lines and operated between Marseilles and ports in French West Africa. In 1970 she was transferred to Nouvelle Compagnie de Paquebots of Marseilles. She was sold to the China Ocean Shipping Company of Guangzhou in 1973 and used on a trade between China and East Africa, as the MINGHUA, carrying mainly railway construction workers and technicians. She was laid up in 1977, but returned to service in 1979 on charters to several Australian interests, who used her for South Pacific cruises out of Sydney. This lasted until February 1983, when she returned to China for lay-up. In 1984 she was sold to a newly formed Hong Kong-Chinese joint venture company called Sea World Ltd, which converted her into a floating hotel in Shekou, near Shenzhen. Nearby land reclamation projects resulted in the sea surrounding the ship being filled in, leaving the ship marooned in the middle of a park, several hundred metres from the sea. The ship was recently given an extensive renovation and continues to serve as a restaurant, entertainment and banqueting facility, marketed as SEA WORLD. IMO 5015957

SS GREAT BRITAIN

The Company The SS Great Britain Trust was established in 1970 to rescue and preserve the ship. The restoration programme was finally completed in 2005.

Address Great Western Dockyard, Gas Ferry Road, Bristol BS1 6TY, England

Telephone +44 1179 260680

Website www.ssgreatbritain.org

Area operated Static museum ship in Bristol, England

GREAT BRITAIN	3270gt	1843	k			m	m	m

GREAT BRITAIN was built in the Great Western Dockyard, Bristol (where she now resides) in 1843. Designed by the great Isambard Kingdom Brunel for the Great Western Steamship Company, she made her maiden transatlantic crossing in July 1845 in a record time of 14 days. Initially intended to be a paddle steamer, she was completed with a single 16 foot diameter iron screw. When launched in 1843 she was by far the largest ship in the world and could carry 252 passengers with a crew of 130. Although technologically successful, the venture was something of a financial failure, and her Atlantic days finished in 1846 after a serious grounding off the coast of Northern Ireland. Between 1852 and 1876 she served the route to Australia via the Cape as an emigrant carrier. Refitted to carry 750 passengers, she had a new engine and sails. A brief interlude in 1855/6 saw her in use as a troopship in the Crimean War. Between 1882 and 1886 she served purely as a sailing ship and it was during a sailing in 1886 carrying Welsh coal to San Francisco that she was forced to take shelter in Port Stanley in the Falkland Islands. Uneconomical to repair, she became a coal and wool hulk. By 1937 she was taking in water and was beached. In 1970 she was salvaged and brought back to Bristol for preservation.

SS MILWAUKEE CLIPPER

The Company SS Milwaukee Clipper Preservation Inc was established in 1997 to rescue and preserve the ship.

President Ray Hilt

Address PO Box 1370, Muskegon, Michigan 49443, United States of America

Telephone +1 231 722 2538

Website www.milwaukeeclipper.com

Area operated Static museum ship at 2098 Lakeshore Drive, Muskegon

MILWAUKEE CLIPPER	4272gt	1905	k	SR1	350p	350p	c	110.0m	13.7m	m	US

MILWAUKEE CLIPPER was built in Cleveland, Ohio by the American Shipbuilding Company (yard number 423) for the Anchor Line (Erie & Western Transportation Company), as the JUNIATA for Great Lakes service. She carried 350 passengers between Buffalo, New York and Duluth, Minnesota. She was withdrawn in 1937 following the introduction of new safety regulations, on account of her wooden superstructure. Sand Products Corporation of Muskegon acquired the ship in 1940 and she was rebuilt by the Manitowoc Shipbuilding Company with a new streamlined steel superstructure. She was renamed MILWAUKEE CLIPPER and in 1941 began service between Milwaukee and Muskegon, which continued until 1970. She was sold in 1977, renamed SS CLIPPER and moved to Chicago, where she operated as a static museum and convention ship. In 1990 she moved to Hammond, Indiana and was renamed MILWAUKEE CLIPPER. She returned to Muskegon under her present owner in 1997. IMO 5235375

SS ROTTERDAM

The Company The SS ROTTERDAM is owned by the Dutch company Rederij De Rotterdam BV, a consortium originally consisting of the housing company Woonbron and the investment company Eurobalance. In 2006 Eurobalance pulled out of the venture, and in 2008, on the instruction of the Dutch minister for housing, Woonbron was required to give up its involvement after a massive overspend on the conversion project. That 80% shareholding had not been sold at the time of writing.

Address 3e Katendrechtse Hoofd 25, 3072 AM, Rotterdam, The Netherlands

Telephone +31 10 741 0900

Website www.derotterdam.com

Area operated Static hotel and conference centre in Rotterdam

ROTTERDAM	39674gt	1959	21.5k	ST2		228.2m	28.7m	9.0m	NL

ROTTERDAM was built by the Rotterdam Dry Dock Company (yard number 300) in Rotterdam, The Netherlands, and launched by Queen Juliana, as the flagship for Holland America Line's transatlantic service, and running mate to the NIEUW AMSTERDAM. In later years she was used exclusively as a cruise ship. Carnival acquired Holland America Line in 1988, and the ROTTERDAM continued to serve her new owners, developing a very loyal following. In 1997, she no longer met SOLAS requirements and was withdrawn from service, quickly snapped-up by Premier Cruise Lines, upgraded and renamed REMBRANDT. She was later going to be renamed BIG RED BOAT IV, but the outcry led to her keeping her name. Premier Cruise Lines failed in 2000 and the REMBRANDT was laid up. She was eventually acquired by Dutch interests with a view to returning her to Rotterdam as a static exhibit and hotel ship. The REMBRANDT was towed to Gibraltar in 2004 for some preliminary work, including asbestos removal, to be carried out. She was renamed ROTTERDAM in 2004. Her then owner, SS Rotterdam B V was declared bankrupt, and as the ship had been the security for loans made by the Port Authority of Rotterdam, ownership passed to the latter. Following attention at a shipyard in Cadiz, she was towed to Gdansk, Poland in the autumn of 2005 for the final restoration work to be completed. A dispute over the asbestos remaining on board led to the ship being removed from Polish waters in

The SS **Rotterdam** comes home *(William Mayes)*

summer 2006 to Wilhelmshaven, where the work was completed. The ROTTERDAM returned to the city of Rotterdam on 4 August 2008 and opened in July 2009, although the hotel and restaurants did not open until September. IMO 5301019

STF A F CHAPMAN

The Company STF A F Chapman is a hostel ship in Stockholm.

Address Flaggmansvagen 8, 11149 Stockholm, Sweden

Telephone +46 8 463 2266 **Fax** +46 8 611 7155

Website www.stfchapman.com

Area operated Hostel ship in Stockholm

A F CHAPMAN	‡1425gt	1888		136p		71.1m	11.4m	3.7m	SE

A F CHAPMAN was built by the Whitehaven Shipbuilding Company (yard number 65) in Whitehaven, England as the DUNBOYNE for Charles E Martin & Co of Dublin, Ireland. In 1915 she was renamed G D KENNEDY by Norwegian owners and took her current name in 1923 when she was acquired by Swedish owners. During the Second World War she served as a barracks in Stockholm and was acquired by the City of Stockholm in 1947. She served as a youth hostel in Stockholm from about 1949. The ship was closed for major renovation from autumn 2005 but has now re-opened. IMO 8639924

SUNBORN INTERNATIONAL

The Company Sunborn Hotels is a Finnish company operating hotels in Finland, Germany and England. The operation included two yacht hotels, until the vessel based in London's Docklands was sold to Nigerian owners in 2008. The company won a contract to operate a yacht hotel in Port Forum, Barcelona. This venture has not yet been established.

Address Matkailijante 2, FI 21100 Naantali, Finland

Telephone +358 244 550 **Fax** +358 244 5561

Website www.sunbornhotels.com

Area operated Naantali, Finland static hotel

SUNBORN PRINCESS	7264gt	2002	0.0k	-	280p		119.0m	18.4m	2.9m	FI

SUNBORN PRINCESS was built by Kvaerner Warnow (yard number 404) at Warnemunde, Germany for Sunborn International and is currently in use as a hotel at Naantali, Finland. IMO 8971833

UNITED STATES COAST GUARD

Area operated Static fire training ship at Mobile, Alabama

STATE OF MAINE	13319gt	1952	k	ST1	p	p	c	162.7m	22.2m	8.4 m	US

STATE OF MAINE was built by New York Shipbuilding (yard number 487) at Camden, New Jersey. Launched as the American President Lines' PRESIDENT HAYES, she was completed as the troopship UPSHUR. She was renamed as the STATE OF MAINE in 1973 and currently serves as a fire training ship. IMO 7517064

UNKNOWN OPERATOR – CHINA

Area operated Static in Tianjin, China

ORIENT PRINCESS	10298gt	1967	21.5k	D2	301p	488p	240c	150.3m	21.0m	6.6m

ORIENT PRINCESS was built by Chantiers de l'Atlantique (yard number N23) at St Nazaire, France as the passenger cargo ship YAO HUA for the China Ocean Shipping Co of Guangzhou. Initially used on the trade between China and East Africa, she was converted into a cruise ship in the late 1970s and often chartered to US-based cruise operators. In 1986 she was sold to Hong Kong-based buyers, Main Fortune Ltd, and used for overnight casino cruises out of Hong Kong as the ORIENT PRINCESS. These continued until 2002, when the vessel was auctioned in Guangzhou for unpaid crew wages. The ship was then sold to Chinese interests who plan to use her as a static attraction in Tianjin. Recent reports suggest that the ship is undergoing conversion for future static use. IMO 6708109

The **Queen Mary** at Long Beach *(Rick Frendt)*

UNKNOWN OPERATOR – CHINA

Area operated Static in Zhanjiang, China

BRAZIL MARU	10216gt	1954	k	D1	156.0m	19.6m	8.7m

BRAZIL MARU was built by Mitsubishi Heavy Industries at Kobe, Japan for Osaka Shosen Kaisha for service between Japan and South America. In 1973 she became a static attraction at Toba, Japan. She was believed to have been broken up after being towed to China in 1996, but has recently been discovered in China, where she is still serving in a static role. IMO 5050866

WONINGSTICHTING ROCHDALE

The Company Woningstichting Rochdale operates a floating student hostel in Amsterdam, The Netherlands.

Address Bos en Lommerplein 303, 1055 RW Amsterdam, The Netherlands

Website www.rochdale.nl

Area operated Hostel in Amsterdam

ROCHDALE ONE	7662gt	1977	18.9k	D2	121.5m	17.5m	4.5m	CY

ROCHDALE ONE was built by Dubigeon-Normandie (yard number 144) at Nantes, France as the AYVAZOVSKIY for the Soviet Danube Shipping Company of Ismail, for service in the Black Sea between Ismail, Yalta and Istanbul, in connection with the Soviet owned Danube cruise vessels. In 1992 her owners were re-styled as the Ukraina Danube Shipping Company. In 1996 she was renamed the KARINA for charter to the German tour operator Phoenix Reisen. She became the PRIMEXPRESS ISLAND; a Cyprus based casino ship in 2000 and was acquired by Kyprosun Marine Services of Limassol in January 2004. She was renamed ROCHDALE ONE for her current service as an accommodation ship housing 200 students for the University of Amsterdam. The charter expires in 2009. IMO 7411959

The **Rochdale On**e in Amsterdam *(William Mayes)*

The **Ambassador II** at Port Canaveral *(Andrew Kilk)*

The **Blue Monarch** in Istanbul *(Douglas Cromby)*

The **Oceanic** in San Francisco *(Andrew Kilk)*

the **leading** *guide to the cruise industry*
section 5

Passenger Ships unlikely to see further service

AMBASSADOR II (buit 1970 gross tonnage 11,940) had her first incarnation as the PRINZ OBERON. Built for Sweden's Lion Ferry by Nobiskrug Werft (yard number 663) at Rendsburg, Germany, she entered service on charter to Prinzenlinien on its Bremerhaven, Germany to Harwich, England service. She was sold to her operator in 1978 and continued to serve her North Sea route. Following the closure of the service she undertook a number of charters before becoming Transnordic Line's NORDIC SUN. In 1986 she was renamed CRUISE MUHIBAH for cruising service from Malaysia. She came back to Europe three years later and joined B & I Line in Dublin as the MUNSTER for Irish Sea ferry service. She was sold to New Olympic Ferries of Greece and renamed AMBASSADOR in 1993, but was re-sold within a year to EPA Invest of Limassol, renamed AMBASSADOR II, and put onto the charter market. Over the next three years she undertook a number of charters in the Mediterranean and Baltic Seas. In 1997 she passed to International Shipping Partners of Monrovia and spent almost two years being converted for use as a casino ship by A&P Appledore in England. She began what is likely to be the last phase of her career as a casino ship for Sterling Casino Lines in June 1999. In 2008 Sterling Casino Lines ceased trading and the ship was laid up at Orange, Texas. IMO 7011515

ARTSHIP (built 1940 gross tonnage 7,987) was built as the type C3P cargo and passenger liner DELORLEANS for Delta Line's New Orleans to Argentina service. Soon afterwards she was renamed as the USS CRESCENT CITY and put into service as a troop transport. She was laid up from 1948 to 1971, when she was refitted to become the California Maritime Academy's training ship GOLDEN BEAR. On her retirement in 1995 she was again laid up until 1999 when acquired by the Artship Foundation and renamed ARTSHIP with the aim of being converted into a floating cultural centre. She is currently laid up at Mare Island, California. IMO 8424666

BAYKAL (built 1962 gross tonnage 5,230) built for the Far East Shipping Company and last reported in Vladivostok. However she is reported by Lloyds Register to have been broken up in 1998 in Vietnam, before the above sighting. IMO 5401352

BETA (built 1962 gross tonnage 5,230) built as the AFGHANISTAN and last reported laid up in Novorossiysk.

BLUE MONARCH (built 1966 gross tonnage 11,429) was one of the last French built passenger ships destined for a French operator. She was built by Chantiers de l'Atlantique (yard number D23) at St Nazaire as the RENAISSANCE for Paquet's subsidiary Compagnie Francaise de Navigation for service between Marseilles and the ports of the Eastern Mediterranean. Liner services in the Mediterranean were in decline and the ship was gradually transferred to cruising. In 1977 she was sold to Epirotiki Lines of Greece who renamed her as the HOMERIC RENAISSANCE. She was chartered to Costa Cruises fairly quickly and renamed WORLD RENAISSANCE. In the early 1980's she was sub-chartered to Curnow Shipping for service between the UK and St Helena and Cape Town. This was less than successful and the ship reverted to her Costa duties. She later operated for Epirotiki, but in 1995 transferred to Club Awani Travel of Djakarta, Indonesia as the AWANI DREAM. When she returned to Epirotiki in 1998, that company had merged most of its business into Royal Olympic Cruises, so that is where the WORLD RENAISSANCE was employed. Royal Olympic Cruises subsequently became Royal Olympia Cruises but collapsed in 2004 and the ship was laid up. Elysian Cruises, part of US based Ravenscroft Shipping, acquired her at auction in April 2005 and she was quickly renamed GRAND VICTORIA. In 2006 she operated for Russian tour company Metropolis Tur. She operated in 2007 as the BLUE MONARCH for Monarch Classic Cruises, but does not appear to have seen service in 2008 or 2009. IMO 6604834

CARIB VACATIONER (built 1971 gross tonnage ‡2,430) was launched by De Merwede (yard number 601) at Hardinxveld in The Netherlands as the KIELER FORDE. She was completed as the cargo vessel CRAIGAVON, but reverted to her launch name in 1972. She became the NASSAU later in 1972, being slightly renamed as NASSAU I in 1978. Two years later she became NASSAU again. She was converted in 1982, and operated until 1986 as the very budget cruise ship VACATIONER. She was sold in 1986 and renamed CARIB VACATIONER. It is thought that she was renamed CORAL PRINCESS in 1992, and it appears that she may have been laid up at Curacao since 1998. IMO 7038214

CARIBBEAN MERCY (built 1952 gross tonnage 2,125) was built as the POLARLYS by Aalborg Vaerft (yard number 98) in Aalborg, Denmark for Det Bergen Dampskibsselskab (The Bergen Line), one of the Norwegian Coastal Express operators, and was one of four ships sold to TFDS in 1979 when that company joined the Hurtigruten. She was re-engined in 1982 and passed to Mercy Ships in 1994 when she was renamed CARIBBEAN MERCY. She was sold in December 2006 to the Sherman Family Charitable Foundation, and it was thought that she would be used for medical seminars at sea. However, she remains laid up with little indication of a return to service. IMO 5280930

GAGE (built 1944 gross tonnage 7,612) was built in 1944 by Oregon Shipbuilding Corporation (yard number 118) in Portland, Oregon as a Haskell class attack transport. She is laid up as part of the US Reserve Fleet in the James River, and is named after Gage County, Nebraska.

GENERAL EDWIN D PATRICK (built 1945 gross tonnage 16,039) was built by the Bethlehem Alameda shipyard (yard number 9505) at Alameda, USA as the troopship ADMIRAL C F HUGHES. She was renamed GENERAL EDWIN D PATRICK in 1946. She has been laid up since 1968. IMO 8332849

GENERAL JOHN POPE (built 1943 gross tonnage 17,927) was built by the Federal Shipbuilding & Drydock Company (yard number 268) at Kearny, New Jersey, USA as a troopship, one of a series of nine similar vessels. She was designed to carry up to 5,000 troops. She was laid up in 1969 and is currently in the Suisun Bay reserve fleet. IMO 8332851

HERMES (built 1956 gross tonnage 2,174) was most recently used as a day cruise ship, operating from Piraeus, Greece. Brodogradiliste (yard number 130) built her at Split, in what was then Yugoslavia, as the JUGOSLAVIA for Jadrolinija for coastal work. She was sold in 1971, becoming the MESSAGER and took her present name in 1976 upon passing to Epirotiki Lines. It is unknown if she is currently operating, but it is thought that she has spent some time laid up in Piraeus. Hermes was the Olympian god of boundaries and the travellers that cross them. IMO 5176713

ISLAND BREEZE (built 1967 gross tonnage ‡4,595) was built by Helsingor Skibsvaerft og Maskinbyggeri (yard number 381) at Helsingor, Denmark as the ro-ro freight ferry STAFFORD for DFDS for service between England and Denmark. In 1984 she was renamed DANA GLORIA, and later that year was sold to Tzamar Voyage and renamed VOYAGER. In 1985 she was converted to a passenger and car ferry and later sold to Cross Med Maritime Co to run from Patras, Greece to Brindisi, Italy as the MONACO for Euroferries. Three years later she was renamed SITIA for service between Piraeus and the island of Crete. In 1990 she was converted at the Avlis Shipyard at Chalkis, Greece, into a casino and cruise ship. At this time she had about 50 luxury cabins installed. During the next year she began running low cost cruises from Miami as the TROPIC STAR. In 1993 she was renamed PACIFIC STAR and began to operate day cruises from San Diego, USA to Ensenda, Mexico for Starlite Cruises. Following arrest over non-payment of bills, this service ceased and the ship returned to Greece in 1995 for lay-up under the name AEGEO STAR. She was finally sold at auction in 1997 to Fortune Ship Investments and renamed NEW YORK FORTUNE 1. In 2002 she was renamed as the ATLANTIS and during the following year started operating day cruises between the Greek islands of Crete and Santorini. She was laid up in 2005 and it was thought unlikely that she would see further service. However, although remaining laid-up she was renamed ISLAND BREEZE in 2007. IMO 6708252

LO SHAN (built 1974 gross tonnage 2,151) was built by Niigata Engineering (yard number 1233) at Niigata, Japan as the LO SHAN for Shun Tak Holding. She is currently laid up. IMO 7355052

MABUHAY SUNSHINE (built 1983 gross tonnage 7,262) was built for Oshima Unyu KK by Mitsubishi Heavy Industries (yard number 858) at Shimonoseki in Japan as the cruise ship SUNSHINE FUJI for domestic Japanese cruises. She was sold to Mabuhay Holiday Cruises of the Philippines in 1995 and rebuilt as the MABUHAY SUNSHINE, re-entering service on cruises out of Manila in 1996. The venture did not prove successful and the ship has been laid up for sale in Cebu since 1998. IMO 8300561

MAN GYONG BONG (built 1971 gross tonnage ‡3,317) was built by the Chongjin Shipyard in North Korea as a passenger cargo ship. She operated an irregular service between North Korea and Japan but was reported sold to unknown owners in 2007. IMO 7111406

MARIA KOSMAS (built 1977 gross tonnage ‡3,344) was built by the HMA Naval Dockyard at Melbourne, Australia as the oceanographic research vessel HMAS COOK. Following grounding in 1990 she was withdrawn from service. In 1993 she was sold to Greek interests and renamed MARIA

KOSMAS for conversion to a cruise ship. She was laid up again in 1996 and in 2002 towed to Dubai. Her current use and whereabouts are unknown. IMO 8872784

NIKOLAYEVSK (built 1962 gross tonnage 5,230) last reported laid up in Sochi.

OCEANIC (built 1950 gross tonnage 26,658) was built by the Bethlehem Shipbuilding Corporation (yard number 1618) at Quincy, Massachusetts, USA for American Export Lines as the INDEPENDENCE, along with her sister, the CONSTITUTION for the New York to Italy service. The INDEPENDENCE was withdrawn from her Atlantic service in 1967, in the face of air competition. During the following year she ran cruises to the Caribbean and Mediterranean for an American tour operator. This proved unsuccessful and was not repeated in the following year. The ship was laid up until purchased by Hong Kong ship owner C Y Tung in 1974. She was renamed as the OCEANIC INDEPENDENCE and cruised briefly from Hong Kong before suffering a further period of lay-up from 1976 as the SEA LUCK I. C Y Tung formed American Hawaii Cruises in 1980 and began operating the ship under the US flag as the OCEANIC INDEPENDENCE on cruises from Honolulu. In 1983, following a major refurbishment, she reverted to her original name. Four years later the company was sold by Tung and following the terrorist attacks on the USA in 2001, the company filed for bankruptcy. She was laid up in San Francisco, but purchased by Norwegian Cruise Line in 2003, with a possible intention of her being returned to service as a US flag ship. However, nothing happened and she remained laid up. In 2005 her ownership changed to California Manufacturing Corporation (with an address in the same building as NCL) and she was renamed OCEANIC. On 4 February 2008 she was towed out of San Francisco, supposedly heading for Singapore, but she has remained at sea until now with sightings reported occasionally, the last being off Dubai. It is clear that she is eventually heading for the scrap yard, but the mysterious route to get there may be as a result of the suggestion that she had been illegally exported from the USA, due to the potentially toxic materials that she may have on board. IMO 5160180

PATRIOT STATE (built 1964 gross tonnage ‡11,188) was built by Bethlehem Steel Company (yard number 4602) at Sparrows Point, USA as the SANTA MERCEDES for Grace Line of New York. She operated on the service from New York around South America. In 1983 she passed to the US Maritime Commission and was converted for use as a training ship for the Massachusetts Marine Academy. She is currently laid up in the James River. IMO 5422409

POLYNESIAN PRINCESS (built 1959 gross tonnage 977) was built by Brodogradiliste Titovo (yard number 361) at Kraljevica in Yugoslavia for the state ferry operator Jadrolinija as the OPATIJA. In 1968 she was acquired by the Government of Kiribati and was renamed NINIKORIA. In 1975 she became the TERAAKA, and is thought to have been renamed POLYNESIAN PRINCESS more recently. She is laid up in Ensenda, Mexico. IMO 5263853

PRINCE (built 1962 gross tonnage 5,145) was built by the Finnboda Shipyard (yard number 375) at Stockholm, Sweden as the SVEA JARL for Silja Line's (Rederi AB Svea) Baltic ferry services. In 1976 she was sold to rival consortium Viking Line (Rederi AB Slite) for use as the cruise ship APOLLO III on the lucrative 24-hour cruise service from Stockholm to Mariehamn in the Aland Islands. With the arrival of the new ATHENA in 1989 she was no longer required, and was sold to Thai owners to become the ANDAMAN PRINCESS. In the summer of 2006 she was sold to Advent Systems, of Tortola, British Virgin Islands, and renamed PRINCE for her final voyage. It was thought that she was going straight for breaking, but recent reports suggest that she first went to Vladivostok. She was last sighted at Vung Tao, Vietnam. IMO 5346502

ROYAL STAR (built 1956 gross tonnage 5,067) was built for the Italian liner and ferry operator Adriatica as the SAN GIORGIO by Cantieri Riunite dell'Adriatico (yard number 1813) at Trieste, Italy and was used on Mediterranean Sea passenger/cargo services from Venice and Trieste to Istanbul, Izmir and Piraeus. Sometimes these voyages were extended to call at Alexandria and other Eastern Mediterranean ports. In 1976 this elegant little ship was sold to the Greek Kyriakis Group and converted for pure cruising in and around the Aegean Sea. She was rebuilt and renamed as the CITY OF ANDROS and operated under the Cycladic Cruises banner. In 1984 she passed to Ocean Cruise Lines, becoming the high-quality OCEAN ISLANDER. She then cruised in European waters in summer and in the Caribbean Sea in winter. Ocean Cruise Lines was sold to Paquet, the French cruise operator in 1990, but the OCEAN ISLANDER was sold to Star Line Cruises, renamed ROYAL STAR and put to work in the Indian Ocean under charter to African Safari Club. The ship's owners appear to have run into financial difficulty and the ship was laid up in Mombassa. IMO 5309906

SOUNDS OF ORIENTS (built 1961 gross tonnage 5,230) built as the KHABAROVSK and last reported at Vladivostok more recently that the 1989 date that Lloyd Register suggests that she was broken up. IMO 5186196

STATE (built 1952 gross tonnage ‡13,319) was built by the New York Shipbuilding Corporation (yard number 485) at Camden, New Jersey, USA. She was laid down for American President Lines as the PRESIDENT JACKSON, but was completed as the troopship BARRETT. In 1973 she was renamed EMPIRE STATE V when she became a training ship for the New York Maritime Academy. In 1978 her name was shortened to EMPIRE STATE, and it was further shortened in 1990 when she became the STATE. She is laid up in the James River. IMO 7941904

XANADU 2 (built 1955 gross tonnage 2,496) was built by Blohm & Voss (yard number 786) in Hamburg, Germany as the WAPPEN VON HAMBURG for the day cruise business from Hamburg and Cuxhaven to Helgoland and Hornum. She carried 1600 passengers as built. In 1960 she was sold to Nomikos Lines of Greece, who had her refitted to carry 186 cruise passengers. She was renamed as the DELOS for cruising in the Greek Islands. In 1967 Westours acquired her for use as the Alaskan cruise ship POLAR STAR. In 1970 she passed to subsidiary company West Lines as the PACIFIC STAR. Only two years later she was sold to Xanadu Cruises and renamed as the XANADU. Eventually unable to compete, she was laid up in Vancouver in 1977. She was sold in the mid 1980's to become the exhibition and trade fair ship EXPEX. She moved to lay up off Los Angeles, but little was done to convert her for her new role. In 1991 she was acquired by Friendships, and renamed FAITHFUL for conversion to a mission ship. That never materialised and she was eventually seized and sold to James Mitchell, who intended to use her as a hospital ship, for which she was renamed XANADU 2. In September 2005 she was towed to Alameda, California where she is to be converted to a luxury yacht. IMO 5088227

ZOE (not completed gross tonnage c50,000) was ordered in 1979, but not laid down until 1986 by Stocznia im Lenina (yard number B494/4) in Gdansk, Poland as the STENA BALTICA, the final member of a class of four large overnight ferries for Stena Line of Gothenburg. By 1989 she was still incomplete and the order for the final two ships was cancelled. The hull was purchased by Regent Cruises and launched in 1990 and was then towed to the Avlis Shipyard at Chalkis in Greece for completion as the REGENT SKY. The hull was lengthened by 53 metres in 1992. Regent Cruises later collapsed and the shipyard was left with what there was of the ship. She was thought to have been sold for scrap in 2004, but remained laid up at Chalkis, Salamina, Greece. Subsequently Kyma Ship Management acquired her in 2007, with a view to completing her as an 800-passenger cruise ship. She has been renamed ZOE, but remains laid up. IMO 7907685

The **Island Breeze,** as the **Atlantis** off Santorini *(Rick Frendt)*

the **leading** *guide to the cruise industry*

section 6

Recent Departures

AL-JAZIRAH (built 1956 gross tonnage 1,542) was built by Philip & Son (yard number 1276) at Dartmouth, England as the SEYYLD KHALIFA. She became the JAMHURI in 1963 and took her new name in 1986. Recent evidence has come to light that suggests that this ship became a total loss after a period of lay up Pemba, Mozambique during the 1990s. IMO 5321526

ANASTASIS (built 1953 gross tonnage 11,701) was built as the VICTORIA for Lloyd Triestino by Cantieri Riunite dell'Adriatico (yard number 1765) at the San Marco shipyard in Trieste, Italy. She was built for the service from Italy to the Far East, which she served for fourteen years, before switching to the Karachi service via Cape Town following the closure of the Suez Canal in 1967. Line voyages were on the decline, so in 1974, in a reorganisation among the fleets controlled by the mighty Finmare Group, she was transferred to Adriatica for local Mediterranean services and cruising. She only lasted another three years before being laid up. In 1978 she was acquired by the American organisation Youth with a Mission, for use as floating church. She was renamed as the ANASTASIS and was refurbished in Piraeus from 1979 to 1982, when she passed to Mercy Ministries of Malta. In 1990 she was registered under the ownership of Mercy Ships. She was replaced by the AFRICA MERCY, and arrived at Alang on 14 July 2007. IMO 5379729

EXPLORER (built 1969 gross tonnage 2,398) was built by Uudenkaupungin Telakka Oy at Nystad, Finland as the LINDBLAD EXPLORER for Lars-Eric Lindblad as the world's first expedition cruise ship. In 1985 she became the SOCIETY EXPLORER, under charter to Society Expeditions and in 1992, while under the ownership of Vienna International Shipping, she was renamed EXPLORER for service with Abercrombie & Kent. She passed to Lambeth Navigation in 1996, then Explorer Shipping during the following year. In late 2003 she was sold to Kyris Shipping and her current owner acquired her in September 2004. She has always been employed on expedition type cruises and her managers since 1992 have been V-Ships. On 23 November 2007, at 3am she collided with ice off Antarctica, was abandoned about two hours later and eventually sank with no loss of life. IMO 6924959

FLYING CLOUD (built 1935 gross tonnage 452) was built by Dubigeon at Nantes-Chantenay, France as the cargo ship AVE DE TAHITI, although her original name was to have been TUXTLA. She later became OISEAU DES ILES and was converted for passenger use in 1966. Windjammer Barefoot Cruises acquired her in 1989 and it is thought that she was renamed FLYING CLOUD in 2002, since when she has been laid up at Port of Spain, Trinidad. She is believed to have been scrapped in 2009. IMO 5409665

GOLDEN PRINCESS (built 1967 gross tonnage 12,704) was built as the ferry FINLANDIA by Wartsila (yard number 383) in Helsinki, Finland. She operated as such for both Finlandia Lines and Finnlines. In 1978 she was converted into the cruise ship FINNSTAR for Mediterranean cruising. This was not a success and she was laid up in 1980. I.M. Skaugen of Norway purchased the ship in 1981, and used her for Far Eastern cruises under the name PEARL OF SCANDINAVIA. The ship, and its operating company Pearl Cruises, was sold to Ocean Cruise Lines in 1987. The ship was again rebuilt, this time becoming OCEAN PEARL, but still operating Far Eastern cruises. Ocean Cruise Lines was sold to Paquet Cruises in 1990, who shortened the ship's name to PEARL in 1994. By this time Paquet was owned by the Costa Line, who took the ship over as COSTA PLAYA in 1995, and used her for cruises from Cuba. The venture was short-lived as Costa was purchased by Carnival Corporation, who shut down the Cuban cruises two years later. In 1995 the ship was sold to Hong Kong casino interests who sailed her in the overnight casino trades as ORIENTAL PEARL and JOY WAVE. The Emperor Group purchased the ship in 2000, and have used her as the GOLDEN PRINCESS in the same trade ever since. She was sold to Chinese breakers in July 2009. IMO 6622458

LOGOS II (built 1968 gross tonnage 4,804) was built as the Spanish ferry ANTONIO LAZARO by Union Naval de Levante (yard number 100) at Valencia, Spain for Cia. Trasmediterranea's Mediterranean Sea car ferry services. She was acquired by Operation Mobilization in 1988 and renamed ARGO. Later that

The **Explorer** in Genoa *(Rick Frendt)*

The **Logos II** *(Mark Amielanczyk)*

The **Lucky Star** in Singapore *(Jonathan Boonzaier)*

year she was renamed again as the LOGOS II. Replaced by the LOGOS HOPE in 2008, she arrived at Aliaga, Turkey on 3 October 2008. IMO 6806834

LUCKY STAR (built 1962 gross tonnage 9,821), completed in 1962 for Companhia Nacional De Navegacao Costeira of Brazil by Soc. Espanola de Construccion Naval (yard number 104) at Bilbao, Spain, the PRINCESA ISABEL entered service as a two-class vessel on the Brazilian coast. By 1969, following the financial difficulties of her owner and the subsequent merger of that company with Lloyd Brasiliero she was sold to the Dominion Far East Line of Hong Kong and towed to the River Clyde in Scotland for refitting by Barclay, Curle & Company. As the MARCO POLO she began cruising to the Far East from Australia in June 1970. In 1978 she was sold to a company associated with the Greek Kavounides family and as the AQUAMARINE proceeded to Greece for a further refit, following which she returned to the Far East to offer cruises from Hong Kong to China and Japan. This proved unsuccessful and she was eventually auctioned, with her mortgage holder, the Commercial Bank of Greece acquiring her. After seven years of lay up, during which auctions and charter attempts had failed, she was acquired by Epirotiki Lines and renamed as the ODYSSEUS. On the merger of that company with Sun Line Cruises she passed into the new Royal Olympic Cruises fleet. A subsequent charter to Legend Cruises as the JOY WAVE proved to be unsuccessful, and so she remained in the ROC fleet. Following the collapse of Royal Olympic Cruises she was sold at auction in April 2005 to Mantovana Holdings and chartered to Everis Capital Holdings, renamed LUCKY STAR and placed on gambling cruises from Hong Kong. After a period of lay-up she arrived at Alang on 25 January 2008 under the name LUCKY. IMO 5284780

MADAGASCAR (built 1960 gross tonnage 3,008) was built by Adler Werft (yard number 19) at Bremen, Germany as the German coastal liner BREMERHAVEN, for service between Bremerhaven and Helgoland. She was purchased by Sun Lines in 1966 and rebuilt as the elegant little STELLA MARIS II. In 1998 she was acquired by Luxembourg-based Viking Cruises and renamed as the VIKING BORDEAUX. Her owners ceased operation in 2003 and the ship was arrested at Eemshaven. In July 2004 it was reported that she had been acquired by Royal African Cruise Line and was to be renamed AFRICAN QUEEN. That never materialised, but later that year she was renamed as the BORDEAUX. In spring 2005 this ship was acquired by Indian Ocean Cruises and was renamed MADAGASCAR. Following some charters in the Mediterranean, the ship moved to Durban from where she began cruising in the Indian Ocean. She was later supposedly purchased by Razzmatazz Cruises, but never entered service, instead being arrested and sold at auction. It is believed that the MADAGASCAR arrived at Alang in July 2008. IMO 5051365

MAXIM GORKIY (built 1969 gross tonnage 24,220) was built by Howaldtswerke-Deutsche Werft (yard number 997) in Hamburg, Germany for Deutsche-Atlantik Line of the same city. Completing the pattern, she was named HAMBURG. She was used on the company's service between Cuxhaven and South America. In 1973 she was renamed HANSEATIC, but later that year was laid up after her owners ran into financial difficulties. In 1974 she was acquired by SOVCOMFLOT and renamed MAKSIM GORKIY for service with the Black Sea Shipping Company of Odessa. She was chartered during the same year for use as the BRITANNIC in the film Juggernaut. In 1988 she underwent a major modernisation by Lloyd Werft at Bremerhaven, but while on a cruise in June of the following year almost sank after sailing into drifting ice off Spitzbergen. Passengers and crew took to the boats after the pressure of the ice on the hull caused leaks and the ship began to sink. With the assistance of the Norwegian Coastguard the hull was patched and eventually the ship was towed to an inlet to allow more thorough repairs to be carried out. About two weeks later she arrived under her own power at Bremerhaven for permanent repairs. In 1991 she was renamed slightly as the MAXIM GORKIY. She has been a long-term member of Phoenix Reisen's chartered fleet. Maxim Gorkiy was the pseudonym of the writer Aleksei Peshkov (1868-1936). In 2008 she finished service with Phoenix Reisen and a charter had been agreed between her owner and a newly revived Orient Lines. However, that charter did not materialise, due to the economic downturn, and despite efforts to save the ship as a tourist attraction for Hamburg, she was beached at Alang on 24 February 2009 under the name MAXIM M. IMO 6810627

PHILIPPINE DREAM (built 1966 gross tonnage ‡9,318) was built by Uraga Heavy Industries (yard number 885) at Yokosuka in Japan for the Japan National Railways as the train ferry TOWADA MARU. She was sold to the Japan Sea Passenger Co in 1989 and extensively rebuilt as the cruise ship JAPANESE DREAM for overnight cruises between Kobe and Yokohama. The ship proved unsuccessful and was laid up in January 1992. She was then sold to Philippine owners who used her as a hotel and casino in Cebu under the name PHILIPPINE DREAM. The hotel closed down several years ago and the ship remained laid up on Mactan Island, near Cebu, in a quagmire of legal problems. In September

The **Maxim Gorkiy** at Flam *(William Mayes)*

The **Princesa Marissa** *(William Mayes Collection)*

The **Princess Rowena** in Hong Kong *(Jonathan Boonzaier)*

2007 she was auctioned on the instructions of the Philippines Internal Revenue Bureau and subsequently arrived in Chittagong, Bangladesh in July 2008. IMO 6618938

PRINCESA MARISSA (built 1966 gross tonnage 10,487) was built by Wartsila (yard number 377) at Helsinki, Finland as the car ferry FINNHANSA for Finnlines' Baltic Sea services. In 1977 she passed to another Baltic operator, Birka Line, for the 24-hour cruise business between Stockholm and Mariehamn. For this route she was renamed PRINCESSAN. She was laid up in 1986 and during the following year acquired by Louis Cruise Lines for its cruise/ferry service from Piraeus to Rhodes, Limassol and Alexandria. She now carried the name PRINCESA MARISSA. Following a period of inactivity, in 2006 and 2007 she operated cruises from Cyprus to Egypt. She went for scrap under the name PRINCE, arriving at Alang on 20 June 2008. IMO 6509371

PRINCESS ROWENA (built 1979 gross tonnage 11,513) was built by Union Navale de Levante (yard number 139) at Valencia, Spain as the CIUDAD DE BADAJOZ for Trasmediterranea's Mediterranean ferry services. She was sold in 2004 and moved to Asia to operate as the gambling ship PRINCESS ROWENA. In 2008 she was sold for scrap, arriving at Alang, India under the name NENA on 13 May. IMO 7707231

REGAL EMPRESS (built 1953 gross tonnage 21,909) was built on a keel originally laid down for an aircraft carrier as the OLYMPIA, the new flagship for the Greek Line, by Alexander Stephen & Sons (yard number 636) in Glasgow, Scotland. She operated sailings for the Greek Line between Piraeus and New York. She was laid up in Piraeus in 1974, not being reactivated until sold to Sally Shipping in 1981. She went to Bremerhaven as the CARIBE for refit where her Parsons steam turbines were replaced by diesels. In 1982 she began operating for Commodore Cruise Line in the Caribbean as the CARIBE I. In 1993 she passed to Regal Cruise Line as the REGAL EMPRESS and was acquired, on the bankruptcy of Regal Cruise Line, by Imperial Majesty Cruise Line in 2003 as a replacement for the OCEAN BREEZE (formerly the SOUTHERN CROSS), without a change of name. She operated her Bahamas cruises until early 2009, when she was sold for scrap. She was last reported anchored off Bombay. IMO 5262835

RTS SINDBAD NUI (built 1971 gross tonnage 2,651) was built by Rolandwerft Dockbetrieb (yard number 973) as the BREMER. She was renamed HORST BISCHOFF in 1971 and became the ARANUI II in 1990 for Compagnie Polynesienne de Transport Maritime of Tahiti. She almost passed to Windjammer Barefoot Cruises as the CARIBE TRADE in 2002, but that deal did not materialise. She was acquired by Zambezi Shipping in 2003 and renamed RTS SINDBAD NUI in the following year. Her passenger accommodation is not currently used. She arrived at Gadani Beach, Pakistan in March 2008. IMO 7104348

SERENADE (built 1957 gross tonnage 14,173) was built by Chantiers de l'Atlantique (yard number 117) at St Nazaire, France as the JEAN MERMOZ for Compagnie de Navigation Fraissinet et Cyprien Fabre of Marseilles, France. She initially operated between her home port and West Africa. In 1965 Nouvelle Compagnie de Paquebots acquired her without a change of name. That company restyled itself, in keeping with changes in sea travel, as Croisieres Paquet in 1970 and the ship was renamed MERMOZ following a conversion to make her more suitable for cruising. In 1998 she was acquired by Prestige Cruises of Nassau, but was sold again at the end of 1999, becoming the SERENADE for Louis Cruise Lines. Latterly she operated short cruises from Limassol, Cyprus. In 2008 she went for scrap under the name SERENA, arriving at Alang on 14 June. IMO 5171115

TEXAS CLIPPER (built 1944 gross tonnage 9,644) was built by Bethlehem Steel (yard number 4421) at Sparrows Point Shipyard in the United States of America for American Export Lines, but completed as the attack transport QUEENS. After decommissioning, in 1948 she became American Export Lines' EXCAMBION and operated between New York and Mediterranean ports until withdrawn and laid up in 1959. In 1965 she became the first training ship for Texas Maritime Academy and was renamed TEXAS CLIPPER. She finished her service with the academy in 1994 and spent two years as a dormitory for the Seaborne Conservation Corps. Laid up for many years, she was sunk as an artificial reef off Port Isabel, Texas in November 2007. IMO 5110616

TEXAS TREASURE (built 1968 gross tonnage 9,337) was built by Swan Hunter & Tyne Shipbuilders (yard number 2029) at Wallsend on Tyne in England as the ST GEORGE for the Harwich, England to Hook of Holland, Netherlands service of British Rail Sealink. Following the arrival of the ST NICHOLAS in 1983, she was laid up and in the following year was sold to the Greek Ventouris Group and became the PATRA EXPRESS. Later, she was the intended ship for new operator British Iberian Line and was to have been renamed as the MAIDEN CASTLE, but in the event she was sold by her owner to Sea Escape Cruises instead and renamed SCANDINAVIA SKY II, and later SCANDINAVIAN DAWN. In 1996 she was renamed as the DISCOVERY DAWN, becoming the ISLAND DAWN in 1998. Her current name first appeared in 2000 when she was acquired by Corpus Christi Day Cruises (trading as Texas Treasure Cruises). She ceased operating in 2008 and was sold for scrap, arriving at Alang, India on 23 September 2008. IMO 6810897

THE TOPAZ (built 1956 gross tonnage 32,327) was built by the Fairfield Shipbuilding and Engineering Company Ltd (yard number 731) at Govan on the River Clyde in Scotland as the EMPRESS OF BRITAIN for Canadian Pacific Steamships' services from Liverpool to Montreal, and Greenock to Quebec. She was launched by Her Majesty Queen Elizabeth II on 22 June 1955 and sailed on her maiden voyage in April 1956. In 1964 she was sold to Greek Line and became the QUEEN ANNA MARIA, and following a major refit at the Mariotti Shipyard in Genoa she entered service between the Mediterranean and New York. She was later used exclusively for cruising and in 1975 Carnival Cruise Lines acquired her, when she became that company's second ship, the CARNIVALE. Displaced by new tonnage in 1993 she was renamed FIESTA MARINA for service with Fiestamarina Cruises of Nassau, The Bahamas, but the following year was transferred to Epirotiki Lines as the OLYMPIC for Mediterranean cruising for the short-lived joint venture with Carnival. In 1998 she became THE TOPAZ for Topaz International Shipping of Piraeus and was chartered to the then British tour operator, Thomson Holidays. At the end of her service with Thomson, she was chartered by the Peaceboat Organization in June 2003 without a change of name. Her charter came to an end in early 2008 when the CLIPPER PACIFIC replaced her. She arrived at Alang under the name TOPAZ on 4 July 2008. IMO 5103924

TIAN JIANG (built 1984 gross tonnage 5,492) was built at Xingang Shipyard (yard number 240) at Tianjin, China. Latterly she operated for China Shipping Passenger Liner, but is believed to have been broken up in China in 2008. IMO 8311869

VICTORIA (built 1962 gross tonnage 3,451) was built by Sudostroitelnyy Zavod im A Zhdanov (yard number 691) in Leningrad, Russia as the BUKOVINA, one of a series of ten attractive little ships built for various Russian owners between 1959 and 1963. The series created the first Soviet-built sea-going passenger ships since 1932. The BUKOVINA began service with the Northern Shipping Company of Archangel, although many of her sisters operated in what is now her home territory of the Black Sea. In later life she moved through a variety of owners and managers before changing her name to CROWN in 2001 while in the ownership of UTA Shipping and Trading and moving to the somewhat unlikely flag of Cambodia. In recent years she operated as the VICTORIA in the Black Sea under the Georgian flag. She arrived at Aliaga, Turkey on 14 July 2008. IMO 6730217

The **Regal Empress** at Gibraltar on her final voyage *(Matthew Davies)*

The **Serenade** arriving at Port Said *(Rick Frendt)*

The **Texas Treasure** *(Rick Frendt)*

The **Topaz** *(Rick Frendt)*

Other Changes since the previous edition

African Safari Club has ceased to offer ocean cruises.

Atlantic Stars Lines is now listed as Classic Cruises of Newport.

Bora Bora Cruises is now listed as Nomade Yachting Bora Bora.

British Columbia Discovery Voyages never started trading.

Chesva Enterprises is not thought to have traded in the cruise business.

Chikara Yacht Club never started trading.

Coco Explorer Cruises ceased operating.

Clipper Cruise Line was merged with Quark Expeditions, both part of TUI, and the name discontinued.

Creative Cruising Australia no longer operates its own programme.

Cruise Ferries, subsidiary of Star Cruises sold the WASA QUEEN and is no longer operating.

Dami Cruises no longer operates the DARLI and is therefore no longer included.

Globalia Travelplan has ceased to operate in the cruise market.

Golden Princess Cruises ceased trading following the sale of the GOLDEN PRINCESS to Chinese breakers.

Hornblower Marine Services failed to acquire the CAPE MAY LIGHT and CAPE COD LIGHT.

Indian Ocean Cruises (South Africa) ceased trading.

Korea Tonghae Shipping no longer operates any vessels that qualify for inclusion in the book.

Louis Hellenic Cruises' ships have been absorbed into the Louis Cruise Lines fleet.

Magic 1 Cruise Line is no longer included as its ship is chartered to Caspi Cruises.

Monarch Classic Cruises has been restyled as Mediterranean Classic Cruises.

NCL is now controlled by Apollo Management.

NCL America is now wholly owned by Apollo Management.

Novoship no longer owns any passenger ships.

Oceania Cruises is now owned by Apollo Management.

Razzmatazz Ocean Cruises did not commence trading.

Regent Seven Seas is now owned by Apollo Management.

Royal Zante Cruises never started operating.

Sea Containers' remaining ship was sold to Louis Cruise Lines.

Sealegend Holdings appears to have ceased trading with the sale of the PRINCESS ROWENA.

Sterling Casino Lines has ceased operating.

Sulpicio Lines is no longer licenced to carry passengers after the loss of THE PRINCESS OF THE STARS.

Swan Hellenic Cruises is now listed under All Leisure Group.

Texas Treasure Cruises has ceased operating.

The Scholar Ship failed to secure the funding needed to continue in operation.

Travelscope ceased trading in early 2008.

Vision Cruceros ceased trading in 2009.

Voyages of Discovery is now listed under All Leisure Group.

World Adventurer is no longer listed as the company succeeded in selling its ship.

Zambezi Shipping no longer operates any passenger-carrying vessels.

Late News

The ASIA STAR (Asia Cruises) has moved from Hong Kong to Singapore.

Easycruise and the EASYCRUISE LIFE have been acquired by Hellenic Seaways.

Indian Ocean Cruises has been reported to have ceased trading, and the OCEAN ODYSSEY sold for scrap.

Saga eventually acquired the ASTORIA which will be renamed SAGA PEARL II.

Ownership of the UNITED STATES has been transferred from NCL America to Star Cruises.

The REGAL EMPRESS was beached on 23 July 2009.

Aegean Experience will become Voyages to Antiquity and the AEGEAN I will be renamed AEGEAN ODYSSEY and is expected to begin trading in May 2010.

New operator Cruise and Maritime Voyages will be operating Transocean Tour's MARCO POLO in the British market from 2010.

Bibliography - *Books*

Bent, Mike *Coastal Express* Conway Maritime Press 1987

Brogen, Klas (ed) *Guide 05,06,07,08,09* Shippax Information 2005-9

Brogen Klas (ed) *Market 09* Shippax Information 2009

Cartwright, Roger and Harvey, Clive *Cruise Britannia* Tempus Publishing 2004

Cooke, Anthony *Emigrant Ships* Carmania Press

Cooke, Anthony *Liners and Cruise Ships- Some notable smaller vessels* Carmania Press 1996

Cooke, Anthony *Liners and Cruise Ships 2- Some notable smaller vessels* Carmania Press 2000

Cooke, Anthony *Liners and Cruise Ships 3- Further notable smaller vessels* Carmania Press 2003

Cowsill, Miles, Hendy, John and Mayes, William *P&O The Fleet* Ferry Publications 2000

Dickinson, Bob and Vladimir, Andy *Selling the Sea* John Wiley & Sons 1997

Dunn, Laurence *Passenger Liners* Adlard Coles 1961 and 1965

Elisio, Maurizio and Piccione, Paolo *The Costa Liners* Carmania Press 1997

Hackmann, Peter (ed) *Passenger Ships for Indonesia* Meyer Werft 2002

Hornsby, David *Ocean Ships 15th Edition,* Ian Allan 2009

Kludas, Arnold *Great Passenger Ships of the World Today,* Patrick Stephens 1992

Kludas, Arnold, Heine, Frank and Lose, Frank *Die Grossen Passagierschiffe der Welt* Koehler 2002

Kludas, Arnold, Heine, Frank and Lose, Frank *Die Grossen Passagierschiffe der Welt* Koehler 2006

Latimer, David W *Passenger Ships of the 20th Century – An illustrated Encyclopaedia* Colourpoint 2002

May, John and Mayes, William *Ferries 2004 Southern Europe* Overview Press 2004

Miller, William H *The Chandris Liners* Carmania Press 1993

Miller, William H *Passenger Liners Italian Style* Carmania Press 1996

Miller, William H *Going Dutch, The Holland America Line Story* Carmania Press 1998

Miller, William H *Passenger Liners French Style* Carmania Press 2001

Peter, Bruce *Passenger Liners Scandinavian Style* Carmania Press 2003

Plowman, Peter *Australian Cruise Ships* Rosenburg Publishing 2007

Rabson, Stephen and O'Donoghue, Kevin *P&O A Fleet History* The World Ship Society 1987

Rothe, Claus *Die Deutschen Traumschiffe* Koehler 1997

Rothe, Claus *Welt der Passagierschiffe unter Hammer und Sichel* DSV-Verlag 1994

Thorsoe, Soren and others *DFDS 1991-2006 – Ship Development Continues* DFDS 2006

Vapalahti, Hannu *Finnish Passenger Ships 1960-1996 Volumes 1 & 2* Judicor 1996

Ward, Douglas *Complete Guide to Cruising and Cruise Ships 2009* Berlitz 2008

Widdows, Nick *Ferries 2009 British Isles and Northern Europe* Ferry Publications 2008

Wilson, E A *Soviet Passenger Ships 1917-1977* The World Ship Society 1978

Worker, Colin *The World's Passenger Ships* Ian Allan 1967

Periodicals

Cruise and Ferry Info Shippax Information

European Ferry Scene and Cruise Ship Review Ferry Publications

Fairplay Lloyds Register-Fairplay

Lloyds Cruise International Informa Publishing

Lloyds List Informa Publishing

Marine News The World Ship Society

Sea Lines The Ocean Liner Society

Ships Monthly IPC Publishing

Steamboat Bill The Steamship Historical Society of America

Other sources

Company brochures

Company websites

Linerslist, a membership site on Yahoo Groups

www.maritimematters.com

Sea Web – the on-line ships register from Lloyds Register-Fairplay

Among these many and varied information sources there are often conflicts in what ought to be factual information. It is therefore possible that some errors have crept into this book. I would appreciate notification of any information that might be suspect, so that the next edition will be an even more accurate portrayal of the cruise ships of the world.

william.mayes@overviewpress.co.uk

Index of companies

Index of former names

CONTINENTAL WORLD	LEISURE WORLD	EASYCRUISEONE	CRUISEONE
CORAL CAT	CORAL PRINCESS II	ECSTASY	CARNIVAL ECSTACY
CORINTHIAN	LAUREN I	ELATION	CARNIVAL ELATION
COSTA EUROPA	THOMSON DREAM	ELBE 2	ATLANTIS
COSTA OLYMPIA	NORWEGIAN SKY	ELOISE	ROYAL IRIS
COSTA PLAYA	GOLDEN PRINCESS	EMERALD EMPRESS	CASINO ROYALE
COSTA TROPICALE	OCEAN DREAM	EMERALD SEA	KRONPRINSESSE MARTHA
CRAIGAVON	CARIB VACATIONER	EMPIRE STATE	STATE
CRESSIDA	YANKEE CLIPPER	EMPIRE STATE V	STATE
CRIMPER	YANKEE CLIPPER	EMPRESS OF BRITAIN	THE TOPAZ
CROWN	ALBATROS	EMPRESS OF THE SEAS	EMPRESS
CROWN	VICTORIA	ENCHANTED SUN	CASINO ROYALE
CROWN DYNASTY	BRAEMAR	ENDEAVOUR	NATIONAL GEOGRAPHIC
CROWN JEWEL	GEMINI		ENDEAVOUR
CROWN MAJESTY	BRAEMAR	ERNEST HEMINGWAY	TURAMA
CROWN MONARCH	ALEXANDER VON HUMBOLDT	EROS	OCEAN ODYSSEY
CROWN ODYSSEY	BALMORAL	EUROPA	BLEU DE FRANCE
CROWN PRINCESS	OCEAN VILLAGE TWO	EUROPAFARJAN I	WIND SOLUTION
CROWN PRINCESS	PACIFIC JEWEL	EUROPEAN STARS	MSC SINFONIA
CROWN PRINCESS		EUROPEAN VISION	MSC ARMONIA
VICTORIA	AMUSEMENT WORLD	EXCAMBION	TEXAS CLIPPER
CRUCERO EXPRESS	MIRAGE I	EXECUTIVE EXPLORER	CONTESSA
CRUISE MUHIBAH	AMBASSADOR II	EXPEX	XANADU 2
CRUISE ONE	DELPHIN VOYAGER	EXPLORER II	MINERVA
CRYSTAL HARMONY	ASUKA II	EXPLORER STARSHIP	LE DIAMANT
CT NEPTUNE	NEPTUNE	FABIOLAVILLE	HAI HUA
CUNARD ADVENTURER	CORAL	FADDEY BELLINGSHAUSEN	OMEGA G
CUNARD CONQUEST	GOLDEN IRIS	FAIRSKY	ATLANTIC STAR
CUNARD COUNTESS	OCEAN COUNTESS	FAITHFUL	XANADU 2
CUNARD COUNTESS	NEW PACIFIC	FANTASY	CARNIVAL FANTASY
CUNARD CROWN JEWEL	GEMINI	FANTASY WORLD	LEISURE WORLD
CUNARD PRINCESS	GOLDEN IRIS	FARAH	EASYCRUISE LIFE
DALMATINO	ORIENTAL PRINCESS	FASCINATION	CARNIVAL FASCINATION
DANA GLORIA	JUPITER	FERNHILL	LE DIAMANT
DANA GLORIA	ISLAND BREEZE	FIESTA MARINA	THE TOPAZ
DANAE	PRINCESS DANAE	FINLANDIA	GOLDEN PRINCESS
DANAOS	SALAMIS GLORY	FINNHANSA	PRINCESA MARISSA
DAPHNE	PRINCESS DAPHNE	FINNSTAR	GOLDEN PRINCESS
DARLI	DICLE	FIRDA	DICLE
DAUNTLESS	SS DELPHINE	FLAMENCO	FLAMENCO I
DELFIN CARAVELLE	TURAMA	FLORIDIAN	NOMAD
DELFIN CLIPPER	PRINCE ALBERT II	FLORNES	SAKARYA
DELFIN STAR	PRINCE ALBERT II	FORCE TIDE	PACIFIC EXPLORER
DELORLEANS	ARTSHIP	FORTUNE STAR	CASINO ROYALE
DELOS	XANADU 2	FRANCA C	DOULOS
DELPHIN RENAISSANCE	AZAMARA QUEST	FRANCE II	LEGACY
DELPHINE	SS DELPHINE	FRANCESCA	THE IRIS
DIAMOND ISLAND	THE EMERALD	FRANKFURT	ALEXANDER
DIAMOND PRINCESS	SAPPHIRE PRINCESS	FRIDTJOF NANSEN	ATHENA
DIAMOND PRINCESS	HAKON JARL	FRONTIER SPIRIT	BREMEN
DISCO II	QUEST	FUTURE SEAS	EMPRESS
DISCOVERY DAWN	TEXAS TREASURE	FYODOR DOSTOEVSKIY	ASTOR
DISKO	POLARIS	G D KENNEDY	A F CHAPMAN
DMITRIY SHOSTAKOVICH	ROYALE STAR	GALAXY	MEIN SCHIFF
DOLMAR	PICTON CASTLE	GANN	SJOKURS
DOLPHIN	AEGEAN I	GANN	SANDNES
DON EUSEBIO	DIPOLOG PRINCESS	GLOMMEN	RTS SINDBAD BITIC
DOUBLE FORCE	PEGASUS	GOLDEN BEAR	ARTSHIP
DREAM	FESTIVAL	GOLDEN ODYSSEY	MACAU SUCCESS
DREAM 21	PRINCE ALBERT II	GOLDEN PRINCESS	BOUDICCA
DREAM PRINCESS	FESTIVAL	GOPLO	SIGNORA DEL VENTO
DREAMWARD	NORWEGIAN DREAM	GRAND LATINO	BOUDICCA
DRO KI CAKAU	REEF ESCAPE	GRAND VICTORIA	BLUE MONARCH
DRONNING INGRID	AFRICA MERCY	GREAT RIVERS EXPLORER	NATIONAL
DUNBOYNE	A F CHAPMAN		GEOGRAPHIC SEA LION
DURR	THE CALYPSO	GREAT SEA	PHILIPPINES
EAGLE	ROYAL IRIS	GRIPSHOLM	SAGA ROSE
EARL WILLIAM	WINDWARD II	GROSSHERZOG	

MERCURY	CELEBRITY MERCURY
MER-JULIA	WINDWARD II
MERMOZ	SERENADE
MESSAGER	HERMES
METANGULA	PRINCESSA ELENA
MIDNATSOL	NATIONAL GEOGRAPHIC EXPLORER
MIDNATSOL II	NATIONAL GEOGRAPHIC EXPLORER
MIKHAIL SUSLOV	OCEAN JEWEL OF ST PETERSBURG
MILLENNIUM	CELEBRITY MILLENNIUM
MINERVA II	ROYAL PRINCESS
MING FAI PRINCESS	METROPOLIS
MING YI	TONG HU
MINISEA	BIRGER JARL
MINOAN PRINCE	GOLDEN PRINCE
MISTRAL	GRAND MISTRAL
MONACO	ISLAND BREEZE
MOONTA	LYDIA
MORMACTIDE	EMPIRE STATE
MORNING STAR	SALAMIS GLORY
MOSTAR	HARMONY II
MOTIVE EXPLORER	HAUMANA
MTS DISCOVERER	OCEAN QUEST II
MUNSTER	AMBASSADOR II
MURRAY EXPLORER	CAPTAIN COOK'S EXPLORER
MUSSON	SEVASTOPOL-1
N F TIGER	EXPEDITION
N KAZANTZAKIS	METROPOLIS
NANTUCKET CLIPPER	SPIRIT OF GLACIER BAY
NARCIS	AEGEAN I
NARVIK	GANN
NASSAU	CARIB VACATIONER
NASSAU I	CARIB VACATIONER
NATASHA	EASYCRUISE LIFE
NAUTICAN	ALEXANDER VON HUMBOLDT
NEVA	IGOR FARKHUTDINOV
NEW FLAMENCO	FLAMENCO I
NEW PACIFIC	OCEAN COUNTESS
NEW SHOREHAM 1	PACIFIC MONARCH
NEW SHOREHAM II	SPIRIT OF COLUMBIA
NEW YORK FORTUNE 1	ISLAND BREEZE
NEWPORT CLIPPER	SPIRIT OF ENDEAVOUR
NIEUW AMSTERDAM	THOMSON SPIRIT
NINIKORIA	POLYNESIAN PRINCESS
NJORD	POLAR STAR
NOORDAM	THOMSON CELEBRATION
NORDIC EMPRESS	EMPRESS
NORDIC PRINCE	AQUAMARINE
NORDIC SUN	AMBASSADOR II
NORPAC II	PACIFIC EXPLORER
NORRONA	LOGOS HOPE
NORRONA 1	LOGOS HOPE
NORTH STAR	NATIONAL GEOGRAPHIC ENDEAVOUR
NORWEGIAN CROWN	BALMORAL
NORWEGIAN DYNASTY	BRAEMAR
NORWEGIAN MAJESTY	LOUIS MAJESTY
NORWEGIAN SEA	SUPERSTAR LIBRA
NORWEGIAN STAR	ALBATROS
NORWEGIAN STAR 1	ALBATROS
NORWEGIAN WIND	SUPERSTAR AQUARIUS
OCEAN COUNTESS	NEW PACIFIC
OCEAN EMPRESS	OCEAN JEWEL OF ST PETERSBURG
OCEAN ISLANDER	ROYAL STAR
OCEAN KING	PHILIPPINES
OCEAN MONARCH	PRINCESS DAPHNE
OCEAN ODYSSEY	PRINCESS DAPHNE
OCEAN PEARL	GOLDEN PRINCESS
OCEAN PRINCESS	OCEANA
OCEAN PRINCESS	SAPPHIRE
OCEAN PRINCESS	ORIENTAL PRINCESS
OCEAN VILLAGE	PACIFIC PEARL
OCEAN VILLAGE TWO	PACIFIC JEWEL
OCEANIC GRACE	CLIPPER ODYSSEY
OCEANIC II	MONA LISA
OCEANIC INDEPENDENCE	OCEANIC
OCEANIC ODYSSEY	CLIPPER ODYSSEY
OCEANIC PRINCESS	OCEANIC DISCOVERER
ODESSA SKY	VAN GOGH
ODYSSEUS	LUCKY STAR
OGASAWA MARU	PRINCESS OF THE CARRIBEAN
OISEAU DE POLYNESIA	POLYNESIA
OISEAU DES ILES	FLYING CLOUD
OKEAN	MINERVA
OLVIA	NEPTUNE
OLYMPIA	REGAL EMPRESS
OLYMPIA COUNTESS	OCEAN COUNTESS
OLYMPIA COUNTESS	NEW PACIFIC
OLYMPIA EXPLORER	EXPLORER
OLYMPIA VOYAGER	GRAND VOYAGER
OLYMPIC	OCEAN MAJESTY
OLYMPIC	THE TOPAZ
OLYMPIC COUNTESS	OCEAN COUNTESS
OLYMPIC COUNTESS	NEW PACIFIC
OLYMPIC EXPLORER	EXPLORER
OLYMPIC VOYAGER	GRAND VOYAGER
OMAR II	MACAU SUCCESS
OMAR III	LONG JIE
OMAR STAR	ASIA STAR
OMEGA	OMEGA G
OPATIJA	POLYNESIAN PRINCESS
OPERA	CRISTAL
ORANGE MELODY	SPIRIT OF ADVENTURE
OREGON	EMPIRE STATE
ORESUND	NATIONAL GEOGRAPHIC POLARIS
ORIENT EXPRESS	AMAZING GRACE
ORIENT VENUS	DELPHIN VOYAGER
ORIENTAL PEARL	GOLDEN PRINCESS
ORLOVA	LYUBOV ORLOVA
OSTFOLD	RTS SINDBAD BITIC
OURANOS	F DIAMOND
PACIFIC NORTHWEST EXPLORER	SPIRIT OF ALASKA
PACIFIC PRINCESS	PACIFIC
PACIFIC SKY	ATLANTIC STAR
PACIFIC STAR	OCEAN DREAM
PACIFIC STAR	AMUSEMENT WORLD
PACIFIC STAR	ISLAND BREEZE
PACIFIC STAR	XANADU 2
PACIFIC SUN	THE EMERALD
PACIFIC WARRIOR	PACIFIC EXPLORER
PALAU	WIND SOLUTION
PALMIRA	EASYCRUISE LIFE
PALOMA I	ROYALE STAR
PARADISE	CARNIVAL PARADISE
PATRA EXPRESS	TEXAS TREASURE
PATRIA	SEA CLOUD
PATRICIA	AMUSEMENT WORLD
PATRIOT	THOMSON SPIRIT
PCE 830	KRISTINA BRAHE
PEACE	SIGNORA DEL VENTO
PEARL	GOLDEN PRINCESS

PEARL OF SCANDINAVIA	GOLDEN PRINCESS	REGAL PRINCESS	PACIFIC DAWN
PEARL OF SEYCHELLES	FIJI PRINCESS	REGENT JEWEL	THE CALYPSO
PEARL WILLIAM	WINDWARD II	REGENT MOON	COSTA ALLEGRA
PEREGRINE MARINER	AKADEMIK IOFFE	REGENT RAINBOW	THE EMERALD
PEREGRINE		REGENT SPIRIT	SALAMIS GLORY
VOYAGER	AKADEMIK SERGEY VAVILOV	REGENT SUN	COSTA MARINA
PERLA	THE AEGEAN PEARL	REGINA MARIS	ALEXANDER
PETR		REGINA RENAISSANCE	CORINTHIAN II
PERVVY	OCEAN JEWEL OF ST PETERSBURG	REMBRANDT	ROTTERDAM
PETREL	CALEDONIA	RENAI I	CORINTHIAN II
PETREL V	CALEDONIA	RENAI II	ISLAND SKY
PETRONELLA	MARE FRISIUM	RENAISSANCE	DABAWI
PHAROS	AMAZING GRACE	RENAISSANCE	BLUE MONARCH
PILGRIM BELLE	SPIRIT OF '98	RENAISSANCE EIGHT	ISLAND SKY
PILOTO PARDO	ANTARCTIC DREAM	RENAISSANCE FIVE	SPIRIT OF OCEANUS
PINTA I	LA PINTA	RENAISSANCE FOUR	CLELIA II
PIONEER	YANKEE CLIPPER	RENAISSANCE SEVEN	CORINTHIAN II
PLATINUM	DISCOVERY	RENAISSANCE SIX	SUNRISE
POLAR STAR	XANADU 2	RENAISSANCE	
POLARIS	NATIONAL GEOGRAPHIC POLARIS	THREE	GALAPAGOS EXPLORER II
POLARLYS	CARIBBEAN MERCY	RENAISSANCE TWO	CRUISEONE
POLII	ARTEMIS	RESEARCHER	USHUAIA
POLYARNYY PIONER	POLAR PIONEER	RHAPSODY	GOLDEN IRIS
POLYNESIA I	POLYNESIA	RIVAGE MARTINIQUE	FIJI PRINCESS
PONGNAE	LONG JIE	RIVAGE ST MARTIN	FANTASEA AMMARI
PORT MELBOURNE	PRINCESS DANAE	RIVAGES	
PORT SYDNEY	PRINCESS DAPHNE	GUADELOUPE	NATIONAL GEOGRAPHIC ISLANDER
PRESIDENT HAYES	STATE OF MAINE	ROMA	DOULOS
PRIDE OF ALOHA	NORWEGIAN SKY	ROYAL MAJESTY	NORWEGIAN MAJESTY
PRIDE OF HAWAI'I	NORWEGIAN JADE	ROYAL MAJESTY	LOUIS MAJESTY
PRIDE OF SAN DIEGO	CASINO ROYALE	ROYAL ODYSSEY	ALBATROS
PRIMEXPRESS ISLAND	ROCHDALE ONE	ROYAL PRINCESS	ARTEMIS
PRINCE	GOLDEN PRINCE	ROYAL SEAS	ISLAND ADVENTURE
PRINCE ALBERT	HARMONY II	ROYAL VIKING QUEEN	SEABOURN LEGEND
PRINCESA ISABEL	LUCKY STAR	ROYAL VIKING SEA	ALBATROS
PRINCESA OCEANICA	SAPPHIRE	ROYAL VIKING SKY	BOUDICCA
PRINCESS ITALIA	SAPPHIRE	ROYAL VIKING STAR	BLACK WATCH
PRINCESS MAHSURI	SPIRIT OF ADVENTURE	ROYAL VIKING SUN	PRINSENDAM
PRINCESSAN	PRINCESA MARISSA	ROYALE OCEANIC	OCEANIC
PRINSESSAN CHRISTINA	WIND SOLUTION	RTS SINDBAD	RTS SINDBAD BITIC
PRINSESSE		RUBY	OCEAN COUNTESS
RAGNHILD	BAHAMAS CELEBRATION	RUBY	NEW PACIFIC
PRINSESSE RAGNHILD	JI MEI	RYFYLKE	KRONPRINSESSE MARTHA
PRINTSESSA YELENA	PRINCESSA ELENA	SAFE CHRISTINA	WIND SOLUTION
PRINZ OBERON	AMBASSADOR II	SAGA PEARL	MINERVA
PRISIDENT	PHILIPPINES	SAGAFJORD	SAGA ROSE
PROFESSOR KHROMOV	SPIRIT OF	SALLY ALBATROSS	CRISTAL
	ENDERBY	SALLY CARAVELLE	TURAMA
PUTRI BINTANG	AMUSEMENT WORLD	SALLY CLIPPER	PRINCE ALBERT II
PYOTR		SAN GIORGIO	ROYAL STAR
PERVVY	OCEAN JEWEL OF ST PETERSBURG	SANTA MERCEDES	PATRIOT STATE
QUEEN ANNA MARIA	THE TOPAZ	SANTA ROSA	THE EMERALD
QUEEN ODYSSEY	SEABOURN LEGEND	SAPPHIRE PRINCESS	DIAMOND PRINCESS
QUEEN VICTORIA	ARCADIA	SAQQIT ITTUK	QUEST
QUEENS	TEXAS CLIPPER	SARPIK ITTUK	OCEAN NOVA
R EIGHT	ROYAL PRINCESS	SCANDINAVIA	ISLAND ESCAPE
R FIVE	NAUTICA	SCANDINAVIA SKY II	TEXAS TREASURE
R FOUR	OCEAN PRINCESS	SCANDINAVIAN DAWN	TEXAS TREASURE
R ONE	INSIGNIA	SCANDINAVIAN SAGA	CASINO ROYALE
R SEVEN	AZAMARA QUEST	SCANDINAVICA	MIRAGE I
R SIX	AZAMARA JOURNEY	SEA BIRD	NATIONAL GEOGRAPHIC SEA BIRD
R THREE	PACIFIC PRINCESS	SEA GODDESS I	SEADREAM I
R TWO	REGATTA	SEA GODDESS II	SEADREAM II
RADISSON DIAMOND	ASIA STAR	SEA LINER	LA PINTA
RAGNVALD JARL	SJOKURS	SEA LION	NATIONAL GEOGRAPHIC SEA LION
RAINBOW	THE EMERALD	SEA LUCK I	OCEANIC
RAPTURE	SAFARI EXPLORER	SEA PRINCE	SAPPHIRE
REEF TREK	HAUMANA	SEA PRINCE V	SAPPHIRE

SEA PRINCESS	MONA LISA	STOCKHOLM AV GOTEBORG	STOCKHOLM
SEA TRAVELLER II	LA PINTA	STORMONT	CHRISTINA O
SEA VENTURE	PACIFIC	SUMMIT	CELEBRITY SUMMIT
SEA WORLD	MINGHUA	SUN	CORINTHIAN II
SEABOURN GODDESS I	SEADREAM I	SUN BAY	XPEDITION
SEABOURN GODDESS II	SEADREAM II	SUN BAY II	LAUREN I
SEABOURN SUN	PRINSENDAM	SUN FIESTA	THE CALYPSO
SEASPIRIT	SPIRIT OF ENDEAVOUR	SUN FIESTA	AMUSEMENT WORLD
SEAWARD	SUPERSTAR LIBRA	SUN FLOWER 7	GOLDEN PRINCE
SEAWING	THE AEGEAN PEARL	SUN JO 1	LA PINTA
SEMINOLE EXPRESS	MIRAGE I	SUN PRINCESS	FLAMENCO I
SENSATION	CARNIVAL SENSATION	SUN VIKING	LONG JIE
SEYYLD KHALIFA	AL-JAZIRAH	SUN VIVA	SPIRIT OF OCEANUS
SHANGRI-LA WORLD	LEISURE WORLD	SUN VIVA 2	SUNRISE
SHEARWATER	POLARIS	SUNBIRD	THOMSON DESTINY
SHIRETOKO MARU	METROPOLIS	SUNBORN	LAGOS YACHT HOTEL
SIKKER HAVN	SAKARYA	SUNDREAM	FESTIVAL
SILJA OPERA	CRISTAL	SUNFLOWER	AL SAID
SITIA	ISLAND BREEZE	SUNNHORDLAND	KRISTINA BRAHE
SITMAR FAIRMAJESTY	OCEAN VILLAGE	SUNSHINE FUJI	MABUHAY SUNSHINE
SITMAR FAIRMAJESTY	PACIFIC PEARL	SUNWARD	BOUDICCA
SJOKURS	SANDNES	SUNWARD II	CORAL
SKULE	RTS SINDBAD BITIC	SUPERSTAR ARIES	BLEU DE FRANCE
SKY	ISLAND SKY	SUPERSTAR CAPRICORN	BOUDICCA
SKY PRINCESS	ATLANTIC STAR	SUPERSTAR EUROPE	BLEU DE FRANCE
SKY WONDER	ATLANTIC STAR	SUPERSTAR GEMINI	GEMINI
SKYWARD	LEISURE WORLD	SUPERSTAR LEO	NORWEGIAN SPIRIT
SOCIETY ADVENTURER	HANSEATIC	SUPERSTAR LIBRA	NORWEGIAN STAR
SOCIETY EXPLORER	EXPLORER	SUPERSTAR SAGITTARIUS	LONG JIE
SOFIA	CASINO ROYALE	SUPERSTAR SCORPIO	NORWEGIAN DAWN
SOL CHRISTIANA	OCEAN MAJESTY	SUPERSTAR TAURUS	CRISTAL
SONG OF AMERICA	THOMSON DESTINY	SVEA CORONA	JUPITER
SONG OF FLOWER	LE DIAMANT	SVEA JARL	PRINCE
SONG OF NORWAY	FESTIVAL	SVYATOY NIKOLAY	GEROI SEVASTOPOLYA
SOROY	RTS SINDBAD BITIC	SWITZERLAND	PRINCESS DAPHNE
SOUTHERN CROSS	FLAMENCO I	TAHITIAN PRINCESS	OCEAN PRINCESS
SOUTHWARD	THE AEGEAN	TAOUEY	ESMERELDA
	PEARL	TAVERNER	PACIFIC AURORA
SOVEREIGN OF THE SEAS	SOVEREIGN	TDI KARADENIZ	DREAM
SPICE ISLANDER	CORAL PRINCESS II	TEMPTRESS EXPLORER	PACIFIC EXPLORER
SPIRIT	THOMSON SPIRIT	TEMPTRESS VOYAGER	SEA VOYAGER
SPIRIT OF GLACIER BAY	PACIFIC MONARCH	TERAAKA	POLYNESIAN PRINCESS
SPIRIT OF LONDON	FLAMENCO I	TETYS	PICTON CASTLE
SPIRIT OF NANTUCKET	SPIRIT OF GLACIER BAY	THE AUSONIA	IVORY
SPORT VENTURE	KRONPRINSESSE MARTHA	THE AZUR	ROYAL IRIS
SS CLIPPER	MILWAUKEE CLIPPER	THE EXPLORER	ATOLL EXPLORER
ST GEORGE	TEXAS TREASURE	THE JASMINE	EASYCRUISE LIFE
ST TROPEZ	CASINO ROYALE	THE MERCURY	DABAWI
STAFFORD	ISLAND BREEZE	THE NEPTUNE	CRUISEONE
STAR ODYSSEY	BLACK WATCH	THE NEPTUNE 2	CRUISEONE
STAR PRINCESS	OCEAN VILLAGE	THE SCHOLAR SHIP	MONA LISA
STAR PRINCESS	PACIFIC PEARL	THE TALISMAN	CASINO ROYALE
STARDANCER	ISLAND ESCAPE	THERIOT OFFSHORE IV	NORDIK EXPRESS
STARLIGHT PRINCESS	PRINCESS DANAE	THERISOS EXPRESS	PRINCESS DANAE
STARSHIP ATLANTIC	MELODY	TIGER	EXPEDITION
STARSHIP MAJESTIC	FLAMENCO I	TOKYU MARU	DIPOLOG PRINCESS
STARSHIP OCEANIC	OCEANIC	TOR HOLLANDIA	F DIAMOND
STARWARD	ORIENT QUEEN	TOSHIMA	O'MEGA
STEINFOREST	PICTON CASTLE	TOWADA MARU	PHILIPPINE DREAM
STELLA DALMATIAE	MONET	TRILLINGEN	SAKARYA
STELLA MARIS II	MADAGASCAR	TRITON	CORAL
STENA ARCADIA	CASINO ROYALE	TROPIC BIRD	CORAL I
STENA BALTICA	REGENT SKY	TROPIC STAR	ISLAND BREEZE
STENA FINLANDICA	GALAPAGOS LEGEND	TROPIC STAR II	CASINO ROYALE
STENA NORDICA	WIND SOLUTION	TROPICALE	OCEAN DREAM
STENA OCEANIC	AMUSEMENT WORLD	TUHAAPAE 3	VAEANU
STENA SAGA	AMUSEMENT WORLD	TURNSTEIN	PICTON CASTLE
STOCKHOLM	ATHENA	TURQUAZ	DIOGENIS V

TYDEMAN	PLANCIUS	VLADIMIR CHIVILIKHIN	KAY
UKRAINA	ISLAND ADVENTURE	VOLKER	ATHENA
UPSHUR	STATE OF MAINE	VOLKERFREUNDSCHAFT	ATHENA
USNS MAURY	GOLDEN BEAR	VOYAGER	GRAND VOYAGER
USNS TANNER	STATE OF MAINE	VOYAGER	ISLAND BREEZE
USS CRESCENT CITY	ARTSHIP	WAKACHIBA MARU	EVOLUTION
USS DAUNTLESS	SS DELPHINE	WAKASHIO MARU	GOLDEN PRINCE
UTSTRAUM	PICTON CASTLE	WALRUS	ALEXANDER VON HUMBOLDT
VACATIONER	CARIB VACATIONER	WAPPEN VON HAMBURG	XANADU 2
VALTUR PRIMA	ATHENA	WELLAMO	JUPITER
VASILIY GOLOVNIN	GEROI SEVASTOPOLYA	WESTERDAM	THOMSON DREAM
VASILIY SOLOVYEV SEDOY	OCEAN JEWEL OF ST PETERSBURG	WESTWARD	BLACK WATCH
VELMA	MANDALAY	WESTWARTS	STRATSRAAD LEHMKUHL
VELMA LYKES	ENTERPRISE	WINDWARD	SUPERSTAR AQUARIUS
VICENTE PUCHOL	ISLANDS CRUISE	WORLD DISCOVERER	PRINCE ALBERT II
VICTORIA	LORD OF THE GLENS	WORLD RENAISSANCE	BLUE MONARCH
VICTORIA	ANASTASIS	XANADU	XANADU 2
VICTORIA	MONA LISA	XI QUE	WU TONG SHANG
VICTORIA II	LORD OF THE GLENS	YANKEE CLIPPER I	YANKEE CLIPPER
VICTORIAN EMPRESS	SPIRIT OF '98	YAO HUA	ORIENT PRINCESS
VIKING BORDEAUX	MADAGASCAR	YORKTOWN CLIPPER	SPIRIT OF YORKTOWN
VIKING II	WINDWARD II	YU JIN XIANG	XIN YU JIN XIANG
VIKING POLARIS	POLARIS	YUSHAR	MONET
VIKING PRINCESS	PALM BEACH PRINCESS	YUWA MARU	EVOLUTION
VIKING SAGA	CRISTAL	ZHAN XIN	XIN SHANG HAI YOU LUN
VIKING SERENADE	ISLAND ESCAPE	ZI DING XIANG	ARAFURA LILY
VIKINGFJORD	SANDNES		
VIRGO	ORIGO		
VISION STAR	GEMINI		
VISTAFJORD	SAGA RUBY		

Index